International Advances in Self Research

A volume in
Research in International Advances in Self Research
Series Editors: Herbert W. Marsh, Rhonda G. Craven,
and Dennis M. McInerney

International Advances in Self Research

Edited by

**Herbert W. Marsh, Rhonda G. Craven,
and Dennis M. McInerney**

INFORMATION AGE
PUBLISHING

80 Mason Street • Greenwich, Connecticut 06830 • www.infoagepub.com

Library of Congress Cataloging-in-Publication Data

International advances in self research : speaking to the future /
edited by Herbert W. Marsh, Rhonda G. Craven, and Dennis M. McInerney.
    p. cm.
Includes bibliographical references.
  ISBN 1-59311-005-7 – ISBN 1-59311-004-9 (pbk.)
  1. Self. I. Marsh, Herbert W. II. Craven, Rhonda. III. McInerney, D.
M. (Dennis M.), 1948-
  BF697.I675 2003
  155.2–dc21

                                                      2003013629

Printed in the United States of America

CONTENTS

part III
MEASUREMENT ISSUES

part IV
APPLIED STUDIES: FOCUS ON SPECIAL EDUCATION

PREFACE

This inaugural volume of "International Advances in Self Research" marks a milestone in the progress of research on the self over the past 40 years. Tremendous progress has been made in the measurement of the self, progress that would have been difficult to imagine by the likes of Ruth Wylie and her seminal review of the self-concept literature. Back then she wrote (Wiley, 1961) that, "when one reads the empirical literature pertaining to self-concept theories, one finds that a bewildering array of hypotheses, measuring instruments, and research designs has been used" (p. 3). She went on to say that "the theories are in many ways ambiguous, incomplete, and overlapping, and no one theory has received a large amount of systematic empirical exploration" (p. 3). Quite clearly, today, this is *not* the case. The work of Herb Marsh, Barbara Byrne, John Hattie, Rhonda Craven, and other colleagues at the SELF Research Centre has gone a long way to change this state of affairs.

But let us return to Wylie. She found that measurement as well as theoretical concerns abounded. She pointed to the then recent work of Cronbach and Meehl (1955) arguing that "construct validity is necessary because self-concept theories explicitly require that we measure a stated class of variables, Ss' conscious processes; and, by definition, Ss' phenomenal fields are private and beyond direct observation... It is *not* sufficient to demonstrate that one's self-concept measure have 'predictive' or 'concurrent' validity in the sense that an MMPI scale, for example, may be shown to discriminate nosological [disease] categories without an explanation of why the association between MMPI scores and diagnostic labels is obtained" (p. 23, italics in original). Again, today this situation is greatly

International Advances in Self Research, pages ix–xv
Copyright © 2003 by Information Age Publishing

changed. We have extensive research on the validity of self-concept interpretations of scores from self-concept instruments.

I now digress, apologizing at the outset, in what, hopefully, becomes relevant later on. This seems a reasonable prerogative for someone asked to
write a preface for sins of his past! I was, at the time of Wylie's influential
work, an acting assistant professor at Stanford having finished my doctor-
ate there in 1970. Wylie's description fit the field of self-research that my
students, Judith Hubner and George Stanton, and I entered into in the fall
of 1971. My training had been in cognitive psychology with Bower and
Atkinson and in psychometrics with Cronbach and Snow. I had a three-year
appointment to teach courses taught by Cronbach who was on sabbatical
leave in Japan and to conduct research on teaching at the Stanford Center
for Research and Development in Teaching (SCRDT) because that was
where some of the money came from to cover my appointment.

My entry into self-research started at the center. I remember sitting
around a table with Dick Snow, the director of the Heuristic Teaching Program, and Carl Thoresen, a counseling psychologist and the second of the
three faculty members in the program; I was the third. Snow said that some
"bureaucrat" in Washington had decided that SCRDT had to have overrid-
ing goals and that the "feds had bought into Jack" (Ernest) Hilgard's ideas
of three major outcomes of education: cognitive, social, and self. Snow
looked around the table and in his gruff voice said, "I'm taking cognitive."
Carl looked around the table and said, "I'm taking social." Snow and
Thoresen looked at me and said, in unison, "You're taking self." And that
was that. I was low man on the totem pole and had been assigned to put
together a set of measures of self concept to be used by the center and
more generally in education to track outcomes.

Hubner, Stanton, and I set to our task of trying to figure out what self
concept was, how it was measured, and how these measurements might be
adapted for the center's use. (To be sure, we had the help of Pat Sears and
Bob Hess, colleagues on the faculty who were conducting self-research).
The obvious first step was to review the literature and for this review we
turned to Wylie (1961) and were immediately discouraged. However, 10
years had passed and we reasoned that she had shaped up the field
through her cogent criticism and advice. Such was not the case. The field
was as much or possibly more in disarray than when she had reported her
review. To be sure, there were many good conceptual ideas out there and
some very interesting instruments. However, the major theorists of that era
such as Brookover, Coombs, Coopersmith, Hamachek, Harris, Piers, Sears
(not to mention James and Rogers!) seemed to talk past one another, or
not to listen to each another, either theoretically or methodologically.

What we had believed to be a straightforward review of literature
became a puzzle to solve. There was misunderstanding on at least three

fronts: theory, measurement, and construct validity. In our review of the field (Shavelson, Hubner, & Stanton, 1976), "Self-Concept: Validation of Construct Interpretations," we attempted to address these issues. We dealt with theory by synthesizing the ideas most prevalent at the time, defining self-concept as "a person's perception of himself ... formed through his experience with his environment ... and influenced especially by environmental reinforcements and significant others" (p. 411). Self-concept, we said, could be characterized as well-organized, multifaceted, hierarchical, stable, developmental, evaluative, and differentiable. We summarized our findings in a now somewhat well known self-concept hierarchy with general self-concept at the apex dividing into academic, social, emotional, and physical self-concepts at the next level, and so on down behavior in specific situations. With respect to measurement, we urged that the development of self-concept scales be linked to a definition of the construct, such as ours. Finally, we concluded that many researchers had still not grasped Cronbach and Meehl's notion of construct validity and so explained construct validation in the context of validating self-concept interpretations of scores.

Somewhat unknowingly, Hubner, Stanton, and I had set out a research and development agenda for the study of self concept, the vestiges of which can be seen in current *issues* as is evident in many chapters in this monograph. The field has made remarkable progress. There seems to be rough agreement on the definition of self-concept which includes multidimensionality, increasing differentiation with age, hierarchical structure, the importance of frames of reference, the relevance of a self-concept as both a desirable outcome and a facilitator of other desirable outcomes, and the like. From where we sat over 30 years ago, this is, indeed, progress! Moreover, there appears to be consensus in the measurement of self-concept, a consensus that derives from the definition of the construct and benefits from psychometric developments in statistically modeling self-concept scores. And finally, there is widespread understanding in how construct validation theory applies to the measurement and interpretation of self-concept instruments.

Together, theory, measurement, and construct validation have worked to advance the field by leaps and bounds. We now have an international community of scholars, as evidenced for example by the authors of chapters in this inaugural volume, conducting sound, scientific research on self. We now have an international research center, the SELF Research Centre, committed to carrying out cutting edge research on the self and to identifying strategies to optimize self-concept and facilitate the attainment and understanding of other valued outcomes in a variety of settings.

Indeed, self-concept research has become truly international in scope, with self-concept researchers from around the world conducting collaborative research based upon common instruments, theoretical perspectives, research paradigms, and policy issues. Such a commonality of international research focus would have been completely unimaginable when my colleagues and I provided our review of self-concept research in 1976. This international perspective is well illustrated by the international conferences hosted by the SELF Research Centre (http://self.uws.edu.au) with its membership of more than 300 researchers from 46 countries and six continents, and by presentations at professional meetings such as the American Educational Research Association. Furthermore, much of this research is cross-cultural and forms a basis for extending tests of the construct validity and generalizability of our measures, theories, theoretical predictions, and application. Importantly, as evidenced by chapters in this monograph, the benefits are reciprocal in that cross-cultural research provides new theoretical insights and areas of application through the broader perspectives that it provides self-concept researchers from all countries.

In closing, it seems appropriate to look beyond the accomplishments of this community, for in success there is also opportunity to develop further. To do this, I turn back to the 1970s, the meeting with Snow and Thoresen, and the work done by Judy Hubner and George Stanton and myself. Our review of the self-concept literature was driven, in part, by a mandate to seek reliable and valid measures of self-concept for SCRDT. Moreover, with 20/20 hindsight, my background in psychometrics, not the cognitive psychology side, greatly influenced our summary of the literature into a hierarchy, which we noted:

> At the apex ... is general self-concept (cf. Spearman's 'g'). General self-concept may be divided into two components: academic and non-academic self-concept (cf. verbal-educational and practical abilities in the Vernon model). Academic self-concept may be divided into subject-matter areas (cf. group factors in the Vernon model)" (p. 412).

What we had conceived, predictable with the psychometrics background, was primarily a structural model of self-concept. If our theory was "right," we should be able to retrieve this multidimensional, hierarchical structure in the pattern of correlations among self-concept measures—and we did! We made tremendous progress and continue to do so. Papers in this volume show that we have now:

- Developed and expanded new theoretical models;
- Matured in our psychometric approach to measurement issues and have extended the number of self-concept facets we can specifically measure;
- Developed new innovative approaches to self-concept that allow us to assess self-concept with children as young as 4 and 5 years of age and

with special populations who were not well-served with traditional measures;

- Advanced to the point that we can apply our understandings in settings of practical significance and help to make a difference in people's lives (e.g., focus on special education in this volume); and
- Been able to test our findings and expand new theories in cross-cultural research to address major international issues (e.g., language of instruction in Hong Kong following its return to China).

The importance of self-concept as both a desirable outcome and a means to facilitate other desirable outcomes is particularly evident in educational settings but in other settings as well. We have established appropriate paradigms and begun to disentangle the causal role of academic self-concept in facilitating the attainment of valued educational outcomes such as enhanced academic achievement, attendance, participation, school enjoyment, and coursework selection. Self-concept research is being done in health (improved physical fitness, commitment to exercise), sport (winning gold medals), and social issues (e.g., enhancing the education of disadvantaged and gifted students; decreasing school violence, bullying and victimization; and improving language instruction; achieving and maintaining health-related physical activity).

As Rosenberg (1979) emphasized many years ago, self-concept provides the individual with the cornerstone upon which all actions and individual behavior (choices, effort, and persistence) are based. More recently Branden (1994) argued that all psychological problems can be traced at least in part to issues of low self-concept. Self-concept makes a difference, people who think positively about themselves are healthier, happier, and more productive. Hence, self-concept is fundamental to enhancing human potential, from early development and school achievement, to physical/mental health and wellbeing, to cultural identity and social justice. Self-concept research sets the stage to address critical societal issues (schooling, antibullying, social support, indigenous issues, physical and mental health, social inequities) with understudied, disadvantaged groups.

However, as a field, we still have challenges. Many researchers still take a "dustbowl" perspective to self-concept (see discussion by Hattie, 1992)—throw it in and see what happens. Despite outstanding reviews of the best self-concept measures currently available (e.g., Byrne, 1996), some researchers continue to use obsolete measures or construct new ad hoc measures without adequate attention to current standards of instrument construction (see Marsh & Hattie, 1996).

Moreover, the substantial focus on structure and the refinement of confirmatory factor analysis to address our concerns meant that we paid too little attention to *processes*, in particular, to cognitive, conative, and affective processes (e.g., Snow, Corno, & Jackson, 1996; see also Shavelson et al., in press) associated with self. We need to give greater consideration to these processes in our future work, doing a first-rate job of linking structure to how the self functions. For example, how might self-concept interact with cognitive processes in problem solving? "Think aloud" protocols (Ericsson & Simon, 1993) might be analyzed not only for cognitive processes but also for affective and conative processes to see how, for example, self-conceptions play out during the problem-solving process. Or, as noted in Hattie's paper (this volume), William James claimed that a person has multiple selves and these selves might very well play out in critical life decisions as suggested by the work of Markus (Markus & Kitayama, 1991; Markus & Nurius, 1986). For as Snow made clear, observed performance, including responses to Likert-type scales, is a function of person-in-situation—a transaction between the affordances and constraints of the task and the "aptitudes," including self, that are brought to bear on and transform the task. Moreover, by doing so, we inevitably will have to grapple with clinical practice and how self-concept plays out in the everyday life of people. Such a link between our research and every day practice will add richness to our theory and methods and even challenge our edifice.

Self-concept research is much better than it once was but it is still not as good as it might become. This monograph series and the work of the SELF Research Centre will continue to help drive the international research agenda and result in making a real difference to theory, measurement and practice in a range of settings and by so doing make a difference in people's lives by helping to maximize individual's full potential.

—Richard J. Shavelson
Stanford University
March 2003

REFERENCES

Branden, N. (1994). *Six pillars of self-esteem.* New York: Bantam.

Byrne, B. M. (1996). Academic self-concept: Its structure, measurement, and relation to academic achievement. In B. A. Bracken (Ed.), *Handbook of self-concept* (pp. 287-316). New York: Wiley.

Cronbach, L. J., & Meehl, P. E. (1955). Construct validity in psychological tests. *Psychological Bulletin, 52,* 281–302.

Ericsson, A. K., & Simon, H. A. (1993). *Protocol analysis. Verbal reports as data* (Rev. ed.). Cambridge, MA: MIT.

Hattie, J. A. (1992). *Self-concept.* Hillsdale NJ: Lawrence Erlbaum Associates.

Markus, H., & Kitayama, S. (1991). Culture and the self: Implications for cognition, emotion, and motivation. *Psychological Review, 98,* 224–253.

Markus, H., & Nurius, P. (1986). Possible selves. *American Psychologist, 41*, 954–969.

Marsh, H. W., & Hattie, J. (1996). Theoretical perspectives on the structure of self-concept. In B. A. Bracken (Ed.), *Handbook of self-concept* (pp. 38–90). New York: Wiley.

Rosenberg, M. (1979). *Conceiving the self.* New York: Basic Books.

Shavelson, R. J., Hubner, J. J., & Stanton, G. C. (1976). Self-concept: Validation of construct interpretations. *Review of Educational Research, 46*, 407–441.

Shavelson, R. J., Roeser, R. W., Kupermintz, H., Lau, S., Ayala, C., Haydel, A., Schultz, S., Quihuis, G., & Gallagher, L. (2002). Richard E. Snow's remaking of the concept of aptitude and multidimensional test validity: Introduction to the special issue. *Educational Assessment, 8*(2), 77–100.

Snow, R., Corno, L., & Jackson, D. (1996). Individual differences in affective and conative functions. In D. Berliner & R. Calfee (Eds.) *Handbook of Research in Educational Psychology,* (pp. 186–242). New York: Macmillan.

Wiley, R. (1961). *The self concept.* Lincoln, Nebraska: University of Nebraska Press.

ABOUT THE MONOGRAPH SERIES

PRIMARY RESEARCH FOCUS

Maximizing self-concept is recognized as a critical goal in itself and a means to facilitate other desirable outcomes in a diversity of settings. The desire to feel positively about oneself and the benefits of this feeling on choice, planning, persistence, and subsequent accomplishments transcend traditional disciplinary barriers and are central to goals in many social policy areas. *International Advances in Self Research* monograph series publishes scholarly works that primarily focus on self-concept research and pertain to a broad array of self-related constructs and processes including self-esteem, self-efficacy, identity, motivation, anxiety, self-attributions, self-regulated learning, and meta-cognition. The research focus of the monograph series includes theory underlying these constructs, their measurement, their relation to each other and to other constructs, their enhancement, and their application in research and practice. Chapters address a wide cross-section of: settings participants and research areas This series has a special interest in self-concept theory and research in settings characterized by diversity, such as special education, linguistic diversity, socioeconomic, and cultural diversity.

International Advances in Self Research, pages xvii–xviii
Copyright © 2003 by Information Age Publishing

THE SELF RESEARCH CENTRE

Contributions to this publication largely derive from invited papers from leading international scholars in the field and selected scholarly works emanating from the Self-concept Enhancement and Learning Facilitation (SELF) Research Centre's International Biennial conference (see website for details http://edweb.uws.edu.au/self/).

The vision of the SELF Research Centre is to be the recognized leading international center for self-concept and identity research. In pursuing this vision, the center strives to:

- Develop and promote strategies to optimize self-concept as an important outcome in itself;
- Promote a greater awareness of the worth of self in various social and cultural contexts; and
- Promote the role of self as a key facilitator in the attainment of other valued outcomes such as: cultural identity; learning and achievement; healthier lifestyles; teaching effectiveness; physical, psychological, educational, social, emotional and occupational development, and well-being.

As such, the SELF Research Centre, with its primary focus on self-concept theory, measurement, research, and practice, is unique internationally. The SELF Research Centre is a Research Centre of the University of Western Sydney, Australia. At the heart of the SELF Research Centre is a membership which includes hundreds of self-researchers from 46 countries and a network of International Satellite Research Units throughout the world (e.g. Chinese University of Hong Kong, Max Planck Institute for Human Development and Education in Berlin, Auckland University, Norwegian University of Technology and Science). Its international importance is demonstrated by the breadth of its International Foundation Members comprising some of the world's leading researchers, the world-class standing of its International SELF Satellite Research Units, and the collaborative links sought by key research bodies. The center has had a substantial impact on transforming the conduct and quality of self-concept research throughout the world, driving the international research agenda.

part I

OVERVIEW

CHAPTER 1

INTERNATIONAL ADVANCES IN SELF RESEARCH

Speaking to the Future

**Herbert W. Marsh, Rhonda G. Craven,
and Dennis M. McInerney**

THE IMPORTANCE OF THE SELF-CONCEPT CONSTRUCT

Maximizing self-concept is recognized as a critical goal in itself and a means to facilitate other desirable outcomes in a diversity of settings. The desire to feel positively about oneself and the benefits of this feeling on choice, planning, persistence, and subsequent accomplishments transcend traditional disciplinary barriers and are central to goals in many social policy areas. Nathaniel Branden (1994, p. xv), an eminent psychologist, attests to the significance of the self-concept/self-esteem construct and outcomes that are mediated by it, stating that:

> I cannot think of a single psychological problem—from anxiety to depression, to under-achievement at school or at work, to fear of intimacy, happiness or success, to alcohol or drug abuse, to spouse battering or child molestation, to codependency and sexual disorders, to passivity and chronic

International Advances in Self Research, pages 3–14
Copyright © 2003 by Information Age Publishing

aimlessness, to suicide and crimes of violence—that is not traceable, at least in part, to the problem of deficient self-esteem.

As appropriately illustrated by Branden, self-concept research is highly relevant to important individual and societal issues, particularly those that stem from low self-concept. The universal importance and multidisciplinary appeal of self-concept as one of the most important constructs in the social sciences is established. This importance of self-concept is manifested in diverse settings, including education, child development, mental and physical health, social services, industry, and sport/exercise. For example, educational policy statements throughout the world list self-concept enhancement as a central goal of education and emphasize self-concept as an important mediating factor that facilitates the attainment of other desirable learning, psychological and behavioral outcomes.

EXPANDING THEORETICAL MODELS

Self-concept theory, research, and practice are all inextricably intertwined, whereby neglect of any one area will undermine the other areas. Significant advances in self-concept theory over the last 20 years have resulted in the development of psychometrically sound self-concept measurement instruments and increasingly sophisticated research. The latter has served to further inform and refine the theory on which these instruments and research have been based. As Richard Shavelson acknowledges in the preface to this volume, self-concept researchers today are now extending the boundaries of self-concept theory to more fully explain the self-concept construct and its relation to other constructs. Given the importance of theory, underpinning all the chapters in this volume is a strong theoretical basis. In particular in part 1 of this volume, new theoretical perspectives are presented that serve as an impetus for important new directions in self-concept theory, research, and practice.

Herbert Marsh and Olaf Köller in their chapter, integrate and extend the two major theoretical models of relations between academic self-concept and achievement that have been studied extensively in educational research as separate models. First, they test the reciprocal effects model whereby self-concept is hypothesized to influence subsequent academic achievement, and academic achievement is also hypothesized to influence subsequent self-concept. Second, they test the internal/external frame of reference model, which was developed to explain the near zero correlations between math and verbal self-concept. In pursuing this aim they evaluate the cross-cultural generalizability of predictions based on integrating these two models using longitudinal data from large nationally representative cohorts of 7th grade students from East Germany and West Germany that were collected from the start of the reunification of the school systems following the fall of the Berlin Wall. Consistent with a priori predictions from reciprocal effects model Marsh and Köller demonstrate that: prior self-concept had significant effects on subsequent achievement beyond the effects of prior achievement in both German and mathematics; and that prior achievement also had significant effects on subsequent self-concept in both school subjects. Consistent with the internal/external frame of reference model, the authors demonstrate that: math achievement had a positive effect on math self-concept but a negative effect on German self-concept; and German achievement had a positive effect on German self-concept but a negative effect on math self-concept. Consistent with the integration and extension of these two models, prior self-concept in each school subject had positive effects on achievement in the same subject, but negative effects on achievement in the other school subject. Multigroup structural equation models showed these effects of academic self-concept and achievement to be the similar for East and West German students, providing support for the cross-cultural generalizability of the results and strong support for the integration of these two theoretical approaches.

The importance of validating self-concept theory and research by testing the cross-generalizability of the results is also emphasized in Kit Tai Hau, Chit-Kwong Kong and Herbert Marsh's chapter. Given current self-concept measures and models have been primarily developed based on Western cultural contexts, they have been criticized as being culturally bound to the ideology of individualism and may not be applicable to collective cultures. In this chapter, the authors undertake a large-scale, 6-year longitudinal research study of the applicability of Western self-concept models in regard to Chinese students in Hong Kong. Confirmatory factor, multitrait-multitime, and factorial invariance analyses were conducted. The authors also extend previous research to study self-concept of native and nonnative languages, to use truly longitudinal data in determining causal ordering of achievement and self-concept, and to separate the positive reflected glory assimilation effect from the negative social contrast effect in attending high-ability schools. Taken together the series of analyses presented by Hau, Kong, and Marsh demonstrate the robustness of the Chinese version of the popular Self-Description Questionnaire (SDQ) instruments in non-Western cultures. Furthermore, the cross-cultural applicability and generality of the self-concept and its related theoretical models have also been supported in the Chinese culture, offering good external validity for self-concept theory in an Eastern cultural context. The material in the latter two chapters should be read in the context of Barbara Byrne's chapter on cross-cultural methodologies.

Einar Skaalvik and Mimi Bong compare theoretical arguments and findings from self-concept and self-efficacy theories, in order to elucidate important differences and similarities between these prominent self theories. It is acknowledged that students hold different beliefs about themselves. They differ in their beliefs of what kind of person they are, how satisfied they are with themselves, how capable they are compared with others, and how confident they feel, to successfully perform given tasks. It is often these beliefs, rather than objective competence and characteristics, that determine their subsequent motivation, affect, and behaviors. They argue that although both self-concept and self-efficacy theory reflect generalizations from past experiences, self-concept represents multidimensional yet aggregated judgments of ability with stronger past orientation, heavier emphasis on social comparison, and relative temporal stability. In contrast, they suggest that self-efficacy represents highly context-specific and goal-oriented appraisals of capability that are relatively malleable, and as such, function as an active precursor of self-concept beliefs. The authors also contend that perceptions of competence constitute the single most critical element in both belief systems, which predict important educational outcomes to varying degrees. Hence, this analysis has the potential to serve as a basis for combining these important theoretical approaches.

Rhonda Craven, Herbert Marsh, and Paul Burnett acknowledge that enhancing self-concept across the life span is recognized internationally as a highly desirable goal in diverse settings ranging from the preschool classroom to the retirement village. The authors also recognize that despite the importance placed on the value of enhancing self-concept and the assumption that self-concept enhancement will enhance other desirable outcomes such as academic achievement, a plethora of self-concept interventions have failed to enhance self-concept. In this chapter Craven, Marsh, and Burnett encourage researchers to crack this self-concept enhancement conundrum. They present research evidence demonstrating that enhancing self-concept causally impacts on subsequent academic achievement and other desirable educational outcomes, putting to the test the causal ordering debate. They provide a persuasive rationale for enhancing self-concept underpinned by recent research findings that serves as an impetus for researchers to unravel the self-concept enhancement conundrum. The authors also identify historical methodological weaknesses in self-concept theory and research to assist researchers to avoid pitfalls that continue to plague enhancement research, and provide an overview of recent advances that researchers can capitalize upon to develop and effectively test promising interventions. Importantly the authors present valuable guidelines to assist researchers to develop the next generation of self-concept enhancement research. The compelling results and blueprint for future research presented in the chapter provide an impetus and sound framework for researchers to indeed begin to crack the self-concept enhancement conundrum.

John Hattie revisits William James' chapter on "The Consciousness of Self" (James, 1890), and considers how self-researchers in the twentieth century have selectively ignored much of his advice, such that research has addressed some minor parts of James's program extremely well while continuing to ignore many major issues. Hattie notes that researchers have also attempted to recast some of James' critical questions, which has resulted in self-concept researchers finding excellent answers to wrong questions. Hattie's chapter starts with an overview of James' claims, builds on the 100 years of research since, and outlines an ambitious research program more appropriate to the next 100 years. Hence, the chapter provides self-concept researchers with a thoughtful analysis of issues that need to be addressed in future self-concept research.

MEASUREMENT ISSUES

An important legacy of the classic review by Shavelson and colleagues (1976) has been the emphasis on measurement and construct validation in self-concept research. This emphasis is, arguably, the most important development in self-concept research in the quarter century following their review. Self-concept research was previously known for its "one-shot wonders" in which there were nearly as many self-concept instruments as self-concept studies. Self-concept instruments were typically an ad hoc collection of self-referent items with little attention to measurement issues such as dimensionality, factor structure, reliability, stability, and construct validity. As evidenced by even a casual inspection of the self-concept literature, those days are thankfully gone. Measurement issues are clearly an integral part of an ongoing self-concept research program. As frequently noted by Marsh and colleagues, measurement, instrument construction, construct validation, theory building, research, and application are all intertwined such that each will suffer if any one is neglected. They argue that the determination of theoretically consistent and distinguishable domains of self-concept should be prerequisite to the study of how self-concept is related to other variables. This emphasis on rigorous measurement is clearly evident in all chapters in this monograph, but is particularly important in the two chapters in this section.

In his chapter on music self-concept and self-perceptions, Walter Vispoel extends his exciting work on multidimensional self-concepts in the performing arts arena. Vispoel notes that over the last two decades, considerable advances have been made in self-concept theory and instrument development. Among these advances are extensions of self-theory and instrumentation into new content domains. In this chapter, he synthesized recent developments in the theory and measurement of self-perceptions of musical ability. The issues addressed include the psychometric features of music self-concept instruments, the integration of music self-concept into hierarchical models of self-concept, and the structure of music self-perceptions. In addition, Vispoel tackles the perennial problem of the role that domain importance plays in moderating relations between facets of music self-concept and overall self-esteem. Despite the long history of the importance weighted average model that dates back to the original writings of William James, there has been surprisingly little empirical support for it. Based on psychometrically sound measures of music self-concept, Vispoel provides what appears to be the strongest support for the important weighted-average ever published.

Inés Tomás-Marco and Vicente González-Romá compare the Physical Self-Description Questionnaire (PSDQ) factor structure based on responses by the original Australian sample and by a matched set of Spanish adolescents. In this chapter they combine state-of-the-art measurement procedures and issues in the translation of instruments from one language to another in order to tackle a challenging cross-cultural research issue. They note that there is general agreement among self-concept researchers regarding the idea that the development and evaluation of multidimensional instruments that are specific to self-concept domains needs to be based on theory, followed by factor analytic investigations that offer further support for the hypothesized factor structure. Moreover, the development of translated versions of the questionnaires into other languages offers further evidence of the construct validity of the instruments, and of the generalizability of the factor structure across several cultures. Results from previous research provide support for the reliability and construct validity of the questionnaire for Australian adolescents. The purpose of their study was to develop a translated version of the PSDQ into Spanish in order to study the construct validity of the questionnaire and assess the generalizability of its factor structure across a different culture. They found that the factor structures based on responses by Spanish and Australian adolescents were very similar. These results not only support their new Spanish version of the PSDQ, but also provide strong support for the generalizability of results based on the original English version of the PSDQ instruments.

This measurement focus emphasized in this section is also an important component in several other chapters in the monograph. Hau, Kong, and Marsh, in their chapter on self-concept responses by Hong Kong adolescents, start with a strong emphasis on factor structure and multidimensionality before focusing on more substantive issues. Hattie, in his chapter reviewing the relevance of William James's early writings to current self-concept research, provides provocative challenges to the way we measure self-concept. Each of the chapters in the section Applications to Special Education—particularly the Tracey, Marsh, and Craven chapter—tackles important measurement issues that have hindered self-concept research in this area. Finally, measurement issues are at the heart of the chapters dealing with cross-cultural issues.

APPLICATIONS TO SPECIAL EDUCATION

Self-concept has always played an important role in special education research. Here, perhaps more so than any in other area of education, researchers, policy makers, and practitioners have all endorsed the importance of a positive self-concept as an important goal for educational programs. This importance is particularly evident in the heated debates about whether children with special needs are best educated in special classes developed for these students, in regular (mainstream) classes, or some combination. Interestingly, proponents of very different approaches to this critical issue in special education research have all claimed support for their favored approach in terms of enhancing self-concept. Results based on chapters in this section provide some of the clearest evidence available to address this important policy issue. The research also demonstrates the important synergy between self-concept measurement, theory, research, and application.

The chapter by Danielle Tracey, Herbert Marsh, and Rhonda Craven begins by emphasizing that a major debate in special education is whether students with mild intellectual disability are best placed in regular classes or special classes. They note that self-concept has played a key role in this debate. From a methodological standpoint, they note that unidimensional perspectives on self-concept are still prevalent in special education research even though a multidimensional perspective in most other areas of research has supplanted it. These authors, however, provide clear support for a multidimensional perspective of self-concept. Responses based on the newly developed individualized administration procedure with the SDQI self-concept instrument demonstrated strong psychometric properties (reliability, multidimensional factor structure, convergent and discriminant validity). From a theoretical standpoint, they argued that the two major theoretical positions—labeling theory and the big-fish-little-pond effect (BFLPE)—offered diametrically opposed predictions about the direction of placement effects on self-concept. Their results, based on both a large cross-sectional study and a longitudinal study provided support for the BFLPE. In particular, students placed in special classes reported significantly higher academic (reading, mathematics, general-school) self-concepts compared to their counterparts placed in regular classes. Qualitative interviews elaborated these findings, demonstrating that students with mild intellectual disabilities felt excluded—not included—when placed in regular classes rather than special classes with other students with similar disabilities. These findings have important educational implications because while the inclusion of students with disabilities in regular classes continues to gain international momentum, these results question the appropriateness of this movement. Placing preadolescents with mild intellectual disability in regular classes is detrimental to their academic self-concept.

The chapter by Waheeda Tabassam and Jessica Grainger also focuses on the importance of the multidimensionality of self-concept in special education research. They note that the self-perception of students with learning difficulties has been a research focus over the last three decades. Whereas mounting research evidence shows that students with learning difficulties (LD) have lower self-estimations compared to their normally achieving peers, this difference is mostly evident in academic components of self-concept. The authors conducted research to examine an intervention for the enhancement of academic self-concept for students with learning and attention difficulties. Their intervention utilized an indirect self-concept enhancement approach, using attributional retraining techniques. The basic concept in the intervention program was derived from the suggested reciprocal links between self-concept and self-attributions, which assumed that a positive change in academic attributions would be associated with a positive change in academic self-concept. The results verified the close link between academic attributional beliefs and academic self-perceptions, and provided a support for the effectiveness of attributional retraining technique in the enhancement of academic self-concept.

In Jason Crabtree's chapter, the focus is to provide a strong research basis for what may be the most important policy issue in special education. He notes that students with mild learning disabilities (MLD) are the focus of current educational inclusion initiatives, moving from special education to mainstream education. His research examined the self-concepts of MLD students attending either of these two different types of school setting. In particular, he considered the social comparison processes these students appear to use to maintain positive self-conceptualisations. The findings demonstrate the importance of social comparison groups in the construction of self-concept. When MLD students are in special schools, their social comparisons are with other MLD students so that they maintain positive self-concepts. Conversely, when MLD students are placed in regular schools, their social comparisons are with non-MLD students so it appears that their self-concepts are lower. He concluded MLD students who are integrated into regular classrooms suffer from greater levels of stigmatization and lower levels of self-concept than do MLD students who attend special schools.

Taken together, these two studies on placement effects—one from Australia and the other from the United Kingdom—offer compelling new support for controversial predictions based on the big-fish, little-pond effect and social comparison processes. Both studies argue that special education students with learning disabilities are likely to have higher academic self-concepts in special school settings with other, similar students than if integrated into regular classes with nonlearning disabled students. Whereas most previous research in support of the BFLPE has been based on the effects of attending schools where the average ability level is very high, this research demonstrates the applicability of these theoretical developments for special education research and policy.

CROSS-CULTURAL RESEARCH

Psychology as a discipline is essentially a Western phenomenon. Until relatively recently, research methodologies based on American or Western European models were considered transferable across cultures, with few modifications. Diverse cultural and social groups were, and still are to some degree, assessed on a range of criteria related to constructs such as intelligence, anxiety, motivation, and self-concept, on assumptions derived from research with middle class, protestant, white Americans, or their European counterparts. There has been considerable effort over the last twenty years to reformulate research constructs and methodologies to make them more appropriate cross-culturally. The drive for this has come from a growing realization of the potentially different nature of psychological processes in non-Western societies and from many cross-cultural studies which indicate the inherent weaknesses in using Western constructs, tests, and methodologies in societies and cultures which have different sociocultural bases. With the growing interest in testing the universality of motivational and self-concept constructs in diverse cultural settings it is important that researchers critically evaluate their theories and methodologies to ensure their cultural relevance. The following chapters deal with both methodological and substantive issues when self-concept and motivational research is conducted in non-Western societies.

In her chapter Barbara Byrne discusses the need to test for the equivalence of self-concept measures across cultures. Although mean differences in self-concept scores across culturally diverse groups have been of interest for many decades, the examination of the extent to which these self-concept measures are theoretically and metrically equivalent across such groups is a relatively recent phenomenon. Of particular concern is the use of self-concept instruments that have been translated into another language for use with a cultural group that differs from the one for which they were developed. Barbara addresses this practice and sets out to identify and elaborate on the issue of bias in cross-cultural research. In particular, she examines issues related to construct, instrument, item, administration, and sampling bias and explores the issue of equivalence in cross-cultural research. Specifically, Byrne examines both the measurement and theoretical equivalence of self-concept instruments outlining procedures for testing the equivalency of self-concept measurements across cultures.

As is suggested in the chapter by Byrne, psychological processes may be different across cultural groups. For example, school motivation and achievement for an individual are the products of a complex set of interacting motivational goals, sense of self and self-concept variables. Motivational goals may, therefore, be differentially salient to individuals from different cultural backgrounds, and sense of self, including academic self-concept, may vary across cultural groups. Dennis McInerney's chapter describes a project that examines the nature of motivational goals held by Aboriginal students; the nature of their academic self-concepts, and the nature of their sense of self within school settings. In particular, the chapter examines the similarities and differences between Aboriginal and Anglo students on achievement motivation and academic self-concept, and the comparative ability of these to predict valued school outcomes such as students' intentions to complete further education, whether they like and value school, their level of academic achievement, and school attendance. His results call into question many assumptions about Aboriginal students and their motivation at school, which should give strong cause to educators to reexamine the stereotypes they might hold of Aboriginal students.

The chapter by David Sam and Erkki Virta focuses on the self-esteem of adolescents with immigrant background with special emphasis on its relationship with ethnic identity. With respect to this relationship, Sam and Virta examine whether this relationship is moderated or mediated by perceived discrimination and majority identity. In addition, they compare the level of reported self-esteem among these immigrant adolescents with that of their majority host counterparts. From social identity theory, it has been argued that identity and self-esteem are positively related. It is further argued that disparaged minority group members will have a lower self-esteem than their host majority counterparts because of prejudice, negative stereotypes, and discrimination. However, research testing these assumptions has shown mixed findings. This background serves as the basis for Sam and Virta's development of their chapter. First, they identify the possible reasons for these mixed findings, and argue that perceived discrimination and the degree of the minority group member's identification with the majority group (for example, majority identity) may be either mediating or moderating the relationship between ethnic identity and self-esteem. Second, they suggest that the level of the minority group member's self-esteem might be related to the way they simultaneously identify with their own group and that of the majority group. These hypotheses are examined among three distinct ethnic groups with an immigrant background in Norway and Sweden. While the mediating/moderating roles of the majority identity and perceived discrimination are rejected, the study suggests that a high identification with one's ethnic group as well as with the majority group may lead to high self-esteem. Alternatively, a simultaneous low identification with both the ethnic and majority groups led to low levels of self-esteem. These findings might be useful when planning strategies in helping ethnic minority group members in their adjustment in a settlement country.

The chapter by David Watkins and his colleagues challenges the view of Markus and Kitayama that the independent model of self, depicted in the literature, is not appropriate for non-Western people. Watkins and colleagues consider that the research basis for such a claim is not convincing. The research program reported in their chapter was designed to provide such a database. Two studies are described in the chapter. Study 1, involved content analyzing the responses to the Twenty Statements Test of 2,391 college and 459 school students from 16 countries. Study 2, involved ecological factor analysis and multidimensional scaling analysis of responses of 1,662 adults and 5,124 college students from 25 countries to the Adult Sources of Self-Esteem Inventory. Watkins and colleagues conclude that cultures do differ in the basis of self-conceptions but such differences cannot be explained in terms of Western versus non-Western or a cultural dimension such as Individualism-Collectivism.

Also relevant to this cross-cultural theme in this section are earlier chapters such as the Marsh and Köller's chapter that compares results of theoretical models in East and West Germany at the time of the fall of the Berlin Wall, the Hau, Kong, and Marsh chapter that tests in China the construct validity of the SDQ instrument and theoretical models derived from a Western setting, and the Tomás-Marco and González-Romá chapter that makes rigorous comparisons of responses to the PSDQ instrument by Spanish and Australian high school students. More generally, the diverse settings and countries represented in this monograph are a testament to the cross-cultural appeal of research into self-concept, motivation, and related constructs.

THE SELF RESEARCH CENTRE

Contributions to this series largely derive from invited papers from leading international scholars in the field and selected scholarly works emanating from the Self-concept Enhancement and Learning Facilitation (SELF) Research Centre's International Biennial conference (see website for details http://self.uws.edu.au).

REFERENCES

Branden, N. (1994). *Six pillars of self-esteem*. New York: Bantam.

James, W. (1890/1963). *The principles of psychology*. New York: Holt, Rinehart and Winston.

Markus, H.R., & Kitayama, S. (1991). Culture and the self: Implications for cognition, emotion, and motivation. *Psychological Review, 98*, 224–253.

Shavelson, R. J., Hubner, J. J., & Stanton, G. C. (1976). Self-concept: Validation of construct interpretations. *Review of Educational Research, 46*, 407–441.

part II

EXPANDING THEORETICAL MODELS

CHAPTER 2

BRINGING TOGETHER TWO THEORETICAL MODELS OF RELATIONS BETWEEN ACADEMIC SELF-CONCEPT AND ACHIEVEMENT

Herbert W. Marsh and Olaf Köller

The importance of self-concept as a relevant outcome variable is evident in diverse settings, including education, child development, mental and physical health, social services, organizations, industry, and sport. For example, educational policy statements throughout the world list self-concept enhancement as a central goal of education and an important vehicle for addressing social inequities experienced by disadvantaged groups. Here we integrate two self-concept theories that have been studied extensively in educational research as separate theories and test their cross-cultural generalizability. The theme of this chapter is unification and reunification. Our theoretical goal is to integrate and extend the two major theoretical models of relations between academic self-concept and achievement that have been studied extensively in educational research as separate models.

The reciprocal effects model has to with the relationship between academic self-concept and academic accomplishments. Academic self-concept is correlated with academic achievement. However, does academic self-con-

International Advances in Self Research, pages 17–47

cept merely reflect prior performance or does it contribute to the prediction of future performance beyond what can be explained in terms of prior performance? In this chapter we argue that self-concept reflects more than merely a (possibly imprecise) indicator of performance. Hence, the theoretical question is: What comes first—academic self-concept (how I think and feel about myself academically) or academic achievement (how well I perform in academic settings)? Not surprisingly, "either-or" answers to this question are too simplistic and a growing body of research shows that academic self-concept both affects and is affected by academic achievement. In pursuing this argument, we describe theoretical, methodological, and empirical research to address the critical "chicken or the egg" problem of causal ordering.

The internal/external frame of reference (I/E) model was designed to explain why math and verbal self-concept responses are nearly uncorrelated even though the corresponding areas of achievement are highly correlated. Whereas individuals who have good mathematical skills also tend to have good verbal skills, people tend to think of themselves as a "verbal person" or a "numbers person." According to the I/E model, for example, math self-concept is based in part on math skills but also skills in other school subjects. Good math skills lead to good Math self-concepts, but good verbal skills lead to poorer math self-concepts (if my verbal skills are much better than my math skills, I will have a higher verbal self-concept and a lower math self-concept).

The theme of this chapter is unification and reunification. Our theoretical goal is to integrate and extend the two major theoretical models of relations between academic self-concept and achievement that have been studied extensively in educational research as separate models. What is new in this chapter is the unification of these two theoretical models that have formed the foundation of theoretical and empirical research into relations between academic self-concept and achievement. In bringing together these two theoretical frameworks we demonstrate that the critical interplay between academic self-concepts in different domains—mathematics and verbal—is important to understanding relations between academic self-concept and achievement.

Equally exciting is the unique setting that we have to evaluate support for predictions based on each model separately and the new integrated model. In pursuing our goal of theoretical unification, we evaluate the cross-cultural generalizability of predictions based on this integrated model using longitudinal data from large nationally representative cohorts of students in East and West Germany that was collected from the start of the reunification of the school systems following the fall of the Berlin Wall.

MULTIDIMENSIONAL ACADEMIC SELF-CONCEPTS AND THEIR RELATION TO ACHIEVEMENT

Historically, self-concept measurement, theory, research, and application have emphasized a largely atheoretical, global component of self-concept, and reviewers have noted the lack of theoretical models for defining and interpreting the construct (e.g., Shavelson, Hubner, & Stanton, 1976; Wells & Marwell, 1976; Wylie, 1974, 1979). In an attempt to remedy this situation, Shavelson and colleagues (1976) reviewed existing research and self-concept instruments and provided a theoretical definition and model of self-concept that has had a profound influence on subsequent research (see review by Marsh & Hattie, 1996). In the Shavelson and colleagues model, self-concept is posited to be a multidimensional, hierarchical construct. Global self-concept, at the apex of the hierarchy, is divided into nonacademic (e.g., social, physical, emotional) and academic components. Of particular relevance to the present investigation, academic self-concept is divided into self-concepts in particular content areas such as math and verbal self-concepts. Support for the construct validity of self-concept interpretations and its multidimensionality requires that: (a) academic achievement is more highly correlated with academic components of self-concept than with global and nonacademic components of self-concept; (b) academic achievement in particular domains is more highly correlated with academic self-concepts in the matching domain (e.g., math achievement and math self-concept) than self-concepts in nonmatching domains (e.g., math achievement and general or verbal self-concept).

Reciprocal Effects Model: Causal Ordering of Self-concept and Performance Accomplishments

Self-concept, in addition to being an important outcome variable, is an important mediating construct that facilitates the attainment of other desirable psychological and behavioral outcomes. From a social-cognitive perspective, self-concept is a "hot" variable that makes things happen. The need to think and feel positively about oneself, and the profound benefits of these positive cognitions on choice, planning, and subsequent accomplishments transcend traditional disciplinary barriers and are central to goals in many social policy areas. These basic ideas can easily be translated into many different disciplines. Thus, for example, Marsh (2002) demonstrated that physical self-concept contributed to the prediction of the performances of elite swimmers at international events beyond what could be explained in terms of their previous performances (personal bests and international rankings). In an organizational setting, Parker (1998) summarized research showing that employees who feel more able to perform particular tasks will actually perform better on these tasks, will persist in the face of adversity, and will cope more effectively with change. Judge and Bono (2001) presented a meta-analysis showing that components of a positive self-concept construct were among the best predictors of job performance and job satisfaction.

The major research question in the study of academic self-concept is the "chicken or the egg" question of whether academic self-concept "causes" academic achievement or achievement "causes" academic self-concept. Parents, teachers, and researchers typically assume that self-concept and academic achievement are substantially related and, perhaps, that a positive self-concept fosters academic striving behaviors (e.g., academic choice) that can enhance academic achievement (Marsh & Craven, 1997). Byrne (1996) noted that much of the interest in the self-concept/achievement relation stems from the belief that academic self-concept has motivational properties that affect subsequent academic achievement.

Theoretical Models

Calsyn and Kenny (1977) contrasted self-enhancement and skill development models of the self-concept/achievement relation. The self-enhancement model posits self-concept as a primary determinant of academic achievement (i.e., academic self-concept causes achievement). This model supports self-concept enhancement interventions explicit or implicit in many educational programs. In contrast, the skill development model (i.e., academic achievement causes self-concept) implies that academic self-concept emerges principally as a consequence of academic achievement. According to this model, the best way to enhance academic self-concept is to develop stronger academic skills.

Despite the importance of this issue, well-established paradigms for testing these models did not exist prior to the 1980s. Because self-concept and academic achievement are not readily amenable to experimental manipulations, most research relies on longitudinal panel data in which both self-concept and achievement are measured on at least two occasions (see Figure 2.1A). In this model, it is expected that the primary determinant of subsequent measures of each construct (academic self-concept and achievement) is the prior measure of the same construct (the paths with "++" in Figure 2.1A). The critical paths, however, are the cross paths leading from prior achievement to subsequent self-concept and from prior self-concept to subsequent achievement (the paths with "+" in Figure 2.1A).

Due in part to methodological limitations in the statistical tools available to test these models, early research compared the relative sizes of paths from self-concept to achievement and from achievement to self-concept (i.e., a "winner takes all" strategy). Thus, for example, if the path from prior achievement to subsequent self-concept was larger than the path from prior self-concept to subsequent achievement, the results were claimed to support the skill development model. This approach to evaluating these causal-modeling studies has persisted, despite recent advances in the application of structural equation modeling (Byrne, 1996; Marsh, Byrne, & Yeung, 1999) that mean it is no longer necessary. In a critique of this strategy, Marsh (1990a, 1990b, 1993; also see Marsh, Byrne, & Yeung, 1999) argued that this approach was methodologically unsound and inconsistent with academic self-concept theory. For example, if both paths (from self-concept to achievement and from achievement to self-concept) are significantly positive, then it makes no sense simply to ignore the smaller one. Furthermore, he emphasized that it is widely accepted that prior academic achievement is one determinant of academic self-concept. Hence, the critical path is the one from prior academic self-concept to subsequent achievement (the path with a "+" shaded in grey in Figure 2.1A). A more realistic compromise between the self-enhancement and skill-development models is a "reciprocal effects model" in which prior academic self-concept affects subsequent achievement and prior achievement affects subsequent academic self-concept (the two paths with "+" in Figure 2.1A).

Research Findings

Marsh and Yeung (1997; also Byrne, 1990; Marsh, Byrne, & Yeung, 1999) updated previous reviews of research in this area, but found only nine relevant longitudinal causal modeling studies. Despite limitations in most of these studies, they concluded that this research provided reasonably consistent support for a reciprocal effects model. Apparent exceptions were: the Shavelson and Bolus (1982) study that reported only significant paths from self-concept to achievement; Newman (1984) who reported only significant paths from achievement to self-concept (but Marsh [1988] reported some evidence for self-concept effects in his reanalysis of the data); and Byrne (1986) who found no cross-paths at all (but see Marsh, Byrne & Yeung, 1999, for a reanalysis of this study). Marsh (1990a) suggested that paths from self-concept to achievement might be stronger for school-based performance measures compared to standardized achievement measures, but Helmke and van Aken (1995) did not support this suggestion. Skaalvik and Hagtvet (1990) suggested that paths from self-concept to achievement might be stronger for studies based on older students and there was some support for this proposal.

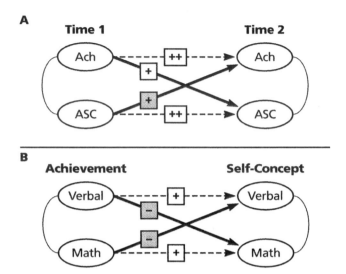

Figure 2.1.   Predictions derived from the reciprocal effect model of Academic Achievement (ACH) and Academic Self-concept based on at least two waves of data ("++" and "+" refer to the relative size of predicted path coefficients leading from Time 1 constructs to Time 2 constructs). In both figures the critical paths for testing the model are presented in gray boxes. Figure 2.1B. Predictions derived from the I/E model relating verbal and math achievements and verbal and math self-concepts are based on a single wave of data. ("+" and "–" refer to the predicted direction of the path coefficients).

Internal/External Frame of Reference (I/E) Model: Domain Specificity of Multiple Self-concepts

The Shavelson and colleagues (1976) model assumes that there is a strong higher-order academic self-concept such that there is a substantial correlation between verbal and math self-concepts. This prediction also follows from the typically large correlation between math and verbal academic achievements (typically .5 to .8, depending on how achievement is measured). Early research, however, demonstrated that math and verbal self-concepts were much more differentiated than the corresponding achievement scores (Marsh, 1986). In contrast to the expectation of high correlations between math and verbal self-concepts, math and verbal self-concepts were nearly uncorrelated. Furthermore, this near-zero correlation was consistent across different measures of the math and verbal self-concepts and a diversity of settings (Marsh & Craven, 1997; Marsh & Yeung, 1997). In response to these seemingly paradoxical results, the I/E model was developed to explain why math and English self-concepts are almost uncorrelated even though corresponding areas of academic achievement are substantially correlated.

Theoretical Model

According to the I/E model, academic self-concept in a particular school subject is formed in relation to two comparison processes or frames of reference. The first is the typical *external* (normative or social comparison) reference in which students compare their self-perceived performances in a particular school subject with the perceived performances of other students in the same school subject and other external standards of actual achievement levels. If they perceive themselves to be able in relation to other students and objective indicators of achievement, then they should have a high academic self-concept in that school subject. Because objective math and verbal accomplishments are substantially correlated, this first process leads to the expectation that math and verbal self-concepts should also be highly correlated. The second is an *internal* (ipsative-like) reference in which students compare their own performance in one particular school subject with their own performances in other school subjects. Hence, according to this internal comparison process, students may have a favorable math self-concept if math is their best subject even if they are not particularly good at math relative to other students and external standards. Because ipsative measures are necessarily negatively correlated, this second process leads to the expectation that math and verbal self-concepts are negatively correlated. The joint operation of these processes, depending on the relative weight given to each, is consistent with the near-zero correlation between math and verbal self-concepts that led to the revision of the Shavelson and colleagues (1976) model. It is, however, important to emphasize that support for the I/E model does not require that the correlation between math and verbal self-concepts be zero, but only that it be substantially less than the typically substantial correlation between math and verbal achievement.

To clarify how these two processes operate, consider a student who accurately perceives him or herself to be below average in both verbal and math skills (an external comparison), but who is better at mathematics than verbal and other school subjects (an internal comparison). The student's math skills are below average relative to other students and objective indicators of math achievement (the external comparison), and this should lead to a below-average math self-concept. However, this student's math skills are above average relative to his or her other school subjects (an internal comparison) and this should lead to an above-average math self-concept. Depending on how these two processes are weighted in the formation of self-concept, this student may have an average or even above-average math self-concept even though he or she has below-average math skills. The I/E model also predicts that this student would have a better math self-concept than another student who did equally poorly at mathematics but who did better in all other school subjects (i.e., math was his or her worst subject). Similarly, a student who is very bright in all school subjects may have an average or even below-average math self-concept if the student perceived mathematics to be his or her worst subject. For example, a student whose *best* subject is mathematics may have a higher math self-concept than other students who are equally good at mathematics but even better at other school subjects.

Stronger tests of the I/E model are possible when math and English achievements are related to math and English self-concepts (see Figure 2.1B). The external comparison process predicts that good math skills lead to higher math self-concepts and that good verbal skills lead to higher verbal self-concepts (the "+" paths in Figure 2.1B). The internal comparison process, however, leads to more interesting predictions that are apparently unique to the I/E model. According to this process, better math skills should lead to *lower* verbal self-concept and better verbal skills should lead to *lower* math self-concept. For example, in order to have a good math self-concept one needs good math skills (the external comparison process) and math skills that are better than one's verbal skills (the internal comparison process). If, however, one has particularly good verbal skills then the math skills are unlikely to be better than the verbal skills and these good verbal skills will detract from one's math self-concept. Hence, the critical paths in testing the I/E model are the negative cross-paths leading from math achievement to verbal self-concept and from verbal achievement to math self-concept (the "−" paths in grey boxes in Figure 2.1B that reflect the internal comparison process).

It is also important to clarify what is actually being tested in the I/E model. Typically, math and verbal achievements are substantially positively correlated with each other (the typical "big-G" that underlies almost all measures of achievement) and typically each is positively correlated with both math and verbal self-concepts. Clearly, math achievement is more correlated with math self-concept than verbal self-concept (and verbal achievement is more correlated with verbal self-concept than math self-concept). The critical prediction for the I/E model, however, is in terms of the path coefficients. In other words, it is the effect of math achievement on verbal self-concept *after* controlling for the effect of verbal achievement. Hence, once we control for the positive effect of math achievement (and the big-G component shared by math and verbal achievement) on math self-concept, then the unique component of verbal achievement is negatively associated with math self-concept. Thus, the size of the negative effect of math achievement on verbal self-concept should be a function of the discrepancy between the math and German language achievement scores. Hence, the operative construct is a residual score that is conceptually like the difference score (without some of the statistical problems associated with raw difference scores to which the reviewer alluded). Thus, a B average in mathematics may induce an average or even below-average mathematics self-concept for the student who earns A's in most other school subjects, but may lead to an above-average math self-concept for the student who earns C's in other subjects. In the language of path analysis, it is the direct effect of math achievement on verbal self-concept that is predicted to be negative—not the correlation between math achievement and verbal self-concept.

Research Findings

It is not surprising, of course, that good verbal skills are associated with good verbal self-concepts and that good math skills are associated with good math self-concepts (the positive paths in Figure 2.1B). More surprising—even paradoxical—are the negative paths from verbal achievement to math self-concept and from math achievement to verbal self-concept (i.e., being more mathematically able detracts from verbal self-concept whereas being more verbally able detracts from math self-concept). In a review of 13 studies that considered students of different ages and different academic achievement indicators, Marsh (1986) reported that: (a) correlations between indicators of verbal and math achievement were substantial (.42 to .94); (b) correlations between measures of verbal and math self-concepts were much smaller (-.10 to +.19); (c) path coefficients from verbal achievement to verbal self-concept, and from math achievement to math self-concept were all significantly positive; (d) path coefficients from math achievement to verbal self-concept, and from verbal achievement to math self-concept, were significantly *negative*. This pattern of results was subsequently replicated for responses to each of three different self-concept instruments by Canadian high school students (Marsh, Byrne, & Shavelson, 1988), for the nationally representative sample of U.S. high school students in the High School and Beyond Study (Marsh, 1989), and for the nationally representative sample of U.S. high school students in the National Longitudinal Study (Marsh, 1994b). Although most of this support is based on responses by students from United States, Canada, and Australia where the native language is English, there is also some support for the cross-cultural or cross-nationality generalizability of these results where verbal self-concept is in relation to a native language other than English (e.g., Norwegian: Skaalvik & Rankin, 1995; Chinese: Marsh, Kong, & Hau, 2001; Yeung & Lee, 1999). In their critique of research in this area, Marsh and Yeung (1997) noted the need to pursue longitudinal studies in which achievement and self-concept measures are collected on multiple occasions.

Unification of the Reciprocal Effects Model and the I/E Frame of Reference Model

The unification of the reciprocal effects model and the I/E frame of reference model (Figure 2.2) provides an important extension to previous theory and empirical research based on each model separately. Tests of the reciprocal effects model are typically based on longitudinal causal models of the reciprocal effects of academic self-concept and achievement across multiple waves of data. Although these models are not inconsistent with the extreme domain specificity shown in the I/E model, the causal models have typically been based on a single academic domain (i.e., a global academic self-concept or self-concepts in one particular school subject such as mathematics). Based on research leading to the internal/external frame of reference model, however, there is a critical interplay between academic self-concepts in different domains that is important to understanding relations between academic self-concept and achievement. Tests of the I/E model are typically based on a single wave of data. They focus on the extreme domain specificity of the effects of math and verbal achievement on math and verbal self-concepts, particularly the negative effect of math achievement on verbal self-concept and the negative effect of verbal achievement on math self-concept (the grey arrows in Figure 2.2). Although there is an implicit assumption in the I/E model that achievement affects self-concept, the model is not inconsistent with a reciprocal

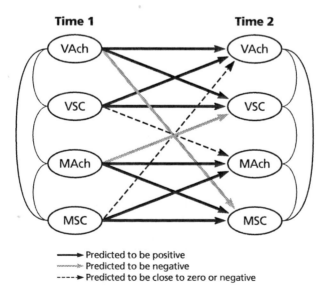

Time 1   Time 2

VAch   VAch
VSC   VSC
MAch   MAch
MSC   MSC

⟶ Predicted to be positive
⟶ Predicted to be negative
----▶ Predicted to be close to zero or negative

Figure 2.2.   Integration of the reciprocal effects model (Figure 2.1A) and the internal/external frame of reference model (Figure 2.1B).

effects model and tests of causal ordering cannot be adequately pursued when data is available from only one wave of data. Putting the two models together highlights potential limitations of each model that are well established strengths of the other—the reciprocal effects of self-concept and achievement (demonstrated in the longitudinal causal models but not largely ignored in I/E models) and the extreme domain specificity of effects (demonstrated in the I/E models but largely ignored in longitudinal causal models).

This unification of the I/E and longitudinal causal models also reveals a critical gap in the complementary theoretical perspectives that has important substantive and theoretical implications. Specifically, neither model offers predictions about either the effects of prior verbal self-concept on subsequent math achievement or the effects of prior math self-concept on subsequent verbal achievement. Extending the logic of the I/E model and consistent with the reciprocal effects in the longitudinal causal models, we predict that the extreme domain specificity in paths leading from math and verbal achievement to math and verbal self-concepts will also be evident in the corresponding paths leading from math and verbal self-concept to math and verbal achievement. In particular, compared to paths leading from self-concept to achievement in matching areas, paths leading from math self-concept to verbal achievement and from verbal self-concept to math achievement (the paths with dashed lines in Figure 2.2) will be very small, and may even be negative. Hence, the domain specificity in academic self-concept that has been the focus of the I/E model will reinforce the domain specificity in subsequent achievement that will further reinforce the domain specificity in subsequent academic self-concept. Tests of the unification of the two theories and new predictions based on their combination constitute a major theoretical contribution of the present investigation. The present investigation also tests predictions based on the unification of these two models for data from two different cultures—students from the former East and West Germany.

Cross-cultural Comparisons: Testing Self-concept Models with East and West German Students

Cross-cultural comparisons provide researchers an extremely valuable, heuristic basis to test the external validity and generalizability of their measures, theories, and models. In their influential overview of cross-cultural research, Segall, Lonner, and Berry (1998, p. 1102) stated that cross-cultural researchers' three complementary goals were:

to transport and test our current psychological knowledge and perspectives by using them in other cultures; to explore and discover new aspects of the phenomenon being studied in local cultural terms; and to integrate what has been learned from these first two approaches in order to generate more nearly universal psychology, one that has pan-human validity.

Similarly, Sue (1999) argued that research has not taken sufficient advantage of cross-cultural comparisons that allow researchers to test the external validity of their interpretations and to gain insights about the applicability of their theories and models. In cross-cultural research, there is an ongoing and growing interest in the relation between culture and the self. This is an inevitable consequence of the symbolic construction of self-image by using the meaning system that is culture (Kashima, 1995). Indeed, Singelis (2000) argues that this emphasis on self has been the primary basis for why other disciplines are increasingly embracing cross-cultural perspectives. However, there exists a schism between the overaching cultural relativist and universalist perspectives of cross-cultural research (Kagitcibasi & Poortinga, 2000). The broad cultural relativist (idiographic, emic, indigenous, qualitative) perspective emphasizes the uniqueness of the individual case that defies comparison. In contrast the broad universalist (nomothetic, etic, positivist, quantitative) perspective emphasizes what is common between cultures with an emphasis on theoretical predictions, replicability of methods, and empirical testing. Because neither of these apparently mutually exclusive metatheoretical positions is defensible in the extreme, there is a need to bridge this dichotomy. Thus, for example, Kashima (1995) noted the need for future research to identify universal as well as culture-specific antecedents and consequences of self-conceptions. In an emerging consensus on the cultural-mind relation, Kashima (2000) emphasizes a system of reciprocal effects whereby agents generate culture but are also shaped by culture. Similarly, Kitayama and Markus (1999) argue for the mutual construction of culture and self.

In their taxonomy of cross-cultural research, Van de Vijer and Leung (2000) discussed generalizablity studies with a strong theoretical framework for generating testable hypotheses and an emphasis on the universality of structures and theoretical propositions. Within this context, they noted the need to use new multiple group structural equation modeling approaches that allows researchers to make fine-grained comparisons of factor structures and patterns of relations between multiple constructs in different cultural groups. Within this framework, there is a focus on similarities as well as differences and an emphasis on the explanation of observed differences. Because of the traditional focus on null hypothesis testing, there is an unfortunate tendency to provide elaborate interpretations for (sometimes very small) differences and largely to ignore similarities that may argue for generalization across cultures. From this perspective, cross-cultural research can be seen as an extremely important variation on the traditional multimethod approach to the evaluation of construct validity. Van de Vijer and Leung emphasize that the endemic problems of replicability in cross-cultural research will improve with greater emphasis on theory development and testing coupled with the more appropriate use of new statistical tools.

In cross-cultural research, a perennial problem is whether cross-cultural differences represent the effects of culture, the potentially infinite number of variables that are confounded with culture, or, perhaps, the representativeness of the specific groups used to represent the different cultures. Hannover (1995) noted that comparisons between East and West Germans prior to or shortly after the fall of the Berlin Wall provided the unique opportunity to compare two groups of individuals who had been living in different cultures for many years but were similar on many variables that are typically confounded with culture (e.g., language, geographic location, cultural history, gene pool). Because the school cultures of the former East and West German school systems were so different, they provided a particularly important basis for testing the generalizability of our predictions based on our academic self-concept models. In particular, Oettingen, Little, Lindenberger, and Baltes (1994) and others (e.g., Hannover, 1995) emphasized three differences in the East and West German school systems that mirror the broader East and West German cultures: (a) the age of onset of grading systems; (b) the nature and emphasis on performance feedback; and (c) the dimensionality or standardization in teaching strategies. East German students were given highly differentiated performance feedback in the form of school grades from the very start of school (in first grade) and this feedback was provided in a manner that emphasized social comparison. Thus, for example, feedback emphasized an accurate representation of the relative performances of different children and was given publicly in front of the entire "class collective" throughout the school day and in public settings outside of school. This was consistent with the educational goal of fostering accurate self-evaluations by students and peers. In addition, the more unidimensional and highly centralized teaching strategies in East Germany reinforced self-evaluation through social comparison. Thus, for example, all East German teachers followed a highly prescriptive curriculum in which all students at a given grade level received the same materials, tasks, pace of studying, and assessment procedures. Within this system, there was no explicit grouping of students into homogeneous ability at the level of school, class, or groups within classes (i.e, not selective schools nor special classes for the brightest or most disadvantaged students). The West German system placed less emphasis on social comparison in that performance feedback was more private, teaching strategies were more differentiated to meet the needs of individual students, and there was no explicit goal to foster accurate and highly differentiated self-evaluations. The former West German system was characterized by the liberal notion that a variety of school careers should be offered to students by providing different paths for achieving final qualifications. This system was characterized by early and selective assignment to different tracks of secondary schools, that is: Hauptschule, Realschule, and Gymnasium. In the present investigation, we ask the research question of whether such substantial differences in these two school systems affected support for predictions based on our extension of the two major theoretical models of relations between academic self-concept and achievement and their unification as proposed here.

METHOD

Data

The empirical basis for our investigation was a subsample of the longitudinal study Learning Processes, Educational Careers and Psychosocial Development in Adolescence and Young Adulthood. This study was conducted by a research alliance between the Max Planck Institute for Human Development in Berlin and the Institute for Science Education at the University of Kiel. Of particular importance is the opportunity to study the development of academic self-concept in federal states that were part of the German Democratic Republic (East Germany) prior to reunification. Hence, it becomes possible to investigate systematically the role of the transition from a unitary to a differentiated school system with all the consequences for academic self-concepts in changing frames of references.

Data were collected from two states of the former German Democratic Republic and one from the former Federal Republic of Germany, all secondary school types, that is, Hauptschule (lowest track), Realschule (middle track), Gymnasium (upper track), and Gesamtschule (comprehensive school) were included. A total of 4,049 7th graders (mean age = 13.4 years) were tested at three measurement points (at the beginning, in the middle, and at the end of the school year 1991/1992) and then again at the end of grade 10. In order to obtain representative samples of all federal states considered here, the sample was stratified by state and school type. Within each state and school-type classification, random samples of schools were selected. Within each school, two 7th grade classes were randomly sampled. In this way the final sample was reasonably representative of the different federal states. (For more general descriptions of the study and resulting data base, see Baumert et al., 1996, Köller, 1998; Schnabel, 1998;

a detailed description of the study is also available via Internet, address: http://www.mpib-berlin.mpg.de/EuB/program/areas/projectII-1.htm).

Measures

Students were assigned school grades that varied along a 5-point response scale in each school subject. Grades in the present investigation were based on student self-reports of their grades at the end of 6th grade (T1, but reported at the start of 7th grade), in the middle of 7th grade (T3), and in 10th grade (T5). For each school subject, the self-concept variable was measured by means of a 5-item scale that was reliable (coefficient alpha > .8) and shown by previous research (Möller & Köller, 1998) to have convergent and discriminant validity in relation to classroom-based performance in different school subjects. The wording of the items (I would prefer math if it weren't so hard. Nobody's perfect, but I'm just not good at math. With some of the topics in math that I don't understand, I know from the start that I just won't get them. Even if I do my best in math, I do not perform very well. Although I really try, math seems harder for me than for many of my classmates.) was strictly parallel except for the specific school subject (e.g., math or German). Students responded to each item on a 4-point (agree-disagree) response format. Math and German self-concept scales were collected, at the start of 7th grade (T2) and at the end of 7th grade (T4).

Statistical Analysis

Structural equation models (SEM) were conducted with LISREL 8 (Joreskog & Sorbom, 1993) using maximum likelihood estimation. A detailed presentation of the conduct of SEM is beyond the scope of the present investigation and is available elsewhere (e.g., Bollen, 1989; Byrne, 1998; Joreskog & Sorbom, 1993; Schumacker & Lomax, 1996). Following Marsh, Balla, and Hau (1996), and Marsh, Balla, and McDonald (1988) we emphasize the Tucker-Lewis index (TLI), but also present the relative non-centrality index (RNI), the root mean square error of approximation (RMSEA), the χ^2 test statistic, and an evaluation of parameter estimates. The TLI and RNI vary along a 0-to-1 continuum in which values greater than .9 are typically taken to reflect an acceptable fit (see Marsh et al., 1996; Schumacker & Lomax, 1996). Browne and Cudeck (1993; also see Joreskog & Sorbom, 1993) suggest that RMSEAs less than .05 are indicative of a "close fit" and that values up to .08 represent reasonable errors of approximation. The RNI contains no penalty for a lack of parsimony so that the addition of new parameters leads to an improved fit that may reflect capitalization on chance, whereas the TLI and RMSEA contain a penalty for a lack of parsimony. Model comparison is also facilitated by positing a nested ordering of models in which the parameter estimates for a more restrictive model are a proper subset of those in a more general model (for further discussion see Bentler, 1990). Under appropriate assumptions, the difference in χ^2s between two nested models has a χ^2 distribution and so can be tested in relation to statistical significance. Whereas tests of statistical significance and indices of fit, aid in the evaluation of the fit of a model, there is ultimately a degree of subjectivity and professional judgment in the selection of a "best" model.

Multiple Group Structural Equation Models

When the researcher has parallel data from more than one group—the East and West German samples in this study—it is possible to test the invariance of the solution for each group by requiring any one, any set, or all parameter estimates to be the same in the two groups. Tests of factorial invariance (for further discussion see Bollen, 1989; Joreskog & Sorbom, 1993; Marsh, 1994a) traditionally posit a series of partially nested models in which the end points are the least restrictive model with no invariance constraints and the most restrictive (total invariance) model with all parameters constrained to be invariant across all groups. A minimal condition of factorial invariance is the invariance of the factor loadings. In the present investigation, the invariance of the path coefficients is of central concern, although invariance tests of the uniquenesses, correlated uniquenesses, correlations among variables, and residual variances are also of interest. All tests of invariance were conducted on separate covariance matrices constructed for participants from each group.

Missing Data

Particularly for longitudinal data, the inevitable missing data is an important issue. In the present investigation, we began with students ($N = 4,047$) who had complete data for school grades (from 6th grade) and self-concept measures (at the start of 7th grade). For subsequent data collections, however, there were increasing amounts of missing data (e.g., $Ns = 3,206$ and $3,184$ for T3 school grades in German and math; $2,640$ and $2,592$ for T4 German and math self-concepts). Particularly at 10th grade (T5), more than three years after the start of the study, there were data for only 948 and 962 students for school grades in German and math, due in part to the fact that for some German states 9th grade is a standard school leaving time for students not planning to attend university. We explored a variety of increasingly restrictive filters for missing data varying from pairwise deletion for missing data to listwise deletion for missing data for all but the final wave of data. The pattern of results, however, was similar in each of these analyses. There is, however, a growing body of research emphasizing the potential inappropriateness of both pairwise and listwise strategies for dealing with missing data (e.g., Brown, 1994; Graham & Hoffer, 2000; Little & Rubin, 1987; Wothke, 2000). For this reason we chose a more methodologically defensible approach of using the expectation maximization algorithm (SPSS, 1999) to impute values for missing data prior to the construction of the covariance matrix. Again, however, solutions based on pairwise deletion for missing data and application of the expectation maximization algorithm resulted in essentially the same conclusions. Hence, we only present results based on the expectation maximization algorithm.

The large amount of missing data for academic achievement measures collected at T5 pose an important problem in the present investigation. An inevitable feature of longitudinal research is that the longer the research continues, the smaller the numbers of the original cases remain. This is particularly true given that the T5 (Grade 10) data were collected three years after the T4 (Grade 7) data and this was done at a time when there was a lot of change in the former East and West Germany. In addition, however, there are three major reasons for the substantial dropout between grades 7 and 10. First, Hauptschule students (nonacademic school track) typically leave school at the end of grade 9. Second, in each year 5–10% of all German students have to repeat the school year because of their poor achievement levels. Third, a few schools who had volunteered to be in the study decided not to continue their participation after the collection of data in Grade 7. Although the amount of missing data was similar in the East and West German samples, the students with T5 data clearly differed from the original sample. Because students who were not in the study in Year 10 were not equivalent to those who remained in the study, there is a concern about the generalizability of the results. As already noted, we fitted the data based on increasingly restrictive filters (varying from pairwise to listwise deletion for missing data) and based on imputation for all missing data using the expectation maximization algorithm (SPSS, 1999). Using both pairwise and listwise deletion for missing data, relations between T5 achievement scores and earlier measures are based on only those students who had T5 achievement scores. In contrast, using imputation for missing data, these relations were based on the actual T5 achievement scores for those students with scores and imputed scores (based on earlier data) for those students without T5 achievement. The juxtaposition between these two approaches—particularly because the pattern of results is similar—provides some support for the appropriateness of interpretations based on the alternative approaches.

Inclusion of A Priori Correlated Uniquenesses

All analyses were conducted on responses to separate self-concept items that allow us to test a priori models with correlated uniquenesses to account for method effects associated with the parallel wording of items in the different self-concept scales and those associated with the same items administered on different occasions. Correlated uniquenesses result when there is unique variance associated with responses to one measured variable that is related to responses to another measured variable that cannot otherwise be explained by the proposed factor structure. Marsh and Hau (1996; also see earlier discussion by Joreskog, 1979) emphasized that if the same measurements are used on multiple occasions as is typical in longitudinal research, the corresponding residual error variables will tend to be correlated and, in order to get accurate estimates of relations among the constructs, correlations among errors must be included in the model. Similarly, correlated uniquenesses are likely to exist between items that are designed to measure different domains but have the same wording. In preliminary analyses, the inclusion of these correlated uniquenesses was supported by modestly better fits to the data and, in particular, because their exclusion would positively bias the corresponding correlation estimates. Their inclusion, however, had no substantively important effect on the pattern of parameter estimates, suggesting that the inclusion of correlated uniquenesses in this study was not a critical issue. In order to facilitate the substantive import of the results, only the models with correlated uniquenesses are presented.

RESULTS

The Reciprocal Effects of Academic Self-concept and Academic Achievement

The a priori model based on the total group of East and West German students (Table 2.1) is well defined in that all factor loadings are statistically significant and substantial (Table 2.1), the solution is fully proper, and the goodness of fit indices are very good (e.g., TLI = .951, Table 2.2). The results summarized in Figure 2.3 provide a convenient overview of the results. For purposes of illustration, only selected parameter path coefficients are presented in Figure 2.3 (but all parameter estimates are presented in Table 2.1) and those that provide critical tests for the two models of self-concept/achievement relations are highlighted with grey shading and thicker paths.

Table 2.1.   Longitudinal Path Model of Relations Between German and Math Achievement and German and Math Self-concept

Indicator	Time 1		Time 2		Time 3		Time 4		Time 5	
	GAch	MAch	GSC	MSC	GAch	MAch	GSC	MSC	GAch	MAch
Factor Loadings										
1	1	1	.59	.63	1	1	.71	.75	1	1
2			.72	.80			.85	.87		
3			.75	.81			.85	.88		
4			.39	.63			.70	.80		
5			.73	.81			.77	.86		
Uniquenesses										
1	0	0	.66	.60	0	0	.50	.44	0	0
2			.48	.37			.28	.25		
3			.44	.34			.28	.22		
4			.85	.61			.51	.35		
5			.47	.35			.41	.26		
Path Coefficients										
T1GAch	0	0	0	0	0	0	0	0	0	0
T1MAch	0	0	0	0	0	0	0	0	0	0
T2GSC	.44	−.16	0	0	0	0	0	0	0	0
T2MSC	−.30	.53	0	0	0	0	0	0	0	0
T3GAch	.43	.16	.27	−.04	0	0	0	0	0	0
T3MAch	.18	.33	−.02	.36	0	0	0	0	0	0
T4GSC	.05	−.01	.47	.08	.24	−.16	0	0	0	0
T4MSC	−.02	.06	.05	.50	−.07	.16	0	0	0	0
T5GAch	.35	.13	.10	−.01	.21	.18	.14	−.16	0	0
T5MAch	.16	.20	−.06	.15	.07	.35	−.09	.23	0	0
Factor Variance/Covariances										
Vars	1.00	1.00	.87	.83	.55	.58	.63	.62	.38	.34
Covar	.63		.19		.20		.18		.11	

Note. GAch = German achievement, MAch = math achievement, GSC = German self-concept, MSC = Math self-concept, T1, T2, T3, T4, T5 = times 1 to 5. There are 5 indicators (items) for each self-concept factor, but only a single indicator for each achievement score (school grades in each subject). All parameter estimates are presented in completely standardized form and parameters with values of 1 or 0 are fixed. Because of the large sample size ($N = 4047$) all estimated parameters greater than .03 are statistically significant ($p < .05$).

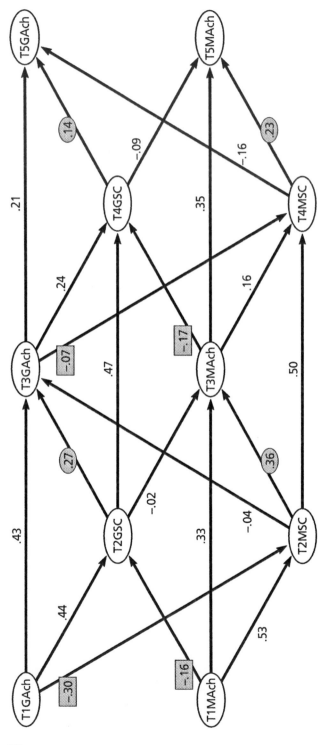

Figure 2.3. Path diagram showing the most important path coefficients relating German and math achievement (GAch & MAch) and German and Math self-concepts (GSC & MSC) collected at times 1–5. All path coefficients were equal in the West and East German samples (see Table 2.2 for a complete presentation of the factor solutions). Consistent with predictions based on the reciprocal "causal" effects model, the effects of prior self-concept on subsequent achievement (coefficients in circles) are all positive. Consistent with predictions based on the internal/external frame of reference model, paths leading from German achievement to math self-concept and from math achievement to German self-concept (coefficients in boxes) are all negative.

Reciprocal Effects Model

There is clear support for the reciprocal effects model. Of particular theoretical and practical importance, there is clear support for the effects of prior T2 self-concept on subsequent T3 achievement after controlling for the effects of prior T1 achievement. This contributes to the growing body of research indicating that prior academic self-concept does influence subsequent achievement. Furthermore, the sizes of these effects (.27 for German and .36 for math) are substantial in relation to previous research and, at least for math, as large as the effect of prior (T1) math achievement on T3 math achievement (.33). An important strength of this study is that there are distal measures of academic achievement at T5 (10th grade, three years after the T2-T4 materials that were collected in 7th grade). Even after controlling for the effects of measures at T1 academic achievement, T2 academic self-concept, and T3 academic achievement, the effects of T4 academic self-concepts (collected at the end of 7th grade) on school grades in 10th grade were still highly significant (.14 for German and .23 for math).

Furthermore, these effects of prior self-concept on T5 achievement were only somewhat smaller than the effects of T3 achievement (.21 for German and .35 for math). These findings are particularly impressive because the effects of prior self-concepts were on T5 achievement that was collected nearly three years after the T4 self-concept measures and because the effects of two waves of prior achievement (T1 and T3) and one wave of prior self-concept (T2) were controlled. Hence, the results provide strong support for the effects of prior self-concept on subsequent achievement after controlling for the effects of prior achievement.

Due to the nature of the data considered here, tests of the effects of prior achievement on subsequent self-concept are not as easy to interpret. Whereas there are substantial effects of T1 achievement on T2 self-concepts (.44 for German, .53 for math), these effects do not control for the effects of prior self-concept. There are, however, also highly significant effects of T3 achievement on T4 self-concepts (.24 for German, .16 for math) even after controlling for the effects of T1 achievements and T2 self-concepts. Hence, as predicted by the reciprocal effects model, the results also support the effects of prior achievement on subsequent self-concept after controlling for the effects of prior self-concept. In summary, the results provide strong support for the reciprocal effects model.

Internal/External (I/E) Frame of Reference Model

There is also clear support for the I/E model. The results most directly analogous to the typical test of the I/E model (as depicted in Figure 2.1B) are those relating T1 achievements to T2 academic self-concepts. As predicted, T1 German achievement has a positive effect on T2 German self-concept (.44), but a negative effect on T2 math self-concept (–.30). Also consistent with predictions, T1 math achievement had a positive effect on T2 math self-concept (.53) but a negative effect on T2 math self-concept (–.16).

The effects of T3 academic achievements on T4 academic self-concepts—because the effects of T1 achievements and T2 academic self-concepts were controlled—provides a more demanding test of the I/E model than those in most previous research. Nevertheless, the pattern of effects support the I/E model in that the effects of German achievement are positive on German self-concept (.24) but negative on Math self-concept (–.07), whereas the effects of math achievement are positive on math self-concept (.16) but negative on German self-concept (–.16). Because of the results supporting the I/E at T1 and T2, these effects represent additional I/E effects at T3 and T4 beyond those that were shown at T1 and T2.

Table 2.2.   Summary of Goodness of Fit Statistics: Total Group and Two-group Tests of Invariance

Model	DF	χ^2	RNI	TLI	RMSEA	Model Description
Total Group Analysis						
1	230	2388.75	.965	.951	.048	Total Group a priori model
Two Group Invariance Tests						
2a	460	2708.57	.964	.949	.049	No Invariance (inv)
2b	476	2796.87	.962	.949	.049	Factor Loading (FL) inv
2c	516	2903.25	.961	.951	.048	FL, path coeff (PC) inv
2d	491	3320.00	.954	.939	.053	FL, factor variance/covariance(FCV)
2e	526	2936.00	.961	.952	.048	FL, uniqueness (U)
2f	531	3404.14	.953	.943	.052	FL, PC, FCV
2g	566	3040.52	.960	.954	.046	FL, PC, U
2h	541	3444.16	.953	.944	.051	FL, FCV, U
2i	581	3529.53	.952	.947	.050	FL, PC, FCV, U (total inv)

Note: RNI = relative noncentrality index, TLI = Tucker-Lewis index, RMSEA = root mean square error of approximation, DF = degrees of freedom, EM = expectation maximization algorithm (SPSS, 1998). Results are presented for the EM imputation for missing data (the preferred approach used here) and, for purposes of comparison, pairwise deletion for missing data.

The Integration of the Reciprocal Effects and Internal/ External Frame of Reference Models

The present investigation is apparently the first to integrate the reciprocal effects and I/E models. Hence, the juxtaposition of the support for both models is important. The results extend support for the extreme domain specificity of academic self-concept in that the effects of prior math self-concept are positive for subsequent math achievement but not German achievement whereas the effects of prior German self-concept are positive for subsequent German achievement but not math self-concept. Furthermore, also consistent with the logic of the I/E model, the effects of prior self-concept on nonmatching domains of subsequent achievement tend to be negative. For T3 achievements these negative effects were small (−.04, the effect of T2 German self-concept on T3 math achievement) or not significant (−.02, the effect for T2 math self-concept on T3 German achievement). For T5, however, effects were more negative and statistically significant (−.09, the effect of T4 German self-concept on math achievement; −.16, the effect of T4 math self-concept on German achievement). Hence, the extreme domain specificity of the academic self-concept measures contributed to the increasing domain specificity of the corresponding achievement measures, which reinforced the domain specificity of subsequent self-concept.

Cross-cultural Generalizability: Comparison of East and West German Samples

The present investigation provided a unique opportunity to evaluate the cross-cultural generalizability of support for the reciprocal effects model, the I/E model, and their integration based on responses by East and West German students. Multigroup structural equation models provide a particularly powerful approach whereby it is possible to constrain any one, any group, or all parameters to be invariant (i.e., identical) across the two groups. To the extent that models requiring parameters to be invariant across samples are able to fit the data as well as samples allowing the parameters to be estimated independently in each sample, there is support for the more parsimonious model imposing invariance constraints. Because of the large sample sizes, such comparisons are most appropriately based on goodness of fit indices that control for parsimony (i.e., the RMSEA and TLI indices used here).

We fit a variety of models (Table 2.2) in which different sets of parameter estimates were constrained to be equal in the two samples. The baseline model (Model 2a) imposing no invariance constraints (i.e., all parameters were free to vary across the two samples) provided a good fit to the data (TLI = .949 and RMSEA = .049) according to traditional guidelines of acceptable fit. Although there was some evidence for the noninvariance of the parameter estimates in some models considered here, even the model of complete factorial invariance (Model 2i in Table 2.2 in which every estimated parameter was constrained to be equal in the two samples) provided a reasonable fit to the data (TLI = .947 and RMSEA = .050). Furthermore, the fit of this model was only marginally poorer than the fit of Model 2A with no invariance constraints. An inspection of the alternative models (Table 2.2) indicates good support for the invariance of factor loadings (M2B) and the factor loadings in combination with path coefficients (M2C) that are of particular relevance to the present investigation and with uniquenesses and correlated uniquenesses that represent measurement error (M2D). In fact, the only models that failed to fit the data as well as M2A (according to the TLI and RMSEA, that take into account model parsimony) are models that imposed invariance constraints on residual factor variances and covariances. Inspection of the solutions for various models and LISREL's modification indices indicated that factor variances were somewhat larger for most latent constructs in the West German sample. Because factor loadings, path coefficients, and uniquenesses were required to be invariant across the best-fitting model (Model 2g in Table 2.2), the parameter estimates were similar to those in Table 2.1 based on the total sample. In summary, despite the substantial differences between the East and West German school systems prior to the start of the present investigation, there was a remarkable similarity across the East and West German samples in parameter estimates representing the integration of the reciprocal effects and I/E models. These results provide good support for the generalizability of the results based on the total sample across responses by East and West German students at this particularly important point in history.

DISCUSSION

The results of the present investigation provide an important replication and extension in a German setting of support for theoretical predictions about the reciprocal effects of academic self-concept and achievement that have been tested primarily in English-speaking countries. Consistent with a priori predictions, there were effects of prior achievement on subsequent self-concept and of prior academic self-concept on subsequent achievement. Similarly, although there is growing support for predictions based on the I/E model, there have been few longitudinal studies of the predictions—particularly ones that have also evaluated the causal ordering of academic self-concept and achievement. Whereas the pattern of results in support of the I/E model for T1 achievement and T2 self-concepts was particularly strong, the apparently smaller path coefficients from T3 achievement to T4 self-concept may be theoretically more important. The path coefficients were only smaller because, in the context of the path model tested here, these effects were controlled for T1 achievement and T2 self-concept. Hence, the results indicated continued support for the I/E predictions even after controlling for the strong I/E effects observed for the prior measures of these constructs. This implies that the processes underlying the I/E model—the counter-balancing internal and external frames of reference—had new effects at T3 and T4 beyond the earlier effects at T1 and T2. Because the I/E model is rarely tested with longitudinal data such as that considered here, these results provide a useful extension of previous research.

Even more important, however, are new predictions based on the integration of the I/E and reciprocal effects models proposed for purposes of the present investigation. Whereas previous tests of the I/E model have emphasized the effects of academic achievement on self-concept, the present investigation demonstrated this extreme and seemingly paradoxical pattern of effects leading from prior self-concept to subsequent achievement. Thus, for example, T4 Math self-concept had a positive effect on T5 math achievement but had a small negative effect on T5 German achievement, whereas T4 German self-concept had a positive effect on T5 German achievement but a smaller negative effect on T5 math achievement. Therefore, the domain specificity of self-concept reinforces the domain specificity in subsequent achievement that further reinforces the domain specificity of subsequent self-concept. Hence, this extension of I/E model has theoretically and substantively important implications about the development of academic self-concept and its relation to achievement.

The results of the present investigation also provide remarkably strong support for the generality of the results across students from the former East and West German school systems. Indeed, it is interesting to speculate about why such apparently substantial differences in the cultures of the two school systems did not influence the support more strongly for the integration of the two theoretical models of self-concept/achievement relations that we evaluated. It might be, for example, that the highly competitive environment that reinforced social comparison processes in the East German system would have accentuated the external comparison process in the formation of academic self-concept. Because the first collection of academic self-concept measures took place about one month into the first school year after the reunification of the two school systems, it may be that the changes in the former East German school systems were so salient that East German students had already adapted new frames of reference that were similar to those of West German students. Also, at least some of the differences between the two school systems that we discussed may have been more dramatic for younger students in primary school grades than for the older students considered in the present investigation (see Little, Oettingen, Stetsenko, & Baltes, 1995; Oettingen, 1995; Oettingen et al., 1994). Alternatively, the processes underlying the I/E and reciprocal effects models may be so robust that they are clearly evident despite important differences in the school systems, as the present investigation seems to imply. In summary, results of the present investigation provide strong support for predictions based on research conducted mostly in English speaking countries about the causal ordering of academic self-concept and achievement, the I/E model, a new integration of the two models, and the generality of results across two very different cultural settings.

Implications for Educational Practice

The results of the present investigation have important implications for educational practice. The critical question leading to the reciprocal effects model is whether better self-concept leads to better achievement or whether better achievement leads to better self-concepts. If better self-concept leads to better achievement, then there is justification in pursuing self-concept enhancement programs as a means to facilitate improved achievement as well as enhancing a desired outcome variable. If, however, better achievement leads to better self-concepts, then schools should focus on the development of academic skills because the successful development of such skills would lead to better self-concepts. Based on support for the reciprocal effects model demonstrated here, however, both these scenarios are too simplistic. Support for the reciprocal effects model implies that self-concept enhancement will lead to better academic skills and the development of better academic skills will lead to better academic self-concepts. There are, however, further implications of the reciprocal effects model. Although academic skill development may result in short-term gains in academic achievement, these achievement gains are unlikely to be maintained unless there are corresponding gains in academic self-concept. Conversely, although self-concept enhancement programs may have short-term gains in academic self-concept, these effects are unlikely to be maintained unless there are corresponding gains in achievement. Hence, the most effective way to have lasting effects on either achievement or academic self-concept is to develop interventions that simultaneously enhance both constructs.

The extreme domain specificity of academic self-concepts that led to the development of the I/E model also has practical implications for educational practice. Teachers, in order to understand the academic self-concepts of their students in different content areas, must understand the implications of the I/E model. When teachers were asked to infer the self-concepts of their students (see discussion by Marsh & Craven, 1997), their responses reflected primarily the external comparison process so that their inferred academic self-concept ratings were highly correlated with the student's achievement. Thus, teacher's inferences are not nearly so domain specific so that students who are bright in one area tend to be seen as having good academic self-concepts in all areas, whereas students who are not bright in one area are seen as having poor academic self-concept in all areas. In contrast to teachers' inferences about their students, student's academic self-concepts in different domains are extremely differentiated. Even bright students may have an average or below average self-concept in their weakest school subject that may seem paradoxical in relation to their good achievement (good relative to other students, but not their own performance in other school subject). Similarly, even poor students may have an average or above average self-concept in their best school subject that may seem paradoxical in relation to their below-average achievement in that subject. Particularly for poorer students, understanding these principles should assist teachers to give positive feedback that is credible to students.

The integration of the reciprocal effects and I/E models also led to new predictions that have practical implications for educational practice. In particular, the negative effects of math achievement on verbal self-concept and of verbal achievement on math self-concept (as predicted by the I/E model) are also reflected in the negative effects of math self-concept on verbal achievement and of verbal self-concept on math achievement. Hence, a pattern of reciprocal effects reinforces the domain specificity of these constructs and the multidimensionality of academic self-concepts. This domain specificity is likely to reinforce a web of related variables associated with intrinsic and extrinsic motivation, coursework selection, subject interest, persistence, and attributions for success and failure that influence and are influenced by academic achievement.

REFERENCES

Baumert, J., Roeder, P. M., Gruehn, S., Heyn, S., Köller, O., Rimmele, R., Schnabel, K., & Seipp, B. (1996). Bildungsverläufe und psychosoziale Entwicklung im Jugendalter (BIJU) [Educational careers and psycho-social development during adolescence (BIJU)]. In: K. P. Treumann, G. Neubauer, R. Möller, & J. Abel (Eds.), *Methoden und Anwendungen empirisch pädagogischer Forschung* (pp.170–180). Münster: Waxmann.

Bentler, P. M. (1990). Comparative fit indices in structural models. *Psychological Bulletin, 107*, 238–246.

Bollen, K. A. (1989). *Structural equations with latent variables.* New York: Wiley & Sons.

Brown, R. L. (1994). Efficiency of the indirect approach for estimating structural equation model with missing data: A comparison of five methods. *Structural Equation Modeling, 1,* 287–316.

Browne, M. W., & Cudeck, R. (1993). Alternative ways of assessing model fit. In K. Bollen & R. Stine (Eds.), *Testing structural equation models* (pp. 136–162). Newbury Park, CA: Sage.

Byrne, B. M. (1986). Self-concept/academic achievement relations: An investigation of dimensionality, stability, and causality. *Canadian Journal of Behavioural Science, 18,* 173–186.

Byrne, B. M. (1996). Academic self-concept: Its structure, measurement, and relation to academic achievement. In B. A. Bracken (Ed.), *Handbook of self-concept* (pp. 287–316). New York: Wiley.

Byrne, B. M. (1998). *Structural equation modeling with LISREL, PRELIS, and SIMLIS: Basic concepts, applications and programming.* Mahwah, NJ: Erlbaum

Calsyn, R., & Kenny, D. (1977). Self-concept of ability and perceived evaluations by others: Cause or effect of academic achievement? *Journal of Educational Psychology, 69,* 136–145.

Graham, J. W., & Hoffer, S. M. (2000). Multiple imputation in multivariate research. In T. D. Little, K. U. Schnable, & J. Baumert (Eds.), *Modeling longitudinal and multilevel data: Practical issues, applied approaches, and specific examples* (pp. 201–218). Mahwah, NJ: Erlbaum.

Hannover, B. (1995). Self-serving biases and self-satisfaction in East versus West German students. *Journal of Cross-Cultural Psychology, 26,* 176–188.

Helmke, A., & van Aken, M. A. G. (1995). The causal ordering of academic achievement and self-concept of ability during elementary school: A longitudinal study. *Journal of Educational Psychology, 87,* 624–637.

Joreskog, K. G. (1979). Statistical estimation of structural models in longitudinal investigations. In J. R. Nesselroade & B. Baltes (Eds.), *Longitudinal research in the study of behavior and development* (pp. 303- 351). New York: Academic Press.

Joreskog, K. G., & Sorbom, D. (1993). *LISREL 8: Structural equation modeling with the SIMPLIS command language.* Chicago: Scientific Software International.

Judge, T. A., & Bono, J. E. (2001). Relationship of core self-evaluations traits—self-esteem, generalized self-efficacy, locus of control, and emotional stability—with job satisfaction and job performance: A meta-analysis. *Journal of Applied Psychology, 86,* 80–92.

Kagitcibasi, C., & Poortinga, Y. H. (2000). Cross-cultural psychology: Issues and overarching themes. *Journal of Cross-Cultural Psychology, 31,* 14–32.

Kashima, Y. (1995). Introduction to the special section on culture and self. *Journal of Cross-Cultural Psychology, 26,* 603–605.

Kashima, Y. (2000). Cross-cultural psychology: Issues and overarching themes. *Journal of Cross-Cultural Psychology, 31,* 129–147.

Kitayama, S., & Markus, H. R. (1999). Yin and yang of Japanese self: The cultural psychology of personality coherence. In D. Cervone & Y. Shoda (Eds.), *The coherence of personality: Social cognitive bases of personality consistency, variability, and organization* (pp. 242–302). New York: Guilford.

Köller, O. (1998). *Zielorientierungen und schulisches Lernen* [Goal orientations and academic learning]. Müenster/New York: Waxmann.

Little, R. J. A., & Rubin, D. B. (1987). *Statistical analysis with missing data.* New York: Wiley.

Little, T. D., Oettingen, G., Stetsenko, A., & Baltes, P. B. (1995). Children's action-control beliefs about school performance: How do American children compare with German and Russian children? *Journal of Personality and Social Psychology, 69,* 686–700.

Marsh, H. W. (1986). Verbal and math self-concepts: An internal/external frame of reference model. *American Educational Research Journal, 23,* 129–149.

Marsh, H. W. (1988). Causal effects of academic self-concept on academic achievement: A reanalysis of Newman (1984). *The Journal of Experimental Education, 56,* 100–103.

Marsh, H. W. (1989). Sex differences in the development of verbal and math constructs: The High School and Beyond study. *American Educational Research Journal, 26,* 191–225.

Marsh, H. W. (1990a). The causal ordering of academic self-concept and academic achievement: A multiwave, longitudinal panel analysis. *Journal of Educational Psychology, 82,* 646–656.

Marsh, H. W. (1990b). A multidimensional, hierarchical self-concept: Theoretical and empirical justification. *Educational Psychology Review, 2,* 77–171.

Marsh, H. W. (1993). Academic self-concept: Theory measurement and research. In J. Suls (Ed.), *Psychological perspectives on the self* (Vol. 4, pp 59–98). Hillsdale, NJ: Erlbaum

Marsh, H. W. (1994a). Confirmatory factor analysis models of factorial invariance: A multifaceted approach. *Structural Equation Modeling, 1,* 5–34.

Marsh, H. W. (1994b). Using the National Educational Longitudinal Study of 1988 to evaluate theoretical models of self-concept: The Self-Description Questionnaire. *Journal of Educational Psychology, 86,* 439–456.

Marsh, H. W. (2002). Physical self-concept: Theory, measurement, and research. Keynote Address to International Congress of Sport Psychology, Skiathos, Greece. Reprinted in *Psychology: The Journal of the Hellenic Psychology Society, 9,* 459–493.

Marsh, H. W., Balla, J. R., & Hau, K.-T. (1996). An evaluation of incremental fit indices: A clarification of mathematical and empirical processes. In G. A. Marcoulides & R. E. Schumacker (Ed.), *Advanced structural equation modeling techniques* (pp. 315–353). Hillsdale, NJ: Erlbaum.

Marsh, H. W., Balla, J. R., & McDonald, R. P. (1988). Goodness of fit indexes in confirmatory factor analysis: The effect of sample size. *Psychological Bulletin, 103,* 391–410.

Marsh, H. W., Byrne, B. M., & Shavelson, R. (1988). A multifaceted academic self-concept: Its hierarchical structure and its relation to academic achievement. *Journal of Educational Psychology, 80,* 366–380.

Marsh, H. W., Byrne, B. M., & Yeung, A. S. (1999). Causal ordering of academic self-concept and achievement: Reanalysis of a pioneering study and revised recommendations. *Educational Psychologist, 34,* 155–167.

Marsh, H. W., & Craven, R. (1997). Academic self-concept: Beyond the dustbowl. In G. Phye (Ed.), *Handbook of classroom assessment: Learning, achievement, and adjustment* (pp. 131–198). Orlando, FL: Academic Press.

Marsh, H. W., & Hattie, J. (1996). Theoretical perspectives on the structure of self-concept. In B. A. Bracken (Ed.), *Handbook of self-concept* (pp. 38–90). New York: Wiley.

Marsh, H. W., & Hau, K.-T. (1996). Assessing goodness of fit: Is parsimony always desirable? *Journal of Experimental Education, 64,* 364–390.

Marsh, H. W., Kong, K. W. & Hau, K.-T. (2001). Extension of the internal/external frame of reference model of self-concept formation: Importance of native and non-native languages for Chinese students. *Journal of Educational Psychology, 93,* 543–553.

Marsh, H. W., & Yeung, A. S. (1997). Causal effects of academic self-concept on academic achievement: Structural equation models of longitudinal data. *Journal of Educational Psychology, 89,* 41–54.

Möller, J., & Köller, O. (1998). Dimensionale und soziale Vergleiche nach schulischen Leistungen [Dimensional and social comparisons of academic achievements]. *Zeitschrift für Entwicklungspsychologie und Pädagogische Psychologie, 30,* 118–127.

Newman, R. S. (1984). Achievement and self-evaluations in mathematics. *Journal of Educational Psychology, 76,* 857–873.

Oettingen, G. (1995). Explanatory style in the context of culture. In G. M. Buchanan, & M. E. P. Seligman (Eds.), *Explanatory style* (pp. 209–224). Hillsdale, NJ: Erlbaum

Oettingen, G., Little, T. D., Lindenberger, U., & Baltes, P. B. (1994). Causality, agency, and control beliefs in East versus West Berlin children: A natural experiment on the role of context. *Journal of Personality and Social Psychology, 66,* 579–595.

Parker, S. K. (1998). Enhancing role breadth self-efficacy: The roles of job enrichment and other organizational interventions. *Journal of Applied Psychology, 83,* 835–852.

Schnabel, K. U. (1998). *Prüfungsangst und lernen* [Test anxiety and learning]. Münster/New York: Waxmann.

Schumacker, R. E., & Lomax, R. G. (1996). *A beginner's guide to structural equation modeling.* Mahwah, NJ: Erlbaum.

Segall, M. H., Lonner, W. J., & Berry, J. W. (1998). Cross-cultural psychology as a scholarly discipline: On the flowering of culture in behavioral research. *American Psychologist, 53,* 1101–1110.

Shavelson, R. J., & Bolus, R. (1982). Self-concept: The interplay of theory and methods. *Journal of Educational Psychology, 74,* 3–17.

Shavelson, R. J., Hubner, J. J., & Stanton, G. C. (1976). Self-concept: Validation of construct interpretations. *Review of Educational Research, 46,* 407–441.

Singelis, T. M. (2000). Some thoughts on the future of cross-cultural social psychology. *Journal of Cross-Cultural Psychology, 31,* 76–91.

Skaalvik, E. M., & Hagtvet, K. A. (1990). Academic achievement and self-concept: An analysis of causal predominance in a developmental perspective. *Journal of Personality and Social Psychology, 58,* 292–307.

Skaalvik, E. M., & Rankin, R. J. (1995). A test of the internal/external frame of reference model at different levels of math and verbal self-perception. *American Educational Research Journal, 35,* 161–184.

SPSS. (1999). *SPSS for Windows* (Release 10.0.5). Chicago: SPSS.

Sue, S. (1999). Science, ethnicity and bias: Where have we gone wrong? *American Psychologist, 54,* 1070–1077.

Van de Vijer, F.J. R., & Leung, K. (2000). Methodological issues in psychological research on culture. *Journal of Cross-Cultural Psychology, 31,* 33–51.

Wells, L. E., & Marwell, G. (1976). *Self-esteem: Its conceptualization and measurement.* Beverly Hills, CA: Sage Publications.

Wothke, W. (2000). Longitudinal and multigroup modeling with missing data. In T. D. Little, K. U. Schnable & J. Baumert (Eds.), *Modeling longitudinal and multilevel data: Practical issues, applied approaches, and specific examples* (pp. 201–218). Mahwah, NJ: Erlbaum.

Wylie, R. C. (1974). *The self-concept.* (Rev. ed., Vol. 1) Lincoln, NE: University of Nebraska Press.

Wylie, R. C. (1979). *The self-concept.* (Vol. 2). Lincoln, NE: University of Nebraska Press.

Yeung, A. S., & Lee, F. L. (1999). Self-concept of high school students in China: Confirmatory factor analysis of longitudinal data. *Educational & Psychological Measurement, 59,* 431–450.

CHAPTER 3

CHINESE SELF-DESCRIPTION QUESTIONNAIRE

Cross-cultural Validation and Extension of Theoretical Self-Concept Models

Kit-Tai Hau, Chit Kwong Kong, and Herbert W. Marsh

In an educational setting, self-concept has often been used as one of the important indicators of students' social development. High self-concept is advantageous not only because it is a desirable outcome, it is also an important mediator in enhancing other positive psychological variables and academic achievement (e.g., see review Marsh, 1990, 1993). Previous studies with Western students supported a multidimensional and hierarchical structure, an internal/external frame of reference (I/E model), and a significant effect of prior self-concept on subsequent academic achievement. In this chapter, we will first present the major theoretical models related to self-concept and its related constructs. Then, we will review and examine a series of analyses on a large-scale longitudinal study of these major theoretical models among Chinese students who are from a collectivistic culture where learning goals and self-improvement (vs. competition) are strongly valued. Our studies also extend previous Western research by separating the potentially positive and negative effects on self-concept for students studying in high ability schools. Furthermore, the disparate relations

International Advances in Self Research, pages 49–65
Copyright © 2003 by Information Age Publishing
All rights of reproduction in any form reserved.

between native and nonnative language achievements on their respective domain specific self-concepts will be explored.

MAJOR CHARACTERISTICS WITH WESTERN STUDENTS

Internal-External Frame of Reference

In schools, particularly in a setting in which academic performance is strongly emphasized, students constantly compare their ability with others in their immediate environment (e.g., classmates) as one of the main bases of formulating their self-concept. Thus, high ability students who outperform their peers in internal school tests and public examinations, tend to have more positive self-concept than their classmates. Prior to the 1980s, self-concept was usually considered as a unidimensional, general, and global construct. However, there has been growing recognition of the need to take into consideration its multidimensional and content specific nature, with instruments generating a set of profile scores for each student. With these multidimensional measures, much stronger relationships ($r = .45$ to $.70$) have been found, for example, between self-concept and achievement of matching subject areas (e.g., between science self-concept and science achievement) (Tay, Licht, & Tate, 1995).

As academic achievements themselves (e.g., math achievement with verbal achievement) and achievement and their matching domain self-concept (e.g., math achievement with math self-concept) are substantially correlated, it is expected that their respective self-concepts (e.g., math self-concept and verbal self-concept) will also be highly correlated. However, empirical research has shown that these two self-concepts are typically uncorrelated. Marsh (1990, 1993) has explained these seemingly paradoxical results by using an internal/external frame of reference model. It has been postulated that students compare their verbal ability with that of other students (external comparison) as well as against their own mathematics ability (or other abilities in other school subjects, internal comparison). The former external comparison leads to a positive relation between verbal and mathematics self-concepts whereas the latter internal comparison results in a negative one. The joint effects, as demonstrated in studies in Australia, Canada, and the United States based on responses to a variety of different instruments, are: (i) a strong positive path from verbal ability to verbal self-concept (matching subject), (ii) a weak negative path from verbal ability to mathematics self-concept (cross-subject), and (iii) a close to zero relation between verbal and mathematics self-concepts (Marsh, 1993).

Big-Fish-Little-Pond Effect (BFLPE) and Assimilation Effect

The above internal/external frame of reference model suggests that students' self-concept is formulated through comparison with classmates as well as with own other abilities. Particularly due to the former type of comparison, research shows that attending schools of high average ability may have negative effects on students' self-concept (Marsh, 1990, 1993). For students of similar levels of ability, those attending high average ability schools will have lower academic self-concept than equally able students studying in low ability schools. This phenomenon is called the little fish in the big pond effect, or conversely, the more well known big-fish-little-pond effect (BFLPE). This shows that students attending high average ability schools are constantly comparing their ability unfavorably with other high ability classmates (contrast effect). In empirical studies, the BFLPE has been demonstrated as a negative effect of school-average ability on students' academic self-concept (Marsh, 1990, 1993).

Despite the above possible negative contrast effect, attending schools of high average ability may have potentially positive impact on self-concept through assimilation or identification (Felson & Reed, 1986). This is because schools of high average ability are socially valued and preferentially selected by many parents. Being a student in these schools is an indication of high academic ability and hence, perhaps, of high social status. There has been ample evidence showing that people enjoy "basking in the reflected glory" of successful others by merely associating with honorable people or joining highly valued social groups (Brown, Novick, Lord, & Richards, 1992). Thus, the identification with schools of high average ability may have a positive effect on one's self-perception. As the negative contrast effect acts simultaneously with the positive assimilation effect (Felson & Reed, 1986; Marsh, 1990, 1993), the BFLPE is necessarily a net result of the two effects, which in previous studies has been generally negative, indicating a stronger contrast component to most students. In other words, the positive "basking in the reflected glory" is usually not large enough to compensate for the negative contrast effect. Being a student in a prestigious school may make one feel good, but the competition with high ability classmates has a much stronger undesirable effect than the net effect of studying in prestigious schools and thus is still negative.

Despite the observation of the negative BFLPE on self-concept, GPA and possibly standardized achievement tests (Marsh, 1990, 1993), there is also another set of literature on ability grouping and tracking which suggests the contrary (e.g., Gamoran, Nystrand, Berends, & LePore, 1995). Some of these studies argue with evidence that students assigned to higher-ability tracks learn and perform better than those in the lower-ability tracks. This is because in the higher-ability tracks, more advanced topics are sometimes covered in a faster pace and the teachers are comparatively more enthusiastic.

CULTURAL GENERALITY AND SPECIFICITY

Cultural Differences in Perception of Self

As current self-concept measures and theoretical models have been primarily developed under Western cultural contexts, they have been criticized as being culturally bound to the ideology of individualism and may not be applicable to people in a collective culture (e.g., Yang, 1991). Two lines of research are particularly relevant to this issue. One is the contrast between the independent and the interdependent views of the construal of self (Markus & Kitayama, 1991). The other is the distinction between the private and the collective self (Triandis, 1989).

Markus and Kitayama (1991) have contrasted the differences in the construal of self between people from individualistic (e.g., Western) and collectivistic cultures (e.g., Asian). In an individualistic culture, the person is viewed as "an independent, self-contained, autonomous entity who comprises a unique configuration of internal attributes" (Markus & Kitayama, 1991, p. 226). Based on these values, the self-concept model in an individualistic culture is characterized by a description of personal attributes and traits. However, people in a collectivistic culture emphasize the interdependence and harmonious relatedness among one another (e.g., family members, working partners). In these cultural contexts, it is important to be harmonious with others, to fulfill and create obligation, and to become part of various interpersonal relationships. Due to such differential cultural emphases, it has been challenged that the Western self-concept models have not captured the salient interdependent and related components of self-concept in the Chinese or other collectivistic cultures.

Some empirical studies appeared to support this argument (e.g., Meredith, Wang, & Zheng, 1993; Tam & Watkins, 1995). For example, Meredith and colleagues (1993) used a modified version of Harter's Self-Perception Profile for Children (Harter, 1982) to investigate mainland Chinese children's perceptions of the salient components of self-concept. The salient scales (scholastic competence, social acceptance, athletic competence, and physical appearance) were not perceived as the most important. Instead, the scales of behavior conduct, social acceptance and group orientation appeared to be of greater importance for Chinese children.

From another perspective, some theorists have attempted to operationalize the differences in the cross-cultural conception of self in terms of differences in cognitions. Baumeister (1986) has proposed that self-information can be organized in a systematic structure consisting of three aspects of self, namely, the private, the public, and the collective self. They refer respectively to "the cognitions about traits, states, or behaviors of the person" (e.g., "I am kind"), "the generalized other's view of the self" (e.g., "Most people think I am kind"), and "the view of the self that is found in some collective contexts" (e.g., "My family thinks I am kind"). Triandis (1989) suggested that these three kinds of self are presented with different probabilities in different cultures. In an individualistic culture, people show mostly the private self, while in a collectivist culture, people show mainly the collective one. Triandis (1989) has further proposed that when the collective self is invoked, people are more likely to behave according to norms, rules, and customs. On the other hand, when the private self is invoked, people are more likely to behave according to their attitudes, feelings, beliefs, or personal philosophy.

Self-Concept in Collectivistic and Individualistic Societies

Researchers have also attempted to measure the collective self and investigated its validity. For example, Luhtanen and Crocker (1992) adopted the definition of collective self in social identity theory as—"that part of an individual's self concept which derives from his knowledge of his membership in a social group(s)" (p. 302)—and designed a measure to tap collective self-esteem. They found that collective self-esteem, in addition to personal self-esteem, was an individual difference variable that moderated the attempt to maintain a positive social identity. More importantly, they demonstrated that collective self-esteem could explain aspects of psychological well-being that otherwise could not be explained by its relation to personal self-esteem (Crocker, Luhtanen, Blaine, & Broadnax, 1994). In subsequent studies, Bettencourt and Dorr (1997) further illustrated the important role of collective self-esteem in predicting human behavior. McFarland and Buehler (1995) also showed that people from a collectivistic cultural-heritage had higher collective self-esteem and were less susceptible to the BFLPE in their reactions to performance feedback than people from individualistic cultural-heritage.

Obviously, these two lines of research have pointed out the potential differences in the conception of self between people from individualistic and collectivist cultures. However, the central question is whether such cultural differences are big enough to lead to very different self-concept structures between the two cultures. Perhaps, the similarities across different cultures are not so great that a general model is applicable to both cultures. The independent and interdependent views of the construal of self are, therefore, not necessarily contradicting each other; instead, they are complementary in giving a more comprehensive description of human characteristics and self-perceptions (Markus & Kitayama, 1991).

From the perspective of the three aspects of self (private, social, and collective self; Baumeister, 1986), there is a common consensus that the cognition about one's traits, states, or behaviors (private self) is the most central and universal characteristic of self-concept. Therefore, current self-concept models and measures have focused primarily on this particular aspect of self. For people in Western and Chinese cultures, the similarities rather than the distinctiveness of their self-concept seem to dominate. If that is the case, it can be hypothesized that the imported self-concept measure as well as the related theoretical models will still be applicable in the Chinese culture.

Chinese Students and the Examination System in Hong Kong

In this paper, we will summarize a series of analyses of a large-scale longitudinal research on the self-concept of Chinese students in Hong Kong. Hong Kong was a British colony but has become a special administrative region of the People's Republic of China since July 1, 1997. It is a prosperous commercial and international financial center where Chinese culture and values are still strongly felt and emphasized. There seems to be converging evidence suggesting that Chinese students in Hong Kong as well as in other societies attribute their examination results more to effort than to ability and that they concentrate on their own improvement rather than on comparison with other students as determinants of academic achievement (Hau & Salili, 1991, 1996). Taken to the very extreme, the total concentration on an internal frame of reference and the ignorance of any external comparison with other students may suggest, though not logically necessary, that (i) the interrelations among different specific academic self-concepts would be negative and (ii) the negative BFLPE on self-concept and achievement would not be found among Chinese students.

In Hong Kong, nine-year compulsory and free education up to junior secondary, Grade 9, has been enforced since 1978. However, high school places are allocated according to parental choice in the order of merit of students' internal school examination results in the last two years of primary education, moderated by their public examination performance. Due to the above school place allocation mechanism, which is based largely on academic merit, it is not surprising to find that Hong Kong secondary schools are highly segregated in terms of students' ability as compared to a lot of Western countries (Lo et al., 1997), that is, there is a relatively small within school variation in ability, whereas the between school variation is extremely large.

Emic Measures and Correlates with Psychosocial Constructs

Using open-ended questions and structured questionnaires, Tam and Watkins (1995) attempted to identify the important self-concept dimensions of nondisabled and physically disabled Chinese adults in Hong Kong. The responses to the open-ended questions were content analyzed. For the nondisabled adults, family, friendship, work, marriage, study, material possessions, and leisure were perceived as the most important areas of self-concept. Whereas for the disabled adults, functional independence in daily living tasks stood out as the most important, followed by family, friendship, health, work, leisure, material possessions, and rehabilitation. It is interesting to note that honest family relationships, family responsibilities, and close relationships were identified as the most important for both non-disabled and disabled adults. In sum, the results reflected the cultural emphasis on the importance of human relationships and the interdependence of close others. With the above important relationship dimensions, Tam (1997) developed a self-concept questionnaire for Chinese people in Hong Kong (SCQHK) to measure nine factors: academic self, work self, material self, personal competence, physical self, social influence, social relationship, family influence, and family relationship. The instrument was validated with Chinese adults in Hong Kong, but only nine factors were identified with an exploratory factor analysis. Thus, the model was only partially supported.

In a number of between-construct studies with Chinese subjects, the multidimensional nature of self-concept has been assumed. For example, Lau (1989) showed in a study with Chinese adolescents in Hong Kong that a multidimensional measure of self-concept (an adapted Chinese version of SDQ-I) helped to capture the specific relation between sex role orientations and different domains of self-concept. In a series of studies on Chinese adolescent delinquency using a more refined measure of self-concept (an adapted Chinese version of SDQ-I), Lau and Leung (1992) also demonstrated that parent-child relation tended to have a closer linkage to adolescents' social development, whereas school-student relation was related more to their academic achievement. It was shown that adolescents' delinquency was related to specific components rather than to a global measure of general self-concept (Leung & Lau, 1989). The results were in congruence with Chan and Lee's (1993) finding that psychological symptoms could be accounted for by specific self-concepts.

In another study with Chinese junior high school children, Leung and Leung (1992) found that life satisfaction was more strongly associated with the self-concept in relation with parents, but less so to that with teachers. Distinctive developmental patterns across grades in specific self-concepts were also observed with the adoption of multidimensional measures of self-concept among Chinese students. For example, Lau (1990) found that self-concept of academic ability increased with age, whereas that of appearance decreased with age. In addition, the two specific self-concepts were related differently with other psychological variables such as locus of control, test anxiety and extraversion. In summary, all these studies showed that the inclusion of measures of specific and multidimensional components of self-concept revealed more refined relations, and hence a better under-standing of the relations among constructs.

Despite the above evidences of the usefulness of the multidimensional model of self-concept, there was insufficient validation study of the internal structure of self-concept among the Chinese. In a number of construct val-idation studies based on Chinese students, Watkins and his colleagues identified six out of the seven factors of the SDQ-1 measure by exploratory factor analysis (EFA). However, the general-self dimension was always sub-merged and intermingled with other factors (Chung & Watkins, 1992; Wat-kins & Dong, 1994; Watkins, Dong, & Xia, 1995). This is understandable because their use of EFA, rather than CFA, in model testing had strong lim-itations in that they could not evaluate and compare the a priori model against other alternatives. Moreover, previous self-concept research with Chinese subjects primarily relied on the SDQ-I measure, even though stu-dents would be more appropriately measured with SDQ-II. Furthermore, stronger statistical techniques, including multilevel regression analyses, structural equation modeling and other related techniques should be used to provide stronger tests of various theoretical models.

VALIDATION AND EXTENSION STUDIES
WITH CHINESE STUDENTS

We will summarize below a series of analyses on the SDQ-II with Chinese high school students. This large-scale research started a number of years ago with over 10,000 students followed longitudinally for 6 years (for details, see Hau, Kong, Marsh, & Cheng, 2000; Marsh, Kong, & Hau, 1999, 2000, in press). Students' academic achievements at Grade 6 [Time 0 (T0), pretest achievement test scores collected prior to the start of high school in Grade 7] to Grade 9 (i.e., T0 to T3) measured by standardized tests, as well as their public examination results at Grade 11 (i.e., T5) were gathered.

The English SDQII for adolescents was translated and administered to the students each year from Grade 8 (T2) to Grade 11 (T5).

Factorial Structure

The factorial structure of SDQ-II was first examined. CFA has provided very strong support for the construct validity of the Chinese version of the SDQ-II measure used in this study. The 12 factors, including the added Chinese verbal self-concept factor, were clearly identified and distinguishable from one another. CFA showed that all the self-concept factors were clearly defined. The factor loadings on the target factors were very high and statistically significant (median values = .74, and .78 for Grades 8 and 9, respectively). In addition, the factor loadings on each target factor were consistent across grades, indicating that the factor structure was replicable across the two years. The various goodness-of-fit indices showed that the baseline a priori model fitted the data very well. The RMSEA was small (0.0246), and the NNFI and CFI were substantially high (.942 and .946, respectively).

Reliabilities as estimated by Cronbach's alpha were satisfactory, ranging from .73 (Honesty) to .92 (Mathematics) with a median of .84 for Grade 8 (T2), and from .77 (Honesty) to .94 (Mathematics) with a median of .87 for Grade 9 (T3). These are comparable to the reliability coefficients from the Australian Normative Archive SDQ-II Sample (N=5494, 2658 males and 2836 females), which ranged from .84 (Honesty) to .91 (Physical Appearance) with a median of .87 (Marsh, 1990).

The correlations among the latent self-concept factors based on these CFA were relatively low as hypothesized (median correlations = .26 and .25 for Grades 8 and 9 respectively). The results showed that the different subscales of self-concept were quite independent and differentiable from each other and thus lent strong support for the multidimensional structure of self-concept. The convergent and divergent validity of the measure has been further demonstrated by the multitrait-multitime analysis. The correlations between the same self-concept factors at different occasions were consistently high (high convergent validities, or stability over time in this application), whereas the correlations between different self-concept factors at the same test occasion were much lower and became even lower across different test occasions (high divergent validity).

Factorial Invariance Analysis

The psychometric properties of the measure and the construct validity have been demonstrated further in the factorial invariance analysis. This was tested by placing equality constraints across grade levels, on all factor loadings (M2), factor covariances (M3), factor variances (M4), and item uniquenesses (M5) on the baseline model (M1). The fit of each model was compared with that of the preceding one. Furthermore, the corresponding modification indexes and expected changes for these constrained parameters were inspected to reveal the impacts of the invariance constraints on the whole model.

Judging from the overall goodness-of-fit indices and the modification indexes, it can be concluded that the invariance of factor loadings, factor covariances and factor variances across grades was substantiated while that of uniquenesses was not; for M2 vs. M1, $\Delta\chi^2$ (44) = 288.83; for M3 vs. M2, $\Delta\chi^2$ (66) = 238.62; for M4 vs. M3, $\Delta\chi^2$ (12) = 172.51; for M5 vs. M4, $\Delta\chi^2$ (56) = 3267.46; for all comparison except M4 vs. M5, ΔRMSEA = .000, ΔNNFI= .001, ΔCFI < .001, TC = .999; for M4 vs. M5, ΔRMSEA = .016, ΔNNFI = .008, ΔCFI = .008, TC = .989.

Factor loadings represent the relations between the indicators and the underlying latent constructs that they are posited to measure. Hence the invariance of factor loadings across grades supports that the responses to the items are equally valid for the participants at Grade 8 and 9. Factor covariances and variances reflect the relations among constructs and the invariance of factor covariances and variances indicates that the relations among the different facets of self-concept are stable over time. Furthermore, the invariance of factor correlations over time also suggests that the factor correlations do not drastically decline from Grade 8 to 9, as has been shown to occur between Grades 2 and 5 (Marsh, Byrne, & Shavelson, 1992).

Item uniquenesses are related to the reliability of measurement. In this investigation, the item uniquenesses are not invariant across time, indicating that the items have unequal reliabilities in measuring the self-concept for the same subject at different occasions. The results are consistent with findings discussed earlier showing that the SDQ-II responses were slightly more reliable at T3 (Grade 9, Median reliability = .87) than at T2 (Grade 8, Median reliability = .84). There is no sufficient information to account for this pattern; however, it is suspected that students realize their own attributes a little bit better when they are one year older and hence respond more consistently to the questionnaire items when they are in Grade 9 than when they are in Grade 8.

Internal/External Frame of Reference, Causal Relation and Its Extension

We examine and extend the internal/external frame of reference (I/E) model of self-concept formation by relating Chinese, English, and math achievement to Chinese, English, and math self-concepts. Tests of the I/E model are typically based on math and English constructs for a single wave of data in previous Western countries. We extend this research, testing its cross-cultural generalizability to a non-Western country, including native and nonnative languages as well as mathematics, and evaluating longitudinal effects over a five-year period. Hong Kong provides an ideal setting for testing this extension in that both Chinese (the native, first language) and English (the nonnative, second language) are so important in the high school curriculum and, indeed, in Hong Kong society more generally.

The results clearly support a priori hypotheses that nonnative language—as well as native language and mathematics—provides an important basis for the formation of self-concepts in specific school subjects. Although math, English, and Chinese achievements were all highly correlated ($r = .67$ to $.79$), the respective self-concepts were all nearly uncorrelated ($r = -.07$ to $.13$).

There was also support for new predictions based on the logic of the I/E model that were extended to include nonnative as well as native language. We evaluated the predictions based on the extended I/E model separately for each wave of data. The fit of the a priori (extended) I/E model is extremely good for separate analyses of data from T2 (TLI = .968), T3 (TLI = .968), and T4 (TLI = .980). Critical parameter estimates provide strong support for the I/E model in separate analyses of each of the three waves of data, namely, (i) mathematics achievement has a substantial positive effect on Math self-concept (path coefficients of .63 to .79), but smaller negative effects on English self-concept and Chinese self-concept (path coefficients of −.35 to −.14); (ii) English achievement has a substantial positive effect on English self-concept (path coefficients of .48 to .62), but smaller negative effects on Math self-concept and Chinese self-concept (path coefficients of −.26 to −.10) self-concepts; and (iii) Chinese achievement has a substantial positive effect on Chinese self-concept (path coefficients of .50 to .61), but smaller negative effects on Math self-concept and English self-concept (path coefficients of −.40 to −.06)). Furthermore, there was clear support for this pattern of results for self-concepts collected on each of three different occasions up to four years after the collection of achievement at T0. These results provide very strong support for the extended I/E model and the stability of the effects over time.

The issue of whether self-concept affects achievement or achievement determines self-concept has always been a topic of academic and educational interest. Consistent with previous Western studies, there are reciprocal effects of achievement on self-concept. Specifically, prior self-concept influences subsequent achievement and self-concept on and beyond the effects of prior achievement; similarly, prior achievement influences subsequent achievement and self-concept beyond the prediction of prior self-concept.

Longitudinal Extension of the I/E Model

The present investigation is important because it is a true longitudinal study based on data collected over a five-year period. Particularly because the achievement scores were collected (T0) two years prior to the first wave of self-concept data and each of the three waves of self-concept data (T2, T3, T4) was separated by a full year, there is a clearly established temporal ordering of these variables. Although much of the effects of T0 achievement on T3 self-concepts were mediated by T2 self-concepts, the predicted pattern of results was still evident even after controlling the effects of T2 self-concept. Even more surprising, the weak patterns of effects of achievement on T4 self-concepts beyond the effects that were explained in terms of T2 and T3 self-concepts still provided some support for the I/E predictions. Indeed, for separate analyses of each wave of self-concept data, the strength of the I/E effects were nearly the same at T2 and T3 (two and three years after the collection of the achievement data) and were only diminished slightly at T4 (four years after the collection of the achievement data).

Although clearly supportive of the I/E model, the strength of these effects at T3 and even T4 are somewhat surprising. In particular, even though the achievement scores were collected shortly prior to the start of high school, there was still good support for the I/E predictions in analyses of T4 self-concept measures collected in the fourth year of high school. Part of the explanation, is that academic achievement is a very stable construct. Furthermore, the particular T0 achievement scores considered in the study were very important to students in that they were the basis of determining whether students were able to attend the high schools of their choice. As this is such a critical rite of passage in the school life of Hong Kong students (and their parents), the scores that are the basis for this decision are likely to be strong indicators of academic ability that have a long-lasting impact on how students feel about themselves.

BFLPE and Its Extension

Culture may also have an impact on the assimilation and contrast effects. It has been demonstrated that people in a highly collective culture are less susceptible to the negative BFLPE and have a greater tendency to value their social group than those in an individualistic setting (McFarland & Buehler, 1995). If Chinese students do value strongly being members of a high average ability school (stronger assimilation effect) and that their collective orientation reduces the attention to the undesirable social comparison (weaker contrast effect), the negative BFLPE may disappear or become substantially reduced. In other words, in the Chinese culture where one's face—the reputation obtained through success and ostentation—is of great concern (e.g., Ho, 1976), the gain in status and face of attending a high-ability school (assimilation) may possibly overcompensate the loss in prestige due to comparison with high ability classmates. Thus, the originally negative BFLPE in Chinese students could be less negative or even become positive.

Results from our studies showed that consistent with a priori predictions based on the BFLPE, being in schools where school-average achievement was high led to initially lower academic self-concepts and further declined over time (social comparison contrast effects) (beta = −.22 to −.24 after controlling for initial achievements). Prior self-concept also had a positive effect on subsequent achievement even after controlling for prior achievement.

This study also extended previous BFLPE research by including a measure of perceived school status to tap the potentially positive effects on academic self-concept in attending high-ability schools. Consistent with the a priori prediction, perceived school status was positively related to the school-average achievement and had positive effects on subsequent students' academic self-concept (reflected glory assimilation effects). Also in line with the theoretical hypotheses, when the perceived school status was controlled, the negative social comparison contrast effects on academic self-concept in attending high-ability schools became even more negative. These results have provided strong empirical support for the argument that BFLPE is a net effect of counterbalancing positive reflected glory effects and negative social comparison effects. Students in high-ability schools are facing a more demanding comparison from classmates. But they are also enjoying the pride for being members in these prestigious schools.

By including a separate measure of perceived school status, we partialled out some of the reflected glory effects associated with school-average achievement so that it became a better (less confounded) basis for inferring social comparison contrast effects leading to a more negative

BFLPE. These results also imply that previous research may have underestimated the size of the negative contrast effect. However, because reflected glory effects were predicted to be particularly important in Hong Kong, further research is needed to determine the generality of counter-balancing assimilation and contrast effects.

CONCLUSION

Strong support has been found for the applicability of Western self-concept instruments, theories, and models with Chinese students. In the large-scale 6-year longitudinal study, the validity of a Chinese version of a widely used self-concept instrument (SDQ-II) was first evaluated by CFA, multitrait-multitime analysis, and factorial invariance analysis. The psychometric properties of the Chinese instrument were found to be as strong as or even stronger than those of the original Australian (English) version. It is fascinating to see that an instrument developed in an Australian context can perform so well in a Chinese context.

Unlike previous validity studies using Chinese participants (e.g., Chung & Watkins, 1992; Watkins & Dong, 1994; Watkins et al., 1995), this study is able to distinguish the global, general self-factor from other more specific self-concept factors using methodologically more appropriate CFA. The results suggest that knowledge or information of oneself is organized in a systematic way and this information can be retrieved and assessed accordingly. The results support the description of the characteristics of self-concept as structured, hierarchical, and stable. Consistent with the theoretical predictions, the general self-factor correlated substantially high with almost every self-concept factor. Thus, results from CFA, multitrait-multitime analysis and factorial invariance analysis have converged to provide a very strong support for the generality of the multidimensional model of self-concept and the validity of the SDQ-II measure in self-concept research across cultures—in particular Chinese secondary students in Hong Kong.

Other major relationships among self-concept and related constructs have also been found in the Chinese culture. Specifically, results similar to Western findings were replicated in the relationships between self-concept and achievement of matching and nonmatching domains in the internal/external frame of reference model, the relationship between school average ability and students' self-concept in the BFLPE model, and the cross-lag relationships between achievement and self-concepts in determining causal relationships. In contrast to previous Western research, we have also extended to study self-concept of native and nonnative languages, to use truly longitudinal data in determining causal ordering of achievement and self-concept, and to separate the positive reflected glory assimilation effect from the negative social contrast effect in attending high-ability schools. Taken together the series of analyses demonstrate the robustness of the SDQ instruments in non-Western cultures. Furthermore, the cross-cultural applicability and generality of the self-concept and its related theoretical models have also been supported in the Chinese culture.

REFERENCES

Baumeister, R. F. (1986). *Public self and private self.* New York: Springer.

Bettencourt, B. A., & Dorr, N. (1997). Collective self-esteem as a mediator of the relationship between allocentrism and subjective well-being. *Personality and Social Psychology Bulletin, 23,* 955–964.

Brown, J. D., Novick, N. J., Lord, K. A., & Richards, J. M. (1992). When Gulliver travels: Social context, psychological closeness, and self-appraisals. *Journal of Personality and Social Psychology, 62,* 717–727.

Chan, D. W., & Lee, H. C. B. (1993). Dimensions of self-esteem and psychological symptoms among Chinese adolescents in Hong Kong. *Journal of Youth and Adolescence, 22,* 425–440.

Chung, C. H., & Watkins, D. (1992). Some evidence of the reliability and validity of a Chinese version of the Self Description Questionnaire. *Bulletin of the Hong Kong Psychological Society, 28–29,* 39–48.

Crocker, J., Luhtanen, R., Blaine, B., & Broadnax, S. (1994). Collective self-esteem and psychological well-being among white, black, and Asian college students. *Personality and Social Psychology Bulletin, 20,* 503–513.

Felson, R. B., & Reed, M. D. (1986). Reference groups and self-appraisals of academic ability and performance. *Social Psychology Quarterly, 49,* 103–109.

Gamoran, A., Nystrand, M., Berends, M., & LePore, P. C. (1995). An organizational analysis of the effects of ability grouping. *American Educational Research Journal, 32,* 687–715.

Harter, S. (1982). The perceived competence scale for children. *Child Development, 53,* 87–97.

Hau, K. T., & Salili, F. (1991). Structure and semantic differential placement of specific causes: academic causal attributions by Chinese Students in Hong Kong. *International Journal of Psychology, 26,* 175–193.

Hau, K. T., & Salili, F. (1996). Prediction of academic performance among Chinese students: Effort can compensate for lack of ability. *Organizational Behavior and Human Decision Processes, 65,* 83–94.

Hau, K. T., Kong, C. K., Marsh, H. W., & Cheng, Z. J. (2000, April). *Chinese students' self-concept: Multidimensionality, big-fish-little-pond effects and casual ordering.* Paper presented at American Educational Research Association Annual Meeting, New Orleans, LA.

Ho, D. Y.-F. (1976). On the concept of face. *American Journal of Sociology, 81,* 867–884.

Lau, S. (1989). Sex role orientation and domains of self-esteem. *Sex Roles, 21,* 415–422.

Lau, S. (1990). Crisis and vulnerability in adolescent development. *Journal of Youth and Adolescence, 19,* 111–131.

Lau, S., & Leung, K. (1992). Relations with parents and school and Chinese adolescents' self-concept, delinquency, and academic performance. *British Journal of Educational Psychology, 62,* 21–30.

Leung, K., & Lau, S. (1989). Effects of self-concept and perceived disapproval of delinquent behavior in school children. *Journal of Youth and Adolescence, 18,* 345-359.

Leung, J. P., & Leung, K. (1992). Life satisfaction, self-concept, and relationship with parents in adolescence. *Journal of Youth and Adolescence, 21,* 653–665.

Lo, L. N-K., Tsang, W. K., Chung, Y. P., Cheng, Y. C., Sze, P. M.-M., Ho, E. S.-C., & Ho, M. K. (1997). *A survey of the effectiveness of Hong Kong secondary school systems.* Hong Kong: Chinese University of Hong Kong.

Luhtanen, R., & Crocker, J. (1992). A collective self-esteem scale: Self-evaluation of one's social identity. *Personality and Social Psychological Bulletin, 18,* 302–318.

Markus, H. R., & Kitayama, S. (1991). Culture and the self: Implications for cognition, emotion, and motivation. *Psychological Review, 98,* 224–253.

Marsh, H. W. (1990). A multidimensional, hierarchical self-concept: Theoretical and empirical justification. *Educational Psychology Review, 2,* 77–172.

Marsh, H. W. (1993). Academic self-concept: Theory, measurement, and research. In J. Suls (Ed.), *Psychological perspective on the self* (Vol. 4). Hillsdale, NJ: Erlbaum.

Marsh, H. W., Byrne, B. M., & Shavelson, R. J. (1992). A multidimensional, hierarchical self-concept. In T. M. Brinthaupt & R. P. Lipka (Eds.), *The self: Definitional and methodological issues* (pp. 44–95). New York: State University of New York.

Marsh, H. W., Kong, C. K., & Hau, K. T. (1999). Longitudinal multilevel modeling of the Big Fish Little Pond Effect on academic self-concept: Counterbalancing social comparison and reflected glory effects in Hong Kong high schools. *Journal of Personality and Social Psychology, 78,* 337–349.

Marsh, H. W., Kong, C. K., & Hau, K. T. (2000). Extension of the internal/external frame of reference model of self-concept formation: Importance of native and nonnative languages for Chinese students. *Journal of Educational Psychology, 93,* 543–553.

Marsh, H. W., Hau, K. T., & Kong, C. K. (2002). Multilevel causal ordering of academic self-concept and achievement: Influence of language of instruction (English vs. Chinese) for Hong Kong students. *American Educational Research Journal, 37,* 245–282.

McFarland, C., & Buehler, R. (1995). Collective self-esteem as a moderator of the frog-pond effect in reactions to performance feedback. *Journal of Personality and Social Psychology, 68,* 1055–1070.

Meredith, W. H., Wang, A., & Zheng, F. M. (1993). Determining constructs of self-perception for children in Chinese cultures. *School Psychology International, 14,* 371–380.

Tam, A. S. F., & Watkins, D. (1995). Towards a hierarchical model of self-concept for Hong Kong Chinese adults with physical disabilities. *International Journal of Psychology, 30,* 1–17.

Tam, S. F. (1997). Development and validation of a self-concept questionnaire for Hong Kong Chinese adults. *Psychologia, 40,* 121–130.

Tay, M. P., Licht, B. G., & Tate, R. L. (1995). The internal/external frame of reference in adolescents' math and verbal self-concepts: A generalization study. *Contemporary Educational Psychology, 20,* 392–402.

Triandis, H. C. (1989). The self and social behavior in different cultural contexts. *Psychological Review, 96,* 506–520.

Watkins, D., & Dong, Q. (1994). Assessing the self-esteem of Chinese school children. *Educational Psychology, 14,* 129–137.

Watkins, D., Dong, Q., & Xia, Y. (1995). Towards the validation of a Chinese version of the self-descriptive questionnaire–1. *Psychologia, 38,* 22–30.

Yang, C. F. (1991). A review of studies on self in Hong Kong and Taiwan: Reflections and future prospects. In C. F. Yang & H. S. R. Kao (Eds.), *Chinese and Chinese heart* (pp.15–92). Taipei, Taiwan: Yuan Liu.

CHAPTER 4

SELF-CONCEPT AND SELF-EFFICACY REVISITED

A Few Notable Differences and Important Similarities

Einar M. Skaalvik and Mimi Bong

One of the strong beliefs held by both researchers and practitioners in the field of education is that self-perceptions, the various attributions and beliefs that students assign to themselves, provide a basic foundation of behavior and motivation. Individuals who are otherwise similar feel differently about themselves and choose different courses of action, depending on how they perceive themselves, such as what attributes they think they possess and what they believe they are capable of. These are beliefs and perceptions about self that are heavily rooted in one's past experiences. Yet it is these subjective convictions about oneself, once established, which play a determining role in individuals' further growth and development (Bandura, 1997; Markus & Nurius, 1986). As Rosenberg (1979) noted in his classic book on self-concept, the individual's behavior is based not on what he or she is actually like but on what the individual *thinks* he or she is like.

There have been two separate research traditions in the study of academic self-perception: (a) self-concept tradition and (b) self-efficacy tradition. Research in personality and social psychology during the past couple

International Advances in Self Research, pages 67–89
Copyright © 2003 by Information Age Publishing
All rights of reproduction in any form reserved.

of decades has focused extensively on these constructs. However, investigators within the two traditions not only define the constructs differently but also explain the development and the effect of the constructs in different ways. They also use different measures, hardly ever referring to each other. In rare instances where such references do occur, their purpose is usually to emphasize the distinctiveness of the given construct (e.g., Bandura, 1986). Still, several attempts have been made to analyze, theoretically or empirically, the difference between the constructs (see Bong & Clark, 1999). The purpose of this chapter is to illuminate some of the similarities and differences between these two conceptions.

CONCEPTUAL DEFINITIONS

Consider the following scenario. A high school student, who has received mostly A's and occasional B's in her previous math courses, nonetheless feels that mathematics is not one of her strong subjects. She recognizes that her ability to learn and perform in mathematics is clearly above average but thinks that her linguistic skills are far superior to her mathematical capabilities. Indeed, she has been receiving slightly better grades in verbal subjects such as English literature or composition. When presented with a set of core math problems, however, she expresses strong confidence to successfully solve them. Her confidence stems mostly out of her prior experiences with similar tasks in various math courses she has taken before. When judging her chances of success on these familiar tasks, she is less concerned about her vague feelings of insecurity in the domain of mathematics. Instead, she conjures up and focuses on her previous successful encounters with analogous problems.

According to the current views, the first half of the scenario—evaluation of capability in reference to that of others, comparison of one's own math and verbal abilities, self-perceptions of competency and general feelings of confidence or inadequacy in the given domain—describes characteristics typically assigned to self-concept beliefs. The latter half—appraisals of competence in relation to specific tasks and convictions for success on the basis of prior mastery experiences—is better ascribed to self-efficacy beliefs.

Self-concept is colloquially defined as a composite view of oneself. Rosenberg (1979) defined self-concept as "the totality of the individual's thoughts and feelings having reference to himself as an object" (p. 7). Shavelson, Hubner, and Stanton (1976, p. 411) defined self-concept as "a person's perception of himself," which is formed through experiences with the environment and is influenced especially by environmental reinforcements and significant others. Self-concept research in the past tended to involve a global construct such as global self-esteem. Therefore, a composite score was computed for each individual by summing his or her self-concept responses toward various aspects of life. This score was then treated as an indicator of the person's general self-concept (see Marsh, 1990, for an overview). Several researchers have criticized this method, arguing that it overlooks both the multidimensionality of self-concept and the psychological centrality of different dimensions (e.g., Harter, 1982). Based largely on the work of Herbert Marsh and his associates (e.g., Marsh, 1993), the field has come to recognize that any sound understanding of self-concept and its impact must take into account the multidimensional nature of the construct.

Research in self-efficacy can be characterized by its relatively short history compared to self-concept research. Bandura (1977, p. 3) defined self-efficacy as "beliefs in one's capabilities to organize and execute the courses of action required to produce given attainments." Self-efficacy differs from self-concept in that it is concerned less with the skills and abilities one thinks one has but more with what one can do with whatever skills one possesses (Bandura, 1986). Thus, self-efficacy is based on expectations of what one can do and has been conceptualized as an important aspect of perceived control. For example, the expectation that one can successfully solve specific math problems is an efficacy judgment. It is not a judgment of whether a person feels competent in mathematics in general but a judgment of how strongly the person believes that he or she can successfully carry out required actions that lead to correct solutions of particular math problems under the given circumstances. Self-efficacy researchers thus emphasize the role of specific contexts in efficacy appraisals.

Conceptual definitions of self-concept and self-efficacy often do not point to specific dimensions on which they are believed to differ. The distinction between the two constructs becomes much easier when operational definitions of each are compared. Therefore, we start with what may seem to be a backward strategy of analyzing measurement instruments to tease out theoretical differences. We emphasize, however, that operational definitions of constructs are explicit and manifested forms of implicit, underlying theories. In some sense, this also indicates that differences between the two self-beliefs might have been exaggerated in the literature due to the different assessment and analytic strategies (Bong & Clark, 1999; Skaalvik & Rankin, 1996a).

OPERATIONAL DEFINITIONS

A self-report is by far the most frequently used assessment method for both constructs. Typical self-concept items include "Schoolwork is easy for me," "I have always done well in *subject*," and "Compared to others my age, I'm good at *subject*." Different views exist among researchers regarding whether self-concept also taps emotional reactions such as interest, enjoyment, and satisfaction. Some regard these as an important part of self-concept, whereas others consider them a distinct construct. Researchers with the former view add items such as "I'm hopeless when it comes to *subject*," "I am interested in *subject*," and "I look forward to *subject*" (Marsh, 1999a, 1999b).

Self-efficacy is typically assessed by presenting specific problems to respondents and asking them to report their convictions for successfully performing on each (e.g., Bandura & Schunk, 1981). Written descriptions of problems or tasks may also be presented in lieu of actual problems, for example, "How sure are you that you can correctly spell all words in a one-page story or composition?" (Pajares, Miller, & Johnson, 1999) and "How confident are you that you can successfully solve equations containing square roots?" (Bong, 2002). Self-efficacy may also be measured beyond the specific problem level. One example is, "How confident are you that you will get a grade better than a B in mathematics at the end of this term?" (Zimmerman & Bandura, 1994).

Several differences quickly become noticeable: (a) Orientation toward the past versus orientation toward the future, (b) general versus specific measurements, (c) relativistic versus absolute evaluation of capability, (d) integration versus separation of cognition and affect, and (e) temporal stability versus malleability. It is important to note that these differences are more a question of the degree rather than all-or-none characteristics. A critical issue that distinguishes self-concept and self-efficacy is the extent to which the target behavior or outcome is defined or made explicit. Moreover, items reveal not only differences but important similarities as well. Most importantly, both call for a subjective judgment of perceived academic competence.

SOME NOTABLE DIFFERENCES

Past versus Future Orientation

As alluded to earlier, self-concept focuses on general ability perceptions, whereas self-efficacy focuses on expectations of being able to execute specific actions. Most academic self-concept items begin with phrases that read, "I *am* good," "I *am* hopeless," or "I *have done* well" (see Byrne, 1996). Self-efficacy items usually start with "How confident are you that you *can*...?" "How well *can* you ...?" or "I am confident that I *will be able to* ..." (see Pajares, 1996). The examples show that the wording of self-concept items tends to direct the attention of respondents toward their past accomplishments, asking them to answer the question, "Am I good at it?" Self-efficacy items make the respondents focus on their future expectancies by answering the question, "Can I do it?" (see Skaalvik, 1997a, for a related discussion).

Although self-concept and self-efficacy are both products of one's past experiences, they make salient slightly different time frames. As pointed out by Markus and Nurius (1986), self-concepts are past-oriented because relevant information and experiences need to be processed by self-schemas and these schemas are created from individuals' past experiences in a particular domain. Self-efficacy expectations are also in large part results of self-schemas that are created from their earlier mastery experiences (see Bandura, 1986). Yet these perceptions are inherently future-oriented because they represent individuals' confidence for successfully accomplishing the imminent tasks. The student in the beginning scenario demonstrated high expectations for solving the problems correctly, which has yet to occur, despite her lack of confidence toward mathematics in general.

The relative emphasis on the past versus future is inevitably intertwined with how much specific aspects of the prospective situation should be taken into account in forming the ability judgments. When the bases of judgments called for are mostly experiences in the past, neither the researchers nor the respondents are compelled to pay closer attention to particulars of the current situation. Individuals' overall views of themselves in the area based on the past self-schema will not change much by the specifics of any single event. In contrast, if students are to report their likelihood of success on some impending tasks that are yet to be performed, it is to their benefit to consider all the variables operating in the context. Otherwise, they risk forming inaccurate assessments of self, which may result in ineffective execution plans and unsuccessful performance.

Levels of Specificity and Implicit versus Explicit Reference to Target Performance

Traditional measures of self-concept and self-efficacy also differ with respect to the level of generality of the self-judgments (Pajares, 1996). Academic self-concept, even when assessed in reference to particular domains, has been measured at more general levels. Students typically report their general feelings of doing well or poorly in given subject areas. Consequently, self-concept items rarely specify what constitutes successful performance in the given academic pursuits. This forces respondents to come up with aggregated evaluations of themselves in the particular domain. In the previous scenario, the student demonstrates an insecure sense of self-confidence when her thoughts focus on the broader domain of math. When she is presented with a specific set of problems and thereby becomes able to assess her capabilities in reference to the particular courses of action required under the particular circumstances, she reaches a different conclusion.

According to Rosenberg (1968), "a man's global self-esteem is not based solely on his assessment of his constituent qualities; it is based on his self-assessments of qualities that count" (p. 339). This statement is not only true for global self-esteem but also applicable to domain-specific self-concepts. Students are asked to make evaluations of their competence in academic domains without being provided with explicit information regarding what facets of performance need to be given primary consideration. Competence information that is most salient and readily accessible in students' self-schemas in the domain of interest tends to determine the perceptions of self.

Beliefs of self-efficacy have usually been examined at more specific levels. Because efficacy questions correspond directly to target performance, important features of tasks that could wield tangible influence on performance outcomes are clearly spelled out (Bandura, 1997). The problem of aggregating different dimensions and impressions becomes fairly irrelevant. Consistent with this assumption, stronger relations of self-efficacy beliefs to performance have been reported when the content and specificity of self-efficacy measures corresponded closely with criterial performance (e.g., Pajares & Miller, 1995).

The purported differences between domain-level self-concept and task-level self-efficacy are widely recognized (e.g., Marsh, Walker, & Debus, 1991; Pajares, 1996). Nevertheless, they may not reflect inherent differences between the two constructs. More recent investigations in both camps moved forward to a less familiar territory. Some researchers have assessed domain-level self-efficacy (e.g., Bong, 2002; Pajares & Miller, 1995; Zimmerman, Bandura, & Martinez-Pons, 1992), while a few others ventured the notion of task-specific academic self-concepts (e.g., Yeung et al., 2000).

More generally, it is interesting that while the focus of self-concept research has changed from global composite measures (self-esteem) to area specific measures, self-efficacy assessments in some research have become more general. For instance, self-efficacy has come to refer to judgments of being able or not able to complete certain courses or learn certain subjects (e.g., Zimmerman, Bandura, & Martinez-Pons, 1992) or manage certain unfamiliar jobs (e.g., Lent, Brown, & Larkin, 1986). Questions such as "How well can you learn general mathematics?" and "How well can you learn science?" neither state what defines successful performance in each of these areas nor specify the courses of action required to reach the desired outcome. They depart substantially from judgments toward particular tasks in that (a) completing a course is not equivalent to completing any one particular task, (b) one does not know beforehand the whole array of tasks one will be required to manage, and (c) one often has no means of knowing exactly what specific actions are necessary for each type of unknown task (Skaalvik, 1997a). Therefore, self-efficacy for learning differs from self-efficacy for performance and may not be distinguishable from area-specific self-concept. An important characteristic distinguishing self-efficacy from self-concept therefore seems to be the specification of target behavior in self-efficacy items. The specification of target behavior or lack of such specification may result in differences in what constitutes subjective feeling of success.

Frames of Reference for Self-Evaluation

Self-related perceptions are formed through experiences with the environment, which involve self-evaluation. Self-evaluations require certain criteria or frames of reference against which one's own performances and attributes are gauged. Marsh and Craven (2000) noted that self-concept cannot be adequately understood if frames of reference are ignored because, "The same objective characteristics and accomplishments can lead to disparate self-concepts depending on the frame of reference or standard of comparison that individuals use to evaluate themselves" (p. 75). Self-concept researchers typically emphasize reflected appraisals from significant others and social comparisons as major reference frames.

Social comparison theory suggests that people appraise themselves by using significant others in their immediate environment as the bases of comparison, when objective standards of comparison are not readily available (Festinger, 1954). Marsh, Byrne, and Shavelson (1988) hence explained that students compare their own achievement with perceived achievements of other students and use this external, relativistic impression as one basis of their academic self-concept. Marsh (1987) proposed a similar notion termed the "big-fish-little-pond effect" (BFLPE). This effect occurs "when equally able students have lower self-perceived academic skills and lower academic self-concepts when they compare themselves with more able students, and higher self-perceived academic skills and academic self-concepts when they compare themselves with less able students" (p. 281). The BFLPE has been supported in a number of studies reporting the direct negative effect of school or classroom average ability on students' self-concept, after controlling for individual achievement (see Marsh & Craven, 2000, for an extensive review of this research).

Marsh (1986) proposed yet another comparative frame of reference that is thought to be in use in academic self-concept formation. He argued that students base their academic self-concepts in a particular subject not only on how their ability compares with those of other students (i.e., social or external comparison) but also on how their ability in that subject compares with their abilities in other subjects (i.e., internal comparison). The ipsative nature of internal comparison is presumed to result in negative direct effects of achievement in one domain on self-concept in other domains. High math achievement lowers verbal self-concept and vice versa. The joint effects of internal and external comparisons cancel each other out, producing a relationship between verbal and math self-concepts that is much weaker than that between verbal and math achievements. Both these predictions of the frames of reference model on self-concept have been supported in a number of studies (for an overview, see Skaalvik, 1997a).

According to Bandura (1977), people rely on four major sources of information for gauging their self-efficacy: Enactive experiences, vicarious information, verbal persuasion, and physiological reactions. Among these sources, self-efficacy judgments are assumed to be most heavily affected by one's previous encounters with the same or similar tasks (Bong, 1997; Bong & Clark, 1999). Because required performances and standards against which to assess their confidence are clearly spelled out, there is less reason to engage in vigorous social comparison, at least for self-efficacy judgments at a problem specific level. Consistent with this assumption, predictions of the frames of reference model (Marsh, 1986) have not received support with self-efficacy measures (e.g., Bong, 1998; Marsh et al., 1991; Skaalvik & Rankin, 1990). Verbal and math self-efficacy perceptions usually correlate highly, the degree of which is commensurate with the corresponding correlation between verbal and math achievements. Further, high achievement in one area does not necessarily lower efficacy judgments in other areas. Two studies are particularly interesting because predictions from the frame of reference model were tested for both self-concept and self-efficacy judgments in the same samples (Marsh, Walker, & Debus, 1991; Skaalvik & Rankin, 1995). Both studies gave support to the frame of reference model when measuring math and verbal self-concepts by means of SDQ measures, but not when measuring math and verbal self-efficacy at a problem specific level.

Although the internal comparison process does not seem relevant in efficacy estimation, social comparison, and reflected appraisals are implicit in the theory and research of self-efficacy. Pajares (1997) pointed out that vicarious experiences involve social comparisons made with other individuals and that "a model's failure has a more negative effect on the self-efficacy of observers when observers judge themselves as having comparable ability to the model" (p. 5). Thus, the relative performance of others may have different effects on self-concept and self-efficacy. Whereas the failure of others may affect a particular student's self-concept positively (a contrast effect) it may affect self-efficacy negatively (an assimilation effect). However, if the observer judges his or her ability to be superior to the model's capability, failure of the model might not have negative impact on his or her feelings of efficacy. Therefore, the assimilation effect of social comparison on a student's self-efficacy is assumed to be restricted to comparisons with models having comparable ability to the student in question. Reflected appraisals are also implicit in self-efficacy judgments. Verbal persuasion by credible others is known to influence perception of self-efficacy. Verbal persuasion, in effect, is a concrete manifestation of how a person is perceived or evaluated by significant others. When the task is novel or when the criteria for success are not clear, individuals estimate their efficacy perceptions primarily on the basis of social comparative information (Bandura, 1977). Under such circumstances, their efficacy beliefs will also be more heavily swayed by verbal persuasion of credible others. The difference between self-concept and self-efficacy regarding social comparison and reflected appraisals, therefore, seems to be one of degree.

Integration versus Separation of Cognition and Affect

It has long been recognized by many researchers in the field that self-concept reflects more than one's competence perceptions. Scheirer and Kraut (1979) argued that self-concept consists of at least four distinguishable aspects, including emotional attitudes toward the self called self-esteem. Skaalvik (1997a) made a distinction between descriptive, evaluative, and affective/motivational aspects of self-concept. He claimed that, whereas self-description and self-evaluation components may not be clearly separated from each other, they can be distinguished from affective/motivational components. Knowledge that one learns mathematics easily, for example, is both a description and evaluation of self. That one is proud of one's own mathematics ability or that one likes mathematics is, on the other hand, a motivational statement that is related to yet separable from the former self-knowledge. Consistent with this reasoning, empirical research was able to extract two correlated but independent factors from students' self-concept responses (Skaalvik & Rankin, 1996b; Tanzer, 1996). Marsh, Craven, and Debus (1999) also found that the competency and the affective components of self-concept could be separated. Still, they found high correlations around .7 to .8 suggesting that differential effects of these components may be limited. The content in the cognitive dimension of self-concept is believed to generate affective and motivational reactions to the recognized attributes of self (Bong & Skaalvik, 2003).

We may also make a distinction between descriptive and evaluative aspects of self-efficacy and the resultant affective and motivational responses. However, self-efficacy theorists and researchers make conscious effort for separating one's efficacy perceptions, which are primarily cognitive and evaluative, from resultant emotions (Bong & Clark, 1999). Self-efficacy measures ask individuals make judgments on how well they believe they can execute the set of behaviors required for a desired outcome, without explicitly prompting to their feelings about carrying out those tasks. Apparently, although such judgments are primarily cognitive they require subjective evaluations of what one is or is not able to do. Like self-concept judgments therefore, the cognitive and the evaluative components of self-efficacy may not be separated from each other. To repeat, self-efficacy researchers separate the cognitive/evaluative component from resultant emotions. However, the motivational and emotional responses resulting from self-efficacy judgment may be as important for behavior and for subsequent achievement as the self-efficacy judgment itself.

Relative Stability versus Malleability

Temporal stability is another major difference between self-concept and self-efficacy beliefs. Shavelson and colleagues (1976) identified stability as one of the most important characteristics to the definition of self-concept. In fact, several studies reported that general as well as subject matter specific self-concepts demonstrated high stability coefficients that were even stronger than the stability coefficients of corresponding achievements (Marsh & Yeung, 1998; Shavelson & Bolus, 1982). The time lag in these investigations ranged from four months to two years.

Stability of self-efficacy has not been investigated systematically, although experimental evidence suggests that these perceptions quickly respond to changes in experience. Schunk's series of experiments with elementary school children demonstrated repeatedly that self-efficacy beliefs of these students improved significantly after participating in the experiments, even in the area where they had not been successful (e.g., Schunk & Swartz, 1993). Bandura (1997) stated that, once established, perception of self-efficacy is resilient to temporary failures. Nevertheless, he warned that it is fundamentally a context-specific construct that should not be viewed as one of the stable personality traits. Pajares and Graham (1999) also reported a higher stability coefficient for self-concept than self-efficacy. Students' math self-efficacy judgments had changed significantly during the course of six months, whereas their self-concept scores essentially stayed the same.

Whether self-perceptions are resistant or amenable to change upon new experiences has important implications for educational practice. As research of self has demonstrated, success of instructional strategies such as providing adaptive attributional feedback or attainable short-term goals depends largely on whether students modify their beliefs in response to the new information. Compared to the success in self-efficacy manipulation experiments, attempts to bolster students' self-concept have produced only modest success, presumably due to its relatively unchanging nature (e.g.,

Craven, Marsh, & Debus, 1991). Stability of self-concept appears age-related such that self-concepts of younger children are more flexible, whereas those of older students are more rigid and more highly correlated with their achievement and others' evaluation of their competence (Skaalvik & Hagtvet, 1990; Wigfield et al., 1997).

IMPORTANT SIMILARITIES

Up to this point, we have discussed some of the notable distinctions between self-concept and self-efficacy beliefs. We should emphasize that most of these differences involve differences in the degree to which each construct displays the particular characteristics under consideration, rather than the absolute all-or-none situation. Despite differences in time orientation, measurement and context specificity, frames of reference, construct composition, and temporal stability, the two belief systems share some important similarities. It is these similarities that we now turn to.

Centrality of Perceived Competence

Perceived competence in well-defined domains or activities comprises the single most critical element in both self-concept and self-efficacy. Perceptions of competence comprise the key element in most contemporary theorizing of academic self-concept (e.g., Harter, 1982; Wigfield et al., 1997). Perceived capability in reference to specific tasks and domains is also the principal component of academic self-efficacy judgments.

At the domain level of specificity, self-concept and self-efficacy beliefs may not be separable (e.g., Pajares, 1996). Thus far, researchers have reported that students' responses to the Self Description Questionnaire, one of the most popular self-concept scales, formed two separate factors, cognitive and motivational (Skaalvik & Rankin, 1996a; Tanzer, 1996). The cognitive self-concept factor was empirically indistinguishable from self-efficacy (Skaalvik & Rankin, 1996a). Because few studies have systematically addressed the equivalence of self-concept and self-efficacy responses, it is still premature to draw any firm conclusion regarding the nature of the relationship between these two constructs. Nevertheless, it seems reasonable to assume, on the basis of limited available evidence, that there is at least considerable overlap in self-concept and self-efficacy and that perception of competence is the major common denominator between the two.

Multidimensional and Hierarchical Structure

Shavelson and colleagues (1976) argued that self-concept is a multidimensional construct that is hierarchically structured, with the most general perceptions at the apex of the hierarchy. Therefore, a more general self-concept in the given domain of functioning subsumes many subarea-specific self-concepts, which in turn subsume task- or activity-specific self-concepts. Among the four major domains that Shavelson and colleagues proposed (i.e., academic, social, emotional, and physical), academic self-concept was later found to be more highly differentiated than the researchers originally hypothesized. More specifically, students' self-concepts are so clearly defined along the line of verbal and math subjects; they cannot be adequately represented by a single academic self-concept factor. The academic portion of the hierarchy was thus revised to incorporate verbal and math higher-order self-concept factors (Marsh, 1990; Marsh, Byrne, & Shavelson, 1988).

Whereas most researchers agree on the multidimensional nature of self-concept, some express different views on the hierarchical structure of self-concepts. For example, Harter (1998) questioned the validity of self-concept hierarchy, stating that "one has to ask whether the statistical structure extracted does, in fact, mirror the psychological structure as it is phenomenologically experienced by individuals" (p. 579). The issue still needs to be resolved but evidence tends to support the revised hierarchy (Byrne & Worth Gavin, 1996; Marsh & Yeung, 1998).

Self-efficacy perceptions are also reliably differentiated between domains and activities (Bong, 1997; Bong & Hocevar, 2002). The degree of such differentiation partly depends on age, gender, and prior experience (Bong, 1999). As was the case with academic self-concept, academic self-efficacy beliefs in primarily verbal areas diverge from those in quantitatively oriented subjects. However, questions still remain as to whether the internal structure of self-efficacy belief resembles the hierarchical organization of self-concept. While Bong's series of studies (Bong, 1997, 1999, 2001a, 2001b) provided enough evidence to confirm the multidimensionality of academic self-efficacy beliefs, they have not yet provided evidence that directly pertains to the question of hierarchy. It remains to be demonstrated, as self-concept researchers have (Yeung et al., 2000), whether the common factor underlying more specific self-efficacy beliefs is equivalent in content to more general self-efficacy beliefs.

Content-Specificity

In his critique of self-concept research, Bandura (1981) contended that the global nature of self-concept detracts from its power to explain behavior. However, modern research in self-concept acknowledges the multidimensional nature of the construct and the need for domain specific measures of self-concept. As a result, academic self-concept researchers have repeatedly demonstrated that students' self-concept in a particular school subject relates most strongly with achievement indexes in the same subject area. Its relations to achievement measures in other school subjects are considerably weaker (e.g., Marsh et al., 1988; Skaalvik & Rankin, 1995; Skaalvik & Valås, 1999).

Self-efficacy investigators typically include measures that belong to the same domain and, as such, are less interested in whether the within-domain relations between self-efficacy and performance are stronger than their cross-domain relations. However, several recent studies reported evidence of strong content-specificity of self-efficacy beliefs that is comparable to that obtained in self-concept research. In Joo, Bong, and Choi (2000), for instance, students reported their self-efficacy toward biology and use of Internet in web-based biology classes. Self-efficacy for biology learning predicted end-of-session biology performance on the written test, whereas self-efficacy for Internet use predicted Internet search performance on biology topics. Neither of the cross-task prediction paths (e.g., biology self-efficacy to Internet performance) was significant. In another investigation, English self-efficacy only predicted English achievement, while math self-efficacy only predicted math achievement, despite the high correlation between self-efficacy and achievement in the two areas (Bong, 2002). Again, relations of self-efficacy in one domain to achievement in the other were not significant. Therefore, evidence is pretty consistent that both self-concept and self-efficacy beliefs are tied to specific content areas.

Prediction of Motivation, Emotion, and Performance

Both academic self-concept and self-efficacy researchers claim that their construct is important both as a desirable outcome and as a mediator of academic motivation and performance (e.g., Marsh et al., 1991). Supporting this view, numerous studies have documented strong relations of the two self-beliefs with various indexes of motivation and performance. Self-concept has been shown to relate significantly to effort (Skaalvik & Rankin, 1995), help-seeking (Ames, 1983), course-selection (Marsh & Yeung, 1997b), intrinsic motivation (Harter, 1982; Skaalvik, 1997b; Skaalvik & Rankin, 1996b), achievement (Marsh & Yeung, 1997a; Shavelson & Bolus,

1982; Skaalvik & Hagtvet, 1990), and teachers' ratings of engagement and persistence in classroom activities (Skaalvik & Rankin, 1996b; Skinner, Wellborn, & Connell, 1990). Self-efficacy beliefs have related significantly to choice of tasks (Bandura & Schunk, 1981; Pajares & Miller, 1995), career selection (Betz & Hackett, 1983), persistence and performance (Pajares & Miller, 1994; Schunk & Swartz, 1993), grade goals (Zimmerman, Bandura, & Martinez-Pons, 1992; Zimmerman & Bandura, 1994), strategy use (Pintrich & De Groot, 1990), task-value (Bong, 2001b), mastery goal orientation (Bong, 2001a; Skaalvik, 1997b), and intrinsic interest and self-satisfactions (Zimmerman & Kitsantas, 1999).

As can be seen from the above examples, self-concept and self-efficacy have been used to predict somewhat different outcomes in the past research (Bong & Clark, 1999). Even when achievement is the target of prediction, slightly different indexes are favored in each research tradition. Self-concept research typically uses course grades or standardized test scores. Self-efficacy research commonly includes performance indicators on specific tasks. However, choice of these outcomes obviously depends on the measurement specificity of the construct itself and does not represent an inherent difference between the two constructs. Because self-concept is most often assessed at the school subject level and beyond, course grades or GPAs are the preferred achievement indexes. Likewise, self-efficacy toward particular tasks is most logically linked to performance on those specific tasks.

Bong and Clark (1999) argued that self-concept might predict affective reactions such as anxiety, satisfaction, and self-esteem better than self-efficacy, whereas self-efficacy better predicts actual performance. We may also speculate that self-concept predicts future learning better than self-efficacy whereas self-efficacy predicts achievement in test-like situations better than self-concept. However, these are mere speculations and few studies analyze the relative predictive value of self-concept and self-efficacy for different outcomes. Moreover, whereas self-concept research is heavily based on correlational data self-efficacy researchers use both correlational and experimental designs (see Pajares, 1997, for an overview). Self-concept research strongly supports a reciprocal effects model of the relations between self-concept and achievement whereas self-efficacy research most often is designed to let self-efficacy predict achievement. Nevertheless, self-efficacy theory is based on the assumption of a reciprocal effects model. Such relative differences notwithstanding, recent investigations relate both constructs to a similar set of outcomes. A common underlying theme of self-concept and self-efficacy research is that the perceived self is the major determinant of intrinsic motivation, positive emotion, and performance.

SUMMARY AND DISCUSSION

Analyses of conceptual and operational definitions of self-concept and self-efficacy reveal many differences. Some of the differences are more deeply ingrained in the theoretical conceptualizations, whereas others are more artifacts of standard assessment and analytic strategies associated with each research tradition. Self-concepts are conceptualized as aggregated judgments of past experiences and are typically assessed at domain-specific levels. When making these judgments, individuals do not necessarily think in terms of particular performance outcomes. Instead, self-concept in a given domain is conceptualized as aggregated perceptions of reflected appraisals in the domain, perception of relative standings in comparison with others in the given domain, and perception of one's performance level in the domain compared to that of other domains. Thus, self-concept beliefs reflect one's general evaluation of ability in particular domains, but have also been conceptualized as reflecting emotions that are directed toward the domain and self. These beliefs are general impressions of self that are resistant to change.

Beliefs of self-efficacy are also constructed largely on the basis of one's prior mastery experiences. In theory, the critical difference of efficacy judgments from self-concept judgments is that, in estimating efficacy, individuals judge their expectations of succeeding at some impending tasks using information from past experiences with similar types of tasks, rather than dwelling on general feelings of their abilities in the area in question. The focus on one's capability to carry out the present or immediate future tasks is aided by the specific information on the eventual target performance made available at the time of making these judgments. The desired outcomes and specific features associated with them function as standards against which to gauge the likelihood of success. Though these judgments may be as potent as feelings of self-concept in generating positive or negative emotions, the resultant affective responses are treated as correlates and not part of self-efficacy beliefs. Efficacy beliefs are more amenable to change than self-concept beliefs upon availability of new information.

Both self-concept and self-efficacy represent important dimensions of self-perception or perceived competence. Little research has been conducted across the two traditions that may explain why we have not seen many reports that emphasize the similarities between the constructs. In our analysis we have examined several similarities; both constructs emphasize the centrality of perceived competence, both constructs are multidimensional, and both constructs predict motivation, emotion, and performance. Moreover, a careful analysis of the literature reveals that there exist different orientations even within each research tradition and that the nature of the differences between the two constructs is often that of the degree. To some extent, the differences are a function of both fundamental differences and disparate research practices. For instance, although self-efficacy items are normally more future-oriented than self-concept items, this may not be an inherent difference. Self-concept may include both feelings of doing well or poorly in the domain as well as beliefs that one will do well or poorly in the future. It is also generally true that self-concept items entail rather global evaluations of one's own abilities even within a specific target domain and self-efficacy assessment normally requires making competence judgments toward particular tasks. However, self-efficacy items sometimes tap more general estimation of confidence, especially when there is not enough prior experience upon which to build expectations.

After careful examination of the constructs in question, we conclude that there is a need for systematic empirical analysis of the similarities and differences between self-concept and self-efficacy proposed in this chapter and elsewhere (Bong & Clark, 1999; Bong & Skaalvik, 2003). Empirical studies should explore whether any of the purported differences are inherent in construct definitions or merely artifacts of different research traditions. For example, Skaalvik and Rankin (1996a) suggested that the primary difference between the two constructs is that they measure self-evaluations at different levels of generality and that the differences in time orientations and format of questions, asking for either ability judgments or mastery expectations, are less important. On the other hand, in this chapter we have argued that an important distinction, possibly underlying differences in level of generality, is how success is defined in self-concept and self-efficacy judgments.

A particularly important issue for future research is therefore to examine the frames of reference used by students in their self-concept and self-efficacy appraisals. Self-concept researchers emphasize external and internal comparisons as important frames of reference for evaluating one's own abilities, whereas self-efficacy researchers emphasize mastery experiences as the most important determinant of self-efficacy expectancies. This difference in perspective when reflecting on antecedents of self-concept and self-efficacy raises a number of problems for future research. We start by considering frames of reference in self-concept research. Within this tradition quite a number of studies to date have investigated the impact of external and internal comparisons for self-concept development. This research convincingly confirms that external comparison predicts a positive relation between achievement and self-concept in a given domain whereas internal comparison predicts that high achievement in one area negatively influences self-concept in the competing area. Still, more research is needed to explore the complexity of external and internal frames of reference. For instance, Skaalvik and Skaalvik (2002) analyze four possible frames of reference related to external comparisons: (a) school-average ability, (b) class average ability, (c) selected students in class, and (d) selected students outside of class. They also propose four different types of internal comparisons related to schoolwork: (a) comparison of achievements in different school subjects at a given time, (b) comparison of achievements in the same subject across time, (c) comparison of achievements with goals and aspirations, and (d) comparison of achievements in different school subjects with applied effort in those subjects. By analyzing the eight frames of reference in relation to five sources of information they illustrate the complexity of internal and external comparisons that students may make.

Hence, investigations are needed that unveil psychological processes involved when internal and external comparisons are made. How are achievements in different activities, for instance two school subjects, compared to each other? What happens when two verbal or two math domains are involved? Does high achievement in one area (e.g., algebra) still hurt self-concept in the other area (e.g., geometry)? Or does it have additive effects such that individuals' overall "math" or "quantitative" self-concepts increase? Under what circumstances do the effects of external and internal comparisons most vividly play out? Do different students use different frames of reference in their internal and external comparisons? How does the learning environment affect frames of reference used by the students in their self-evaluations?

Turning to self-efficacy, researchers within this tradition emphasize mastery experiences as the most important determinant of self-efficacy expectancies. In practice, however, few experiences can be dichotomized clearly into mastery versus non-mastery categories solely on the basis of absolute standards of success. Judgments on the degree of mastery often have to be made against some relativistic criteria. Thus, mastery experiences, the major information source for efficacy formation, involve subjective judgments of success and failure made against some criterion or frames of reference. Different tasks or activities may evoke different criteria for success and hence render frames of reference effects more or less salient. Consider the following two tasks: Lighting a fire in the stove and writing an English essay. The criterion for success for the former is quite self-evident. There is no compelling reason to compare one's performance to those of others or to seek information on one's performance in other tasks. Simply making it burn suffices. Success on the latter activity is more difficult to judge and the feeling of mastery may depend on the grade received on the essay, comments made by the teacher, or even comparison of one's own grades with those of other students.

More research examining frames of reference in both self-concept and self-efficacy judgments seems important from a practical as well as a theoretical point of view. For instance, studies clearly show that placement of academically disadvantaged or academically gifted students into special classes or regular classrooms has bearing on the students' academic self-concepts. A review of research by Marsh and Craven (2000) demonstrates that ability grouping, as in special classes for gifted or academically disadvantaged students, has consequences for students' self-concept, partly because students compare and contrast their performance with that of other students (social comparison), and partly because students may assimilate their self-perceptions into the context in which they are placed (either basking in glory or suffering from labelling). Marsh and Craven (2000) suggest that the contrast effect predominates over the assimilation effect. More research is needed and future research should examine effects of ability grouping for both self-concept and self-efficacy.

To increase understanding of frames of reference, both for self-concept and self-efficacy development, we need research using a variety of approaches to measurement. In particular, more research is needed using introspection and retrospection in different learning contexts. These data would capture external and internal comparison processes that are conscious and below the level of awareness in students, as well as which frames of reference that different students hold salient. Students may participate in unstructured or semi-structured interviews, for example, in which they describe how they think their schoolwork is going, how well they think they have been doing in particular areas, and how certain they are that they can conduct particular tasks, followed by questions about how and why they know this. Such interviews could be conducted profitably in different activities and school subjects as well as in different achievement contexts outside of school.

We have noted that there has been a distinct difference in the types of outcomes linked to self-concept and self-efficacy beliefs. In addition to whether this discrepancy represents an innate construct difference, we also need to address the question why positive self-concepts or strong senses of efficacy sometimes do not lead individuals to making the most logical decisions—selecting challenging tasks, investing effort, and persisting in the face of temporary obstacles. Too often, highly competent students avoid important academic tasks, slacken their effort prematurely, fail to persevere and give up altogether when presented with what appear to be small and innocuous stumbling blocks. Findings from the expectancy-value and achievement goal research may have much to offer in answering some of these questions.

Self-concept and self-efficacy may be used for different practical purposes. Because self-efficacy is typically assessed by presenting specific problems to respondents and asking them to judge how certain they are that they can successfully perform similar tasks, self-efficacy may best predict achievement related to particular tasks, for instance a mathematics test. In comparison, self-concept reflects more general ability perceptions related to specified domains and may therefore best predict attitudes, emotions, learning strategies, and choices of activities. However, due to limited research involving both self-concept and self-efficacy in the same projects these reflections are merely speculations which call for empirical research involving both constructs. Because efficacy beliefs seem to be more amenable to change than self-concept beliefs a tempting conclusion could be to advise teachers to concentrate on strengthening student's self-efficacy. Again, however, we know too little about the effect of raising self-efficacy on self-concept. An obvious conclusion however, is that both constructs are affected by student's subjective feeling of mastery. Therefore, arranging the learning situation in order for each student to work with tasks that give him or her optimal challenge and in order to minimize social comparisons seems to be the most important challenge for educators.

From a practical standpoint, conclusions such as this give rise to debate over best grouping practices in schools—whether they be mainstreaming individual students or developing selective schools. The debate cannot be resolved as yet, however, because firm conclusions remain unavailable about the merits of practices such as mainstreaming versus selective schools. There is a need for studies exploring the impact of instructional strategies within different contexts on the frames of reference that students use and how these frames influence aspects of self-concept and self efficacy.

ACKNOWLEDGMENT

We would like to thank Herb Marsh for his suggestion to prepare this chapter and for helpful comments on an earlier version of the chapter.

REFERENCES

Ames, R. (1983). Help-seeking and achievement orientation: Perspectives from attribution theory. In B. DePaulo, A. Nadler, & J. Fisher (Eds.), *New directions in helping* (pp.165–188). New York: Academic Press.

Bandura, A. (1977). *Social learning theory.* Englewood Cliffs, NJ: Prentice-Hall.

Bandura, A. (1981). Self-referent thought: A developmental analysis of self-efficacy. In J. H. Flavell & L. Ross (Eds.), *Social cognitive development: Frontiers and possible futures* (pp. 200–239). New York: Cambridge University Press.

Bandura, A. (1986). *Social foundations of thought and action: A social cognitive theory.* Englewood Cliffs, NJ: Prentice-Hall.

Bandura, A. (1997). *Self-efficacy: The exercise of control.* New York: Freeman.

Bandura, A., & Schunk, D. H. (1981). Cultivating competence, self-efficacy, and intrinsic interest through proximal self-motivation. *Journal of Personality and Social Psychology, 41,* 586–598.

Betz, N. E., & Hackett, G. (1983). The relationship of mathematics self-efficacy expectations to the selection of science-based college majors. *Journal of Vocational Behavior, 23,* 329–345.

Bong, M. (1997). Generality of academic self-efficacy judgments: Evidence of hierarchical relations. *Journal of Educational Psychology, 89,* 696–709.

Bong, M. (1998). Tests of the internal/external frames of reference model with subject-specific academic self-efficacy and frame-specific academic self-concepts. *Journal of Educational Psychology, 90,* 102–110.

Bong, M. (1999). Personal factors affecting the generality of academic self-efficacy judgments: Gender, ethnicity, and relative expertise. *Journal of Experimental Education, 67,* 315–331.

Bong, M. (2001a). Between- and within-domain relations of academic motivation among middle and high school students: self-efficacy, task-value, and achievement goals. *Journal of Educational Psychology, 93,* 23–34.

Bong, M. (2001b). Role of self-efficacy and task-value in predicting college students' course performance and future enrollment intentions. *Contemporary Educational Psychology, 26,* 553–570.

Bong, M. (2002). Predictive utility of subject-, task-, and problem-specific self-efficacy judgments for immediate and delayed academic performances. *Journal of Experimental Education, 70,* 133–162.

Bong, M., & Clark, R. E. (1999). Comparison between self-concept and self-efficacy in academic motivation research. *Educational Psychologist, 34,* 139–154.

Bong, M., & Hocevar, D. (2002). Measuring self-efficacy: Multitrait-multimethod comparison of scaling procedures. *Applied Measurement in Education, 15,* 143–171.

Bong, M., & Skaalvik, E. M. (2003). Academic self-concept and self-efficacy: How different are they really? *Educational Psychology Review, 15,* 1–40.

Byrne, B. M. (1996). *Measuring self-concept across the life span: Issues and instrumentation.* Washington, DC: American Psychological Association.

Byrne, B. M., & Worth Gavin, D. A. (1996). The Shavelson model revisited: Testing for structure of academic self-concept across pre-, early, and late adolescents. *Journal of Educational Psychology, 88,* 215–228.

Craven, R. G., Marsh, H. W., & Debus, R. L. (1991). Effects of internally focused feedback and attributional feedback on enhancement of academic self-concept. *Journal of Educational Psychology, 83,* 17–27.

Festinger, L. (1954). A theory of social comparison processes. *Human Relations, 7,* 117–140.

Harter, S. (1982). The perceived competence scale for children. *Child Development, 53,* 87–97.

Harter, S. (1998). The development of self-representations. In W. Damon (Series Ed.) & N. Eisenberg (Vol. Ed.), *Handbook of child psychology: Vol. 3. Social, emotional, and personality development* (5th ed., pp. 553–617). New York: Wiley.

Joo, Y. J., Bong, M., & Choi, H. J. (2000). Self-efficacy for self-regulated learning, academic self-efficacy, and Internet self-efficacy in Web-based instruction. *Educational Technology Research and Development, 48*(2), 5–18.

Lent, R. W., Brown, S. D., & Larkin, K. C. (1986). Self-efficacy in the prediction of academic performance and perceived career options. *Journal of Counseling Psychology, 33,* 265–269.

Markus, H., & Nurius, P. (1986). Possible selves. *American Psychologist, 41,* 954–969.

Marsh, H. W. (1986). Verbal and math self-concepts: An internal/external frame of reference model. *American Educational Research Journal, 23,* 129–149.

Marsh, H. W. (1987). The big-fish-little-pond effect on academic self-concept. *Journal of Educational Psychology, 79,* 280–295.

Marsh, H. W. (1990). The structure of academic self-concept: The Marsh/Shavelson model. *Journal of Educational Psychology, 82,* 623–636.

Marsh, H. W. (1993). Academic self-concept: Theory, measurement, and research. In J. Suls (Ed.), *Psychological perspectives on the self* (Vol. 4, pp. 59–98). Hillsdale, NJ: Erlbaum.

Marsh, H. W. (1999a). *Academic Self Description Questionnaire–I: ASDQ I.* Macarthur, Australia: University of Western Sydney, Self-concept Enhancement and Learning Facilitation Research Centre.

Marsh, H. W. (1999b). *Self Description Questionnaire–II: SDQ II.* Macarthur, Australia: University of Western Sydney, Self-concept Enhancement and Learning Facilitation Research Centre.

Marsh, H. W., Byrne, B. M., & Shavelson, R. J. (1988). A multifaceted academic self-concept: Its hierarchical structure and its relation to academic achievement. *Journal of Educational Psychology, 80,* 366–380.

Marsh, H. W., & Craven, R. G. (2000, October). *Swimming in the school: Expanding the scope of the Big Fish Little Pond Effect.* Paper presented at the 2000 Self Research Centre Conference, Sydney, Australia.

Marsh, H. W., Craven, R. G., & Debus, R. (1999). Separation of competency and affect components of multiple dimensions of academic self-concept: A developmental perspective. *Merrill-Palmer Quarterly, 45,* 567–601.

Marsh, H. W., Walker, R., & Debus, R. (1991). Subject-specific components of academic self-concept and self-efficacy. *Contemporary Educational Psychology, 16,* 331–345.

Marsh, H. W., & Yeung, A. S. (1997a). Causal effects of academic self-concept on academic achievement: Structural equation models of longitudinal data. *Journal of Educational Psychology, 89,* 41–54.

Marsh, H. W., & Yeung, A. S. (1997b). Coursework selection: Relations to academic self-concept and achievement. *American Educational Research Journal, 34,* 691–720.

Marsh, H. W., & Yeung, A. S. (1998). Top-down, bottom-up, and horizontal models: The direction of causality in multidimensional, hierarchical self-concept models. *Journal of Personality and Social Psychology, 75,* 509–527.

Pajares, F. (1996). Self-efficacy beliefs in academic settings. *Review of Educational Research, 66,* 543–578.

Pajares, F. (1997). Current directions in self-efficacy research. In M. Maehr & P. R. Pintrich (Eds.), *Advances in motivation and achievement,* (Vol. 10, pp. 1–49). Greenwich, CT: JAI Press.

Pajares, F., & Graham, L. (1999). Self-efficacy, motivation constructs, and mathematics performance of entering middle school students. *Contemporary Educational Psychology, 24,* 124–139.

Pajares, F., & Miller, M. D. (1994). Role of self-efficacy and self-concept beliefs in mathematical problem solving: A path analysis. *Journal of Educational Psychology, 86,* 193–203.

Pajares, F., & Miller, M. D. (1995). Mathematics self-efficacy and mathematics performances: The need for specificity of assessment. *Journal of Counseling Psychology, 42,* 190–198.

Pajares, F., Miller, M. D., & Johnson, M. J. (1999). Gender differences in writing self-beliefs of elementary school students. *Journal of Educational Psychology, 91,* 50–61.

Pintrich, P. R., & De Groot, E. V. (1990). Motivational and self-regulated learning components of classroom academic performance. *Journal of Educational Psychology, 82,* 33–40.

Rosenberg, M. (1968). Psychological selectivity in self-esteem formation. In C. Gordon & K. J. Gergen (Eds.), *The self in social interaction.* New York: Wiley.

Rosenberg, M. (1979). *Conceiving the self.* New York: Basic Books.

Scheirer, M. A., & Kraut, R. E. (1979). Increasing educational achievement via self concept change. *Review of Educational Research, 49,* 131–150.

Schunk, D. H., & Swartz, C. W. (1993). Goals and progress feedback: Effects on self-efficacy and writing achievement. *Contemporary Educational Psychology, 18,* 337–354.

Shavelson, R. J., & Bolus, R. (1982). Self-concept: The interplay of theory and methods. *Journal of Educational Psychology, 74,* 3–17.

Shavelson, R. J., Hubner, J. J., & Stanton, G. C. (1976). Self-concept: Validation of construct interpretations. *Review of Educational Research, 46,* 407–441.

Skaalvik, E. M. (1997a). Issues in research on self-concept. In M. Maehr & P. R. Pintrich (Eds.), *Advances in motivation and achievement,* (Vol. 10, pp. 51–97). Greenwich, CT: JAI Press.

Skaalvik, E. M. (1997b). Self-enhancing and self-defeating ego-orientation: Relations with task and avoidance orientation, achievement, self-perceptions, and anxiety. *Journal of Educational Psychology, 89,* 71–81.

Skaalvik, E. M., & Hagtvet, K. A. (1990). Academic achievement and self-concept: An analysis of causal predominance in a developmental perspective. *Journal of Personality and Social Psychology, 58,* 292–307.

Skaalvik, E. M., & Rankin, R. J. (1990). Math, verbal, and general academic self-concept: The internal/external frame of reference model and gender differences in self-concept structure. *Journal of Educational Psychology, 82,* 546–554.

Skaalvik, E. M., & Rankin, R. J. (1995). A test of the Internal/External Frame of Reference Model at different levels of math and verbal self-perception. *American Educational Research Journal, 32,* 161–184.

Skaalvik, E. M., & Rankin, R. J. (1996a, April). *Self-concept and self-efficacy: Conceptual analysis.* Paper presented at the annual meeting of the American Educational Research Association, New York.

Skaalvik, E. M., & Rankin, R. J. (1996b, August). *Studies of academic self-concept using a Norwegian modification of the SDQ.* Paper presented at the XXVI International Congress of Psychology, Montreal, Canada.

Skaalvik, E. M. & Skaalvik, S. (2002). Internal and external frames of reference for academic self-concept. *Educational Psychologist, 37,* 233–244.

Skaalvik, E. M., & Valås, H. (1999, April). *Achievement and self-concept in mathematics and verbal arts: A study of relations.* Paper presented at the annual meeting of the American Educational Research Association, Montreal, Canada.

Skinner, E. A., Wellborn, J., & Connell, J. (1990). What it takes to do well in school and whether I've got it: A process model of perceived control and children's engagement and achievement in school. *Journal of Educational Psychology, 82,* 22–32.

Tanzer, N. K. (1996, August). *Interest and competence as components of academic self-concepts for the Self Description Questionnaire I.* Paper presented at the XXVI International Congress of Psychology, Montreal, Canada.

Wigfield, A., Eccles, J. S., Yoon, K. S., Harold, R. D., Arbreton, A. J. A., Freedman-Doan, C., & Blumenfeld, P. C. (1997). Change in children's competence beliefs and subjective task values across the elementary school years: A 3-year study. *Journal of Educational Psychology, 89,* 451–469.

Yeung, A. S., Chui, H. S., Lau, I. C., McInerney, D. M., Russell-Bowie, D., & Suliman, R. (2000). Where is the hierarchy of academic self-concept? *Journal of Educational Psychology, 92,* 556–567.

Zimmerman, B. J., & Bandura, A. (1994). Impact of self-regulatory influences on writing course attainment. *American Educational Research Journal, 31,* 845–862.

Zimmerman, B. J., Bandura, A., & Martinez-Pons, M. (1992). Self-motivation for academic attainment: The role of self-efficacy beliefs and personal goal setting. *American Educational Research Journal, 29,* 663–676.

Zimmerman, B. J., & Kitsantas, A. (1999). Acquiring writing revision skill: Shifting from process to outcome self-regulatory goals. *Journal of Educational Psychology, 91,* 241–250.

CHAPTER 5

CRACKING THE SELF-CONCEPT ENHANCEMENT CONUNDRUM

A Call and Blueprint for the Next Generation of Self-concept Enhancement Research

Rhonda G. Craven, Herbert W. Marsh, and Paul Burnett

I cannot think of a single psychological problem—from anxiety to depression, to under-achievement at school or at work, to fear of intimacy, happiness or success, to alcohol or drug abuse, to spouse battering or child molestation, to co-dependency and sexual disorders, to passivity and chronic aimlessness, to suicide and crimes of violence—that is not traceable, at least in part, to the problem of deficient self-esteem.

—Branden (1994, p. xv).

These words by Nathaniel Branden—an eminent philosopher and psychologist—attest to the significance of the self-concept/self-esteem construct and outcomes that are mediated by it. Due to the benefits of a positive self-concept, enhancing self-concept across the life span is recognized internationally as a highly desirable goal in diverse settings ranging from the preschool classroom to the retirement village. The broad appeal of enhancing self-concept is also readily evidenced by sales figures of self-help and self-

International Advances in Self Research, pages 91–126
Copyright © 2003 by Information Age Publishing
All rights of reproduction in any form reserved.

concept enhancement books and participation rates in self-concept improvement courses and conventions around the world. The development of a positive self-concept is prized as a desirable outcome in and of itself as well as a mediator of an array of valued outcomes including enhanced educational and career aspirations, increased adoption of adaptive striving behaviors, and improved achievement/performance in educational and work settings. This wide-ranging appeal of the self-concept construct has resulted in numerous self-concept interventions developed by researchers from a multiplicity of disciplines.

Despite this importance placed on the value of enhancing self-concept and the presumed impact of self-concept enhancement on other desirable outcomes, a plethora of self-concept interventions have failed to enhance self-concept. In this chapter we encourage researchers to crack this self-concept enhancement conundrum. First, we provide a rationale for enhancing self-concept in order to demonstrate that enhancing self-concept is a highly desirable goal and a vital key to maximizing human potential and happiness. To underpin this rationale we provide an overview of cutting-edge research evidence from the education sector that demonstrates self-concept's causal impact on subsequent academic achievement and other desirable educational outcomes. Second, we present a brief historical overview of self-concept theory and intervention research to illustrate that historically intervention research has been plagued by weak research methodology that continues to dominate enhancement research in this new millennium. Third, we describe advances in self-concept theory, measurement, and research that can be capitalized on to expedite progress in unraveling the self-concept enhancement conundrum. Fourth, we summarize results from important meta-analyses that critically analyze the effects of a range of self-concept interventions, and outline promising interventions, research designs, and methods. Finally, based on a synthesis of information presented in this chapter, we present guidelines to call on and assist researchers to implement the next generation of self-concept enhancement research. It is hoped that the results and guidelines for future research presented in the chapter will help provide an impetus and sound framework for researchers to indeed crack the self-concept enhancement conundrum.

WHY ENHANCE SELF-CONCEPT?: A RATIONALE

The answer to the question "Why enhance self-concept?" is important in order to elucidate the pervasive significance with which the self-concept construct is accorded. In the following section we put forth a rationale to contribute to stimulating ongoing interest in this field of research.

The Pervasive Significance of the Self-Concept Construct

The universal importance of self-concept and multidisciplinary appeal of self-concept as one of the most important constructs in the social sciences is highlighted by the regularity/consistency with which self-concept enhancement is identified as a major focus of concern in diverse settings, including education, child development, mental and physical health, social services, industry, and sport/exercise. This pervasive influence of self-concept has resulted in educational policy statements listing the development of a positive self-concept as one of the key goals of education. For example, in Australia, The Common and Agreed National Goals of Schooling (Australian Education Council, 1989) was the first agreement by the Australian Commonwealth and States and Territories on the aims of Australian education at a national level. The second of the 10 goals identified the need "to enable all students to achieve high standards of learning and to develop self-confidence, optimism, high self-esteem, respect for others, and achievement of personal excellence" (Australian Education Council, 1989). This goal has since been included in the recent Revised Common and Agreed Goals of Schooling (Ministerial Council on Education, Employment, Training and Youth Affairs, 1998) and reflected in State/Territory syllabus documents (e.g., Board of Studies New South Wales, 1998). The pervasive significance of enhancing self-concept as mirrored in education policies is underpinned by the widely held beliefs that enhancing self-concept is a desirable educational goal in itself and is also likely to enhance academic achievement. In the next section we discuss recent research that puts the latter belief to the test by scrutinizing the relation between self-concept and academic achievement.

To Maximize Academic Achievement

Debate has raged as to whether self-concept has a causal impact on academic achievement (the self-concept enhancement model) or whether academic achievement causes self-concept (the skill development model). Support for the self-enhancement model would provide a strong justification for self-concept enhancement interventions. In contrast, support for the skill development model implies that the best way to enhance academic self-concept is to develop stronger academic skills. In her initial classic review of research in this area, Byrne (1984) could only identify three studies (Byrne's doctoral thesis subsequently published in 1986; Shavelson & Bolus, 1982; Newman, 1984) testing the direction of causality of self-concept and achievement with paradoxical results. Potential limitations of these three studies, were discussed by Marsh and Craven (1997, pp. 152–153) who concluded that the findings varied depending on how academic achievement was inferred and suggested that "the effect of prior academic self-concept on subsequent achievement is more likely if achievement is inferred from school grades that may be more responsive to effort and motivational influences than from standardized test scores" (p. 153).

Marsh and Craven (1997) also provided an overview of critical design features in this area of research. Marsh (1990a) in a study that incorporated these key features, found strong support for the effect of prior self-concept on subsequent school grades. This study is important because it was methodologically stronger than previous research and along with the Shavelson and Bolus (1982) study, provided defensible evidence for the effect of prior academic self-concept on subsequent academic achievement. In scrutinizing this study, Marsh and Craven (1997) noted that: "In neither of the intervals did school grades from a prior data wave have a statistically significant direct effect on subsequent academic self-concept. Thus, the effects of academic self-concept are "causally predominant" over those of school grades and these results provide strong support for the self-concept enhancement model of the self-concept/achievement relation. Hence, research suggests that changes in self-concept may cause changes in academic achievement.

It is also likely that the relationship between self-concept and academic achievement is reciprocal (the reciprocal effects model) whereby changes in academic achievement effect academic self-concept and vice versa. For example, Marsh and Yeung (1997a) found that prior achievement in specific subject areas affects subsequent academic related facets of self-concept and prior self-concept affects subsequent achievement after controlling for the effects of prior achievement. These results are critical as they suggest prior self-concept has significant effects on subsequent achievement beyond the effects of prior achievement alone. Marsh, Byrne, and Yeung, (1999; see also Byrne, 1996a; Marsh & Craven, 1997) updated previous reviews of this research area and emphasized that based on existing research using strong methodology (nine causal modeling studies) there was clear support for a reciprocal effects model in which the largest paths were from prior academic self-concept to school grades. These results imply that interventions that successfully produce changes in the appropriate area of self-concept and achievement are more likely to have long-lasting effects than studies that focus exclusively on academic self-concept or academic achievement alone. Marsh and Craven (1997) emphasized that short-term gains in achievement are also unlikely to be maintained unless there are corresponding gains in academic self-concept and concluded that "enhancing a child's academic self-concept is not only a desirable goal but is likely to result in improved academic achievement as well" (p. 155).

Relations between academic self-concept and achievement have not been examined fully from a developmental perspective. Skaalvik and Hagtvet (1990) found support for a reciprocal effects model for older students (sixth and seven grades) but found support for a skill-development model for younger students (third and fourth grades; see also Muijs [1997] for similar results). Skaalvik (1997) also reported support for a skill-development model during elementary school years and reciprocal influences during the high school years. However, Skaalvik and Valas (1999) did not provide support for this developmental perspective. Hence, previous research has suggested stronger support for a skill-development model during the early elementary school years, whereas support for a reciprocal effects model became stronger in later school years.

In order to test the developmental pattern in the causal ordering of these constructs, Marsh and colleagues (1999) recommended the use of multicohort-multioccasion designs (e.g., Marsh, Craven, & Debus, 1998) that combine the advantages of cross-sectional and longitudinal research within the same study. Marsh (2002) reported on an in press study (Guay, Marsh, & Boivin, in press) which, based on a multicohort-multioccasion design evaluated developmental hypotheses about the causal ordering of academic self-concept and academic achievement among elementary school children. Participants (202 girls, 183 boys) were students in grades 2, 3, and 4 from 10 elementary schools. Results from correlational and CFA analyses showed that, as children grow older, their academic self-concept responses became more reliable, more stable, and more strongly correlated with academic achievement. Furthermore, support for these age-related differences was evident for both multicohort (cross-sectional) and multioccasion (longitudinal) comparisons. However, results from stronger statistical tests (invariance analyses) indicated that the developmental effects observed within and between cohorts were not statistically significant. However, the small sample size involved in the three cohorts (Ns of 125, 147, and 113) may explain the absence of significant effects. Hence, although previous research suggested evidence in favor of the skill development model for young children and support for the self-enhancement model or the reciprocal effects model for older children, there was little support for this developmental pattern for the children considered in the present investigation. This recent study is important, because the results of this methodologically strong study for young children (i.e., Grade 2), provide strong support for a reciprocal effects model for all three age cohorts and support for the self-enhancement model was stronger than support for a skill development model for all three waves. The results of this study also support the contention by Marsh et al. (1999) that support for the reciprocal effects model has good generalizability. Marsh (2002) concluded that "the fact that the reciprocal effect model was supported for very young children (i.e., Grade 2) provided support for early interventions based on academic self-concept and achievement and not only on achievement, as suggested by the results of a number of previous studies ... the present results suggest that with young children, teachers should strive to improve simultaneously both academic self-concept and achievement in order to produce positive changes in both these constructs" (p. 3). Hence advances in recent research suggest that a component of the answer to the question "Why enhance self-concept?" is that enhancing self-concept will enhance achievement. Partly because of this role of self-concept in impacting on achievement, another component of the rationale for enhancing self-concept is the presumed belief that enhancing self-concept is fundamental to maximizing human potential, the research basis of which we discuss in the following section.

To Maximize Human Potential

Self-concept is valued as having a powerful mediating influence on human behavior. A positive self-concept is widely considered fundamental for psychological health, personal achievement, and positive relationships. Self-concept is thought to make such a difference, that people who think positively about themselves are healthier, happier, and more productive. Hence, enhancing self-concept is considered necessary to maximizing human potential, from early development and school achievement, to physical/mental health and well-being, to gainful employment and other contributions to society. For over two decades, Marsh has undertaken a research program examining what makes a difference during adolescence. This research is based in part on the extensive educational "census-like" databases of nationally representative samples of thousands of high schools and a diversity of educational and psychological variables collected on multiple occasions during high school and after graduation. This research program has shown that positive and negative effects of some critical life events on subsequent outcomes are mediated through their significant effects on self-concept. Marsh and colleagues have demonstrated that changes in critical outcomes variables (e.g., coursework selection (Marsh & Yeung, 1997b) educational and occupational aspirations (Marsh, 1991), bullying (Marsh, Parada, Yeung, & Healey, 2001), relations with parents (Marsh & Craven, 1991), locus of control (Marsh & Craven, 1997) were related to the effects of academic self-concept. For example, Marsh and Yeung (1997b) demonstrated that coursework selection and persistence are systematically related to academic self-concept, but are nearly uncorrelated (or even negatively related) to nonacademic (social and physical) self-concept responses.

The attainment of a positive academic self-concept has also been shown to mediate positive influences on multiple desirable educational outcomes including: academic behaviors such as persistence on academic tasks, academic choices, and educational aspirations (Byrne, 1996a, 1996b; Marsh, 1990a, 1992a; Marsh, Byrne, & Shavelson, 1988; Marsh & Yeung, 1997a, 1997b). For example, Skaalvik and Rankin (1995) found that math and verbal self-concepts favorably influenced associated measures of intrinsic motivation, effort, and anxiety. Research also suggests that prior academic self-concept influences subsequent course selection and degree of difficulty. Authors of early reviews of research in this area (Meece, Parsons, Kaczala, Goff, & Futterman, 1982; Eccles et al., 1983) that there was considerable theoretical and empirical support for a link between academic self-concept and subject course selection, which has been supported by more recent research. For example, Meece, Wigfield, and Eccles (1990) related school grades and mathematics self concept in one year with intentions to take further coursework in mathematics and subsequent school grades the following year. In a further path analysis of the data Marsh and Yeung (1997b, p. 696) found that coursework selections were significantly impacted on by prior mathematics self-concept and the effect of prior grades was nonsignificant. Similarly, Ethington (1991) presented path analyses relating mathematics school grades, mathematics self-concept and intentions to study mathematics and found that even though mathematics self-concept was based on a single item, it was more highly correlated with intentions to study mathematics than was prior achievement. In a further path analysis of this data, Marsh and Yeung (1997b, p. 697) found that the effects of self-concept on intentions were significant and larger than the effects of prior achievement on intentions. They also compared and contrasted the impact of nine facets of academic self-concept and academic achievement (measured by school grades) on subsequent coursework selection. They found that specific self-concept facets significantly influenced wanting to do a course in the subject area the following year, and actually enrolling in the course. These findings led Marsh and Yeung (1997b, p. 709) to conclude that "self-concepts in specific school subjects are significantly related to subsequent coursework selection—to choices of what subjects students want to study and the choices of what they actually do pursue. These results provide new and additional support to academic self-concept theories predicting that academic self-concept contributes to the prediction of important outcome variables beyond what can be explained by academic achievement." Hence, recent studies have demonstrated that academic self-concept influences other important desirable educational and academic outcomes that are fundamental to maximizing human potential. Research findings therefore offer support for the notion that it is important to enhance self-concept in order to maximize human potential, and attest to the pervasive significance of the self-concept con-struct. In fact, so significant is the construct that enhancing self-concept is also thought to be an important strategy for addressing critical social issues of our time.

To Address Societal Problems

As dramatically illustrated by Branden in the opening of this chapter, enhancing self-concept is highly relevant to important individual and soci-etal problems that stem from low self-concept. Whereas positive self-con-cepts enhance human potential, the effects of low self-concept stifle human potential. As emphasized by Branden (1994, p. xv), low self-con-cept can lead to personal and social ineffectiveness such as disadvantage, academic failure, depression, suicide, violence, criminality and many other social problems. As such, enhancing self-concept is potentially a potent tool for addressing major social problems of our time.

For example, there is growing recognition that bullying, violence, aggression, and victimization in schools are pervasive problems with long-term psychological consequences for bullies, victims, other students, and communities—with links to diminished school performance, poor mental health, and future criminality. So significant is this problem that the Austra-lian National Crime Prevention Strategy contended that bullying interven-tions at the early stages of schooling were a necessary and crucial aspect of Australia's efforts to reduce crime (National Crime Prevention, 1999). Hence enhancing self-concept may help to address dysfunctional patterns of social interaction such as bullying, victimization, and school violence (Marsh, Parada, Yeung, & Healey, 2001) by "breaking the cycle." The implementation of interventions in the early years of school is recognized in Australia as a means to prevent the escalation of violence in schools and reduce the economic and social costs emanating from the pervasive inci-dence of school bullying. Enhancing self-concept of bullies in adaptive ways as opposed to maladaptive self-enhancement strategies whereby bul-lies feel good about themselves by bullying less powerful others, could prove to be a vital key in the success of these interventions. Thus, enhanc-ing self-concept has the potential to address critical social issues. Impor-tantly, enhancing self-concept may also help to address critical social justice issues impacting on the most vulnerable groups in society, as discussed in the next section.

To Address Social Inequities

Enhancing self-concept is important for addressing social inequities experienced by disadvantaged groups. For example, national reports, and all Australian governments have acknowledged that Aboriginal people are significantly educationally disadvantaged (Hughes, 1988; Commonwealth of Australia, 1994, 1995, 1997; Johnston, 1991; Kemp, 1999), which has implications for further education, employment and life opportunities. The New South Wales Department of Aboriginal Affairs has emphasized that: "The key reason for Aboriginal children being disadvantaged educationally, is that the current education system fails to acknowledge the vital importance of maximizing Aboriginal children's self-concept as the critical link between schooling and successful outcomes" (Burney, 2001). Similarly, the National Board of Employment, Education and Training (NBEET, 1995, p. xi) concluded that Aboriginal students need to "develop a strong sense of personal identity and self-esteem" and the Australian Royal Commission into Aboriginal Deaths in Custody (Johnston, 1991) identified low self-esteem as a critical variable contributing to Aboriginal disadvantage and deaths. Hence, in Australia enhancing self-esteem has been acknowledged as a vital key to improving educational outcomes for Aboriginal Australians.

Enhancing self-concept also has important implications for social policy. For example, the movement toward the inclusion of academically disadvantaged students in regular classrooms is a contentious issue that has generated many debates. Illustrating this current dilemma is the fact that Labeling theory suggests that placing academically disadvantaged students in special classes with other low-achieving students will lead to lower self-concepts and create a long lasting stigmatization (Tracey, Marsh, & Craven, 2003). On the basis of this theoretical argument and an economic rationalist perspective, there is widespread integration of academically disadvantaged students into regular classrooms ("mainstreaming"). In contrast, theoretical predictions based on self-concept theory (see Tracey, Marsh, & Craven, 2003) imply that academically disadvantaged students who remain in special classes will have higher self-concepts compared to similarly disadvantaged students in regular (integrated) classroom settings. Providing apparent advantages to disadvantaged individuals through programs such as affirmative action and reverse discrimination is well-intentioned, but may not result in the desired outcomes unless there is an associated shift in the individual's self-concepts and this has important implications for social programs for the disadvantaged. This research (Tracey, Marsh & Craven, 2003) suggests that identifying ideal educational placement settings for special education groups (e.g. learning disabled, students with mild intellectual disabilities) that result in enhancing students' human potential (self-concept, achievement, and life effectiveness) is vital. The broader implications of this research also extend to other important social-policy issues related to moving individuals of all ages to nursing homes, specialized dementia units, and out of special care facilities (e.g., institutions for the mentally impaired, see Dixon, Marsh, & Craven, 2002), into the broader community and how best to enhance self-concept and thereby the individual human potential of those at risk groups in these contexts. Hence, self-concept enhancement research has important social policy implications that can make a real difference to enhancing the potential of the most vulnerable individuals, and can assist in addressing problems experienced by understudied groups who pose special research problems and thereby reduce significant economic and social costs and important social justice issues associated with these groups.

PITFALLS AND ADVANCES IN SELF-CONCEPT THEORY, MEASUREMENT, AND RESEARCH

Historical Pitfalls

Despite the value of enhancing self-concept outlined above, a plethora of self-concept interventions have failed to enhance self-concept. This failure can be directly attributed to methodological flaws in previous research such as: the use of weak interventions; the use of potentially powerful interventions with small sample sizes or weak designs so that effects are unlikely to be statistically significant; and a poor fit between the intended goals of the intervention and the specific dimensions of self-concept used to evaluate the interventions (see Hattie, 1992; Hattie & Marsh, 1996; Marsh & Craven, 1997; Marsh & Richards, 1988). Hattie (1992, p. 254) terms the period from the 1970s to early 1980s as a "dust bowl of empirical relationships" and has noted that most research during this period was of poor quality.

Self-concept is a hypothetical construct and so its usefulness must be established by investigations of construct validity. Within-construct studies attempt to define the structure of self-concept. Between-construct studies attempt to establish a logical, theoretically consistent pattern of relations between measures of self-concept and other constructs (also see Messick, 1989; Shavelson, Hubner, & Stanton, 1976, for more general discussion). Identifying the structure or nature of self-concept is a logical prerequisite to relating self-concept to other variables, yet historically self-concept research has focused on between-construct research prior to addressing within-construct issues. This has resulted in inaccurate theory and paradoxical research findings, and consequently a proliferation of ineffective educational practice.

Historically, research has investigated a unidimensional or overall general self-concept rather than positing multiple different facets of self-concept (e.g. reading self-concept, mathematics self-concept, physical self-concept) even though earlier theoretical accounts recognized the multidimensionality of self-concept (e.g., James, 1890). "This agglomerate use of general self-concept is particularly dubious, and probably has led to many of the contradictory findings which abound in the self-concept research" (Marsh, 1990c, p. 31). For example, Coopersmith (1967, p. 6) based on an instrument that was unable to identify the factors it was supposed to measure concluded that "children make little distinction about their worthiness in different areas of experience or, if such distinctions are made, they are made within the context of the overall, general appraisal of worthiness that the children have already made." Similarly, over a decade later Marx and Winne (1978, p. 900) concluded that: "self concept seems more of a unitary concept than one broken into distinct sub-parts or facets." While some past studies identified multiple factors indicating that the multidimensionality of self-concept was apparent, the observed factor structures were not consistently replicable and did not provide clear support for the multiple dimensions that they were designed to measure, nor the theoretical basis on which they were based. Thus, early reviews of self-concept research prior to the 1980s (e.g., Burns, 1979; Shavelson, Hubner, & Stanton, 1976; Wells & Marwell, 1976; Wylie, 1974, 1979) noted the lack of theoretical basis in most studies, the poor quality of self-concept measurement instruments, methodological problems, and a general inconsistency in reported findings. Similar observations led Hattie (1992) to conclude that the predominant research design in self-concept studies was "throw it in and see what happens."

The vast majority of intervention research today is still characterized by methodological flaws that have prevailed historically in this area of research. As a result, there is no definitive answer as to the most appropriate techniques that can be utilized to enhance self-concept despite a vast literature on the topic. However, recent advances in self-concept theory, measurement and research offer promising new directions.

Advances in Theory

The Shavelson, Hubner, and Stanton Model

Shavelson, Hubner, and Stanton (1976) reviewed theoretical and empirical research, and developed a theoretical model of self-concept that has proved to be of paramount significance. Included in the model were the assumptions that self-concept is: organized or structured; multifaceted; hierarchically arranged; stable at the apex of the model, but as one descends the hierarchy, self-concept becomes increasingly situation specific and as a consequence less stable; facets are increasingly differentiated with age; both evaluative and descriptive; and is differentiable from other constructs. General-self appears at the apex and is divided into academic and nonacademic components that are divided into more specific components. Shavelson and colleagues (1976) also suggested a possible representation of the model with general academic self-concept broken into subject specific facets of self (e.g., mathematics and reading); nonacademic self-concept divided into social, emotional, and physical self-concepts that were further divided into more specific components (e.g., physical self-concept was divided into physical ability and physical appearance). The facets proposed were only considered a possible representation of the hierarchical model, as their emphasis was on the multidimensionality of the structure of self-concept rather than on the number of specific facets.

Perceptions were proposed to be formed through experience with and interpretations of environmental factors. Perceptions were also proposed to move from the subareas (e.g., academic self-concept in mathematics) to encompassing areas (e.g., academic self-concept), and finally to general self-concept (a bottom-up model). Recently, Marsh and Yeung (1998) suggested that the original Shavelson and colleagues (1976) model might also be consistent with a top-down model in which perceptions also moved both from general self-concept, to encompassing areas of specific subareas. In the relatively few proposed tests of this distinction there has been no clear evidence favoring either top-down or bottom-up models (e.g., Marsh & Yeung, 1997a). However, it is likely that the direction of flow is reciprocal (both top-down and bottom-up), but more research and stronger methodological approaches are needed to resolve this theoretical issue. From a self-concept intervention perspective it is logically desirable to target specific facets of self-concept lower in the hierarchy (a bottom-up model) rather than general self-concept alone (a top-down model). For example, if a child had a maladaptive low reading self-concept it would be logical to target reading self-concept specifically rather than general self-concept in the hope that somehow an increase in general self-concept would dissipate down the hierarchy to enhance reading self-concept. Unfortunately a predominant strategy in many schools today is to continue to focus on enhancing general self-concept—a strategy that emanates from earlier unidimensional theoretical perspectives of the structure of self-concept.

At the time Shavelson and colleagues (1976) were unable to measure the multiple facets of self-concept posited by their model due to the unavailability of a suitable instrument but the basic theoretical assumption whereby self-concept was posited as a multidimensional construct was fundamental to the development of a new generation of self-concept measurement instruments and revisions in self-concept theory.

Marsh/Shavelson Model and the Development of Multidimensional
Instruments

Based on the Shavelson model, Marsh developed the Self Description Questionnaire (SDQ) instruments (Marsh, 1990c, 1990d, 1992b). Reviews of self-concept instruments consistently refer to these instruments as "an excellent measure of the various first-order dimensions of self-concept as proposed by Shavelson and colleagues.... The estimates of reliability are consistently high, and tests are based on a multifaceted model of self-concept. The set of SDQs are the best set of measures available" (Hattie, 1992, pp. 82–83) (also see Boyle, 1994; Byrne, 1996b; Wylie; 1989). Numerous factor analyses have identified the facets of self-concept that the SDQ instruments measure (e.g., see Marsh, 1990c, 1992b for summaries). Results of factor analyses provide strong support for the multidimensionality of self-concept, the facets and the hierarchical structure of self-concept (although, the particular form of this higher order structure is more complicated than was previously suggested) proposed by the Shavelson model and construct validity for the SDQ instruments. "Implicit in this approach is the edict that theory building and instrument construction are inexorably intertwined, and that each will suffer if the two are separated" (Marsh, 1990c, p. 19).

Recent reviews (Byrne, 1996a, 1996b; Hattie, 1992; Marsh, Byrne, & Shavelson, 1988; Marsh & Craven, 1997) support the multifaceted structure of self-concept and espouse that self-concept cannot be adequately understood if its multidimensionality is ignored. The multidimensionality of self-concept posited in the Shavelson and colleagues model is now well established but subsequent research has indicated that the hierarchy is more complicated than originally posited, leading to revisions in the model (Marsh, Byrne, & Shavelson, 1988; Marsh & Shavelson, 1985; Vispoel, 1995). Marsh and Shavelson's (1985) findings generally supported the Shavelson and colleagues (1976) model. However, data in several studies (e.g., Marsh, 1986) demonstrated that while verbal and mathematics achievements are substantially correlated, near zero correlations are present in the research literature for verbal and mathematics self-concept. These findings led to the revision (Marsh, Byrne, & Shavelson, 1988; Marsh & Shavelson, 1985; Shavelson & Marsh, 1986) of the original Shavelson and colleagues (1976) model which posited that verbal and math self-concepts combine to form a single, higher order academic self-concept. The revised model postulates that self-concepts, in particular subject areas, form two separate second order academic factors—verbal/academic and math/academic self-concepts—rather than a single order factor. Hence, the development of better measurement instruments has resulted in the emergence of new theoretical understandings of the structure of self-concept that have important implications fundamental to strengthening self-concept intervention research.

META-ANALYSIS INVESTIGATIONS OF THE EFFECTS OF DIFFERENT TYPES OF INTERVENTIONS

Traditional literature reviews of self-concept enhancement research are difficult to undertake and are susceptible to selection bias because of the volume, diversity, and contradictory nature of the findings of self-concept intervention studies. Major scientific issues cannot be resolved by a single or small number of studies; rather advances in knowledge come from the integration of many studies undertaken via meta-analytic studies (Schmidt, 1992). In self-concept intervention research it is disappointing that only two meta-analyses have been undertaken (Hattie, 1992; Haney & Durlak, 1998) to specifically investigate aspects of self-concept intervention research, although other meta-analyses focusing on intervention research have examined the effects of self-concept in relation to specific types of intervention programs (e.g. outdoor education inventions). Taken together, these crucial meta-analyses offer vital insights into strengthening intervention research.

Hattie's Meta-Analysis

A meta-analysis to investigate whether cognitively oriented intervention programs had more of an effect on self-concept change than affectively oriented programs was conducted by Janet Hattie (1986) on pre-1983 studies and reported in John Hattie's (1992) seminal work on self-concept. Although 650 studies from Psychological Abstracts were located, only 89 contained sufficient data for meta-analysis. "That so many studies had to be rejected is a reflection of the quality of research conducted in the area of self-concept change" (Hattie, 1992, p. 227). From the 89 articles, 485 effect sizes were calculated with the average size being .37 (SD =.12). Hattie (1992, p. 227) concluded that 10 percent of those who experienced an intervention increased their self-concept compared with the control group. This conclusion was based on the differences between change scores for experimental (65% of people in self-concept programs enhanced their self-concept) and control participants (55% of people in the control group enhanced their self-concept). Hattie (1992) also found that effect sizes were higher for: adults (z = .52) than children (z = .31); lower socioeconomic groups than middle socioeconomic groups; groups with previously diagnosed problems (z = .55) relative to groups without problems ($z = .26$); and other settings ($z = .50$) compared to educational settings ($z = .36$) (see Hattie, 1992, pp. 228–230). The results also indicated of the total sample, adults with previously diagnosed problems had the highest average effect-size ($z = .87$). Of particular concern is the finding that the effectiveness of teachers as self-concept change agents was considerably lower than average ($z = .26$).

In 66 percent of the studies selected by Hattie (1992) the global term self-concept was used and 20 percent used the term self-esteem. Academic scales were used on 13 occasions ($z = .22$) and global measures were used on 10 occasions ($z = .08$). Hattie (1992, p. 232) concluded, "programs to change a particular dimension appear to have little effect on the global self." Differences between more global measures of self and specific scales indicate that caution is needed when using global measures to assess change in a particular dimension of self-concept. Only 36 of the 485 effect sizes included a delayed posttest and these came from only four studies. A significant difference was present between studies that were followed up ($z = .16$) and those without ($z = .40$). These results suggest that the effect size decreases over time. Marsh, Richards, and Barnes (1986a, 1986b) suggest that participants may experience a short-term euphoric effect as a result of an intervention that dissipates in time, that could explain such a decrease in effect size based on only four studies.

In examining enhancement approaches Hattie (1992, p. 233) found that cognitively oriented interventions appear to be effective with a mean effect-size of .47. Though transactional analysis had a relatively high mean effect-size of .81, Hattie (1992, p. 233) cautions that it is based on only one study with 9 effect sizes. The mean effect-size of .12 for affective programs indicates that the effects of these types of enhancement programs are relatively low with the exception of creative self-awareness programs, which had a high mean effect size of .40. Hattie (1992, p. 234) notes that there is considerable variation in effect-sizes for different studies within affective categories, which is probably attributable to the quality of the therapist. For other types of programs the average effect-size was .37 with variation according to the category. "There were no major differences between studies in which direct self-change was the aim (.32; e.g., therapy); studies where change was brought about by indirect methods (.29; e.g., enhancing academic achievement); those studies in which the intervention was direct and indirect (.44; e.g., a reading program combined with a self-concept program such as counseling); and, finally, those studies in which intervention was not associated with self-change (.42; e.g., longitudinal studies)" (Hattie, 1992, p. 235).

Hattie's (1992) meta-analysis is a valuable contribution to the self-concept literature. As Hattie (1992, p. 236) has pointed out, "there were too many fair and poor studies, too many studies were rejected because they evaluated programs by intuition, too few studies with follow-ups, and too few studies that included control groups." To these concerns Marsh and Craven (1997, p.179) have added that too few studies "have used well-validated, multidimensional self-concept instruments in which at least some of the scales are closely matched to the intended goals of the intervention."

Haney and Durlak Meta-Analysis

Recently Haney and Durlak (1998) conducted a meta-analysis of 116 self-concept/self-esteem pre-1992 studies for children and adolescents to: address whether interventions lead to significant improvement in self-concept, identify factors that moderate outcomes, and test whether improvements in self-concept are associated with other desirable outcomes. Studies identified were selected based on whether they involved children or adolescents with a mean age of 18 or younger; included at least one measure of self-concept or self-esteem, and contained a control group from the same population as the intervention group. Studies were coded based on the methodology employed, theoretical basis, general features of the study, and characteristics of the participants. Two types of interventions were operationalized: studies that focused on enhancing self-concept and studies that had another major focus but that included a self-concept measure. Interventions were also categorized as to whether students had any presenting problems. Studies where no presenting problems were present were coded as preventive studies and studies where presenting problems were present were coded as treatment studies. A single effect size was calculated for each intervention, however the authors noted, "for studies using more than one SE/SC [self-esteem/self-concept] measure effects were averaged to yield one effect per intervention" (Haney & Durlak, 1998, p. 425). Similarly, effects for other outcome measures were averaged for studies using more than one outcome measure.

The mean effect size for studies focused on enhancing self-concept was significantly ($p < .01$) higher (.57) than the mean effect size from studies focusing on other outcomes (.10). Except for children with internalizing problems where both interventions that targeted self-concept and other outcomes did equally well (mean effect sizes in the mid .50s), all other categories of students (externalizing, mixed and no previously diagnosed problems) display more improvement in the mean effect size for other outcomes if they are participating in an intervention that targets self-concept rather than other outcomes. However, the authors note that this pattern of results does not hold for three categories of outcomes (behavior, personality and academic) considered in their study but noted these comparisons were limited due to small cell sizes.

Nonrandomized designs resulted in significantly lower effect sizes (.04) than randomized studies (.38). Studies with no treatment control groups had significantly higher effect sizes (.34) than studies with attention-placebo controls (.10). Interventions that were developed based on prior research findings produced the highest effect size of .71, interventions based on a specific self-concept theory resulted in an effect size of .43, interventions that were based on other theory .53, studies based on another rationale produced an effect size of .26 and studies based on no rationale resulted in an effect size of .11. The authors also found that effects were stronger for treatment studies (.47) than prevention studies (.09). These results suggest that self-concept enhancement researchers can potentially maximize the impact of interventions on self-concept by: employing randomized designs, capitalizing on previous research findings and theory to develop interventions, and targeting particular categories of students who are most likely to benefit from a self-concept enhancement intervention.

Hancy and Durlak (1998) also created 3 categories of studies to test if positive changes in self-concept were associated with changes in other outcomes consisting of group 1 (studies with the highest mean changes in self-concept—.50 or greater), group 2 (studies with what the authors term intermediate effects from .20-.49), and group 3 (studies with effects less than .20). A single overall mean effect size was created for all outcomes for each study by averaging across all outcomes (p. 428). The authors reported that the results of these analyses showed that group 1 studies had the highest mean effect size across other outcomes (.55), with mean effect sizes for the remaining two groups being .31 and .14 respectively (p. 428). Importantly, based on these results Haney and Durlak (1998, p. 429) concluded, "it is possible to significantly improve children's and adolescents' levels of SE/SC and to obtain concomitant positive changes in other areas of adjustment. There is even the suggestion that SE/SC programs do at least as well as other types of interventions in changing other domains of functioning outcome data thus supports the views of several authors regarding the value of SE/SC interventions." Haney and Durlak (1998, p. 429) also suggested that significant improvements in self-concept are unlikely unless interventions focus on self-concept. This suggestion is supported by the longitudinal causal modeling studies discussed earlier, which demonstrated that the strongest effect on subsequent self-concept is prior self-concept.

The meta-analysis of Hattie (1986) and Haney and Durlak's (1998) have similar overall mean effects (.27 vs. .37), and both suggest students with prediagnosed conditions are likely to benefit more from self-concept interventions. However, while Haney and Durlak (1998) found that studies focused on enhancing self-concept had higher effect sizes than studies that focused on other outcomes, Hattie (1986) found no difference between such studies. Hattie (1986) also found that effect sizes varied according to the type of intervention program and the characteristics of the treatment administrator, while Hanley and Durlak (1998) found that these variables were not significant moderators. Hence, these issues may need to be clarified by further meta-analytic research.

In addition, while Haney and Durlak's (1998) meta-analysis makes an interesting and timely contribution to self-concept enhancement research, there are several important limitations of this study that restrict the validity and generalizability of the interpretations. Haney and Durlak (1998, p. 424) in their background to their study contended, "there is also no agreement about whether SE/SC is best conceptualized in unidimensional, multidimensional, or hierarchical terms. Furthermore, Harter (1982) has introduced the notion of perceived competence that contains a global assessment of self-worth and separate self-perceptions of abilities in different domains (e.g., physical, social, and cognitive). As a result, there is no theoretical or operational consensus regarding self-esteem or self-concept." This conclusion is most surprising in that Harter's (1982) research provides a clear justification for the multidimensionality of self-concept. Furthermore, there is consensus that self-concept cannot be adequately understood if its multidimensionality is ignored (e.g., Byrne, 1996a, 1996b; Marsh, 1990b; Marsh & Craven, 1997). Hattie (1992, p. 232) cautioned, "combining dimensions from personality inventories may result in an inaccurate estimate of self." Marsh and Craven (1997) in their review of self-concept research concluded that "our research has increasingly led to the conclusion that general self-concept—no matter how it is inferred—may not be a particularly useful construct.... General self-concept cannot adequately reflect the diversity of specific self-concept domains. If the role of self-concept research is to better understand the complexity of self in different contexts, to predict a wide variety of behavior, to provide outcome measures for diverse interventions, and to relate self-concept to other constructs, then the specific domains of self-concept are more useful than a general domain" (p. 191). To address these problems we would advocate that research designs of future meta-analysis studies examining self-concept enhancement account for the multidimensionality of self-concept and in so doing capitalize on recent advances in self-concept theory and research. More specifically, we argue that it is important to distinguish between the effects of an intervention on target areas of self-concept that are directly relevant to the goals of the program (e.g., math self-concept for a math intervention), the effects of an intervention on related areas of self-concept where one might predict a transfer effect (e.g., academic self-concept for a math intervention), and the effects of an intervention on non-target areas (e.g., physical self-concept for a math intervention). Based on self-concept theory and empirical research (e.g., Marsh & Craven, 1997), as well as common sense, target effects should be substantially larger than nontarget effects whereas related transfer effects should be intermediate. By failing to make this distinction, we argue that the Haney and Durlak (1998) meta-analysis is likely to have substantially underestimated the effects of interventions on targeted areas of self-concept, particularly for academic intervention studies that were evaluated in relation to changes in global self-concept, self-esteem, or nonacademic components of self-concept. Also given that Hattie's meta-analysis was based on pre-1983 studies and Haney and Durlak's on pre 1992 studies, it is important to note that these meta-analyses are largely based on studies that current self-concept enhancement researchers would mostly consider to be methodologically weak and would not incorporate recent advances in self-concept research.

Meta-Analyses Examining the Impact of Outdoor Education Programs

Meta-analyses focusing on the impact of outdoor education programs in relation to a broad range of constructs frequently include enhanced self-concept as an outcome measure. For example, Cason and Gillis (1994) conducted the first meta-analysis in this area based on 43 studies and 147 effect sizes, and found that 26 percent of the outcomes measured were self-reported self-concept scales. An effect size of .40 was found for the impact of outdoor education programs on self-concept. They noted that the considerable focus on self-esteem, had produced mixed, but generally positive findings. A significant positive correlation was found between length of program and the effect size ($r = .17$, $p = .001$) whereby longer outdoor education programs yielded higher outcomes. Larger outcomes were also more evident for younger adolescents, less rigorous studies, clinical outcome instruments, and more recent studies. Cason and Gillis commented that "the wide variance in findings raises questions about the validity of quantitative research for this field, the reliability of instruments used for assessment of pre- and post-program changes, and the host of unknown variables that may be influencing both positive and negative effects of adventure programming" (p. 46).

Hattie, Marsh, Neill, and Richards (1997) undertook a further meta-analysis to identify the outcomes most influenced by outdoor education programs and to examine the differences in outcomes for particular types of studies, programs, groups and participants. They identified 96 studies and 1,728 effects based on 12,057 participants. The largest category in terms of number of effects was self-concept. The greatest self-concept effects were for the constructs of independence, confidence, self-efficacy, and self-understandings. Furthermore, the effects of outdoor education programs on self-concept (.28) were large and consistent, and were long lasting, and greater than is typically found for classroom-based programs on self-concept. In particular they found that the largest effects occurred for Outward Bound Programs, the characteristics of which we discuss in a later section reviewing promising self-concept enhancement interventions. However, first we discuss advances in self-concept enhancement research methodology that are central to analyzing self-concept interventions.

ADVANCES IN SELF-CONCEPT INTERVENTION RESEARCH METHODOLOGY

The Construct Validity Approach

Fundamental to advances in self-concept enhancement research methodology were the Marsh, Richards, and Barnes (1986a, 1986b) studies which presented a construct validity approach to the study of intervention effects. They argued that specific dimensions of self-concept that are most relevant to the intervention should be most affected, while less relevant dimensions should be less affected. For example, if an intervention in a school setting targeted reading self-concept it would be logical to test whether the intervention affected: reading self-concept (target variable), school self-concept as reading self-concept is related to this construct (transfer variable), and nontarget facets of academic (e.g., mathematics) and nonacademic (e.g., physical appearance) self-concept (nontarget variables).

Testing for Diffusion Effects

Craven, Marsh, Debus, and Jayasinghe (2001) (also see Craven, 1996) developed a recent extension of this approach in educational settings that incorporated full experimental designs within-classes. Full experimental designs within-classes typically involve randomly assigning students in each class to an experimental group that receives a teacher-mediated intervention and to a control group or a nonexperimental group. Naturally the major focus in such research is the effects of a teacher-mediated treatment on the target participants. Nevertheless in classroom settings in which a teacher-mediated intervention is to some extent usually public, the possibility that the treatment has inadvertently affected nontarget participants is generally overlooked. Yet "if the classroom ecology is to be disturbed, it is important to assess how changes in teacher behavior affect *all* students" (Good & Brophy, 1974). Hence, Craven (1996; Craven, Marsh, Debus, & Jayasinghe, 2001) has advocated that enhancement researchers using within-class experimental designs need to test for what she terms "diffusion effects" of the treatment to nontarget participants in the context of a construct validity approach to the study of intervention effects. Such research designs enable the examination of: diffusion effects on target and nontarget participants, which has important implications for within-class control groups, and the impact of the intervention on target and nontarget facets of self-concept relevant to the goals of the intervention.

Interventions employing these research methods clearly demonstrate that the multidimensionality of self-concept as defined in the Shavelson model is vital to consider in research designs that aim to enhance self-concept. These advances in research methodology in combination with recent developments in theory and measurement instruments have provided the basis for overcoming some of the limitations of past self-concept enhancement research by ensuring considerations of measurement instruments, interventions, research methods, and theory are intertwined. To illustrate some recent advances in self-concept research an overview of some promising new generation enhancement studies is discussed in the next section.

PROMISING INTERVENTION STUDIES

Outward Bound Interventions

The Outward Bound Standard Course is a 26-day residential program comprised of physically and mentally demanding outdoor activities for 17–25 year olds. Hence, the program goals are primarily nonacademic. Marsh, Richards, and Barnes (1986a; 1986b) studies of this program found that participation in the standard course had a significant effect on the nonacademic (SDQ-III) dimensions of self-concept most related to the course goals. Applying a construct validity approach they demonstrated that gains were significantly larger for the SDQ-III scales predicted a priori to be most relevant to the goals of the program. Of critical importance, an 18-month follow-up showed that there was no decrement in these gains (Marsh, Richards, & Barnes, 1986b). Therefore, it was predicted and found that the program affected primarily nonacademic self-concepts and had much less impact on academic self-concepts. In order to provide a clear test of these predictions, the director of the Outward Bound program classified the 13 SDQIII scales into three categories those most relevant, those moderately relevant, and those least relevant to the goals of the Outward Bound program. In evaluating the effects of the program, Marsh and colleagues (1986b) showed that the intervention effects were significantly more positive for the most relevant self-concept factors, less positive for the moderately relevant self-concept factors, and least positive for the least relevant goals. Furthermore, this clearly differentiated pattern of results was also maintained during the 18-month follow-up period (Marsh et al., 1986a). Hattie (1992) based on a meta-analysis of self-concept enhancement studies found this enhancement effect to be among the largest and most consistent in published research.

The Outward Bound Bridging Course is a 6-week residential experience conducted in an isolated environment away from school. The course design was based on the Outward Bound philosophy and McClelland's (1965) achievement motivation theory. The Outward Bound Bridging Course was developed for underachieving boys to improve math and reading achievement and self-concept and self-esteem. Program goals were primarily academic. The Marsh and Richards (1988) study was like the Standard Course study in that: it evaluated the effect of a course run by Outward Bound on multiple dimensions of self-concept as measured by one of the SDQ instruments; a short multiple time series design was used; the generality of effects was examined across different course offerings of the same (or a similar) program; and a construct validity approach was used to assess the validity of the findings. The study differs from the Standard Course study in that: the primary focus of the Bridging Course was on educational objectives rather than the nonacademic goals of the standard course; participants were 13 to 16-year old low-achieving males rather than self-selected 17 to 25-year olds; participants responded to the SDQ-I rather than the SDQ-III; and the academic nature of the intervention made it appropriate to assess the intervention with achievement tests as well as with multiple dimensions of self-concept. It was predicted and found that the program affected primarily academic self-concepts and had much less impact on nonacademic self-concepts and corresponding effects were present for reading and mathematics achievement.

The juxtaposition of the two studies is important. The Standard Course study (Marsh, Richards, & Barnes, 1986a) predicted and found more change in nonacademic than academic self-concepts. In contrast, the Bridging Course study (Marsh & Richards, 1988) predicted and found greater change in the academic than in the nonacademic self-concepts. There were also changes for reading and math achievements corresponding to the changes in academic self-concepts. Taken together, the two studies provide stronger support for the domain specificity of each of the interventions than was possible in considering either one in isolation, and attest to the importance of utilizing a construct validity approach, and accounting for the multidimensionality of self-concept in intervention studies.

Marsh and Peart Study

Marsh and Peart (1988) conducted a study of aerobics training, physical fitness, and physical self-concept with randomly assigned competitive, cooperative, and control groups. The cooperative group participated in exercises undertaken in pairs and feedback that was provided to students emphasized individual improvement. This intervention resulted in an increase in physical self-concept and physical fitness. The competitive/social comparison group participated in individual exercises and feedback provided emphasized comparisons with the best students. This treatment resulted in an increase in physical fitness but a decrease in physical self-concept. Students in the competitive group knew they were fitter at the end of the study, but this was offset by more critical standards used to evaluate their performances. The authors concluded that competitive environments—where there are a few winners and lots of losers—leads to lower self-concepts. Importantly, the study also demonstrates the rationale for developing both skill level and the corresponding area of self-concept. Of central relevance to our discussion, the results provide an important example of why it is important to consider multiple dimensions of self-concept. An aerobics intervention designed to enhance physical fitness affected physical fitness and Physical self-concept. The self-concept effects were domain specific in that other facets of self-concept were not influenced by the intervention. This supports the construct validity of interpretations of the intervention and the self-concept responses.

The results of the Marsh and Peart (1988) study demonstrated that self-concept effects were domain specific in that other facets of the intervention were not influenced by the intervention, hence providing support for the construct validity interpretation of the intervention effects and the self-concept responses. To illustrate the potential generality of this finding, consider a study in which participants with poor performances in some particular domain—physical, social, or academic—are identified and randomly assigned to experimental and control groups. The experimental group is given a training program and the control group receives no treatment. Even if the intervention positively affects the performance deficit, it may have no positive effect on the corresponding area of self-concept if the intervention also serves to make more obvious the participants' deficits in that area. Application of the reciprocal effects model of self-concept and achievement implies that failing to enhance self-concept will lead to deterioration of performance levels. Hence, interventions should be designed to enhance both self-concept and performance to ensure the intervention has long lasting effects on both constructs.

Craven, Marsh, and Debus Study

Craven, Marsh, and Debus (1991), and Craven (1989) implemented an enhancement intervention in a primary setting that aimed to enhance reading and mathematics self-concept. Secondary effects were predicted to occur in self-attributions and academic achievement. Participants were primary school students who were low on academic self-concept as measured by the SDQ-I. The intervention was a combination of a researcher-devised treatment designed to enhance self-concept directly (internally focused performance feedback) and an indirect self-concept treatment designed to enhance self-concept via training students to change their self-attributions in success and failure situations (attributional retraining). The intervention focused on both reading and math self-concepts. Brophy's (1981) guidelines for effective praise were utilized in delivering the intervention by ensuring both feedback forms were delivered contingent to appropriate improvements in performance to ensure the feedback was perceived as credible by students. The treatment was applied in educational settings and was administered by teachers in the regular classroom and by researchers in withdrawn assistance groups conducted within the school setting.

The researcher-administered treatment was successful in enhancing reading and mathematics self-concepts (target facets), school and general self-concept (transfer facets), and some logically related self-attributions (e.g., attributing success to effort). The researchers also found that nontarget facets of self-concept that were unrelated to the goals of the intervention were not affected. The findings provide support for: (a) the importance of applying a construct validity approach to test the effectiveness of the intervention on target, transfer and nontarget facets of self-concept, (b) the usefulness of the self-concept enhancement intervention; (c) the critical importance of accounting for multiple dimensions of self-concept in intervention studies; and (d) the necessity of utilizing the strongest available multidimensional self-concept measurement instruments with demonstrated reliability and validity.

Despite the effectiveness of the similar researcher-administered treatment, the intervention administered by teachers in the context of the regular classroom did not result in significant changes in self-concept. To address this paradoxical result Craven and colleagues (1991) and Craven (1989) suggested that future research based on teacher-administered interventions should consider: (a) strategies to maintain the frequency of reinforcement delivered by teachers; (b) introducing the intervention at the beginning of the school year to ensure feedback was perceived as salient by students; and (c) extending the treatment implementation period.

Craven Study

Craven (1996) incorporated the design features suggested above to maximize teacher-generated effects on self-concept. The purpose of this large-scale study was to investigate the effectiveness of an intervention to enhance academic self-concept and the related constructs of self-attributions and academic achievement. Participants for the longitudinal analysis were 1,300 middle and working class children from 8 schools in metropolitan Western Sydney from each of the grades of 3, 4, and 5. From each of the 50 classes participating in the study, 18 participants with the lowest combined academic self-concept scores measured by the Self Description Questionnaire-I (SDQ-I) were selected from the longitudinal pool to participate in the enhancement component of the study.

The self-concept enhancement intervention was a combination of internally focused feedback and attributional feedback targeted at reading or mathematics or a combination thereof. The intervention was delivered over a period of 14 weeks by primary school teachers in the regular classroom context and by research assistants in educational settings as an analogue to withdrawn assistance groups. Six students from each of the 42 experimental classes were assigned to the within-class control group. One additional class from each of the 8 participating schools was randomly assigned to be an experimental diffusion control group and did not receive either the teacher-mediated or researcher-mediated intervention. This control group was incorporated in the research design to test for possible diffusion effects of the teacher-mediated intervention to non-target participants in the within-class control group.

The results demonstrated that the researcher-mediated intervention was successful in enhancing several targeted facets of self-concept and some logically related self-attributions and areas of academic achievement. For example, the researcher-mediated intervention in mathematics enhanced mathematics self-concept, some mathematics attributions and mathematics achievement. The single domain teacher-mediated interventions were successful in affecting some aspects of self-concept, self-attributions and academic achievement relevant to the goals of the intervention, though the teacher-administered intervention was less potent than the researcher-administered intervention. Students experiencing the combined teacher-mediated intervention showed gains in some aspects of reading achievement but the intervention did not enhance self-concept or self-attributions.

Comparison of academic self-concept and self-attribution scores of the within-class control group with the external diffusion control group revealed that the within-class control group had higher academic self-concepts and self-attribution scores at posttest than the external diffusion control group. Comparison of self-concept scores of the within-class control group with the external diffusion control group at time 2 revealed main effects for group were present for school, general and combined academic self-concept. Participants in within-class control groups had higher self-concepts in school, general and combined academic self-concept at time 2. Main effects for group were not present for reading and mathematics self-concept at time 2, however significant aptitude treatment interaction effects were present for mathematics and reading self-concept with prior levels of self-concept at time 2. These significant aptitude treatment inter-action effects suggest that diffusion effects in mathematics and reading self-concept for students in the within-class control group are greater for some categories of students at time 2.

The presence of this diffusion effect suggests that teachers can enhance self-concept over a relatively short period. The findings provide support for: (a) the effectiveness of the intervention as a means to enhance self-concept particularly for treatments mediated by researchers, and mediated by teachers in single academic domains, (b) the importance of including multiple dimensions of self-concept in intervention studies, and (c) the need to test for diffusion effects when utilizing within-class full experimental designs.

BURNETT'S RESEARCH PROGRAM:
THE ROLE OF CHILDREN'S SELF-TALK AND
TEACHER FEEDBACK IN SELF-CONCEPT ENHANCEMENT

Burnett has developed and evaluated the role of self-talk strategies in enhancing upper primary school students' self-concepts. Burnett defines self-talk as "what a student says to him/herself with particular emphasis on the words used to express thoughts, beliefs, values and attitudes about the world and oneself" (Burnett, 1994, p.182). Burnett (1995, 1997) building on Hattie's (1992) finding that cognitive behavioral based interventions were the most successful enhancers of self-esteem and self-concepts, developed two eight-week cognitive behavioral programs. One program was based on Cognitive-Behavioral Therapy strategies while the other was based on Rational Emotive Education activities. Burnett (1995, 1997) noted that Cognitive-Behavioral Therapy strategies programs are based on the notion that negative thoughts and beliefs about life result in negative self-talk that leads to negative thoughts and feelings about oneself and one's characteristics. Rational Emotive Education programs emphasize the limitation of skills and cognitive training without first challenging and focusing on a person's irrational and unproductive beliefs. In terms of self-enhancement, Cognitive-Behavioral Therapy strategies use cognitive and behavioral techniques to help children think more positively about themselves and behave more confidently, while Rational Emotive Education focuses on developing rational self-accepting beliefs as the primary technique of enhancement. Burnett (1995, 1997) developed a series of materials and activities based on the theoretical distinction between Cognitive-Behavioral Therapy strategies and Rational Emotive Education and a Masters level School Counsellor administered these in two classes in two schools. The findings indicated that neither program had an impact on children's self-esteem or self-concepts. However, both programs were associated with an increase in positive self-talk and Cognitive-Behavioral Therapy strategies were linked to a decrease in negative self-talk. It seemed that self-talk was changed for the positive in the short-term but not self-esteem or self-concepts. Given that self-esteem was found to correlate with positive self-talk ($r = 0.39$) and with negative self-talk ($r = -0.36$), it was postulated that self-esteem may increase in the longer term as a result of changes in the frequencies of positive and negative self-talk. Janet Hattie (1992) reported that it was difficult to enhance preadolescent's self-esteem and self-concepts using short-term intervention programs and Burnett's findings confirmed this. However, one important finding to emerge from these studies was the significant relationships between positive and negative self-talk and self-esteem and the fact that the program seemed to have an impact on changing children's self-talk in a positive way.

Burnett's recent studies have also highlighted the importance of what significant others say to children in generating adaptive self-talk statements in primary aged children (Burnett 1996, 1999, Burnett & McCrindle, 1999). For example, Burnett (1996) administered the Significant Others Statements Inventory (SOSI) and the Self-Talk Inventory (STI) to 635 primary school students in Grades 3 to 7 and found that positive statements made by teachers were the best predictor of positive self-talk. The next predictors in order were positive statements made by peers, parents and siblings. A perceived low rate of positive statements from teachers was a predictor of negative self-talk behind negative statements from siblings and peers and a low rate of positives from peers. The results of this study indicated that significant relationships existed between the perceived frequency of positive and negative statements made by others and positive and negative self-talk. In a subsequent study, Burnett and McCrindle (1999) found that general positive statements made by teachers had a direct effect on children's general positive self-talk which in turn had a direct effect on children's self-esteem and their self-esteem related behavior. Also of note was the finding that negative statements from peers were directly related to negative self-talk. Similarly, in a further study based on data collected in six rural elementary schools ($n = 747$), Burnett (in press) found a mediating effect of self-talk between teachers' subject specific feedback and students' mathematics and reading self-concepts. These findings support the Craven, Marsh and Debus (1991) internal mediating model and Burnett's (1999) study that found that general positive self-talk mediated between teachers' general praise and students' self-concept in reading. Findings from Burnett's research program are important in suggesting that self-concept may be enhanced by encouraging students to use adaptive self-talk strategies and the latter may be best achieved by training teachers and peers to increase their administration of positive feedback and reduce negative feedback. Given that Hattie (1992) based on a meta-analysis has concluded that feedback is the most powerful single moderator that improves affective and achievement outcomes, and that promising interventions discussed above include feedback, incorporating feedback in future self-concept interventions is a useful consideration for incorporation in the next generation of self-concept enhancement research. Some guidelines are presented next.

GUIDELINES FOR CREATING THE NEXT GENERATION OF SELF-CONCEPT ENHANCEMENT RESEARCH

Taken together this chapter's analysis of historical pitfalls and recent advances in self-concept theory, measurement, and research provides a blueprint for the next generation of self-concept enhancement research whereby researchers need to consider:

1. Utilizing the strongest available self-concept theory as a basis for designing self-concept enhancement studies. Based on over a decade of research experience we judge the original Shavelson and colleagues model and the Marsh and Shavelson revision of this model (1985; also see Marsh, 1990b; 1990e; 1990f) to be the best available structural theory. We also anticipate that self-concept researchers will also need to build nomological theoretical models articulating the direction of relations between self-concept and other critical variables (e.g., reciprocal effects models of relations between academic self-concept and academic achievement) over the next decade as a foundation for between-construct studies that relate self-concept to other variables and as a basis for disentangling the processes and identifying the constructs that contribute to enhancing self-concept.

2. Employing measurement instruments that account for the multidimensionality of self-concept and demonstrate the reliability and validity of the self-concept instruments employed in each investigation. The latter should help to ensure that appropriate attention is given to within-construct issues and hence internal validity is demonstrated

prior to proceeding to relating self-concept measures to other constructs and their use as outcome measures in intervention studies. It is inadequate to quote the reliability and validity reported in test manuals, rather researchers need to demonstrate their measures are reliable measures of multiple facets of self-concept based on the sample under examination, preferably by utilizing CFA approaches. This procedure is particularly important when researchers are using new instruments, adaptations of existing instruments or when targeting a new sample population with an established instrument.

3. Devising and implementing potentially powerful interventions that can be justified in the context of previous theory and research as opposed to ad hoc idiosyncratic interventions. Internally focused feedback, attributional retraining, and self-talk interventions are some potentially potent strategies deserving of further research. As mentioned previously, we would also suggest that a key element of self-concept interventions needs to be feedback/reinforcement. Interventions deriving from promising self-concept enhancement studies often seem to share this characteristic. In addition, when implementing a range of interventions we have observed that participants respond positively to both positive reinforcement/feedback and constructive feedback. It also needs to be noted that Hattie, based on the findings of a thorough meta-analysis contends that the most important ingredient underlying successful academic learning is feedback (Hattie, 1992). For these reasons, we suspect that in the near future it will also be possible to demonstrate that one of the most critical strategies for enhancing self-concept will be the provision of feedback.

It is also important to note that the actual procedures of new self-concept interventions need to be presented in adequate detail for: (a) replication so that future researchers can offer further support, strengthen or refute findings and thereby ensure "one shot" studies do not continue to dominate the field; and (b) inclusion in future meta-analytic studies that can serve to elucidate the most powerful next generation interventions (i.e. report means, standard deviations and sample sizes for each effect on specific target, transfer and non-target variables for both control and experimental groups).

4. Capitalizing on the strongest available research methodology by: (a) utilizing adequate sample sizes that allow for the strongest statistical tools (e.g., SEM, Joreskog & Sorbom, 1993) to be employed to analyze intervention effects; (b) focusing interventions on specific facets of self-concept and stating hypotheses and their associated rationales in sufficient detail to identify and justify target, transfer and nontar-

get self-concept facets and other outcomes. This should ensure an appropriate fit between the goals of the intervention and the specific dimensions of self-concept and measures of other outcomes used to evaluate interventions; (c) employing a construct validity approach to the study of intervention effects (e.g., Marsh, Richards, & Barnes, 1986a, 1986b); (d) ensuring in studies where possible diffusion effects may be present, that the research design includes controls to test for effects on target and non-target participants, and such effects are tested for and reported prior to undertaking further data analysis and reporting further results (e.g., Craven, 1996); and (e) where possible conducting studies that employ longitudinal designs and include a long-term follow-up test of intervention effects.

5. Capitalizing on the implications of the results of causal modeling studies (e.g., Marsh & Yeung, 1997a) by designing interventions to enhance both self-concept and desirable outcomes (e.g., academic achievement) as implied by the reciprocal effects model in studies that aim to produce long lasting effects of the intervention. For example, the Marsh and Richards (1988) study provides an excellent example of a study that simultaneously enhanced and affected math and reading self-concepts and corresponding areas of achievement.

In addition, given that Hattie (1992) has found that, compared to other instructors, teachers are least likely to enhance self-concept and given the importance of identifying effective self-concept techniques for the classroom, future new generation research needs to consider focusing intervention designs incorporating the features above on educational settings. Thus far, the value of interventions embedded in ecologically undisturbed settings (e.g., classrooms), mediated by ecologically natural agents (e.g., teachers) has not been fully explored or adequately supported by a body of studies with strong research designs and instrumentation. Designing interventions to be administered in naturalistic settings is a desirable goal since this is the target setting where interventions have most direct practical significance. Thorough training methods may need to be instigated for the schooling sector to ensure teachers comprehend how to implement a sophisticated self-concept intervention, the key features of the intervention, and perhaps most importantly recognize the value in doing so.

SUMMARY

In this chapter we have attempted to demonstrate some aspects of the rationale for enhancing self-concept. We also have emphasized that enhancing self-concept is a vital goal in itself and an important mediating variable that impacts on a variety of desirable outcomes in a variety of settings. We have also suggested that the results of promising self-concept enhancement studies are providing the basis for important directions in self-concept theory, research, and practice, and have suggested some new directions to begin to foster the next generation of self-concept enhancement studies. Throughout this chapter we have attempted to illuminate that consideration of theory, measurement instruments, intervention design based on previous research results, research methodology, and practice are intertwined such that weaknesses in any one area will adversely affect the other areas. We trust that attention to the design features described above assists researchers to ensure the next generation of self-concept enhancement studies avoid and overcome previous methodological flaws and capitalize on recent developments in theory, measurement and research to solve the enhancing self-concept conundrum.

REFERENCES

Australian Education Council. (1989). *The common and agreed national goals of schooling.* Canberra: AGPS.

Board of Studies New South Wales. (1998). *Human society and its environment K–6.* Sydney, Australia: Board of Studies NSW.

Boyle, G. J. (1994). Self-Description Questionnaire II: A review. *Test Critiques, 10,* 632–643.

Branden, N. (1994). *Six pillars of self-esteem.* New York: Bantam.

Brophy, J. (1981). Teacher praise: A functional analysis. *Review of Educational Research, 51,* 5–32.

Burnett, P. C. (1994). Self-talk in upper elementary school children: Its relationship with irrational beliefs, self-esteem, and depression. *Journal of Rational-Emotive and Cognitive-Behavior Therapy, 12*(3), 181–189.

Burnett, P. C. (1995). Cognitive behaviour therapy vs rational-emotive education: Impact on children's self-talk, self-esteem and irrational beliefs. *Australian Journal of Guidance and Counselling, 5,* 59–66.

Burnett, P. C. (1996). Children's self-talk and significant others' positive and negative statements. *Educational Psychology, 16,* 57–68.

Burnett, P. C. (1997). Self-esteem and self-talk enhancement in upper primary school children. *Set: Research Information for Teachers, 2,* 1–4.

Burnett, P. C. (1999). Children's self-talk and academic self-concepts: The impact of teachers' statements. *Educational Psychology in Practice, 15,* 195–200.

Burnett, P. C. (2003). The impact of teacher feedback on self-talk and self-concept in reading and mathematics. *Journal of Classroom Interaction, 38,* 11–16.

Burnett, P. C., & McCrindle, A. (1999). The relationship between significant others' positive and negative statements, self-talk and self-esteem. *Child Study Journal, 29,* 39–48.

Burney, L. (2001). Unpublished letter from Linda Burney, Attorney-General, New South Wales Department of Affairs to the New South Wales Minister for Education and Training.

Burns, R. B. (1979). *The self-concept: Theory, measurement, development, and behaviour.* London: Longman.

Byrne, B. M. (1984). The general/academic self-concept nomological network: A review of construct validation research. *Review of Educational Research, 54,* 427–456.

Byrne, B. M. (1986). Self-concept/academic achievement relations: An investigation of dimensionality, stability, and causality. *Canadian Journal of Behavioral Science, 18,* 173–186.

Byrne, B. M. (1996a). Academic self-concept: Its structure, measurement, and relation to academic achievement. In B. A. Bracken (Ed.), *Handbook of self-concept* (pp. 287–316). New York: Wiley.

Byrne, B. M. (1996b). *Measuring self-concept across the life span: Issues and instrumentation.* Washington, DC: American Psychological Association.

Cason, D., & Gillis, G. H. L. (1994). A meta-analysis of outdoor adventure programming with adolescents. *Journal of Experiential Education 17*(1), 40–47.

Commonwealth of Australia. (1994). *National review of education for Aboriginal and Torres Strait Islander peoples.* Canberra: Australian Government Publishing Service.

Commonwealth of Australia. (1995). *The Commonwealth Government's response to the National Review of Education for Aboriginal and Torres Strait Islander peoples.* Canberra: Australian Government Publishing Service.

Commonwealth of Australia. (1997). *Australian Reconciliation Convention.* Canberra: AGPS.

Coopersmith, S. A. (1967). *The antecedents of self-esteem.* San Francisco: WH Freeman.

Craven, R. G. (1989). *An examination of self-concept: The interrelationship of teachers, parents and children's perceptions of self-concept, and their influence in enhancing self-concept.* Unpublished thesis, University of Sydney, Australia .

Craven, R. G. (1996). *Enhancing academic self-concept: A large-scale longitudinal study in an educational setting.* USA: UMI. (Doctoral thesis submitted to the University of Sydney).

Craven, R. G., Marsh, H. W., & Debus, R. (1991). Effects of internally focused feedback and attributional feedback on the enhancement of academic self-concept. *Journal of Educational Psychology, 83, 17–26.*

Craven, R. G., Marsh, H. W., Debus, R. L., & Jayasinghe. U. (2001). Diffusion effects: Control group contamination threats to the validity of teacher-administered interventions. *Journal of Educational Psychology, 93,* 639–645.

Dixon, R. M., Marsh, H. W., & Craven, R. G. (2002, August). Moving out: The impact on the self and other related variables for people with mild intellectual disabilities. In H. W. Marsh, R. G. Craven, & K. Simpson (Eds.), *Self-concept research, driving international agendas.* Collected papers of the Self-Concept Enhancement and Learning Facilitation (SELF) Research Centre Second International Conference, Sydney, Australia.

Eccles, J. S., Adler, T. F., Futterman, R., Goff, S. B., Kaczala, C. M., Meece, J. L., & Midgley, C. (1983). Expectancies, values, and academic behaviours. In J. T.

Spence (Ed.), *Achievement and achievement motivation* (Vol. 32, pp. 75–146). San Francisco: Freeman.

Ethington, C. A. (1991). A test of a model of achievement behaviors. *American Educational Research Journal, 28,* 155–172.

Good, T. L., & Brophy, J. E. (1974). Changing teacher and student behavior: An empirical investigation. *Journal of Educational Psychology, 66,* 390–405.

Guay, F., Marsh, H. W., & Boivin, M. (2003). Academic self-concept and academic achievement: Development perspectives on their causal ordering. *Journal of Educational Psychology, 95,* 124–136.

Haney, P., & Durlak, J. A. (1998). Changing self-esteem in children and adolescents: A meta-analytic review. *Journal of Clinical Child Psychology, 27,* 423–433.

Harter, S. (1982). The perceived competence scale for children. *Child Development, 53,* 87–97.

Hattie, J. A. (1992). *Self-concept.* Hillsdale, NJ: Lawrence Erlbaum Associates.

Hattie, J. A., & Marsh, H. W. (1996). Future directions in self concept research. In B. A. Bracken (Ed.), *Handbook of self-concept* (pp. 421–462). New York: Wiley.

Hattie, J. C. (1986). *Enhancing self concept.* Unpublished master's thesis, University of New England, Australia.

Hattie, J., Marsh, H. W., Neill, J. T., & Richards, G. E. (1997) Outward Bound and adventure education: Out-of-class experiences that make a lasting difference. *Review of Educational Research, 67,* 43–87.

Hughes, P. (1988). *Aboriginal education policy task force report.* Canberra: Commonwealth of Australia.

James, W. (1890/1963). *The principles of psychology.* New York: Holt, Rinehart, & Winston.

Johnston, E. (1991). *Royal Commission into Aboriginal deaths in custody.* Canberra: Commonwealth of Australia.

Joreskog, K. G., & Sorbom, D. (1993). *LISREL 8: Structural equation modeling with the SIMPLIS command language.* Chicago: Scientific Software International.

Kemp, D. (1999). Speech. Australian College of Education: Indigenous Education Forum, Alice Springs, 3 November 1999. Presentation by Dr. David Kemp. Commonwealth Minister for Education, Training and Youth Affairs. Canberra: DETYA.

Marsh, H. W. (1986). Verbal and math self-concepts: An internal/external frame of reference model. *American Educational Research Journal, 23,* 129–149.

Marsh, H. W. (1990a). The causal ordering of academic self-concept and academic achievement: A multiwave, longitudinal path analysis. *Journal of Educational Psychology, 82,* 646–656.

Marsh, H. W. (1990b). The structure of academic self-concept: The Marsh/Shavelson model. *Journal of Educational Psychology, 82,* 623–636.

Marsh, H. W. (1990c). *Self Description Questionnaire (SDQ) I: A theoretical and empirical basis for the measurement of multiple dimensions of preadolescent self-concept: A test manual and a research monograph.* Sydney: University of Western Sydney.

Marsh, H. W. (1990d). *Self Description Questionnaire (SDQ) II: A theoretical and empirical basis for the measurement of multiple dimensions of adolescent self-concept: An interim test manual and a research monograph.* San Antonio, TX: The Psychological Corporation (Republished in 1992, Publication Unit, Faculty of Education, University of Western Sydney, Macarthur).

Marsh, H. W. (1990e). A multidimensional, hierarchical self-concept: Theoretical and empirical justification. *Educational Psychology Review, 2,* 77–172.

Marsh, H. W. (1990f). The structure of academic self-concept: The Marsh/Shavelson model. *Journal of Educational Psychology, 82,* 623–636.

Marsh, H. W. (1991). The failure of high ability high schools to deliver academic benefits: The importance of academic self-concept and educational aspirations. *American Educational Research Journal, 28,* 445–480.

Marsh, H. W. (1992a). The content specificity of relations between academic achievement and academic self-concept. *Journal of Educational Psychology, 84,* 43–50.

Marsh, H. W. (1992b). *Self Description Questionnaire (SDQ) III: A theoretical and empirical basis for the Measurement of multiple dimensions of late adolescent self-concept: A test manual and a research monograph.* Publication Unit, Faculty of Education, University of Western Sydney, Macarthur.

Marsh, H. W. (2002, August). *Causal ordering of academic self-concept and achievement.* Paper presented at the 2nd Biennial International Conference of the Self-concept Enhancement Learning Facilitation Centre, Sydney, Australia. (http://self.uws.edu.au)

Marsh, H. W., Byrne, B. M., & Shavelson, R. (1988). A multifaceted academic self-concept: Its hierarchical structure and its relation to academic achievement. *Journal of Educational Psychology, 80,* 366–380.

Marsh, H. W., Byrne, B. M., & Yeung, A. S. (1999). Causal ordering of academic self-concept and achievement: Reanalysis of a pioneering study and revised recommendations. *Educational Psychologist, 34,* 155–167.

Marsh, H. W., & Craven, R. G. (1991). Self-other agreement on multiple dimensions of preadolescent self-concept: Inferences by teachers, mothers, and fathers. *Journal of Educational Psychology, 83,* 393–404.

Marsh, H. W. & Craven, R. G. (1997). Academic self-concept: Beyond the dustbowl. In G. Phye (Ed.), *Handbook of classroom assessment: Learning, achievement and adjustment.* Orlando, FL: Academic Press.

Marsh, H. W., Craven, R. G., & Debus, R. (1998). Separation of competency and affect components of multiple dimensions of academic self-concept: A developmental perspective. *Merrill-Palmer Quarterly, 45,* 567–601.

Marsh, H. W., Parada, R. H., Yeung, A. S., & Healey, J. (2001). Aggressive school troublemakers and victims: A longitudinal model examining the pivotal role of self-concept. *Journal of Educational Psychology, 93*(2), 411–419.

Marsh, H. W., & Peart, N. (1988). Competitive and cooperative physical fitness training programs for girls: Effects on physical fitness and on multidimensional self-concepts. *Journal of Sport and Exercise Psychology, 10,* 390–407.

Marsh, H. W., & Richards, G. (1988). The Outward Bound Bridging Course for low achieving high-school males: Effect on academic achievement and multidimensional self-concepts. *Australian Journal of Psychology, 40,* 281–298.

Marsh, H. W., Richards, G., & Barnes, J. (1986a). Multidimensional self-concepts: The effect of participation in an Outward Bound program. *Journal of Personality and Social Psychology, 45,* 173–187.

Marsh, H. W., Richards, G., & Barnes, J. (1986b). Multidimensional self-concepts: A long-term follow-up of the effect of participation in an Outward Bound program. *Personality and Social Psychology Bulletin, 12,* 475–492.

Marsh, H. W., & Shavelson, R. J. (1985). Self-concept: Its multifaceted, hierarchical structure. *Educational Psychologist, 20,* 107–125.

Marsh, H. W., & Yeung, A. S. (1997a). The causal effects of academic self-concept on academic achievement: Structural equation models of longitudinal data. *Journal of Educational Psychology, 89,* 41–54.

Marsh, H. W., & Yeung, A. S. (1997b). Coursework selection: The effects of academic self-concept and achievement. *American Educational Research Journal, 34,* 691–720.

Marsh, H. W., & Yeung, A. S. (1998). Top-down, bottom-up, and horizontal models: The direction of causality in multidimensional, hierarchical self-concept models. *Journal of Personality and Social Psychology, 75,* 509–527.

Marx, R., & Winne, P.H. (1978). Construct interpretations of three self-concept inventories. *American Educational Research Journal, 15,* 99-108.

McClelland, D. C. (1965). Towards a theory of motive acquisition. *American Psychologist, 20,* 321–333.

Meece, J. L., Parsons, J. E., Kaczala, C. M., Gott, S. B., & Futterman, R. (1982). Sex differences in math achievement: Toward a model of academic choice. *Psychological Bulletin, 91,* 324–348.

Meece, J. L., Wigfield, A., & Eccles, J. S. (1990). Predictors of math anxiety and its influence on young adolescents' course enrollment intentions and performance in mathematics. *Journal of Educational Psychology, 82,* 60–70.

Messick, S. (1989). Validity. In R. L. Linn (Ed.). *Educational measurement* (3rd ed., pp. 13–104). New York: Macmillan.

Ministerial Council on Education, Employment, Training, and Youth Affairs. (1998). *Revised national goals for schooling.* Australian Curriculum Studies Association newsletter.

Muijs, R. D. (1997). Predictors of academic achievement and academic self-concept: A longitudinal perspective. *British Journal of Educational Psychology, 67,* 263–277.

National Board of Employment, Education and Training. (1995). *Meeting the educational needs of Aboriginal adolescents.* Canberra: AGPS.

National Crime Prevention. (1999). *Pathways to prevention: Developmental and early intervention approaches to crime in Australia.* National Crime Prevention, Attorney-General's Department: Canberra.

Newman, R. S. (1984). Children's achievement and self-evaluations in mathematics: A longitudinal study. *Journal of Educational Psychology, 76,* 857–873.

Schmidt, F. L. (1992). What do data really mean? Research findings, meta-analysis, and cumulative knowledge in psychology. *American Psychologist, 47,* 1173–1181.

Shavelson, R. J., & Bolus, R. (1982). Self-concept: The interplay of theory and methods. *Journal of Educational Psychology, 74,* 3–17.

Shavelson, R. J., Hubner, J. J., & Stanton, G. C. (1976). Self-concept: Validation of construct interpretations. *Review of Educational Research, 46,* 407–441.

Shavelson, R. J., & Marsh, H. W. (1986). On the structure of self-concept. In R. Schwarzer (Ed.), *Anxiety and cognitions.* Hillsdale, NJ: Lawrence Erlbaum.

Skaalvik, E. M. (1997). Issues in research on self-concept. In M. L. Maehr & P. R. Pintrich (Eds.), *Advances in motivation and achievement* (Vol. 10, pp. 51–98). Greenwich, CT: JAI Press.

Skaalvik, E. M., & Hagtvet, K. A. (1990). Academic achievement and self-concept: An analysis of causal predominance in a developmental perspective. *Journal of Personality and Social Psychology, 58,* 292–307.

Skaalvik, E., & Rankin, R. J. (1995). A test of the internal/external frame of reference model at different levels of math and verbal self-perception. *American Educational Research Journal, 35,* 161–184.

Skaalvik, E. M., & Valas, H. (1999). Relations among achievement, self-concept, and motivation in mathematics and language arts: A longitudinal study. *The Journal of Experimental Education, 67,* 135–149.

Tracey, D., Marsh, H. W., & Craven, R. G. (2003). Self-concepts of preadolescent students with mild intellectual disabilities: Issues of measurement and educational placement. In H. W. Marsh, R. G. Craven, & D. McInerney (Eds.), *International advances in self research* (Vol. 1, pp. 000–000). Greenwich, CT: Information Age Publishing.

Vispoel, W. P. (1995). Self-concept in the arts: An extension of the Shavelson model. *Journal of Educational Psychology, 87,* 134–145.

Wells, L. E., & Marwell, G. (1976). *Self-esteem: Its conceptualization and measurement.* Beverly Hills, CA: Sage Publications.

Wylie, R. C. (1974). *The self-concept* (Rev. ed., Vol. 1). Lincoln: University of Nebraska Press.

Wylie, R. C. (1979). *The self-concept* (Vol. 2). Lincoln: University of Nebraska Press.

Wylie, R. C. (1989). *Measures of self-concept.* Lincoln: University of Nebraska Press.

CHAPTER 6

GETTING BACK ON THE CORRECT PATHWAY FOR SELF-CONCEPT RESEARCH IN THE NEW MILLENNIUM

Revisiting Misinterpretations of and Revitalizing the Contributions of James' Agenda for Research on the Self

John Hattie

This chapter revisits Williams James' chapter on "The Consciousness of Self" (James, 1890), which very much set the agenda for research on self-concept for the subsequent 100 years. James' two books, the longer two-volume *The Principles of Psychology* (1890) and the shorter version *Psychology: A Briefer Course* (1892), affectionately known as James and Jimmy, changed the prevailing view from a reliance on "habit," mental philosophy, and overlearned behaviors, to a more cognitive model emphasizing the person as thinker.

It is fascinating to note how self-researchers in the twentieth century have often selectively ignored much of James' advice, such that research has often addressed some minor parts of James' program extremely well

International Advances in Self Research, pages 127–148
Copyright © 2003 by Information Age Publishing
All rights of reproduction in any form reserved.

while ignoring some of the major issues. Researchers also have recast some of his critical questions and thus have led research down paths of finding excellent answers to wrong questions. This chapter addresses seven of James' major claims.

1. The core of the self: Self is the sum total of all that he or she CAN call his or hers.

James included in this sum total "not only his body and his physic powers, but his clothes and his house, his wife and children, his ancestors and friends, his reputation and works, his land and horses, and yacht and bank account." This notion of the "sum total" has led many to seek what is to be summed, as if self-concept is a summation of concepts, of nouns, or attributes. For example, Coopersmith (1967) proposed that the global self was some amalgam of the specific self-concepts. Such notions have led to the massive search for the various dimensions or components of self and in this we have been most successful.

This summation, however, has led us to ignore that self-concept is a process—it is NOT conceptions or set of beliefs about one's self, but a process of how we interpret these conceptions. We have listened too carefully to James and sought this inner core as a "sum total" and thus been led astray. Instead, we should be considering the core as a dynamic process involving appraisals, the processes of integration, the interrelations among the parts, and the way we select, bias and interpret that which is part of the "sum total." That is:

> Our self-concepts or conceptions of our self are cognitive appraisals, expressed in terms of descriptions, expectations and/or prescriptions, integrated across various dimensions that we attribute to ourselves. The integration is conducted primarily through self-testing or self-status quo tendencies. These attributes may be consistent or inconsistent depending on the type or amount of confirmation or disconfirmation our appraisals received from ourselves or from others. (Hattie, 1992)

The emphasis needs to be placed on the appraisals, as they are not merely "cognitive" processes, but they also involve values; our thoughts about our selves relate to value statements and these may be good or bad, rational or irrational, frustrating or not frustrating, adaptive or maladaptive, appropriate or inappropriate, reasonable or unreasonable, justified or unjustified. Our self-concepts involve constructions about how we construe the significance of an encounter for our well-being. As James (1890) so eloquently argued, we are less involved with making explanations and more often involved in making choices.

We have erroneously chosen to concentrate on the "sum total" aspect of James' work, whereas, we need to be more reliant on James' edicts to consider "man as a chooser." As James (1890) remarked,

> People can be viewed as continually attempting to impose some sort of order and coherence on the events in which they find themselves immersed. In order to survive we must extract some meaning from our experiences so that we can understand, anticipate, and, thus, exercise some control over life's experiences. We do this by making choices—choices about how to interpret events, choices among alternative courses of actions, (and) choices among evaluations of our actions. (p. 56)

These arguments place much emphasis on choice, decision making, and interpretation of the environments we find ourselves in and project ourselves into. The manner in which we do this, while maintaining or enhancing a conception of self, needs much more research. This also highlights the, often, post hoc place of self-concept. It may be less informative as explaining "Why" people do, think or act, but may be more important for a person to explain to themselves "Why" they did, think, or acted like that.

These remarks place attention on the person as an appraiser who makes decisions and choices on the basis of beliefs about his or her self. Using the vast literature in cognitive processing, it is most likely that individuals select, bias, and retain information, and we may do so differently from each other.

Hence, I would suggest that James' misled us in his claim that:

"Self is the sum total of all that he or she CAN call his or hers"

and could have more constructively claimed:

Self is the appraisal of all that which we choose to interpret as I.

There is more emphasis on the perpendicular pronoun and less on the self as a kind of separate collection of entities. This should lead us to research endeavours about "How do individuals make choices about what to value about themselves?"

2. The core or role of personal identity.

> All men must single out from the rest of what they call themselves some central principle of which each would recognize the foregoing to be a fair general description—for some the soul, for others nothing but a fiction the imaginary being denoted by the pronoun I, and many between.

> I have said all that need be said of the constituents of the phenomenal self, and of the nature of self-regard. Our decks are consequently cleared for the struggle with that pure principle of personal identity. (James, 1890)

There has been centuries of debate about the core of the person, the essence of self-identity, and thus the role that self-concept plays in the larger picture of the person. Mostly this debate has centred on finding the "core." Obviously this core can vary in terms of time, development, situation, mood, and purpose. Thus to think of a core as a single attribute is of little value and more difficult to defend: it grows, it changes, it adapts, and it reacts. We know so little about the development of this core, and to consider self without a reference to time and place is surely absurd. There is no immaculate perception, no universal generalization, and no single core entity. It is neither genetic nor environmental, it is thought about—by the person in a time and place.

Perhaps the research on self-concept has played too little attention to the place of self-concept in the greater picture of the person. It is interesting to note how the literature on self-concept during the latter part of the twentieth century seems to take place outside the realms of personality, from whence it grew post-James. It is time to place it back into that larger domain of the "person." Or more relevant, we need to consider self-concept not as a personality attribute, but rather as closer to various goal strivings (Emmons, 1986)—in that they are nomothetic, idiographic, and personalized motives. That is, the goals a person chooses are tied to the life tasks, such that we strive to attain these goals, which invoke various self-strivings, or seeking life tasks.

Thus, with respect to the Jamesian agenda, I suggest we reiterate the first part and ask what are the primary principles that various people use to consider the essence of self, rather than assume, as many of our models of self-concept and self-identity do, that there is an inner core.

> All persons must single out from the rest of what they call themselves some central principles of which each would recognize the foregoing to be a fair general description—for some the soul, for others nothing but a fiction the imaginary being denoted by the pronoun I, and many between. (James, 1890)

As to the second part, I would suggest we listen clearly to James—enough said of multidimensionality, and more said about personal identity, the values and cultural systems that impinge on personal identity, the way we reflect on ourselves, and the way we consider ourselves in time and place. We are but an arrow, defined in no one moment but are striving toward a target. We need a research agenda related to our strivings as they have more to say about how we reflect on our selves. Research is required on Self as part of the Identity, as part of Wellness As James claimed, we know all that need be said about the constituents of the self, and it is time to struggle with the principles of personal identity. Here I echo the Jamesian agenda—we have hardly started on these aspects.

I have said all that need be said of the constituents of the phenomenal self, and of the nature of self-regard. Our decks are consequently cleared for the struggle with that pure principle of personal identity. We know in subsequent reflection, as part of a stream of thought.

3. Self is multidimensional.

The constituents of the self may be divided into four classes, those which make up respectively: the material self, the social self, the spiritual self, the pure ego.

As noted above, James was quite clear about the constituents of the self. For example, he extensively discussed the material self (body, clothes, family, home, property we collect), the social self (recognition which he gets from his mates), the spiritual self, and the pure ego. It took a long time for researchers in the twentieth century to agree to this James' claim. But, particularly since Shavelson's and Marsh's work we now have a good map of these constituents. If anything we may have over-factored the constituents. It is possible to locate, for example: 18 dimensions of academic self-concept; 6 dimensions of music self-concept; 4 dimensions of arts self-concept; 1 dimensions of classroom self-concept; 2 dimensions of peers self-concept; 2 dimensions of family self-concept; 15 dimensions of physical self-concept; 3 dimensions of religious self-concept, and so on. Clearly, we can have a concept about anything and everything. Let me illustrate the problem with the over attention to the multidimensionality with an extreme case. For most of us our toes would not be considered part of our concept of self, although I could develop a scale for self-toeness:

1. I like my big toe
2. I am proud of my toes
3. I like to show off my toes to others
4. My toes are important to me
5. I could not bear to part with my toes.

Given that there would be high correlations between such items, it would be easy to show via factor analysis and reliability that there is a strong single factor (80% variance explained by the first factor, $AGFI > .95$, alpha < .80, $RMSEA < .05$, etc.), that it is discriminant from other aspects about my self, and that it correlates with other related dimensions (e.g., fingerness, eyeballness, and earness). Psychometrically wonderful, it would seem.

There are four major points illustrated by this example of self-concept of toeness. First, the specific dimensions must derive from a theoretical model of self-concept. Such a model needs to defend a series of dimensions and the relations between them. The alternative method of throwing together a bank of items and "seeing" what dimensions emerge is indefensible and so often has led to spurious dimensions of self (Hattie, 1992). If "self-concept of toeness" is a defensible aspect of a theoretical model then it should be present, well-measured, and related to appropriate outcomes etc.

Second, we need to consider the value, or importance of the dimensions—to what degree are these various dimensions of self important to the "core"? How do various and particular beliefs about this attribute of self become invoked when making decisions that affect the self? How salient are the conceptions when forming an overall concept of the self? And how important, or what value does the individual place, on toeness self-concept—no matter how well measured, differentiated, or developed? For most of us, toeness self-concept would have next to no salience whatsoever. I can imagine situations, however, when it does matter. For example, if you loose your toes, then toeness may become an important factor (or as Reinhold Meisner, the great mountaineer, said when asked about the effects of loosing his toes, "It makes me closer to the mountain").

Third, we have tended to over rely on surveys of self-reports to infer the various constituents of the self. As Bruner (1998) argued, a major problem with the concept of self-esteem "is the belief that individuals are aware of this quality; hence their answers to direct questions are assumed to be accurate" (p. 178). It is not clear that what people, especially children, claim in self-reports about self is necessarily related to how they conceive of conceptions about themselves. We know, for example, that adolescent boys who have no friends and are failing at school often vehemently deny the ascription of low self-esteem when asked via self-reports (Bruner, 1998). We know that adolescent males, certainly much more than girls, are far less likely to ascribe negative attributes preferring to emphasize the positive (Elliott, 1986, 1988; Roberts & Nolen-Hoeksema, 1989). We need more research on alternative ways to measure self-concept, than mainly relying on surveys via Likert scales.

Fourth, the underlying classical model of test theory underlies the development of most scales, and it is time to move on. The classical model has as desirable attributes high alpha, high factor loadings on the first factor, high discrimination between factors, as if there is something in the logic of validity that presumes high correlations. As an extreme, the perfect test consists of a series of items all measuring independent aspects of the behavior domain, in which case alpha = 0, and there can be no single factor. We need more conceptual clarity, and attention to salience and explanatory power of our dimensions before we seek, or claim, multiple dimensionalities. The newer developments of polytomous item response models could make major improvements in our measurement models (Fletcher & Hattie, 1998).

This is not to claim that self is not multidimensional. One of our successes of the late twentieth century is a firm, but not fully agreed, understanding of the constituents of the self. It is the relationships, the importance, and/or the appraisals of these constituents that are far more important that the constituents per se. James (and Shavelson and Marsh) have similarly made this very clear but too often we see researchers creating more scales, more dimensions, and ignoring the relations between them (and between them and other attributes). So, a rewrite of Jamesian prescription for the twenty-first century would be:

> The constituents of the self may be divided into many dimensions, and it is most important to understand how we (re-) assemble these dimensions into a conception of self.

4. Self is hierarchical.

> The aspects of the self are ordered in a hierarchical scale, with the bodily self at the bottom, the spiritual self at top, and the extracorperal material selves and the various social selves between.

This has been one of the more difficult aspects of James' claims to defend. Although James, and later Shavelson, Hubner, and Stanton (1976) claimed that the self was hierarchical, the research on this claim has been fleeting and not convincing. Too often, we have endeavoured to consider hierarchy to be bottom up or top down: Marsh and Shavelson (1985) and Byrne (1996) argued for a bottom-up model whereas Brown (1993) argued for a top-down model.

Herb Marsh and I have noted the confusion in the use of the term global self-concept and we (Marsh & Hattie, 1996) reviewed support for a variety of different ways in which this term can be operationalized which include:

- An agglomerate self-concept, a total score for a typically ill-defined collection of self-report items that has little theoretical rationale nor any basis for understanding how self-concept is formed or how it was related to other constructs, interventions, or life events.
- A weighted-average general self-concept that is a calculated weighted average of specific components of self-concept in which the weights are a function of the saliency, importance, centrality or other features of each component that is particular to the individual respondent. Despite a strong theoretical rationale and a substantial body of empirical research, there is surprisingly weak support for this operationalization, suggesting, perhaps, difficulties in operationalizing constructs such as saliency and importance.

- An actual-ideal discrepancy general self-concept in which general self is a calculated from differences between actual and ideal self-concepts in specific components. Again, despite a strong theoretical rational and intuitive basis, there is limited support for this approach, at least based on studies that actually construct general self-concept scores from separate ratings of actual and ideal self-concept in specific components.
- A hierarchical self-concept, a higher-order self-concept based on factor analysis (as in the Shavelson model). This operationalization refers to an inferred construct that is not measured directly, one that is an empirically weighted-average of the lower-order factors that are considered (e.g., a hierarchical self-concept derived from first-order academic self-concept factors must be a hierarchical academic self-concept).
- A global self-concept scale, a relatively unidimensional scale referring to generalized characteristics that are not specific to a particular domain (e.g., Overall, I have much to be proud of; In general I like the way I am; Overall I am no good). Such global self-concept scales are typically modeled on the widely-used instrument developed by Rosenberg (1979) and are sometimes referred to—albeit ambiguously—as self-esteem. A typical implicit assumption is that respondents base their responses on appropriately weighted self-perceptions in particular areas that take into account features such as their importance, saliency, certainty, and ideal standards. Hence, this approach is not inconsistent with weighted-average, discrepancy, and, perhaps, hierarchical approaches, but does not require the researcher to collect and empirically integrate information about specific components of self-concept.

It is also important to note that some researchers who accept the multidimensionality of self-concept do not necessarily assume that it is also a hierarchically ordered construct (e.g., Harter, 1985, 1986). Hattie (1992; Hattie & Marsh, 1996) also argued that the typical application of factor analysis implies that all people fit the model, whereas individuals may vary in the extent to which self-concept is hierarchically ordered and the relative weight assigned to different domains. Further, the hierarchical integration implied in the Shavelson model is based on a relatively static, structural model, whereas many researchers emphasize a more dynamic process model in which the self is a more active integrator of information and that the manner in which individuals process information about self may vary with processes such as self-consistency, self-enhancement, self-verification, and self-complexity (e.g., Linville, 1982; Markus & Sentis, 1982; Swan, Pelham, & Krull, 1989).

Marsh (2000) completed an innovative study on top-down versus bottom-up hierarchies, using structural equation models of multiwave multivariable models. He found that there was "clear and unambiguous support for the horizontal effects (stability) model and little or no support for the bottom-up, top-down, or reciprocal effects models." This is a major blow to the notion of a hierarchy. A more plausible model is the processing model, as expressed in Wittgenstein's maxim: "The strength of the fibre is not from any one strand but from the overlapping of many fibres." The overlapping of many conceptions of self can lead to a sense of "self", such that we do not wake up each morning and say, "Who am I." This conception does not need a flow up or down, but provides an integrating mechanism for considering self-concept.

The proposition is that there are various *processes of integration* that are used by individuals to achieve a notion of conceptions of self. The use of these processes varies across individuals. There is no need for the presumption that there need be one core, but that there can be many fibres as part of the unity. This is akin to the Jamesian notion of possible selves (see also Markus & Nurius, 1986; Oyserman & Markus, 1993; Rhodewalt, 1986; Rhodewalt & Agustsdottir, 1986). We need to look at the working, online, or accessible self-concepts. Not all conceptions of self will be accessible at any one time. Self-concept is continually active, and some conceptions are "tentative, fleeting and peripheral, others are highly elaborated and function as enduring, meaning-making, or interpretative structures that help individuals lend coherence to their own life experiences" (Oyserman & Markus, 1993, p. 191).

Most current research considers the higher-order conceptions of self-concept as some kind of amalgam of the lower-order concepts, whereas the converse may be the case. It may be that there are critical information-processing competencies that bias, select, and retain information and affectations about self, and these may be different depending on the situation, and on the sources of developing these biases (e.g., cultural and social sources). This is not claiming that individuals distort reality to maintain their self-images of being positive and effective people, as claimed by many (Dunning, Meyerowitz, & Holzberg, 1989; Taylor & Brown, 1988). The individual's perception of reality is a "reality," and the greater concern is the various ways in which individuals select, bias and retains information to maintain this "reality."

Hence, the claim is that we need to reorganize the James' claim to:

> The aspects of the self are interpreted by the individual in manners that can allow for various constituents to become more salient in the interpretations, understandings, and decision making of the person, depending on the deci-

sions, judgements, or interpretations to be made. The unity is thus more related to the processing strategies used than to the constituent parts.{\ex}

5. There are strategies of self.

The longest section of James' chapter on the self concerns the strategies that are used to process information about the self. These processes he recognized as:

- Self-complacency: pride, conceit, vanity, self-esteem, arrogance, vainglory;
- Self-dissatisfaction: modesty, humility, confusion, diffidence, shame, mortification, contrition's personal despair;
- Self-seeking: providing for the future, desire to please, to be recognized by others; and
- Self-preservation: maintaining the present.

This is the aspect of James that is among the least researched, but profitably could be a major focus of the next decade. An exciting research area relates to the many strategies that are used to maintain a concept of self, to enhance self-esteem, and to maintain self-respect. There is a long history of reviews demonstrating that we attribute success to ourselves for positive outcomes and blame others for negative outcomes (Bradely, 1978; Zuckerman, 1979). Snyder, Gangestad, and Simpson (1983) have discussed extensively the manner in which self-esteem can distort information-processing cognitions associated with the attribution of causality, and how we tend toward self-protective attributions especially when these performances are scrutinized by others.

It would be most useful to conduct further research on the various strategies that individuals use to cope with their environment, and beliefs and reactions to their world. Such strategies have been referred to by a variety of generic labels: self-serving biases (Riess, Rosenfield, Melburg, & Tedeschi, 1981; Marsh, 1986); need for approval (Crowne & Marlowe, 1964); self-monitoring (Snyder, 1987); self-deception (Sackheim, 1983), and self-enhancement and self-verification (Sherman, Judd, & Park, 1989; Swann, 1985; Swann, Pelham, & Krull, 1989). Martin (2003) has proposed a model that includes many self-strategies, such as self-sabotage, failure avoidance, low control, and anxiety.

Such strategies explain how individuals can bias, select and retain information that affects their self-concepts. It is likely that we all use the strategies to varying extents to provide predictability in our lives. For example, the various strategies may provide extra predictability as to what to do or how to react in new situations. This effect highlights the enormous difficulties in devising programs to change self-esteem. Daly and Burton (1983) reported high correlations between many irrational beliefs and low self-esteem, particularly problem avoidance, helplessness, high self-expectations, and demand for approval. They noted that individuals with irrational beliefs have a high need to be approved by others, a need to excel in all endeavours to feel worthwhile as a person, obsessive anxiety about possible calamities in the future, and the idea that it is better to avoid problems rather than to face them.

If I was rewriting James agenda, I would recognize:

- Self-enhancement: seeking positive or self-enhancing feedback;
- Self-verification: seeking accurate or self-verifying feedback; and
- Self-strategies: self-handicapping, discounting, distortion, social comparisons, goal setting, negative vigilante.

6. *Self-esteem is that which we back ourselves: I am often confronted by the necessary of standing by one of my empirical selves and relinquishing the rest.*

Yonder puny fellow, however, whom everyone can beat, suffers no chagrin about it, for he has long ago abandoned the attempt to "carry that line," as the merchants say, of self at all.

Self-feeling depends entirely on what we back ourselves to be and do. It is determined by the ratio of our actualities to our supposed potentialities: a fraction of which out pretensions are the denominators and the numerators our success: thus self-esteem = Success/Pretensions.

How pleasant is the day when we give up striving to be young—or slender! (James, 1890, p. 200)

So much has been written in the twentieth century about this notion of self-esteem = success/pretensions. James introduced a model of self in which specific self-concepts are integrated according to their importance, salience, certainty, and relationship to ideals. He argued that our self-worth "depends entirely on what we back ourselves to be and do" (p. 201), and thus global self-esteem was the ratio of one's successes to one's pretensions or aspirations toward success in the various domains of one's life: self-esteem = Success/Pretensions. Hence, we can increase self-esteem by diminishing the denominator or by increasing the numerator. James further argued that we arrange our various conceptions of self "in an hierarchical scale according to their worth" (p. 202). Over the past century since James' writings, we have been most successful measuring and understanding the numerator, know somewhat less about the denominator, and have had little success at putting the two together. This notion that we weight various conceptions of self to form an overall, or general self-worth has been one of the more enduring claims in the psychological literature.

During the subsequent 100 years this importance notion appeared many times. For example, Rosenberg (1979) invoked the notion of psychological centrality—self dimensions vary in the degree to which they are central or peripheral, cardinal or secondary, major or minor parts of self. Stryker and Serpe (1994) also emphasized psychological centrality, or what they termed identity salience, which they defined as a "readiness to act out an identity as a consequence of the identity's properties as a cognitive structure of schema."

There are many attempts to find models that encapture importance. Typically, regression models are used (Hoge & McCrathy, 1984; Pelham and Swan, 1989), and the typical finding has been that there was "little or no support for individually weighted averages" (Marsh, 1993, p. 989), as in no case did any of the weighted models perform much better than the simple unweighted average, and in most cases they performed much poorer. Pelham and Swann (1989) ended with the claim that, if "James were around today, I suspect that he might feel that it has been embarrassingly difficult for us to uncover support for one of his simplest psychological insights" (p. 1165).

If there is additional information to be found by including importance, it probably will be detected when more idiographic (person-level) rather than normative (group-referenced) methods are used, or for those self-concept dimensions that are less common such as religious self-concept, or music self-concept (Vispoel, 2000). In a series of analyses based on 7 different methods of seeking "importance" or centrality, Fletcher and Hattie (1998) failed to find support for this importance dimension.

It is probably much more interesting, as a research question to ask why those with low self-concepts often do not wish to realize this. Those with low self-worth may suffer a dual burden. Kruger and Dunning (1999) argued, in the intellectual domain, that the skills "that engender competence in a particular domain are often the very same skills necessary to evaluate competence in that domain." Thus, less competent individuals lack metacognition, or the ability to know how well one is performing, when one is likely to be accurate in judgement, and when one is likely to be error, and thus they hold inflated views of their performance and ability. One source of evidence they provide for this phenomenon is the "above-average effect," which is when individuals all claim to be above average. This effect is well documented in the self-concept literature (Baumeister, 1982; Dunning, Griffin, Milojkovic, & Ross, 1990; Vallone, Griffin, Lin, & Ross, 1990). Thus, those with low self-esteem are unlikely to "strongly disagree" with positive self-esteem items, partly because they do not recognize they have low self-esteem. This then could lead to a paradox that low self-esteem people have high self-esteem scores on typical questionnaires! We need to spend far more research time with people with low self-esteem to find more defensible methods for assessing their self-esteem more accurately (Crocker, 2002).

James may be correct when he claimed that we should allow for pretensions and success, although for most of us, we tend to have self-concept scores similar to our pretensions. He may have led subsequent research more effectively if he had claimed that self-esteem is less a function of our pretensions, and more a function of our successes and/or failures.

> Why is that "Yonder puny fellow, however, whom everyone can beat, suffers no chagrin about it? "
> Self-esteem = (Success or Failures) + Pretensions.
> What development factors lead to changes in salience, such as when we give up striving to be young—or slender!

7. Self relates to our reputation enhancement

> The Social self is the recognition, which we get from our mates. We have an innate propensity to get ourselves noticed, and noticed favorable, by our kind. No more fiendish punishment could be devised were such a thing physically possible, than that one should be turned loose in society and remain absolutely unnoticed by all the members thereof.

The power or impact of these statements has yet to be realized. Judith Harris' (1999) has certainly underlined the importance of the social self—especially for adolescents. Social self may become more powerful, not because we are fundamentally social animals (many of us are not), but because much of our information about ourselves comes from social circumstances. We are often in the presence of others and thus have to present our selves, and we build and test beliefs/concepts of who we are in social situations. This is particularly so for adolescents. A major topic of research is the way in which we bias, select and retrieve information from others, and how we similarly try to influence others in their conceptions of our selves.

We have developed an integrated model (Figure 6.1) based on the premise that adolescents experience and have access to many resources and opportunities, which can influence the types of self-goals they choose. For example, these resources include socioeconomic status, age, family, ethnicity, and gender. The two major types of self-goals are based on academic and/or social goals, and the social goals can be further divided into: conforming or nonconforming social goals. The choice of these academic, conforming social, and/or nonconforming social goals is critical in the orientation, development, and management of adolescents' peer reputations. These reputations are publicly displayed and maintained, deliberately chosen and promoted, and are more likely to be long- than short-term ori-

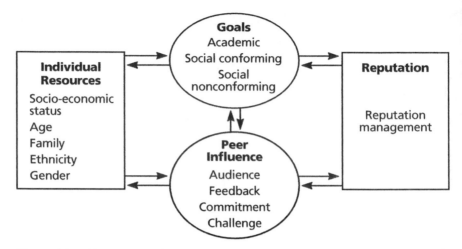

Figure 6.1.   The integrated model of reputation enhancing goals.

ented. Whereas goals can be defined as a generic concept encompassing the essential meanings of such terms as intention, task, purpose, aim, and objective, reputations are different from goals in that they can be conceived of as the outcome of goals, which have been set by individuals and achieved, in most cases, through high levels of commitment. Adolescents regulate their self-identity and self-presentation in ways such that others will perceive them in a certain desired manner. Adolescents who choose nonconforming social goals on which to base their reputations are those most likely to become delinquents (Carroll, Durkin, Houghton, & Hattie, 1996; Carroll, Durkin, Hattie, & Houghton, 1997; Carroll et al., 2001).

Adolescents use various regulating strategies to maintain their reputations, and these strategies include self-concept, social skills, moral reasoning, and future time perspective. A most powerful influence that informs both goal choice and peer reputation is the feedback received from peers. The degree of feedback about goals and reputations provides evidence to adolescents that their reputations are being recognized. The peer audience is extremely influential because friends often generate and facilitate expressions of shared behavioral inclinations (Emler, 1984). The ways in which adolescents visibly present themselves to their peers in their behavior and the values they express communicate a particular identity (Emler, 1984; Goffman, 1959). That is, adolescents may elect to be seen as conforming or nonconforming, respectable or delinquent, and thus choose to display behaviors, which are consistent with the desired reputation. We have conducted over a dozen studies identifying the importance of audience, challenge, commitment, and feedback, and the role of individuals' resources in the management of reputations.

If I were suggesting a rewrite of James, it would be more direct than he suggested:

> We choose to back our reputations in many and often specific ways. The Social self is the recognition, which we get from our mates. We have an innate propensity to get ourselves noticed, and noticed favorable, by our kind. No more fiendish punishment could be devised were such a thing physically possible, than that one should be turned loose in society and remain absolutely unnoticed by all the members thereof.

> "I, who for the time have staked my all on being a psychologist, am mortified if others know much more psychology than I. But I am contented to wallow in the grossest ignorance of Greek." (James, 1890, p. 310).

Our reputations become a major focus of how we interpret our selves, particularly during adolescence and early adulthood.

CONCLUSIONS

Loevinger (1976, p. 113) noted that "scientists are like lovers—they see reminders of their beloved everywhere." Too often our beloved fades with us, and this may be the destiny of the Jamesian agenda for self-concept. The research needs to move onto questions about the mechanisms of self—how do these conceptions of self manifest, impact on, and condition subsequent behaviors, and how do these behaviors manifest, impact on, and condition conceptions of self.

A useful question to ask ourselves every time we reach for the "self-concept" lens is whether the same or a different question would be asked if we left the term "self" out of the question. For example, rather than asking the relation between self-concept of mathematics and achievement we ask the relation between our conceptions of mathematics and achievement. Rather than asking about the development of self-concept of physical attributes, we ask about the development of conceptions of physical attributes. Per Wittgenstein, why do we invoke the concept of self, when it is a given. The question tends to imply that there is some "thing" called self, whereas there is nothing but a language game we involve ourselves in. This highlights the importance of Conceptions as actions rather than concepts as things; highlights the importance of having Conceptions and mis-Conceptions (we can not have mis-concepts), highlights the importance of understanding how we come to have these Conceptions and highlights how having Conceptions impact on knowing, behaving, and caring. I note, that this is one feature that we did not learn from James, as he never used the terms self-concept or self-esteem.

We know so little about the development of our conceptions, and too often we have assumed, in our choice of models, that these conceptions are "there," with no reference to time and place. There is no universal generalization, and no single core entity. It is neither genetic nor environmental, it is thinking about—by the person in a time and place. We are but an arrow defined in no one moment, but striving toward a target.

One of the major changes that James would note if he were present today is the sophistication of our methods. Within 10 years of James' writing we had the critical Spearman articles that spawned factor analysis and classical test theory. Now we have maximum likelihood methods and item response models. But we have not fully harnessed the power of these newer models. We need to move away from the classical test models, move away from a dependence on correlation toward using item response models, generalizability theory, and growth models to more fully understand change, more dependably devise assessments, and more successfully ask about variability across situations.

I am suggesting moving from the twentieth century debates led by the James dictums and asking about self as a strategy not self as a thing; as self as a component of well-being; self as an end in itself not self as a correlate; self as a dynamic and growing not self as static (see Table 6.1). We have the potential of being part of a defining moment in the history of self-concept research: are we going to continue with the old debates, or can we raise new debates that will help set the agenda for this new century in the same way that James did for the twentieth century.

Table 6.1. The James Agenda for the Twentieth and for the Twenty-first Century

No.	Core Notion	James' Claim	The Twenty-first Century Claim
1	The core of the Self	Self is the sum total of all that he or she can call his or hers	Self is the appraisal of all that which we choose to interpret as I
2	The role of personal identity	All men must single out from the rest of what they call themselves some central principle of which each would recognise the foregoing to be a fair general description—for some the soul, for others nothing but a fiction the imaginary being denoted by the pronoun I, and many between.	All persons must single out from the rest of what they call themselves some central *principles* of which each would recognise the foregoing to be a fair general description—for some the soul, for others nothing but a fiction the imaginary being denoted by the pronoun I, and many between.
		I have said all that need be said of the constituents of the phenomenal self, and of the nature of self-regard. Our decks are consequently cleared for the struggle with that pure principle of personal identity.	Self is a part of a person's wellness, and thus serves to a more encompassing sense of personal identity.
3	Self is multidimensional	The constituents of the self may be divided into four classes, those which make up respectively: the material self, the social self, the spiritual self, the pure ego.	The constituents of the self may be divided into many dimensions, and it is most important to understand how we (re-) assemble these dimensions into a conception of self.

143

Table 6.1. The James Agenda for the Twentieth and for the Twenty-first Century (Cont.)

No.	Core Notion	James' Claim	The Twenty-first Century Claim
4	Self is hierarchical	The aspects of the self are ordered in an hierarchical scale, with the bodily Self at the bottom, the spiritual Self at top, and the extracorperal material selves and the various social selves between	The strength of the fibre is not in any one strand but the overlapping of many fibres.
		• Material Self—body, clothes, family, home, property we collect	The aspects of the self are interpreted by the individual in a manner that can allow for various constituents to become more salient in the interpretations, understandings, and decision making, depending on the decision, judgement, or interpretations to be made. The unity is thus more related to the processing strategies used than to the constituent parts.
		• Social Self—we have as many social selves as there are distinct groups of persons about whose opinion we care.	
		• Spiritual Self—a man's inner or subjective being, his psychic faculties or dispositions, "to think ourselves as thinkers"	
5	There are strategies of self	Self-complacency: pride, conceit, vanity, self-esteem, arrogance, vainglory	Self-enhancement: seeking positive or self-enhancing feedback
		Self-dissatisfaction: modesty, humility, confusion, diffidence, shame, mortification, contrition's personal despair	Self-verification: seeking accurate or self-verifying feedback
		Self-seeking: providing for the future, desire to please, to be recognised by others	Self-strategies: self-handicapping, discounting, distortion, social comparisons, goal setting, negative vigilante
		Self-preservation: maintaining the present	

Table 6.1. The James Agenda for the Twentieth and for the Twenty-first Century (Cont.)

No.	Core Notion	James' Claim	The Twenty-first Century Claim
6	Self-esteem is that which we back ourselves	Yonder puny fellow, however, whom everyone can beat, suffers no chagrin about it, for he has long ago abandoned the attempt to "carry that line," as the merchants say, of self at all.	Why is that "Yonder puny fellow, however, whom everyone can beat, suffers no chagrin about it?"
		Self-feeling depends entirely on what we back ourselves to be and do. It is determined by the ratio of our actualities to our supposed potentialities: a fraction of which out pretensions are the denominators and the numerators our success: thus self-esteem = Success/Pretensions	Self-esteem = Success or Failures + Pretensions
		How pleasant is the day when we give up striving to be young—or slender!	What development factors lead to changes in salience, such as when we give up striving to be young—or slender!
7	Self relates to our reputation enhancement	The Social self is the recognition, which we get from our mates. We have an innate propensity to get ourselves noticed, and noticed favorable, by our kind. No more fiendish punishment could be devised were such a thing physically possible, than that one should be turned loose in society and remain absolutely unnoticed by all the members thereof	*We choose to back ourselves/reputation in many and often specific ways.* The Social self is the recognition which we get from our mates. We have an innate propensity to get ourselves noticed, and noticed favorable, by our kind. No more fiendish punishment could be devised were such a thing physically possible, than that one should be turned loose in society and remain absolutely unnoticed by all the members thereof
			I, who for the time have staked my all on being a psychologist, am mortified if others know much more psychology than I. But I am contented to wallow in the grossest ignorance of Greek (James, 1890, p. 310) *Our reputations become a major focus of how interpret our selves, particularly during adolescence and early adulthood.*

REFERENCES

Baumeister, R. F. (1982). A self-presentational view of social phenomena. *Psychological Bulletin, 91*, 3–16.

Bradely, G. W. (1978). Self-serving biases in the attribution process: A re-examination of the fact or fiction question. *Journal of Personality and Social Psychology, 36*, 56–71.

Brown, J. D. (1993). Self-esteem and self-evaluation: Feeling is believing. In J. Suls (Ed.), *Psychological perspectives on the self* (Vol. 4, pp. 27–58). Hillsdale, NJ: Erlbaum.

Bruner, J. (1998). *Three seductive ideas.* Cambridge, MA: Harvard University Press.

Byrne, B (1996). *Measuring self-concept across the lifespan. Methodological issues and selected instrumentation.* Washington, DC: American Psychological Association.

Carroll, A., Durkin, K., Hattie, J., & Houghton, S. (1997). Goal setting among adolescents: A comparison of delinquent, at-risk, and not at-risk youth. *Journal of Educational Psychology, 89*(3), 441–450.

Carroll, A., Durkin, K., Houghton, S., & Hattie, J. (1996). An adaptation of Mak's Self-Reported Delinquency Scale for Australian Adolescents. *Australian Journal of Psychology, 48*(1), 1–7.

Carroll, A., Hattie, J., Durkin, K., & Houghton, S. (2001). Goal-setting and reputation enhancement: Behavioural choices among delinquent, at-risk, and not at-risk adolescents. *Legal and Criminological Psychology, 6*(2), 165–184.

Coopersmith, S. (1967). *The antecedents of self-esteem.* San Francisco: Freeman.

Crocker, J. (2002) The costs of seeking self-esteem. *Journal of Social Issues, 58*(3), 597–615.

Crowne, D., & Marlowe, D. (1964). *The approval motive.* New York: Wiley.

Daly, M. J., & Burton, R. C. (1983). Self-esteem and irrational beliefs: An exploratory investigation with implications for counseling. *Journal of Counseling Psychology, 30*, 361–366.

Dunning, D., Griffin, D. W., Milojkovic, J. D., & Ross, L. (1990). The overconfidence effect in social prediction. *Journal of Personality and Social Psychology, 58*, 568–581.

Dunning, D., Meyerowitz, J. A., & Holzberg, A. D. (1989). Ambiguity and self-evaluation: The role of idiosyncratic definitions in self-serving assessments of ability. *Journal of Personality and Social Psychology, 57*, 1082–1090.

Elliott, G. C. (1986). Self-esteem and self-consistency: A theoretical and empirical link between two primary motivations. *Social Psychology Quarterly, 49*, 207–218.

Elliott, G. C. (1988). Gender differences in self-consistency: Evidence from an investigation of self-concept structure. *Journal of Youth and Adolescence, 17*, 41–57.

Emler, N. (1984). Differential involvement in delinquency: Toward an interpretation in terms of reputation management. In B. A. Maher & W. B. Maher (Eds.), *Progress in experimental personality research* (Vol. 13, pp. 173–237). New York: Academic Press.

Emmons, R. A. (1986). Personal strivings: An approach to personality and subjective well-being. *Journal of Personality and Social Psychology, 51*(5), 1058–1068.

Fletcher, R., & Hattie, J. A. (1998). *Gender differences in physical self-concept: A multidimensional differential item functioning analysis.* Paper presented at the First Biennial

International SELF Conference, Sydney, Australia. [http://edweb.uws.edu.au/self/conferences/2000_Proceedings.pdf]

Goffman, E. (1959). *The presentation of self in everyday life.* New York: Doubleday.

Harris, J. R. (1999). *The nurture assumption: Why children turn out the way they do.* New York: Touchstone.

Harter, S. (1985). *Competence as a dimension of self-evaluation: Toward a comprehensive model of self-worth.* In R. L. Leahy (Ed.), *The development of the self* (pp. 55–122). Orlando, FL: Academic Press.

Harter, S. (1996). Processes underlying the construction, maintenance, and enhancement of the self-concept in children. In J. Suls & A. G. Greenwald (Eds.), *Psychological perspectives on the self* (Vol. 3). Hillsdale, NJ: Erlbaum.

Hattie, J. A. (1992). *Self-concept.* Hillsdale, NJ: Erlbaum.

Hattie, J. A., & Marsh, H. W. (1996). The future of self-concept. In B. A. Bracken (Ed.), *Handbook of self-concept* (pp. 222–254). New York: Wiley.

Hoge, D. R., & McCarthy, J.D. (1984). Influence of individual and group identity salience in the global self-esteem of youth. *Journal of Personality and Social Psychology, 47,* 403–414.

James, W. (1890/1963). *The principles of psychology.* New York: Holt, Rinehart and Winston.

James, W. (1892). *Psychology: A briefer course.* London: McMillan.

Kruger, J., & Dunning, D. (1999). Unskilled and unaware of it: How difficulties in recognizing one's own incompetence lead to inflated self-assessments. *Journal of Personality and Social Psychology, 77,* 1121–1134.

Linville, P. W. (1902). Affective consequences of complexity regarding the self and others. In M. S. Clark & S. T. Fiske (Eds.), *Affect and cognition: The seventeenth annual Carnegie Symposium on Cognition* (pp. 79–109). Hillsdale, NJ: Erlbaum.

Loevinger, J. (1976). *Ego development: Concepts and theories.* San Francisco: Jossey-Bass.

Markus, H., & Nurius, P. (1986). Possible selves. *American Psychologist, 41,* 954–969.

Markus, H., & Sentis, K. (1982). The self in social information processing. In J. Suls (Ed.), *Psychological perspectives on the self* (Vol. 1, pp. 41–70). Hillsdale, NJ: Erlbaum.

Marsh, H. W. (1986). Verbal and math self-concepts: An internal/external frame of reference model. *American Educational Research Journal, 23,* 129–149.

Marsh, H. W. (1993). Relations between global and specific domains of self: The importance of individual importance, certainty, and ideals. *Journal of Personality and Social Psychology, 65,* 975–992.

Marsh, H. W. (2000). *Swimming in the school: Expanding the scope of the big fish little pond effect.* Paper presented at the First Biennial International SELF Conference, Sydney, Australia. [http://edweb.uws.edu.au/self/conferences/2000_Proceedings.pdf]

Marsh, H. W., & Hattie, J. (1996). Theoretical perspectives on the structure of self-concept. In B. A. Bracken (Ed.), *Handbook of self-concept* (pp. 38–90). New York: Wiley.

Marsh, H. W., & Shavelson, R. J. (1985). Self-concept: Its multifaceted, hierarchical structure. *Educational Psychologist, 20,* 107–125.

Martin, A. (2003) *Refining a model of student motivation: Boosters, guzzlers—and mufflers.* Manuscript in review.

Oyserman, D., & Markus, H. R., (1993). The sociocultural self. In J. Suls (Ed.), *Psychological perspectives on the self* (Vol. 4, pp. 187–220). Hillsdale, NJ: Erlbaum.

Pelham, B.W. (1995). Further evidence for a Jamesian model of self-worth: Reply to Marsh (1995). *Journal of Personality & Social Psychology. Vol. 69*(6), 1161–1165.

Pelham, B. W., & Swann, W. B. (1989). From self-conceptions to self-worth: On the sources and structure of global self-esteem. *Journal of Personality and Social Psychology, 57,* 672–680.

Rhodewalt, F. (1986). Self-presentation and the phenomenal self: On the stability and malleability of self-conceptions. In R. Baumeister (Ed.), *Private and public selves.* New York: Springer-Verlag.

Rhodewalt, F., & Agustsdottir, S. (1986). Effects of personality. *Journal of Personality and Social Psychology, 50,* 47–55.

Riess, M., Rosenfield, P., Melburg, B., & Tedeschi, J. T. (1981). Self-serving attributions: Biased private perceptions and distorted public descriptions. *Journal of Personality and Social Psychology, 41,* 224–231.

Roberts, T., & Nolen-Hoeksema, S. (1989). Sex differences in reactions to evaluative feedback. *Sex Roles, 21,* 725–747.

Rosenberg, M. (1979). *Conceiving the self.* New York: Basic Books.

Sackheim, H. A. (1983). Self-deception, self-esteem, and depression: The adaptive value of lying to oneself. In J. Masling (Ed.), *Empirical studies in emotional disorder and psychotherapy* (pp. 51–83). New York: Plenum.

Shavelson, R. J., Hubner, J. J., & Stanton, G. C. (1976). Self-concept: Validation of construct interpretations. *Review of Educational Research, 46,* 407–441.

Sherman, S. J., Judd, C. M., & Park, B. (1989). Social cognition. *Annual Review of Psychology, 40,* 281–326.

Snyder, M. (1987). *Public appearances/private realities.* New York: Freeman.

Snyder, M., Gangestad, S., & Simpson, J. A. (1983). Choosing friends as activity partners: The role of self-monitoring. *Journal of Personality and Social Psychology, 45,* 1061–1072.

Stryker, S., & & Serpe, R. T. (1994). Identity salience and psychological centrality—equivalent, overlapping, or complementary concepts. *Sociological Psychology Quarterly, 57*(1), 16–35.

Swann, W. B. (1985). The self as architect of social reality. In B. Schlenker (Ed.), *The self and social life* (pp. 100–125). New York: McGraw-Hill.

Swann, W. B., Pelham, B. W., & Krull, D. S. (1989). Agreeable fancy of disagreeable truth? Reconciling self-enhancement and self-verification. *Journal of Personality and Social Psychology, 57,* 782–791.

Taylor, S. E., & Brown, J. D. (1988). Illusion and well-being: A social psychological perspective on mental health. *Psychological Bulletin, 103,* 193–210.

Vallone, R. P., Griffin, D. W., Lin, S., & Ross, L. (1990). Overconfident prediction of future actions and outcomes by self and others. *Journal of Personality and Social Psychology, 58,* 582–592.

Vispoel, W. (2000). *Music self-concept: Instrumentation, structure, and theoretical linkages.* Paper presented at the First Biennial International SELF Conference, Sydney, Australia. [http://edweb.uws.edu.au/self/conferences/2000_Proceedings.pdf]

Zuckerman, M. (1979). Attribution of success and failure revisited, or: The motivational bias is alive and well in attribution theory. *Journal of Personality, 47,* 245–287.

part III

MEASUREMENT ISSUES

CHAPTER 7

MEASURING AND UNDERSTANDING SELF-PERCEPTIONS OF MUSICAL ABILITY

Walter P. Vispoel

Self-concept is one of the most enduring and widely researched constructs in education and psychology largely due to the intuitive appeal of notions that positive self-regard is desirable in and of itself and facilitative of other constructive behaviors. Over the last two decades, self-concept theory and instrumentation has expanded into many content domains due in part to an increased focus on self-concept as a multidimensional construct. In this chapter, I discuss recent developments in measuring and understanding self-perceptions of musical ability. As you read the material to follow, you will discover that my views about music self-concept are deeply rooted in my personal experiences as a musician, learner, and researcher. Before I pursued doctoral studies in educational psychology and quantitative methods, I worked for several years as a professional musician. Self-concept theory in general and specifically within the music domain were of great interest to me then and now, because perceptions of my skills in music influenced not only my decision to pursue a career outside of music but also how I felt about myself in general.

International Advances in Self Research, pages 151–179

The Shavelson, Hubner, and Stanton Model of Self-Concept

When I first began to study self-concept, the research literature emphasized a global or unidimensional conceptualization of self-concept, and the most popular assessment measures available at that time such as the *Self-Esteem Inventory* (Coopersmith, 1967), *Piers Harris Children's Self-Concept Scale* (Piers, 1969), and the *Self-Esteem Scale* (Rosenberg, 1965) each yielded a total self-concept score consistent with that view.[1] Gradually, this perspective gave way to theories that placed greater emphasis on the multifaceted nature of self-concept. Of particular importance to me was the work of Shavelson, Hubner, and Stanton (1976), who posited a comprehensive multidimensional model of self-concept that has provided the theoretical framework for much research into self-concept conducted over the last two decades. In that model, self-concept was described as multifaceted, hierarchically structured, and differentiated from other psychological constructs. Further, self-concept was assumed to have both descriptive and evaluative aspects, and global components of it (e.g., academic self-concept) were more stable than specific components (e.g., reading self-concept). Although Shavelson and colleagues did not delineate the specific number, nature, and organization of facets of self-concept; they did propose one possible hierarchical model to guide further research. Within that hierarchy, general self-concept was at the highest level and divided into academic and nonacademic self-concepts at the next level. Academic self-concept in turn was divided into self-concepts in specific content areas (math, science, etc.), whereas nonacademic self-concept was divided into physical (ability and appearance), social (peer and significant other relations), and emotional self-concepts. Further subdivisions of these more specific aspects of self-concept were also hypothesized with components of self-concept becoming increasingly targeted to particular behaviors as one descended the hierarchy.

The Role of Domain Importance in Self-Concept Models

One of the limitations of hierarchical models like the one suggested by Shavelson and colleagues (1976) is that they do not take into account personal and contextual factors that might affect relations between global and specific facets of self-concept. In essence, such models assume that relationships between domain-specific self-concepts (perceptions of math skills, social skills, etc.) and global self-esteem are the same for all individuals. Challenges to such fixed relationships have long been made by self-concept theorists and researchers (see, e.g., Harter, 1986a, 1989; Hattie, 1992; Hoge & McCarthy, 1984; James, 1890/1963; Marsh, 1986, 1993; Marsh & Hattie,

1996; Rosenberg, 1965, 1979; Wylie, 1974). William James (1890/1963), for example, argued that self-appraisals in domains of great personal importance should have a greater impact on overall self-esteem than self-appraisals in domains of irrelevance or unimportance. To quote James:

> I, who for the time have staked my all on being a psychologist, am mortified if others know more psychology than I. But I am contented to wallow in the grossest ignorance of Greek. My deficiencies there give me no sense of personal humiliation at all. Had I "pretensions" to be a linguist, it would have been just the reverse. (p. 310)

Applying James' ideas to music, we would expect a strong relationship between music self concept and self-esteem for individuals who value skill in music, but little relationship between those variables for other individuals.

The perspectives of Shavelson and colleagues (1976), James (1890/1963) and others (e.g., Harter 1986a; Marsh, 1986, 1987) have greatly influenced my thinking about music self-concept. Multifaceted conceptualizations of self-concept within and outside of music are intuitively appealing to me as is the notion that importance affects relations between music self-concept and overall self-esteem. My self-esteem, for example, suffered when I made the difficult decision to end my career as a professional full-time musician. I believe these feelings arose in part because music remained important to me, but I had my doubts about being able to sustain a viable living at it over the long haul. These and other personal experiences provided much of the impetus to pursue research into music self-concept when I became a college professor at the University of Iowa.

When I began to study music self-concept, I adopted a theoretical framework based heavily on the ideas of Shavelson and James (see Vispoel, 1994 for further details). I defined music-concept as self-perceptions of competence in music formed through experiences with the environment and interpretations of those experiences and noted that such self-perceptions are influenced in part by evaluations from others, reinforcements, and causal beliefs about one's performance and accomplishments in music. I also conceptualized music self-concept as organized, multifaceted, hierarchically structured, and distinct from other psychological constructs and hypothesized that the relationships between music self-concept and overall self-esteem would be affected by factors such as the importance ascribed to being highly skilled at music. In the sections to follow, I synthesize some of the research I have done based on this theory of music self-concept. In doing so, I will discuss the measurement of music self-concept, the relations between music self-concept and other facets of self-concept, and how some of these relations are affected by the importance ascribed to being

highly skilled in music. I end the chapter with general conclusions and suggestions for further research into music self-concept.

INITIAL STUDIES INTO THE MEASUREMENT AND
STRUCTURE OF ARTISTIC ASPECTS OF SELF-CONCEPT

Instruments for Measuring Artistic and Music Self-Concepts

When researchers started to emphasize multidimensional over unidimensional models of self-concept, the need arose for new assessment measures. Over recent years, Herbert Marsh has taken the lead in building
psychometrically sound instruments closely aligned with newer multidimensional models of self-concept. The most extensively researched instruments of this type are the Self-Descriptive Questionnaires (SDQ)—an age-
graded series of inventories designed to measure many components of self-
concept posited in the original Shavelson and colleagues (1976) model
(Marsh, 1992a, 1992b, 1992c). Each of the three age levels of the SDQ have
undergone extensive validation research focusing on exploratory and confirmatory factor analysis of item responses, changes in scores over time,
effects of interventions on scores, multitrait-multimethod analysis of scores
across different self-concept measures, and convergent and discriminant
validity analysis of scores with hosts of external criterion measures. Overall,
these results have been highly consistent with the purported nature of the
constructs these inventories are designed to measure. In her recent review
of validity evidence for each SDQ instrument, for example, Byrne (1996,
pp. 117, 153, 207) concluded that researchers, clinicians, counselors and
others could be confident in the validity of score interpretations made
from these multidimensional instruments.

When beginning my research into music self-concept, I used the SDQ
instruments as models in building my own measures designed to assess
important aspects of artistic self-concept. Prior to building these instruments, I had surveyed the relevant research literature and discovered that
most available measures of artistic self-concept either had psychometric
deficiencies or were out of step with contemporary models of self-concept
(see Vispoel, 1994). To address these problems, I decided to build a new
set of inventories intended to measure self-perceptions of artistic abilities
at both general and specific levels. To date, I have constructed two forms
(adolescent and adult/college) of two inventories: the *Arts Self-Perception
Inventory* (ASPI; Vispoel, 1992a, 1992b, 1993a, 1996; Vispoel, Wang, Bleiler,
& Tzou, 1993) and the *Music Self-Perception Inventory* (MUSPI; Vispoel,
1993b, 1993c, 1994).

The ASPI instruments each have four subscales to assess the self-perceptions of overall skill in music, visual art, dance, and dramatic art. These subscales are targeted at a level of generality similar to that of the General School Ability and Physical Ability subscales from Marsh's Self-Description Questionnaires (Marsh, 1992a, 1992b, 1992c) and the Scholastic Competence and Athletic Competence subscales from Harter's Self-Perception Inventories (Harter, 1985, 1986b; Messer & Harter, 1986; Neemann & Harter, 1986). The MUSPI instruments focus exclusively on skills in the music domain but at both general and specific levels. Each MUSPI instrument has one subscale similar to the ASPI's Music scale that assesses perceptions of overall music ability, and six additional subscales that assess perceptions of skill in the subdomains of singing, instrument playing, reading music, composing, listening, and moving to music. Construct validation research for the ASPI and MUSPI instruments has yielded very encouraging results: (a) The internal four-factor structure of the ASPI instruments and seven factor structure of the MUSPI instruments have been supported in confirmatory factor analyses, (b) subscale scores for both instruments have yielded high reliability estimates with alpha coefficients ranging from .92 to .98 and test-retest reliability coefficient in the .80s and .90s over one to four month time intervals, (c) subscale scores for both instruments have reliably separated individuals with noteworthy accomplishments and high achievement in each targeted artistic domain from other individuals, and (d) correlations of subscale scores with external criterion measures have formed logical patterns of relations consistent with the constructs measured by each instrument.

Integrating Artistic and Music Self-Concepts into the Shavelson and Colleagues Model

One of the first important research questions I investigated using the ASPI instruments was how artistic self-concept might be integrated into the Shavelson and colleagues (1976) self-concept hierarchy. Research by Marsh and Shavelson (1985) and Marsh (1987) involving the SDQ-1 and SDQ-3 led to two changes in the original hierarchy proposed by Shavelson and colleagues: (a) academic self-concept was represented better by two general factors (math-academic and verbal-academic) and (b) components of physical (appearance and ability) and social self-concept (same-sex, opposite-sex, and parental relations) did not separate well into distinct higher order factors. Marsh (1987) also found that the self-concept hierarchies he investigated did not account for the majority of variance in many lower-order components of self-concept, implying that facets of self-concept are by and large more distinct from each other than similar.

In my investigations of self-concept hierarchies, I sought to replicate Marsh's findings and extend the analyses to hierarchies that encompassed the four facets of self-concept measured by the ASPI instruments. My main goal was to find the best way to integrate components of artistic self-concept into a self-concept hierarchy. I pursued this question in two investigations, one involving 595 junior high school students who completed the SDQ-2 and the adolescent form of the ASPI (see Vispoel, Brunsman, & Bleiler, 1995), and the other involving 831 college students who completed the SDQ-3 and Adult form of the ASPI (see Vispoel, 1995a). In a preliminary analysis in each study, item clusters from the SDQ and ASPI instruments were subjected to confirmatory factor analysis, and the results provided strong evidence of the distinctiveness of all constructs measured (TLI = .954 & RNI = .961 for junior high; TLI = .935 & RNI = .944 for college). The correlations among factors from these analyses and alpha-reliability estimates for the SDQ/ASPI subscales appear in Tables 7.1 and 7.2 for junior high school and college students respectively. These tables reveal that components of self-concept were measured with high consistency (alpha coefficients ranged from .84 to .94, mdn = .90 for junior high and from .77 to .96, mdn = .92 for college). In addition, components of artistic self-concept were generally more strongly correlated with each other (median r = .32 for junior high and median r = .34 for college) than with non-artistic facets of self-concept (median r = .24 for junior high and median r = .11 for college).

The main research questions in both studies were addressed using hierarchical confirmatory factor analyses. Such analyses are valuable for evaluating the structure of self-concept for the several reasons: (a) Alternative models of the structure of self-concept can be compared, (b) hypothetical constructs can be examined at both superordinate and subordinate levels, (c) relationships among constructs are corrected for measurement error, and (d) indices can de derived for testing model fit, and for estimating the magnitude and direction of relationships among constructs as well as the proportion of systematic variance in each self-concept factor that is unaccounted for by higher order factors in a model. A wide variety of hierarchical models were examined in both studies.

Comparisons of these models revealed that the best way to integrate components of artistic self-concept into the Shavelson and colleagues (1976) model was as a higher order artistic self-concept distinct from the other higher order academic and nonacademic factors identified in previous investigations. The results also replicated Marsh's findings that higher order physical and social self-concept factors were not clearly separated, that academic self-concept was represented better by two higher order factors

Table 7.1. Alpha Coefficients and Correlations among SDQ-2/ASDQ First-Order Factors for Junior High Students (*n* = 595)

	1	2	3	4	5	6	7	8	9	10	11	12	13	14	15
1 General School Ability	**.90**														
2 Math Skill	.59	**.93**													
3 Verbal Skill	.62	.15	**.87**												
4 Physical Ability	.29	.22	.11	**.89**											
5 Physical Appearance	.44	.21	.26	.36	**.91**										
6 Same-sex Relations	.36	.14	.24	.33	.47	**.85**									
7 Opposite-sex Relations	.20	.04	.09	.37	.56	.55	**.91**								
8 Parent Relations	.49	.24	.29	.31	.43	.33	.18	**.89**							
9 Honesty	.47	.33	.41	.13	.18	.28	-.03	.50	**.85**						
10 Emotional Stability	.40	.27	.21	.25	.49	.38	.31	.46	.32	**.87**					
11 Music Skill	.44	.21	.45	.07	.27	.26	.15	.24	.30	.24	**.94**				
12 Visual Art Skill	.29	.21	.29	.21	.33	.13	.14	.24	.24	.23	.32	**.95**			
13 Dance Skill	.14	.05	.18	.10	.24	.25	.28	.07	.13	.06	.27	.23	**.94**		
14 Drama Skill	.30	.14	.39	.15	.32	.26	.32	.14	.16	.18	.40	.31	.38	**.93**	
15 Self-Esteem	.78	.41	.50	.41	.70	.51	.37	.65	.44	.61	.41	.32	.16	.28	**.87**

Note: Diagonal entries are the alpha coefficients for the original subscales. Other entries are correlations among factors from a confirmatory factor analysis.

Table 7.2. Alpha Coefficients and Correlations among SDQ-3/ASPI First-Order Factors for College Students (n = 831)

	1	2	3	4	5	6	7	8	9	10	11	12	13	14	15	16	17
1 Math Skill	.96																
2 Verbal Skill	.03	.86															
3 General School Ability	.36	.67	.90														
4 Problem. Solving.	.36	.56	.60	.84													
5 Physical. Ability.	.19	.03	.09	.16	.96												
6 Physical. Appearance.	.14	.24	.27	.36	.39	.91											
7 Same Sex Relations.	.09	.25	.24	.25	.35	.36	.88										
8 Opposite-sex Relations	.09	.24	.16	.34	.28	.52	.46	.91									
9 Parent Relations	.06	.02	.08	-.01	.25	.21	.37	.20	.91								
10 Spiritual. Values.	.04	.03	.11	.01	.07	.07	.19	.05	.19	.95							
11 Honesty	.11	.34	.40	.20	.01	.14	.21	.13	.28	.22	.77						
12 Emotional Stab.	.18	.28	.31	.30	.28	.44	.39	.40	.28	.04	.25	.90					
13 Dance Skill	-.01	.11	.09	.11	.27	.37	.24	.35	.10	.13	.12	.14	.96				
14 Dramatic Art Skill	-.01	.25	.16	.37	.11	.18	.08	.16	.00	.12	.07	.07	.36	.95			
15 Visual Art Skill	-.02	.15	.12	.28	.09	.18	.01	.07	.06	.04	.06	.04	.26	.38	.96		
16 Music Skill	.07	.22	.22	.21	.01	.15	.11	.16	.08	.18	.13	.12	.33	.35	.29	.96	
17 Self-Esteem.	.23	.33	.38	.44	.32	.70	.50	.56	.36	.14	.25	.68	.26	.22	.12	.17	.95

Note: Diagonal entries are the alpha coefficients for the original subscales. Other entries are correlations among factors from a confirmatory factor analysis.

factors (verbal-academic and math-academic) and that much of the variance in specific facets of self-concept was unaccounted for by higher order factors in all models tested.

Figures 7.1 and 7.2 show the results for a third-order factor model that incorporates a higher order artistic self-concept factor and the changes to the Shavelson and colleagues (1976) model suggested in prior studies by Marsh and Shavelson (1985) and Marsh (1987). The same general model is depicted at both age levels but there are two fewer first-order factors in the junior high school analysis because the SDQ-2 does not include Problem-Solving and Spiritual Values subscale. Honesty and Spiritual Values factors were logically linked together to form a higher order moral self-concept order in Marsh's (1987) study, and they appear that way in Figure 7.2. Such a linkage could not be made at the junior high level due to the absence of the Spiritual Values subscale. In both figures, the Self-Esteem and Emotional Stability first order factors are linked directly to the superordinate General Self-Concept factor and the first-order General School Ability factor is linked to both verbal and math higher order factors. The

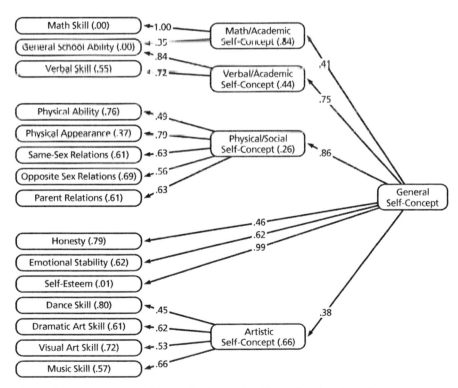

Figure 7.1.   Self-concept hierarchy for junior high school students integrating aspects of artistic self-concept.

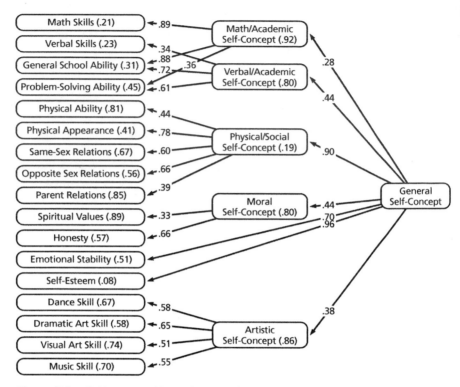

Figure 7.2.   Self-concept hierarchy for college school students integrating aspects of artistic self-concept

values in the ovals for the self-concept facets in Figures 7.1 and 7.2 are residual variance terms, representing the proportion of systematic variance unaccounted for by higher order factors in the model. The values embedded in the lines between facets are standardized regression coefficients (i.e., beta weights). These beta coefficients are identical to correlation coefficients for all paths depicting bivariate relationships.

The hierarchies for junior high and college students shown in Figures 7.1 and 7.2 have many similarities. In both age groups, there was a very strong relationship between the first-order self-esteem factor and the third-order general self-concept factor, suggesting that the SDQ Self-Esteem scale is a reasonable proxy for the general self-concept factor in the models tested here[2]. In addition, general self-concept was highly correlated with physical/social and emotional self-concepts (r_s = .86 and .62 for junior high and r_s = .90 and .70 for college), but most of the variance in specific components of self-concept was unaccounted for by more general components (see the residual terms in the figures). The major difference in the results across age groups was that math-academic, verbal-academic and artistic self-concepts were more strongly correlated with general self-concept at the junior high level (r_s = .41, .75, & .59) than at the college level (r_s = .28, .44 & .38).

The most important finding from these two studies was that components of artistic self-concept formed a distinct general factor in the self-concept hierarchy. However, this general factor was weak in the sense that it failed to account for the majority of variance in music, visual art, dance, and dramatic art self-concepts. These results indicate that self-perceptions of skill in different artistic domains overlap, but they are more distinct than similar. Such findings highlight the importance of measuring self-concept separately in each artistic area rather than inferring them from perceptions of general skill in the arts.

The Multifaceted, Hierarchical Structure of Music Self-Concept

In my next set of studies into the structure of self-concept, I focused exclusively on the music domain and again conducted separate analyses for junior high school (n = 531) and college students (n = 337). My goal was to evaluate the overlap and distinctiveness of self-perceptions of skill in the subdomains of music measured by the MUSPI (instrument playing, reading music, listening, composing, singing, moving to music, and overall music ability). I also explored possible ways of representing the relations among these skill areas with different higher order factor models. In a preliminary analysis within each age group, item clusters from the MUSPI subscales were subjected to confirmatory factor analysis, and the results once again provided compelling evidence supporting the distinctiveness of all constructs measured (TLI = .935 and RNI = .948 for junior high; TLI = .967 and RNI = .974 for college). The correlations among factors from these analyses and alpha-reliability estimates for the MUSPI subscales appear in Table 7.3.

The table shows that all facets of music self-concept were measured with very high consistency (alpha coefficients ranged from .95 to .96 for junior high and from .96 to .98 for college) and correlations among components of music self-concept varied from low to high (.09 to .92) depending on the constructs measured. Overall, however, the correlations among the factors represented by the MUSPI (median r = .56) are much higher on average than those observed among factors measured by the SDQ (median r = .28) and ASPI (median r = .33) in my prior studies.

The main analyses in the MUSPI self-concept structure studies focused on a series of hierarchical confirmatory factor analysis models. Figures 7.3 and 7.4 show results for two of the hierarchical models tested—a simple

Table 7.3.   Alpha Coefficients and Correlations among MUSPI First-Order Factors for Junior High School (*n* = 531) and College Students (*n* = 337)

	Overall Music Ability (OMA)	Instrument Playing (INST)	Reading Music (RM)	Listening (LIS)	Composing (COMP)	Singing (SING)	Moving to Music (MOVE)
OMA	.97/.95	.86	.87	.80	.70	.54	.34
INST	.80	.97/.96	.86	.68	.66	.30	.23
RM	.75	.92	.98/.96	.75	.63	.38	.17
LIS	.73	.62	.62	.97/.95	.74	.47	.26
COMP	.66	.60	.55	.70	.96/.95	.45	.39
SING	.62	.43	.44	.55	.56	.98/.96	.46
MOVE	.39	.11	.09	.23	.27	.28	.98/.96

Note: Diagonal entries represent alpha reliability coefficients; off-diagonal entries represent correlations among factors. Boldface values are for junior high school students: nonboldface values are for college students.

model with one general music self-concept factor (Figure 7.3), and a more complex model with one third-order factor (general music self-concept) and two second-order factors (instrumental performance and auditory cognition; Figure 7.4). Indices outside and within the parenthesis represent results for junior high school and college, respectively. Coefficients in the ovals represent proportions of variance in a facet unaccounted for by higher-order factors, and coefficients embedded in lines represent correlation coefficients. Both models reveal some interesting and intuitively appealing relationships. The single general factor model in Figure 7.3 shows that for both age groups the superordinate music self-concept factor is most strongly correlated with perceptions of overall music ability, instrument playing, reading music, and listening, and it accounts for 53% to 93% of the variance in those factors. The general music self-concept factor is most weakly correlated with singing and moving to music and accounts for only 4% to 30% of the variance in those factors. Adding the two second-order factors in Figure 7.4 improved the accuracy of modeling as evident in the lowering of residual terms (unexplained variance) for all first-order factors. Moreover, the third-order general music self-concept factor was highly correlated with these second order factors (r_s ranging from .82 to .93) and accounted for 73% to 87% of their variances.

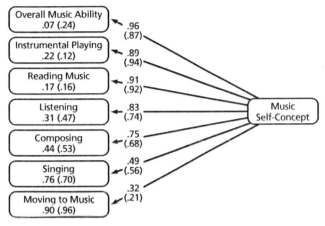

Figure 7.3.   Music self-concept hierarchy with one general factor. Coefficients without and with parentheses represent junior high school (*n* = 531) and college (*n* = 373) students respectively.

Summary of Key Findings from Initial Studies of Artistic and Music Self-Concept

Taken collectively, several important inferences might be made from the studies into artistic and music self-concept discussed thus far. First, there is generally greater support for a self-concept hierarchy within music than outside of music, and this holds at both second- and third-order levels. Second, perceptions of overall skill in music are more closely aligned with skills related to instrumental performance music and auditory cognition than to skills related to singing and moving to music. Third, the low to modest proportions of variance in singing and moving to music accounted for by general music self-concept emphasizes the need to measure such perceptions separately from perceptions of overall skill in music. Finally, there is reasonable consistency in the music self-concept hierarchies across the samples of college and junior high students examined here. The most salient difference may be in the extent to which perceptions of singing and instrumental performance skills relate to perceptions of overall music skill. For example, in the hierarchies depicted in Figure 7.4, there is some evidence that singing's relationship with general music-self concept is stronger and instrumental performance's is weaker at the college level than at the junior high level.

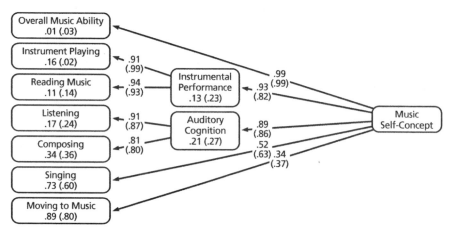

Figure 7.4.   Music self-concept hierarchy with one third-order factor and two second-order factors. Coefficients without and with parentheses represent junior high school ($n = 531$) and college ($n = 373$) students respectively.

STUDIES INTO THE ROLE OF DOMAIN IMPORTANCE

Background

The self-concept hierarchies discussed here provide useful frameworks for organizing facets of self-concept and understanding their interrelationships. However, as noted earlier, such frameworks have been criticized because they imply that the relations among particular facets of self-concept are the same across individuals. In evaluating this notion of uniform relationships, it is important to stress that possible variations in the structuring of components of self-concept from one individual to another are integral parts of the self-concept models discussed by Shavelson and colleagues (1976) and myself (Vispoel, 1994). For example, in my description of music self-concept hierarchies in Vispoel (1994), I emphasized that the structure of music self-concept can vary across individuals or groups as well as change over time. The hierarchical models discussed here only provide snapshots into what may typically be the case when considering the referent group as a whole at a particular point in time. Even within these models, it is clear that much of the variance in many components of self-concept is unexplained by higher order components and that the magnitudes of relationships between different facets of self-concept vary widely. Detecting general trends, comparing competing models, assessing relations among facets of self-concept, and pinpointing strengths and weaknesses in hierarchies are the primary goals of such analyses. This information is useful but unlikely to tell us everything we need to know about the structure and nature of self-concept at either group or individual levels.

One particularly important issue that such hierarchies fail to take into account is the extent to which domain importance and other contributing factors might affect relationships between domain-specific self-concepts and overall self-esteem. James (1890/1963), for example, argued that domain–specific self-concepts should have their greatest effects on self-esteem within domains that are valued by an individual. Addressing this issue, however, has proved to be complicated due to differing definitions of general self-concept and methodological problems in many research studies. Marsh and Yeung (1998, p. 510), for example, noted that there is no widely accepted definition of general self-concept and highlighted four commonly used operational definitions of this construct: (a) an *agglomerate self-concept* represented by a total score derived from an ill-defined set of self-concept items with weak theoretical foundation, (b) an inferred rather than directly measured *hierarchical self-concept factor* such as the general self-concept factor in the Shavelson and colleagues (1976) model and related models considered here (see Figures 7.1 & 7.2), (c) a *weighted-average general self-concept* calculated by combining specific components of self-concept and weighting them by their importance, saliency, centrality and other relevant components, particular to the individual respondent, and (d) a *global self-concept* measured directly from a relatively unidimensional instrument such as the Rosenberg (1965) *Self-Esteem Scale* or scales modeled after it from Marsh's *SDQs*, (Marsh, 1992a, 1992b, 1992c) and Harter's *Self-Perception Profiles* (Harter, 1985, 1986b; Messer & Harter, 1986; Neemann & Harter, 1986) in which items are targeted at general characteristics that are not linked to particular domains (e.g., "I have a good overall self-concept," "I am self-accepting," "I have a number of good qualities," and so forth).

Such distinctions among definitions of general self-concept are important to remember, because they can lead to different conclusions about the nature of self-perceptions. For present purposes, it is especially important to keep in mind the distinctions among the inferred *hierarchical general self-concept* factor in Shavelson and colleagues' (1976) model, *global self-concept* scores measured directly from scales targeted at general feelings about self, and *weighted-average general self-concepts* that are calculated by combining domain-specific self-concepts according to their perceived importance and other relevant features. In studies of domain importance, global self-esteem scores usually represent the key dependent variable of interest, based on the assumption that respondents make their global appraisals of self by appropriately weighting domain-specific aspects of self-concept according to their personal relevance. Global self-esteem scores are then correlated with composite scores based on various theoretically driven methods for combining domain-specific self-concept scores with ratings of their importance and other attributes (saliency, certainty of ratings, actual-ideal discrepancies, and so forth; see Marsh, 1993 for a detailed discussion of a wide variety of weighted-average models and their empirical support).

To evaluate the effects of domain importance on relations between domain-specific and global aspects of self-concept, Marsh (1993) recommended a generalized multiple regression procedure in which the simplest models are tested first, followed by increasingly more complex ones. This approach is based on the time-honored principle of parsimony in which simpler models are preferred over complex ones if both models have the same explanatory power. My discussion here is limited to comparisons of three models included in Marsh's recommended set: (a) a baseline regression model in which only domain-specific self-concept scores are included as independent variables, (b) a mediation or additive model in which corresponding ratings of domain importance are then added to the model, and (c) a moderation or multiplicative model in which Domain Self-Concept × Importance interaction terms are further added to the model.[3] In the baseline model, weights for different self-concept domains can vary but the weight for a given domain is the same across individuals. In the additive model, weights for a given domain self-concept or importance rating are still the same across individuals but domain importance provides an additional main effect that improves the explanatory power of the model. In the multiplicative model, adding the interaction terms increases the explanatory power over the additive or baseline models by allowing the relationships (or weights) between domain specific self-concepts and self-esteem to vary depending on the perceived importance of the domain.

Both the additive and multiplicative models have supporting rationales. The additive model is closely aligned with Harter's (1986a, 1989) proposal to use discrepancies between importance ratings and domain self-concept scores in interpreting results from her *Self-Perception Profiles* (Harter, 1985, 1986b; Messer & Harter, 1986; Neemann & Harter, 1986). The notion here is that self-esteem should decrease when importance ratings exceed domain self-concept ratings. In the music domain, for example, low perceptions of music skill would have a negative impact on self-esteem if one placed a high premium on being skilled at music. Consequently, interpreting results from Harter's self-concept inventories, one would look for marked discrepancies between importance and self-concept ratings in each area of interest (i.e., places where the importance rating greatly exceeds the self-concept rating). In supporting the use of such procedures, Harter (1986a) reported correlations of −.76 and −.67 between mean discrepancy and global self-worth scores for samples of early adolescents. Unfortunately, Harter (1986a) did not report whether the discrepancy scores improved prediction of self-esteem over models that used domain self-concept scores alone.[4]

The multiplicative (or interaction model) has been discussed much more extensively by self-concept theorists and researchers (see, e.g., Byrne, 1996; Hattie, 1992, 2000; Hoge & McCarthy, 1984; Marsh, 1986, 1993, 1995; Marsh & Hattie, 1996; Pelham, 1995a, 1995b; Rosenberg, 1965, 1979; Wylie, 1974), and is historically linked to the work of James (1890/1963) cited earlier. The key attribute of that model is that relationships between self-esteem and domain-specific self-concepts get stronger as domain importance increases with the highest self-esteem expected for individuals with high domain self-concept and high importance ratings and the lowest self-esteem expected for individuals with low domain self-concept and high importance ratings. In the discrepancy model, the effects for domain-self-concepts and importance are the same across individuals, even though they would be expected to vary from each other in magnitude and direction with domain self-concepts providing positive weights and domain importance ratings providing negative weights.[5]

Despite their strong intuitive appeal and compelling theoretical foundation, models that incorporate domain importance weighting schemes like those described here generally have not provided very meaningful improvements over models based on domain specific scores alone in accounting for variation in self-esteem scores (Hoge & McCarthy, 1984; Forte & Vispoel, 1995, Marsh, 1986, 1993, 1994, 1995; Pelham, 1995a, 1995b; Vispoel, 1995b; Vispoel & Forte, 1994). When statistically significant main or interaction effects for domain importance are found in multiple regression analyses, for example, they generally represent 1% to 2% increments in explained variance. Reasons frequently cited to explain such disappointing findings include psychometric or conceptual flaws in the measures used to assess self-concept and domain importance, homogeneity of traits among the participants sampled, and focus on domains likely to be viewed as reasonably important by most examinees.

Studies of Domain Importance using the ASPI and MUSPI

Undeterred by the weak findings from previous research, I was convinced from my own personal experiences that domain importance effects would emerge in the music domain if I attended to some issues raised in prior studies. Marsh (1986), in a study of 930 high school students and adults who completed the SDQ-3, found the strongest support for domain importance main and interaction effects in the domains of physical ability and spiritual values, and speculated that these results occurred because those domains were narrower and had more variability in importance ratings than did the other domains from the SDQ-3. To elicit stronger domain importance effects in future investigations, he recommended using better measures of domain importance and focusing on narrow self-concept domains that most people find unimportant but a few find very important.

Following up on Marsh's (1986) recommendations, I administering the ASPI music scale, SDQ-2 Self-Esteem scale, and more psychometrically sound measures of domain importance to a sample of 165 middle school students (Forte & Vispoel, 1995) and a sample of 195 junior high school students (Vispoel & Forte, 1994) who varied in their involvement in music-related activities. I found support for domain importance effects, but they were still modest (i.e., domain importance's main and interaction effects accounted for an additional 3% to 4% of variance in self-esteem beyond the effects of music self-concept).

I followed up these studies with two additional ones (see Vispoel, 2000a) that focused on even narrower subdomains of music self-concept measured by the MUSPI (instrument playing, singing, etc.). One study involved 461 junior school students (including 38% who participated in a school choir, band, or orchestra) and the other involved 337 college students (including 12% who had professional music performing experience). Both groups completed age-appropriate versions of the MUSPI, SDQ Self-Esteem scale, and multi-item domain importance rating scales. Prior to the main analyses in these studies, separate confirmatory factor analyses were run for the self-concept and importance scales within each age group. Good model fits were obtained in all instances (*TLIs* ranged from .92 to .97 and *RNIs* ranged form .93 to .98). Alpha-reliability estimates across studies for the self-concept and importance subscales ranged from .88 to .98 (*mdn* = .96).

To evaluate the effects of domain importance on the relations between music self-concept and self-esteem in each age group, seven hierarchical multiple regression equations were derived—one for each of the six domain-specific areas of self-concept (singing, instrument playing, etc.) and one combining the six sub-domain areas. The Self-Esteem score from the SDQ was the dependent variable in each analysis. In each domain-specific regression analysis, the sub-domain self-concept scale was entered first, followed by the importance rating score, followed by the sub-domain self-concept by importance rating interaction term. In the combined sub-domain analysis, the six MUSPI sub-domain self-concept scores were entered in the first step, the six importance ratings in the second step, and the six interaction terms in the final step. The final residual term was used to test all effects in each analysis.

The key tests in these regression analyses focused on the main and interactive effects of domain importance on self-esteem after the main effects of music self-concept were taken into account. The discrepancy (or additive) model is supported if a significant main effect for domain importance is found in a negative direction after the main effects of music self-concept are taken into account. A significant main effect for importance with no interaction would indicate that domain importance effects are the same independent of one's music self-concept score. In that model, self-esteem would decrease when importance ratings exceed music skill ratings. The interaction (or multiplicative) model is supported if a significant interaction effect is found that contributes positively to the explained variance in self-esteem beyond the main effects of music self-concept and domain importance. If the interaction model prevails, relationships between music-concept and self-esteem should be stronger for individuals with high importance ratings than those with low importance ratings. Following the principle of parsimony, interaction models were considered first, followed by the additive model with music-self-concept and domain importance main effects, followed by the model with only music self-concept main effects. If the more complex models failed to provide better explanatory power, they were abandoned in favor of the simpler models.

Generalized Multiple Regression Results for Junior High School Students

Table 7.4 shows the multiple regression results for the two age groups. The results for junior high school reveal that the interaction term in four of the seven regression analyses (instrument playing, reading music, listening, combined analysis) reached statistical significance ($p < .05$) and contributed a positive weight to the regression model in all cases (see the semipartial correlations and R^2 change coefficients in Table 7.4). The strongest effects were observed in the combined analyses in which the music self-concept scores, importance ratings and interaction terms accounted for 18% of the variance in overall self-esteem scores ($R = .43$, $R^2 = .18$). The importance ratings and interaction terms in this analysis accounted for an additional 6% of variance in self-esteem scores beyond that accounted for by the music self-concept scores—a figure somewhat higher than those reported in prior studies. In the regression analyses for separate MUSPI subscales, statistically significant interactions accounted for 1% to 3% of the variance in overall self-esteem scores. These findings replicated those from my two prior studies of domain importance with early adolescents (Forte & Vispoel, 1995; Vispoel & Forte, 1994), but pinpointed more specific areas of music self-concept where domain importance seemed to matter.

Generalized Multiple Regression Results for College Students

The multiple regression results for college students showed a very different pattern of relationships between self-esteem and the other variables of interest than those observed with junior high school students. Overall, for college students, the effects for domain importance and the interaction terms were much stronger and the effects of music self-concept scores were much weaker. In the regression analyses for individual music self-concept scales, both the importance terms (weighted negatively) and interaction terms

Table 7.4. Multiple Regression Results for the Effects of Music Self-Concept and Importance on Self-Esteem

Domain	Domain Self-Concept Score		Importance Rating				Interaction				Importance Rating and Interaction
	r/R	r^2/R^2	spr	R^2 Change	R	R^2	spr	R^2 Change	Final R	Final R^2	R^2 Change
Junior High School ($n = 461$)											
Instrument Playing	.34[c]	.12[c]	−.05	.00	.34	.12	.14[b]	.02[b]	.37[c]	.14[c]	.02[b]
Reading Music	.31[c]	.10[c]	.03	.00	.31	.10	.17[c]	.03[c]	.36[c]	.13[c]	.03[c]
Listening Skill	.26[c]	.07[c]	.06	.00	.27	.07	.09[a]	.01[a]	.28[c]	.08[c]	.01[a]
Composing Music	.24[c]	.06[c]	.00	.00	.24	.06	.05	.00	.25[c]	.06[c]	.00
Singing	.14b	.02b	−.04	.00	.14	.02	.04	.00	.15[a]	.02a	.00
Moving to Music	.09	.01	−.04	.00	.10	.01	−.06	.00	.12	.01	.00
Combined	.35[c]	.12[c]		.01	.37	.14		.05[c]	.43[c]	.18[c]	.06[c]
College ($n = 335$)											
Instrument Playing	.02	.00	−.24[c]	.06[c]	.24[c]	.06[c]	.18[c]	.03[c]	.30[c]	.09[c]	.09[c]
Reading Music	.02	.00	−.23[c]	.05[c]	.23[c]	.05[c]	.22[c]	.05[c]	.32[c]	.10[c]	.10[c]
Listening Skill	.00	.00	−.27[c]	.07[c]	.26[c]	.07[c]	.22[c]	.05[c]	.34[c]	.12[c]	.12[c]
Composing Music	−.09	.01	−.25[c]	.06[c]	.26[c]	.07[c]	.18[c]	.03[c]	.32[c]	.10[c]	.09[c]
Singing	.09	.01	−.28[c]	.08[c]	.29[c]	.09[c]	.21[c]	.05[c]	.36[c]	.13[c]	.13[c]
Moving to Music	.07	.00	−.18[c]	.03[c]	.19[c]	.04[c]	.19[c]	.03[c]	.27[c]	.07[c]	.06[c]
Combined	.18[a]	.03[a]		.09[c]	.35[c]	.12[c]		.07[c]	.44[c]	.20[c]	.16[c]

Note: [a] $p < .05$;
[b] $p < .01$;
[c] $p < .001$;
spr = semipartial correlation at the given step in the regression analysis.

(weighted positively) were statistically significant and their contributions were noticeably larger than those for music self-concept. In the combined analysis, for example, approximately 19.6% of the variance in self-esteem was accounted for ($R = .44$, $R^2 = .196$), but over 83% of that (16.3%) was attributable to domain importance's main and interactive effects. A similar pattern held across the separate MUSPI subscale analyses, where the importance and interaction terms accounted for 6% to 12% of the variance in self-esteem— figures consistently higher than those observed in other studies.

Nature of Domain Importance Interactions

All statistically significant interactions for junior high and college showed patterns consistent with theoretical expectations and provided stronger support for the interaction model than the discrepancy model. To illustrate this general trend, the interaction between domain importance and instrument playing self-concept in the junior high school sample is depicted in Figure 7.5. The axes for self-concept and importance ratings in Figure 7.5 represent scale scores averaged across items. This transformation simplifies the interpretation of results by expressing them along the 1 to 6 point scale used to respond to each item. The regression lines in Figure 7.5 represent relationships between self-esteem and instrument playing self-concept at varying levels of perceived domain importance corresponding to percentile ranks of 1, 25, 50, 75, and 99. Consistent with William James' conceptualization of domain importance, the correlation between perceptions of instrument playing skill and self-esteem is weak for individuals who place minimal importance on instrument playing ability but gets

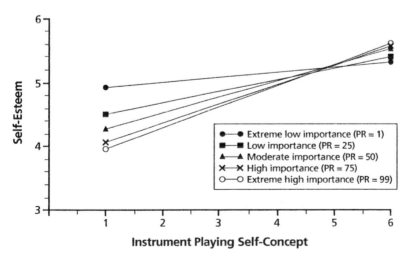

Figure 7.5.   Plot of Instrument playing self-concept × domain importance interaction for junior high school students.

increasingly stronger as domain importance increases. All the interactions found in these two studies, self-esteem was lowest for individuals with low music self–concepts who placed high importance on being skilled at music.

Summary and Implications of Domain Importance Studies in Music

Ultimately, the results reported here for music self-concept represent the strongest evidence to date in support of the moderating role of domain importance and suggest that such effects may be more pronounced for college students than for junior high school students. These findings are in line with Marsh's (1986) speculations that importance effects may be stronger in narrow domains that many respondents rate as unimportant but some rate as very important. MUSPI importance ratings were distributed in this fashion for the college students and understandably skill in the performing arts may be easy for most college students to discount at this stage in life perhaps due to more limited participation in music-related activities. In contrast, a large number of the junior high students participated in formal music ensembles (e.g. 38% were in school choirs, band, or orchestras), and all students were required to take one semester of general music during each school year. Not surprisingly, most junior high students rated music skill as moderately to very important, and the lesser variability in their importance ratings compared to the college students may have been responsible for the weaker interaction effects observed for them. Uniformity in importance ratings (presumably in the high direction) also might explain why Marsh (1993, 1994) failed to find noteworthy importance effects for academic and physical fitness self-concepts in his studies of Australian students in grades 7 to 12. Had he focused on skills in more elective or extracurricular areas in those studies (debating team, competitive sports, etc.), Marsh might have found results more similar to those observed in the current research. Such issues clearly merit further investigation and seemingly hold much potential for enhancing our understanding of self-concept.

CONCLUSIONS AND FUTURE DIRECTIONS

Important Research Findings Regarding Music Self-Concept

The research summarized here shows that significant progress has been made in measuring and understanding self-perceptions of musical ability. Instruments are now available for assessing many aspects of artistic self-concept with psychometric properties that rival those of the best instruments available for assessing nonartistic facets of self-concept. Research has revealed that music self-concept is a component of general artistic self-concept, and music self-concept itself is multifaceted and hierarchically structured. Music self-concept hierarchies, while stronger than those for most other domains of self-concept, still leave much of the variance unexplained in self-perceptions of skill in singing and moving to music. Such findings highlight the distinctiveness of singing and movement self-concepts from other facets of music self-concept and that overall perceptions of musical ability are dominated by perceptions of skill in instrumental performance and auditory cognition. Components of overall artistic and music self-concept have modest correlations with overall self-esteem, and these relations are stronger for junior high students than for college students. However, relations between music self-concept are strengthened when the importance of being skilled at music is taken into account, and this is especially true for college students. The most salient aspect of these relations is that self-esteem is lowest for individuals with low music self-concepts who place great importance on being skilled at music.

The findings discussed here do not touch upon all of the important research that has been done regarding music self-concept and should be interpreted in light of the limited number of studies cited. Some important findings not discussed here, for example, include the following. (a) strong relationships between music self-concept and achievement in music (Austin & Vispoel, 1998), (b) reductions in self-perceptions of music ability that typically occur as children move from first grade to higher grades (Wigfield et al , 1997), (c) consistent sex differences in music self-concept that favor females (Austin & Vispoel, 2000; Eccles, Wigfield, Harold, & Blumenfeld, 1993; Marsh, Craven, & Debus, 1998; Vispoel, 1993a, Vispoel & Forte Fast, 2000), and (d) the ability of very young children (5 to 7 years old) to distinguish self-perceptions of skill and interest in domains both within and outside of music (Austin & Vispoel, 2000; Marsh, Craven, & Debus, 1991, 1998, 1999). Although these findings and others discussed here have clearly moved us forward, there remain many ways in which measurement and understanding of music self-concept might be enhanced further.

Suggestions for Future Research into Music Self-Concept

The development of music self-concept measures certainly can be expanded. The MUSPI instruments, for example, could be extended to include additional subscales (e.g., sight singing, sense of rhythm, improvisation), and simplified forms of the measures could be developed for preschool and elementary school children. Inclusion of domain importance measures in these inventories seems especially warranted at the adult level. The MUSPI instruments could also be computerized to eliminate the need for producing paper-and-pencil questionnaires and answer sheets and to allow for immediate scoring, presentation, and storing of results. Research conducted to date on the computerization of self-concept measures has been quite encouraging in showing that computerized measures have psychometric properties similar to their paper-and-pencil counterparts and that respondents prefer taking the computerized versions (Simola & Holden, 1992; Vispoel, 2000b; Vispoel, Boo, & Bleiler, 2001).

Many substantive questions also are worthy of further exploration. These issues include the following: (a) the short- and long-term effects of interventions designed to enhance music self-concept and achievement, (b) developmental changes in perceptions of domain-specific skills in music from infancy through adulthood, (c) interrelations and potential causal connections between self-concept and achievement in music, and (d) the nature of and reasons for ethnic, cultural, and sex differences in music self-concept and how those differences might affect involvement, motivation, and accomplishments in music.

As a final note, I want to emphasize that music has proved to be a particularly fertile and personally fulfilling area for doing self-concept research. Theoretical notions such as self-concept hierarchies and effects of domain importance have received stronger support in music than in other domains and align well with my own experiences in music. I will continue, and encourage others, to pursue research in this fascinating domain.

ACKNOWLEDGMENTS

I am extremely grateful for the invaluable help my students and colleagues have provided with my research in self-concept. Listed alphabetically, these individuals include James Austin, Timothy Bleiler, Jaeyool Boo, Bethany Brunsman, Ping Chen, Sara Clough, Zhongmin Cui, Ellen Forte Fast, Chuan-ju Lin, Kristen Rizzo, Sid Sharairi, Karen Steger-May, Ahmet Turhan, Hueying Tzou, Tianyou Wang, and Heru Widiatmo. I am especially grateful to Sara Clough for helping me put this chapter together. I also wish to thank Herbert Marsh, Rhonda Craven, and rest of the folks at the Self Research Centre for their inspiration, support and kindness over the years. Herb's research, in particular, has served as a model for all of us to emulate. We would know far less about self-concept today without his groundbreaking contributions to the field.

NOTES

1. The approach used to measure self-concept varies with these instruments. Items from the *Self-Esteem Inventory* (Coopersmith, 1969) and *Piers Harris Children's Self-Concept Scale* (Piers, 1969) come from various content domains (e.g, academic, social, physical), and responses to them are summed together to create a "total score" assumed to reflect self-concept as a whole. Such approaches to measuring self-concept have been criticized because the total scores will depend heavily on the specific content domains assessed and the number of items included within each domain. This approach fails to take into account the relevance of various content domains for particular individuals and typically gives the domains with largest number of items the greatest weight in forming total scores. To address these problems, items from the *Self-Esteem Scale* (Rosenberg, 1965) are phrased in very general ways (e.g., "I have a good overall self-concept") so that respondents focus on the global aspects of self, rather than its individual elements. Distinctions among common ways that self-concept is defined and measured are described later in this chapter.

2. The scale intended to measure overall impressions of self in the SDQ instruments is actually labeled the "General Self" scale. This scale is labeled "self-esteem" throughout this chapter to avoid confusing it with the General Self Concept factor in hierarchical confirmatory factor analysis models. Another reason for changing the SDQ General Self scales' label is to highlight its similarity to Rosenberg's (1965, 1979) *Self-Esteem Scale* from which it was modeled. In the research literature, the terms self esteem and self-concept are often used interchangeably even though it is common to view self-concept as encompassing all perceptions of self (both descriptive and evaluative) and self-esteem as representing only evaluative aspects (see, e.g., Byrne, 1996, pp. 5–7). Distinctions between common definitions of general self-concept important for the research discussed here are described later in this chapter.

3. Marsh (1993) described more elaborate models than the three mentioned here including ones that took into account certainty of ratings and similarities between self-concept and important ratings and allowed weighting factors to vary both within and between individuals. However, these schema generally did no better and usually worse than those discussed here in accounting for variation in self-esteem scores.

4. It is important to point out that Harter's discussions of domain importance have sometimes emphasized the use of a discrepancy score for all domains (Harter, 1986a, p. 155) and at other times for only those domains considered important to an individual (Harter, 1989, p. 76). The latter view implies an interaction model in which the potency of a discrepancy score would vary depending on the perceived importance of the domain in question.

5. A discrepancy model could also be supported in the presence of a Domain Self-Concept × Importance interaction as long as positive discrepancies between importance and domain self-concept ratings signal decreases in self-esteem over the sampled range of responses. However, the interaction model would represent such data better, because the effects of discrepancies on self-esteem are allowed to vary at different levels of domain self-concepts.

REFERENCES

Austin, J., & Vispoel, W. P. (1998). How American adolescents interpret success and failure in classroom music: Relationships among attributional beliefs, self-concept and achievement. *Psychology of Music. 26*, 26–45.

Austin, J. R., & Vispoel, W. P. (2000). Children's ability self-perceptions and interests: Grade level, gender and race differences in music, reading, and math. In R. G. Craven & H. W. Marsh (Eds.), *Self-Concept, theory, research and practice: Advances for the new millennium* (pp.133–142). Sydney, Australia: Self-concept Enhancement and Learning Facilitation Research Centre.

Byrne, B. M. (1996). *Measuring self-concept across the lifespan: Methodological issues and selected instrumentation.* Washington, DC: American Psychological Association.

Coopersmith, S. (1967). *The antecedents of self-esteem.* San Francisco: Freeman.

Eccles, J. S., Wigfield, A., Harold, R. D., & Blumenfeld, P. (1993). Age and gender differences in children's self- and task perceptions during elementary school. *Child Development, 64*, 830–847.

Forte, E. E., & Vispoel, W. P. (1995, April). *Domain importance and involvement: Relations between domain self-concepts and general self-esteem in preadolescence.* (ERIC Document Reproduction No. ED387 668).

Harter, S. (1985). *Manual for the self-perception profile for children.* Denver, CO: University of Denver.

Harter, S. (1986a). Processes underlying the construction, maintenance, and enhancement of the self-concept in children. In J. Suls and A. G. Greenwald (Eds.), *Psychological perspectives on the self* (Vol. 3). Hillsdale, NJ: Lawrence Erlbaum Associates.

Harter, S. (1986b). *Manual for the Self-Perception Profile for Adolescents.* Denver: University of Denver.

Harter, S. (1989). Causes, correlates, and the functional fole of global self-worth: A life-span perspective. In J. Kolligan & R. Sternberg (Eds.), *Perceptions of competence and incompetence across the lifespan* (pp. 67–87). New Haven, CT: Yale University Press.

Hattie, J. (1992). *Self-concept.* Hillsdale NJ: Lawrence Erlbaum Associates.

Hattie, J. (2000). Getting back to the correct pathway for self-concept research in the new millennium: Revisiting misinterpretations of and revitalizing the contributions of James' agenda for research on the self. In R. G. Craven & H. W. Marsh (Eds.), *Self-concept, theory, research and practice: Advances for the new millennium* (pp. 42–66). Sydney, Australia: Self-concept Enhancement and Learning Facilitation Research Centre.

Hoge, D. R., & McCarthy, J. D. (1984). Influence of individual and group identity salience in the global self-esteem of youth. *Journal of Personality and Social Psychology, 47*, 403–414.

James, W. (1963). *The principles of psychology.* New York: Holt, Rinehart and Winston. (Original work published 1890).

Marsh, H. W. (1986). Global self-esteem: Its relation to specific facets of self-concept and their importance. *Journal of Personality and Social Psychology, 51*, 1224–1236.

Marsh, H. W. (1987). The hierarchical structure of self-concept and the application of hierarchical confirmatory factor analysis. *Journal of Educational Measurement,* *24,* 17–39.

Marsh, H. W. (1992a). *Self-Description Questionnaire (SDQ) I: A theoretical and empirical* *basis for the measurement of multiple dimensions of preadolescent self-concept: A test* *manual and research monograph.* Macarthur, New South Wales, Australia: University of Western Sydney, Faculty of Education.

Marsh, H. W. (1992b). *Self-Description Questionnaire (SDQ) II: A theoretical and empiri-* *cal basis for the measurement of multiple dimensions of adolescent self-concept: An* *interim test manual and research monograph.* Macarthur, New South Wales, Austra- lia: University of Western Sydney, Faculty of Education.

Marsh, H. W. (1992c). *Self-Description Questionnaire (SDQ) III: A theoretical and empiri-* *cal basis for the measurement of multiple dimensions of late adolescent self-concept: An* *interim test manual and research monograph.* Macarthur, New South Wales, Austra- lia: University of Western Sydney, Faculty of Education.

Marsh, H. W. (1993). Relations between global and specific domains of self: The importance of individual importance, certainty, and ideals. *Journal of Personality* *and Social Psychology, 65,* 975–992.

Marsh, H. W. (1994). The importance of being important: Theoretical models of relations between specific and global components of physical self-concept. *Journal of Sport and Exercise Psychology, 16,* 306–325.

Marsh, H. W. (1995). A Jamesian model of self-investment and self-esteem: Com- ment on Pelham (1995). *Journal of Personality and Social Psychology, 69,* 1151–1160.

Marsh, H. W., Craven, R. G., & Debus, R. (1991). Self-concepts of young children 5 to 8 years of age: Measurement and multidimensional structure. *Journal of Edu-* *cational Psychology, 83,* 377–392.

Marsh, H. W., Craven, R. G., & Debus, R. (1998). Structure, stability, and develop- ment of young children's self-concepts: A multicohort-multioccasion study. *Child Development, 69,* 1030–1053.

Marsh, H. W., Craven, R. G., & Debus, R. (1999). Separation of competency and affect components of multiple dimensions of academic self-concept: A devel- opmental perspective. *Merrill-Palmer Quarterly, 45,* 567–601.

Marsh, H. W., & Hattie, J. (1996). Theoretical perspectives on the structure of self- concept. In B. A. Bracken (Ed.), *Handbook of self-concept: Developmental, social,* *and clinical considerations* (pp. 38–90). New York: Wiley.

Marsh, H. W., & Shavelson, R. J. (1985). Self-concept: Its multifaceted, hierarchical structure. *Educational Psychologist, 20,* 107–125.

Marsh, H. W., & Yeung, A. S. (1998). Top-down, bottom-up, and horizontal models: The direction of causality in multidimensional, hierarchical self-concept mod- els. *Journal of Personality and Social Psychology, 75,* 509–527.

Messer, B., & Harter, S. (1986). *Manual for the Adult Self-perception Profile.* Denver, CO: University of Denver.

Neemann, J., & Harter, S. (1986). *Manual for the Self-perception Profile for College Stu-* *dents.* Denver, CO: University of Denver.

Pelham, B. W. (1995a). Self-investment and self-esteem: Evidence for a Jamesian model of self-worth. *Journal of Personality and Social Psychology, 69,* 1141–1150.

Pelham, B. W. (1995b). Further evidence for a Jamesian model of self-worth: Reply to Marsh (1995). *Journal of Personality and Social Psychology, 69,* 1161–1165.

Piers, E. V. (1969). *Manual for the Piers-Harris Children's Self-Concept Scale.* Nashville, TN: Counselor Recordings and Tests.

Rosenberg, M. (1965). *Society and the adolescent self-image.* Princeton, NJ: Princeton University Press.

Rosenberg, M. (1979). *Conceiving the self.* New York: Basic Books.

Shavelson, R. J., Hubner, J. J., & Stanton, G. C. (1976). Self-concept: Validation of construct interpretations. *Review of Educational Research, 46,* 407–441.

Simola, S. K., & Holden, R. R. (1992). Equivalence of computerized and standard administration of the Piers-Harris Children's Self-Concept Scale. *Journal of Personality Assessment, 58,* 287–294.

Vispoel, W. P. (1992a). *Arts Self-Perception Inventory (Adolescent Form).* Iowa City, IA: Author.

Vispoel, W. P. (1992b). *Arts Self-Perception Inventory (Adult/College Form).* Iowa City, IA: Author.

Vispoel, W. P. (1993a). The development and validation of the Arts Self-Perception Inventory for Adolescents. *Educational and Psychological Measurement, 53,* 1023–1033.

Vispoel, W. P. (1993b). *Music Self-Perception Inventory (Adolescent Form).* Iowa City, IA: Author.

Vispoel, W. P. (1993c). *Music Self-Perception Inventory (Adult/College Form).* Iowa City, IA: Author.

Vispoel, W. P. (1994). Integrating self-perceptions of music skill into contemporary models of self-concept. *Quarterly Journal of Music Teaching and Learning, 5,* 42–57.

Vispoel, W. P. (1995a). Self-concept in artistic domains: An extension of the Shavelson, Hubner, and Stanton (1976) model. *Journal of Educational Psychology, 87,* 134–153.

Vispoel, W. P. (1995b). *Relations between global and domain-specific aspects of self-concept: The role of importance, involvement, and school subject areas.* Unpublished manuscript.

Vispoel, W. P. (1996). The development and validation of the Arts Self-Perception Inventory for Adults. *Educational and Psychological Measurement, 56,* 731–757.

Vispoel, W. P. (2000a). Music self-concept: instrumentation, structure, and theoretical linkages. In R. G. Craven & H. W. Marsh (Eds.), *Self-concept, theory, research and practice: Advances for the new millennium* (pp. 100–107). Sydney, Australia:Self-concept Enhancement and Learning Facilitation Research Centre.

Vispoel, W. P. (2000b). Computerized versus paper-and-pencil assessment of self-concept: Score comparability and respondent preferences. *Measurement and Evaluation in Counseling and Development, 33,* 130–143.

Vispoel, W. P., Boo, J., & Bleiler, T. (2001). Computerized and paper-and-pencil versions of the Rosenberg Self-Esteem Scale: Psychometric features and respondent preferences. *Educational and Psychological Measurement, 61,* 461–474.

Vispoel, W. P., Brunsman, B., & Bleiler, T. (1995, April). *The multifaceted, hierarchical structure of early adolescent self-concept.* Paper presented at the annual meeting of the American Educational Research Association (AERA), San Francisco, CA.

Vispoel, W. P., & Forte, E. E. (1994, April). *Predicting general self-esteem from domain specific self-concepts: The role of importance and involvement.* Paper presented at the annual meeting of the American Educational Research Association, New Orleans, LA.

Vispoel, W. P., & Forte Fast, E. E. (2000). Response biases and their relation to sex differences in multiple domains of self-concept: *Applied Measurement in Education, 13,* 79–97.

Vispoel, W. P., Wang, T., Bleiler, T., & Tzou, H. (1993, April). *Validation studies for early-adolescent and adult versions of the Arts Self-Perception Inventory.* Paper presented at the annual meeting of the American Educational Research Association, Atlanta, GA.

Wigfield, A., Eccles, J. S., Yoon, K. S., Harold, R. D., Arbrerton, A. J. A., Freedman-Doan, C. F., & Blumenfeld, P. D. (1997). Change in children's competence beliefs and subjective task values across the elementary school years: A 3-year study. *Journal of Educational Psychology, 89,* 451–469.

Wylie, R. (1974). *The self-concept: A review of methodological considerations and measuring instruments* (Rev. ed., Vol. 1). Lincoln, NE: University of Nebraska Press.

CHAPTER 8

TESTING THE GENERALIZABILITY OF THE FACTOR STRUCTURE UNDERLYING THE PSDQ WITH SPANISH ADOLESCENTS

Inés Tomás-Marco and Vicente González-Romá

Self-concept research has offered empirical evidence supporting the multi-faceted nature of self-concept and has indicated the need to develop multi-dimensional instruments that are specific to self-concept domains. The validation process of a measurement instrument begins with the definition of the construct being measured, derived from psychological theory or prior research. Construct definition also implies the formulation of a hypothesized factor structure, which will also guide the test construction process. The previous ideas point out that the development and evaluation of multidimensional instruments that are specific to self-concept domains need to be based on theory, followed by factor analytic investigations that offer empirical support for the hypothesized factor structure. Furthermore, the use of self-concept instruments in one culture may be different from the one in which they were developed and normed. Importantly comparison across different cultures would offer further evidence of the construct validity and generalizability of the factor structure. Needless to say,

International Advances in Self Research, pages 181–200
Copyright © 2003 by Information Age Publishing

the use of an instrument for populations whose language differs from the one in which the instrument was originally developed necessarily leads to the development of a translated version.

The ideas exposed in the previous paragraph summarize the framework of the topic addressed in the present chapter. Our interest in the measurement of physical self-concept (one of the multidimensional self-concept domains), and the issue of whether or not its content and structure differ across socio-cultural contexts led us to the development of this investigation. The questions to be answered focus on the construct validity of multidimensional self-concept instruments when they are translated into distinct languages and applied to different cultural groups. In the present study we point out the importance of cross-cultural comparisons for purposes of construct validation of instruments and offer a practical example. Concretely, we developed a translated Spanish version of one of the most widely used multidimensional physical self-concept instruments, the Physical Self Description Questionnaire (PSDQ, Marsh, Richards, Johnson, Roche, & Tremayne, 1994), to study the generalizability of its factor structure in a culture different form the one in which the instrument was originally developed. Previous to the presentation of the empirical study we carried out, we present a brief literature review on self-concept, its conceptualization and measurement, and we also review results of previous studies that tested the psychometric properties of the PSDQ in the culture in which the questionnaire was originally developed.

In the course of their lives, people develop an empirical aggregation of things objectively known about themselves that has been called self-concept. Individuals' social interactions contribute to the construction of self-concept through an internalization process of what others think about their appearance, motives, deeds, character, and so on. Prior to the 1980s self-concept was considered a unidimensional construct (Marsh & Shavelson, 1985; Marsh, 1990a; Marsh & Hattie, 1996). Consistent with the dominant theoretical orientation, early self-concept measurement instruments were characterized by unidimensionality and an emphasis on global self-concept. Example of such unidimensional scales is the Rosenberg Self-Esteem Scale (Rosenberg, 1965, 1979). In contrast, since the 1980s most self-concept theorists accept the multidimensionality of self-concept, and as a result, most measurement instruments developed subsequently assess several facets of self-concept in addition to a global component. Examples of such multidimensional scales are the Offer Self-Image Questionnaire-Revised (Offer, Ostrov, Howard, & Dolan, 1992), the Self-Perception Profile for Children (Harter, 1982, 1985), the Self-Esteem Index (Brown & Alexander, 1991), the Multidimensional Self Concept Scale (Bracken, 1992), and Marsh's Self-Description Questionnaire instruments SDQI,

SDQII and SDQIII (Marsh, 1988, 1990b, 1992a) (for a review of self-concept instrumentation see Byrne, 1996 and Keith & Bracken, 1996).

An important basis for the theoretical movement toward a multidimensional conceptualization of self-concept was the article by Shavelson, Hubner, and Stanton (1976). The authors posited a multifaceted, hierarchical model of self-concept, which has been subsequently extended (Shavelson & Bolus, 1982), and revised (Marsh & Shavelson, 1985; Shavelson & Marsh, 1986), leading to the Marsh/Shavelson model. The Shavelson and colleagues (1976) model has been the basis for the subsequent development of other multidimensional models of self-concept (Song & Hattie, 1984; Hattie, 1992; Harter, 1982; Pallas, Entwisle, Alexander, & Weinstein, 1990). But surely, serving as the basis for the development of multidimensional self-concept measurement instruments, was the main contribution of the Shavelson and colleagues model. The studies on these instruments have offered empirical evidence supporting the multifaceted nature of the self-concept and have indicated that self-concept cannot be understood adequately if its multidimensionality is ignored (Marsh, 1990a). For example, the different areas of self-concept assessed by Marsh's SDQ instruments are based largely on the Shavelson and colleagues model. The findings of the numerous studies carried out using these questionnaires indicate that the SDQ instruments provide reliable and valid measures of self-concept suitable for testing the Shavelson and colleagues model (e.g., Marsh, 1987a, 1987b; Marsh & Byrne, 1993a, 1993b; Marsh & Hocevar, 1985; Marsh & Shavelson, 1985). These studies also offer support for the use of multidimensional measures of self-concept instead of general measures of self.

The hierarchical nature of self-concept postulated in the Shavelson and colleagues model implies that multidimensional, hierarchical models can be developed for separate domains. More recently, the need to develop multidimensional instruments that are specific to self-concept domains has been recognized (Marsh, 1990a; Marsh & Redmayne, 1994). Thus, researchers have developed self-concept instruments to measure specific aspects within the academic, physical and performing arts domains. Academic self-concept has been the most widely studied. Examples of multidimensional scales designed to measure specific aspects within the academic domains are The Perception of Ability Scale for Students (Boersma & Chapman, 1992), and the Academic Self-Description Questionnaire (Marsh, 1990c, 1992b). The Arts Self-Perception Inventory (Vispoel, 1995) distinguishes between self-concepts in distinct performing arts domains. In the physical domain, the Physical Self Perception Profile (Fox, 1990; Fox & Corbin, 1989), the Physical Self Concept Scale (Richards, 1988), and the Physical Self Description Questionnaire (Marsh, Richards, Johnson, Roche, & Tremayne, 1994), are multidimensional instruments designed to measure specific dimensions of physical self-concept, appropriate for use with participants over the age of 12. More recently, a multidimensional physical self-concept instrument specific to elite athletes has been developed, the Elite Athlete Self Description Questionnaire (Marsh, Hey, Johnson, & Perry, 1997).

There is general agreement among self-concept researchers regarding the idea that multidimensional instruments that measure specific self-concept domains may be more useful than more global measures of self-concept (Marsh, Hey, Johnson, & Perry, 1997; Marsh, Hey, Roche, & Perry, 1997). Within this general framework, theory and practice must work together to posit and evaluate more detailed subdomains that are specific to a particular domain of self-concept. As Marsh, Richards, and colleagues (1994) pointed out, the development and evaluation of multidimensional instruments that are specific to self-concept domains needs to be based on theory, followed by factor analytic investigations that offer further support for the hypothesized factor structure. Moreover, the development of translated versions of the questionnaires into other languages to be used with different cultures would offer further evidence of the construct validity of the instruments, and of the generalizability of the factor structure across several cultures.

The importance of measuring self-concept across culture has been addressed in previous studies (for further details related to the issues and caveats regarding the measurement of self-concept across culture, readers are referred to Byrne, 2000). The present investigation focuses on the measurement of the physical self-concept, and, more concretely, on the construct validity of one of the multidimensional physical self-concept instruments cited above, the Physical Self Description Questionnaire (PSDQ; Marsh, Richards, et al. 1994). The PSDQ was based on the Marsh/Shavelson model (Marsh & Shavelson, 1985; Shavelson & Marsh, 1986), previous research carried out with the SDQ instruments, and a preliminary version of the questionnaire (Marsh & Redmayne, 1994). Thus, the PSDQ was developed to measure nine specific components of physical self-concept (Health, Coordination, Activity, Body Fat, Sports Competence, Appearance, Strength, Flexibility, Endurance/Fitness), and two global components (Global Physical Self-Concept and Self-Esteem). As Marsh (1994a) pointed out, the PSDQ was designed as a hierarchical, multidimensional measure of physical self-concept. Thus, the global physical scale refers to super-ordinate physical self-perceptions in general, and the nine specific scales refer to specific domains of physical self-concept (see Marsh, 1996, for a description of the PSDQ scales).

The psychometric properties of the PSDQ have been tested in several studies. Estimates of the internal consistency and reliability of scores in the eleven PSDQ scales were good for different samples of Australian adolescents (Marsh, Hey, Roche, & Perry, 1997; Marsh, Richards, et al, 1994), varying from .82 to .96. Support for the convergent and discriminant validity for the PSDQ scales has been provided using multitrait-multimethod analysis of the scores of the PSDQ and two other multidimensional physical self-concept instruments (Marsh et al., 1994). The test of the relations of PSDQ responses to external validity criteria (reflecting body composition, physical activity, and other components of physical fitness) has also supported the convergent and discriminant validity of the PSDQ scales (Marsh, 1996). The confirmatory factor analyses (CFA) carried out to test the factor structure of the PSDQ responses have provided clear support for the eleven components of physical self-concept that the PSDQ is designed to measure. The CFAs have also provided support for the replicability of the factor structure over gender (Marsh et al., 1994) and across samples of elite athletes and non-elite high school students (Marsh, Hey, Roche, & Perry, 1997).

In summary, these results demonstrate the appropriateness of the PSDQ and provide support for the reliability and construct validity of the questionnaire for Australian adolescents. The question then arises as to how to evaluate whether or not the factor structure of the instrument can be generalized across different cultural groups. In this regard, the development of translated versions of the PSDQ into other languages would offer the opportunity to study the construct validity of the questionnaire in different cultures and assess the generalizability of its factor structure. However, it is well known among test developers that the use of a test in a culture other than the one in which it was developed requires evidence of the test's reliability and validity in the new setting. The purpose of the present investigation is to test a number of invariance hypotheses regarding PSDQ psychometric properties across two samples of Australian and Spanish adolescents. This will allow us to ascertain to what extent a number of the questionnaire's psychometric properties estimated in an Australian sample are generalizable to a Spanish sample. Concretely, we are concerned with testing the invariance of the factor structure underlying the questionnaire, the invariance of factor loadings and factor correlations, and additionally the invariance of factor variances and uniquenesses across the two samples.

METHOD

Participants and Procedure

Data from a total of 1,972 subjects were used in this study. In Australia, 986 high school students (54% males, 46% females) with a mean age of 13.5 ($SD = 1.11$) years completed the English version of the PSDQ. These data correspond to the two nonelite groups used in the Marsh, Hey, Roche, and Perry (1997) study, discarding only the subjects under the age of 12. In Spain, 986 high school students (51% males, 49% females) with a mean age of 13.3 (SD =1.07) years completed the Spanish translated version of the questionnaire. The ages of the subjects in the Australian and Spanish samples ranged from 12 to 16 years. Moreover, the two samples were equated as much as possible on the demographic variables of gender, age, and grade level. We tested for differences in percentages of males and females in the two samples, but the value obtained for the test was not statistically significant ($z = 1.74$, $p > 0.05$). We also tested for differences in age mean and variance between samples. The difference in age mean was statistically significant ($t = 5.16$, $p < 0.01$), and the difference in age variance was also statistically significant ($F = 13.6$, $p < 0.01$). Taking into account that the differences in age mean and variance between the two samples were very small, the aforementioned significant results may be due to the high statistical power of the tests.

In all cases participation was voluntary. Permission to participate in the study was obtained from the participants and their parents. In the Australian sample, classroom teachers administered the PSDQ to intact classes of no more than 30 students, according to written instructions. In the Spanish sample, the same researcher administered the questionnaire to classroom units of students during one regular class period. Prior to completion of the instrument, the test administrator paraphrased test instructions, and procedural questions were solicited and answered.

Instrument and Tests Translation

The Physical Self-Description Questionnaire (PSDQ) is a 70-item instrument which is designed to measure the following eleven scales: health, coordination, activity, body fat, sports competence, appearance, strength, flexibility, endurance/fitness, global physical self-concept, and global self-esteem. Each scale is represented by 6 or 8 items; each item is a simple declarative statement and participants respond using a 6-point true-false response scale (see Marsh et al., 1994, for a full presentation of the instrument).

In this study, the source English version of the PSDQ and a translation into Spanish of the questionnaire (Tomás, 1998) were used. The PSDQ was translated into Spanish following the back-translation procedure widely described in the literature (Hambleton & Kanjee, 1995; Van de Vijver & Leung, 1996). The test was initially translated from English to Spanish separately by the two authors of the present study and a translator whose first language is Spanish. Translation discrepancies between the three translated forms were discussed in order to develop an initial Spanish version of the questionnaire. A second bilingual translator whose native language is English, and who had not seen the original English version, translated this initial Spanish version of the test from Spanish back to English. The original and back-translated versions of the tests were then compared. Translation differences revealed by the back translation were corrected. Next, a pilot study was carried out in order to test the adequacy of the questionnaire to be used with Spanish teenagers. The Spanish version was administered to a group of 27 Spanish boys and girls whose ages ranged from 12 to 13 years. The questionnaire was applied following the standardized instructions, and afterwards, the students were asked about any expression that would have been difficult to understand. Concretely, the items reporting problems in understanding were those containing expressions in which translation into Spanish had been problematic. English expressions such as "breathe hard" and "huff and puff" used in some of the items of the Activity scale ("I often do exercise or activities that make me breathe hard," "I get exercise or activity three or four times a week that makes me huff and puff and lasts at least 30 minutes"), and the verbs "bend" "twist" and "turn" as they are used in one of the items of the Flexibility scale ("I am quite good at bending, twisting, and turning my body"), did not translate smoothly into Spanish. Because of that, there were some expressions that offered translation discrepancies in the previous stages of the translation process, and curiously, their translation into Spanish appeared difficult for young students to understand. Also the expression "whatever illness is going around" of one of the items of the Health scale ("I usually catch whatever illness is going around") showed problems in understanding in the first pilot study. Once detected, the items showing problems in understanding were reviewed with the suggestions of the adolescents partaking in the first pilot study, consequently some changes were introduced to make the items clearer. Finally, a second pilot study was carried out to test these modifications. This time, no problems in understanding where detected, concluding with a final Spanish version of the PSDQ.

Statistical Analyses

First, descriptive statistics (means, standard deviations, and internal consistency estimates of reliability) for the eleven PSDQ scales were obtained separately in the Australian and the Spanish groups. Second, a series of multisample CFAs were performed with LISREL 8.12 (Jöreskog & Sörbom, 1993) to test the invariance of the factor structure of the PSDQ across the two cultural groups and, additionally, to test the invariance of factor loadings, factor correlations, factor variances, and uniquenesses. Thus, a total of five nested models were tested. Model 1 (M1) tested whether or not an

11 common factor model held in the two samples, but no invariance constraint was imposed in any parameter. This model was used as a baseline for fit comparisons of the later more restricted models. In Model 2 (M2), factor loadings were constrained to be invariant across groups. As pointed out in previous studies (Marsh, 1994b; Marsh, Hey, Roche, & Perry, 1997), the invariance of factor loadings was of primary importance in tests of factorial invariance; however, it may also be important to test for the invariance of relations among factors. Model 3 (M3) tested whether or not factor loadings and factor correlations were invariant across the two cultural groups. The procedure described by Marsh and Hocevar (1985; Marsh, 1987a) for conducting a test for the invariance of factor correlations when factor variances are free was followed. There is no reason to expect that the variability of individuals on each factor should be the same in the two cultural groups, even if relations among the factors are invariant; nevertheless, the invariance of factor variances was also tested. Thus, Model 4 (M4) posited factor loadings, factor correlations, and factor variances to be invariant across groups. Finally, in Model 5 (M5) all estimated parameters (factor loadings, factor correlations, factor variances and uniqueness) were hypothesized to be invariant. For all the models, the analyses were performed on within-group covariance matrices. Maximum likelihood method of estimation was used to estimate the parameters of the models.

To assess the goodness of fit for the models we used three absolute fit indices (the chi-square goodness-of-fit statistic, χ^2; the root mean square error of approximation, RMSEA; and the adjusted goodness-of-fit index, AGFI), and one relative fit index (the nonnormed fit index, NNFI). The chi-square test statistic has been widely used by researchers to assess the fit of the models. It is a test of statistical significance that evaluates whether or not a solution adequately fits the data. However, one of the concerns in the application of the chi-square test statistic to the evaluation of goodness of fit is its sample size dependence (e.g., Jöreskog, 1993; La Du & Tanaka, 1995; Tanaka, 1993). The chi-square statistic is calculated as N-1 times the minimum value of the fit function, where N is the sample size. Thus, in large samples even trivial deviations of a model from the actual structure could be detected and could lead to the rejection of the model. The use of practical fit indices (such as the RMSEA, AGFI and NNFI) has been suggested as an alternative to tests of statistical significance (e.g., Marsh, 1994b; Marsh & Hocevar, 1985; Marsh, Hey, Roche, & Perry, 1997; Reise, Widaman, & Pugh, 1993). The RMSEA (Steiger, 1990) was defined as a measure of the discrepancy per degree of freedom of the model. This badness of fit measure is bounded below by zero and will be zero if the model fits perfectly. Guidelines for interpretation of RMSEA have been recommended. These guidelines suggest that values of about 0.05 or less would indicate a close fit of the model, values of about 0.08 or less would indicate fair fit of the model or a reasonable error of approximation, and values greater than 0.1 would indicate poor fit (Browne & Cudeck, 1993; Browne & Du Toit, 1992). The AGFI (Jöreskog & Sörbom, 1989) is a modification of the GFI by dividing the numerator and denominator terms of the GFI equation by their corresponding degrees of freedom. This index was suggested to avoid a serious limitation reported for the GFI, such as its tendency to increase as more parameters are introduced into the model. Thus, the AGFI applies a penalty for additional parameters. AGFI values near 0.0 indicate poor fit, whereas values near 1.0 indicate good fit. It is fairly conventional to use a threshold value of .90 as indicating good model fit. Finally, the NNFI (Bentler & Bonett, 1980; Tucker & Lewis, 1973) is a relative measure that also applies penalties for a lack of parsimony. It has been suggested that NNFI values of .90 or above indicate good model fit (Bentler & Bonett, 1980). Values near 0.0 indicate poor fit, whereas values near 1.0 indicate good fit.

The comparison of the fit of the competing models was done in terms of the difference in chi-square values ($\Delta \chi^2$). As more restricted models (models 2 to 5) are nested within the baseline model (Model 1), the difference in chi-square values for these models regarding Model 1 can be estimated. For each particular comparison, evidence for the fit of the hypothesized model is given by the degree to which the difference in chi-square value for the model being tested does not differ in a statistically significant way from the baseline model. However, tests of statistical significance of the change in chi-square are subject to the same limitations discussed for the chi-square test statistic. And consequently, the same assertion can be made: the comparison of the goodness of fit of competing models cannot be evaluated solely on the basis of statistical grounds; it should be useful to consider the information provided for the differences in practical fit indices. With these considerations in mind, and taking into account the large sample sizes in this study, we used the differences in NNFI, AGFI, and RMSEA as an alternative to compare the fit of the tested models. Widaman (1985) considered differences between models in NNFI of less than .01 was an indication of unimportant practical differences. Although suggestions for evaluating differences in AGFI have not been developed, La Du and Tanaka suggested that "an incremental change in GFI greater than .01 for a single degree of freedom comparison might be indicative of nontrivial model improvement, particularly for samples sizes greater than 200" (La Du & Tanaka, 1995, pp. 308). As AGFI is a modification of GFI by dividing the numerator and denominator terms of the GFI equation by their corresponding degrees of freedom, a relationship between population values of AGFI and GFI can be established (see, e.g., MacCallum & Hong, 1997). Finally, the RMSEA will decrease if the inclusion of additional parameters substantially reduces the population discrepancy function value (Brown & Du Toit, 1992). However, standards for evaluating differences in RMSEA have not been developed.

RESULTS

The descriptive statistics (means, standard deviations and coefficient alpha estimates of reliability) obtained for the 11 PSDQ scales are presented in Table 8.1. The estimates of internal consistency for the eleven PSDQ scales in the Spanish sample are good, ranging from .79 to .93, with a mean alpha of .87. Reliability estimates for the Australian sample range from .82 to .94, with a mean alpha of .88. In general, the reliability estimates are similar across groups, with differences between groups ranging from .00 to .03.

The outcomes of confirmatory factor analyses are summarized in Table 8.2; in this table, the goodness of fit indices for the five tested models are presented. Results show that the chi-square goodness of fit test for Model 1 is statistically significant, indicating that this model does not hold exactly in the population. However, as has been discussed above, the chi-square is so powerful for large problems with large sample sizes, that the observed chi-square will nearly always be statistically significant even for models with a reasonably good fit to the data. That seems to be the case in this study since the fit of Model 1 would be considered to be acceptable from the point of view of other measures of fit (RMSEA = 0.031; AGFI = 0.90; NNFI = 0.89). Thus, it can be concluded that the same factor model is able to fit the data from each group. And consequently, the freely estimated eleven-factor model (Model 1) will be used as a baseline model to test the fit of additional models that posit some or all of the parameters invariant across the two samples.

Table 8.1. Means, Standard Deviations, and Cronbach's Alpha Estimates of Reliability in Each Group

Scale	Australian group (N = 986)			Spanish group (N = 986)		
	Mean	SD	α	Mean	SD	α
1. Health	4.73	.98	.82	4.68	.86	.79
2. Coordination	4.34	1.04	.84	4.39	.94	.83
3. Activity	4.22	1.29	.86	4.19	1.30	.89
4. Body Fat	4.61	1.46	.94	4.58	1.31	.93
5. Sport Competence	4.18	1.29	.93	4.19	1.14	.91
6. Appearance	3.73	1.24	.89	3.78	1.08	.87
7. Strength	4.18	1.15	.89	3.84	1.14	.89
8. Flexibility	4.19	1.13	.85	3.86	1.10	.86
9. Endurance	3.64	1.37	.90	3.78	1.25	.89
10. Global Physical	4.43	1.28	.93	4.61	1.19	.92
11. Self-Esteem	4.73	.99	.86	4.51	.92	.84

Table 8.2 shows that the difference in chi-square value for Model 2 with respect to Model 1 is statistically significant (χ^2 (59) = 675.2, $p < .01$), indicating that constraining the factor loadings to being invariant across groups leads to a statistically significant decrease in model fit. Taking this result into account, it is clear that Model 2 should be rejected from a strictly statistical viewpoint. However, the chi-square's relation to sample size can lead to the rejection of the model of factor loading invariance even when there are only small or trivial differences between the two groups. Actually, as can be seen in Table 8.2, for small differences in the fit function values between models 2 and 1, a statistically significant change in chi-square is obtained because of the large sample size. Therefore, taking into account the practical fit indices values obtained for Model 2 (RMSEA = 0.032; AGFI = 0.90; NNFI = 0.89), it did not seem unreasonable to accept the adequacy of this model. Furthermore, the RMSEA, AGFI and NNFI values for Model 2 showed minimal differences with respect to values attained for Model 1. Comparison of Model 2 with regard to Model 1 indicated that the decrease in RMSEA for the baseline model was just 0.001. The AGFI and NNFI values for the baseline model and Model 2 were the same (.90 and .89 respectively), indicating that, according to practical fit indices, there were no differences in goodness of fit between models 2 and 1 Thus, it can be concluded that the invariance of factor loadings across the two samples is tenable.

Table 8.2.   Goodness of Fit Indices for Tested Models

Model	Model description	df	χ^2	Δdf	$\Delta\chi^2$	Fit function	RMSEA	AGFI	NNFI
M1	Baseline model	4580	13449.05*			6.83	0.031	0.90	0.89
M2	FL invariance	4639	14124.22*	59	675.20*	7.17	0.032	0.90	0.89
M3	FL + FC invariance	4694	14339.73*	114	890.70*	7.28	0.032	0.90	0.89
M4	FL + FC + FV invariance	4705	14370.14*	125	921.09*	7.29	0.032	0.90	0.89
M5	FL + FC + FV + U invariance	4775	16697.59*	195	3248.54*	8.48	0.036	0.89	0.86

Note. df = degrees of freedom; Δdf = change in degrees of freedom; $\Delta\chi^2$ = change in chi-square statistic; FL = factor loadings; FC = factor correlations; FV = factor variances; U = uniquenesses. * = $p < .01$.

Results for models 3 and 4 yielded similar conclusions as those described for Model 2. As the goodness of fit of these two models was similar, the most parsimonious (Model 4) should be therefore selected. According to results in Table 8.2, it was clear that Model 4 should be rejected from a strictly statistical viewpoint since change in chi-square with respect to Model 1 was statistically significant. However, the practical fit indices provided a different message, suggesting that the fit of Model 4 may be considered acceptable: the RMSEA showed a satisfactory value (.032); the AGFI value (.90) indicated good model fit; and the NNFI (.89) indicated a fairly reasonable level of practical fit. Comparison of Model 4 with regard to Model 1 indicated that the decrease in RMSEA for the baseline model, where no invariance constraints of parameters were imposed, was just 0.001. As has been pointed out above, standards for evaluating differences in RMSEA have not been developed. However, we considered that, for a difference of 125 degrees of freedom, such a small difference in RMSEA could be considered unimportant on practical grounds. Finally, the AGFI and NNFI values for the baseline model and Model 4 were exactly the same, indicating that there were no changes in practical fit with respect to Model 1. Hence, Model 4 should be preferred since it was more parsimonious. Tables 8.3 and 8.4 show the parameter estimates for Model 4.

The fit for Model 5 (which tests the invariance of all parameters constrained to be invariant in Model 4, plus the invariance of uniquenesses) was somewhat poorer than the fit of the models already considered (RMSEA = 0.036; AGFI = 0.89; NNFI = 0.86). For this model, the change in NNFI with respect to Model 1 was .03, indicating a nontrivial decrease in model fit. These results provided support for the selection of Model 4 as the "best model." In summary, taking into account that the indices of practical fit did not show important differences between models 1 and 4, Model 4 was preferred over Model 1 because of its parsimony. Hence, we concluded that the results offered support for the invariance of factor loadings, factor correlations, and factor variances across the two groups. However, the invariance of the uniquenesses was not tenable.

The noninvariance of the uniquenesses implied that there were some differences in the reliabilities across groups at the level of item. An inspection of the uniqueness estimates for the two groups yielded by Model 4 (Table 8.3) indicates that at the level of individual items, there were counterbalancing uniquenesses that were sometimes larger for Australian responses and sometimes larger for Spanish responses. However, at the level of the factors, the coefficient alpha estimates of reliability suggest that reliability estimates for the two groups were very similar (Table 8.1).

Table 8.3.   Factor Loading and Uniqueness Estimates for Model 4

Factor		Item	Factor loading	Uniqueness Australian	Spanish
1.	Health	1	.33	.93	.85
		12	.67	.69	.40
		23	.56	.65	.71
		34	.59	.70	.60
		45	.78	.41	.39
		56	.63	.59	.62
		67	.72	.51	.46
		69	.49	.77	.74
2.	Coordination	2	.58	.77	.56
		13	.53	.64	.79
		24	.77	.47	.35
		35	.74	.41	.49
		46	.74	.55	.36
		57	.72	.49	.48
3.	Activity	3	.47	1.44	.13
		14	.68	.61	.45
		25	.69	.68	?7
		36	.72	.49	.48
		47	.79	.39	.37
		58	.80	.36	.37
4.	Body Fat	4	.88	.20	.23
		15	.79	.35	.40
		26	.90	.21	.19
		37	.87	.25	.24
		48	.84	.32	.26
		59	.77	.43	.39
5.	Sport Comp.	5	.77	.45	.36
		16	.86	.25	.28
		27	.74	.42	.49
		38	.87	.24	.25
		49	.73	.49	.45
		60	.87	.24	.24
6.	Appearance	7	.77	.43	.38
		18	.79	.37	.39
		29	.79	.43	.33
		40	.74	.48	.41
		51	.87	.22	.25
		62	.54	.76	.67

Table 8.3.   Factor Loading and Uniqueness Estimates for Model 4

Factor		Item	Factor loading	Uniqueness	
				Australian	Spanish
7.	Strength	8	.81	.37	.31
		19	.84	.33	.26
		30	.77	.40	.40
		41	.53	.69	.75
		52	.83	.31	.31
		63	.72	.48	.49
8.	Flexibility	9	.45	1.48	.10
		20	.83	.38	.23
		31	.44	.81	.81
		42	.62	.61	.61
		53	.76	.43	.43
		64	.82	.34	.33
9.	Endurance	10	.79	.41	.33
		21	.77	.45	.36
		32	.73	.50	.45
		43	.82	.34	.32
		54	.77	.39	.41
		65	.76	.47	.38
10.	Global Physic.	6	.75	.46	.42
		17	.81	.40	.27
		28	.83	.34	.30
		39	.86	.26	.26
		50	.82	.33	.34
		61	.86	.22	.31
11.	Self-Esteem	11	.53	.79	.64
		22	.61	.64	.61
		33	.59	.65	.65
		44	.70	.51	.51
		55	.64	.60	.59
		66	.75	.41	.45
		68	.69	.50	.54
		70	.64	.58	.60

Note. All parameter estimates are standardized in relation to a common group metric. The solution presented is for Model 4 that holds the factor loadings, factor correlations, and factor variances to be invariant across the two groups. Thus, there is only one set of factor loading estimates presented, and uniquenesses are estimated separately for the Australian and the Spanish groups. All parameter estimates are statistically significant ($p < .01$).

Table 8.4. Factor Correlation and Factor Variance Estimates for Model 4

Factor		1	2	3	4	5	6	7	8	9	10	11
1.	Health	1.00										
2.	Coordination	.22	1.00									
3.	Activity	.07	.64	1.00								
4.	Body Fat	.17	.37	.24	1.00							
5.	Sport Compet.	.15	.79	.66	.34	1.00						
6.	Appearance	.17	.48	.33	.40	.50	1.00					
7.	Strength	.16	.55	.48	.06	.63	.50	1.00				
8.	Flexibility	.15	.70	.49	.34	.57	.44	.41	1.00			
9.	Endurance	.16	.72	.71	.45	.75	.45	.52	.60	1.00		
10.	Global Physical	.20	.59	.43	.53	.59	.68	.46	.43	.54	1.00	
11.	Self-Esteem	.33	.59	.39	.42	.53	.66	.46	.43	.48	.78	1.00
Factor Variances		.96	1.02	1.29	1.20	1.23	1.13	1.08	1.07	1.28	1.19	.91

Note. All the correlation estimates are standardized in relation to a common group metric. All parameter estimates are statistically significant ($p < .05$).

DISCUSSION

The investigation presented in this chapter focused on the construct validity of the PSDQ. The aim of this study was to test a number of invariance hypotheses regarding PSDQ psychometric properties across two samples of Australian and Spanish adolescents. The main purpose was to ascertain to what extent some of the questionnaire's psychometric properties estimated in an Australian sample could be generalized to a Spanish sample. A series of multisample CFAs were carried out to test the invariance of the factor structure underlying the questionnaire, the invariance of factor loadings and factor correlations, and, additionally, the invariance of factor variances and uniquenesses across the two samples. Results provided support for the reliability and construct validity of the questionnaire in the Spanish group. The reliability for the eleven PSDQ scales in the Spanish sample was good, and results of the multi-sample confirmatory factor analyses afforded promising support for the construct validity of the PSDQ for Spanish high school students. The generalizability of the factor structure underlying the questionnaire with Spanish adolescents was supported. Results demonstrated that the hypothesized eleven-factor structure was invariant across responses by the two cultural groups. Moreover, constraining factor loadings, factor correlations, and factor variances to being invariant across the two groups also resulted in a reasonable fit to the data. The invariance of uniquenesses is rejected, but the reliabilities of the 11 scales were similar.

According to the purpose of this study, support for the invariance of factor loadings and factor correlations were substantively important. Support for the invariance of factor loadings indicated that the relation between items and the underlying latent constructs that they are posited to measure, are the same for the Spanish and English versions of the questionnaire. This conclusion implies that the translated version into Spanish of the PSDQ is a useful instrument to be employed in the development of physical self-concept research with Spanish adolescents, and furthermore, that the Spanish version of the PSDQ can be used in cross-cultural comparison research across samples of Australian and Spanish adolescents. As different authors have pointed out (Byrne, Shavelson, & Muthén, 1989; Ghorpade, Hattrup, & Lackritz, 1999; Reise, Widaman, & Pugh, 1993), the only requirement for comparing groups on a latent variable is that factor loading invariance can be established. Thus, comparisons involving scale scores across groups of Australian and Spanish adolescents are psychometrically justified, since the items in the Spanish and Australian versions of the PSDQ appear to relate equivalently to their hypothesized latent factors.

Support for the invariance of factor correlations implies that the pattern of relationships among the 11 factors of the PSDQ was the same for the Australian and Spanish samples. This finding supports the questionnaire's construct validity across the two samples considered, and also offers support to the multidimensionality of the physical self-concept construct.

The invariance of uniquenesses was rejected. The decrement in fit due to constraining item measurement errors (or uniquenesses) to being invariant implies that there are some differences in the reliabilities across groups at the level of item. However, with the exception of two items, the differences between uniquenesses were not important. Furthermore, the coefficient alpha estimates of reliability were very similar for responses from the two countries.

In summary, the results obtained in the present study offer further evidence of the construct validity of the PSDQ, and of the generalizability of its factor structure, factor loadings, factor correlations, and factor variances for a sample of high school students from the Spanish culture. These results support the use of the PSDQ Spanish version for Spanish-Australian cross-cultural research.

To this end, we have pointed out the importance of cross-cultural comparison studies for purposes of construct validation of psychological questionnaires in general and multidimensional self-concept instruments, in particular. The development of these studies will also offer further evidence for the validation of the theories and models underlying the measurement instruments. Future cross-cultural research should pay attention to the construct validity of self-concept instruments in the different cultural contexts involved. Only then, self-concept researchers will know whether those instruments measure the same constructs across different cultural contexts, and consequently, whether perceptions of self generalize, or by contrast differ, across culture.

REFERENCES

Bentler, P. M., & Bonett, D. G. (1980). Significance tests and goodness of fit in the analysis of covariance structures. *Psychological Bulletin, 88*, 588–606.

Boersma, F. J., & Chapman, J. W. (1992). *Perception of Ability Scale for Students*. Los Angeles: Western Psychological Services.

Bracken, B. A. (1992). *Multidimensional Self Concept Scale*. Austin, TX: Pro-Ed.

Brown, L., & Alexander, J. (1991). *Self-Esteem Index*. Austin, TX: Pro-Ed.

Browne, M. W., & Cudeck, R. (1993). Alternative ways of assessing model fit. In K. A. Bollen & J. S. Long (Eds.), *Testing structural equation models* (pp. 136–162). Newbury Park, CA: Sage.

Browne, M. W., & Du Toit, S. H. C. (1992). Automated fitting on nonstandard models. *Multivariate Behavioral Research, 27*(2), 269–300.

Byrne, B. M. (1996). *Measuring self-concept across the lifespan: Issues and instrumentation*. Washington, DC: American Psychological Association.

Byrne, B. M. (2000). Measuring self-concept across culture: Issues, caveats, and practice. In R. G. Craven & H. W. Marsh (Eds.), *Self-concept, theory, research and practice: Advances for the new millennium* (pp. 30–41). New South Wales, Australia: Self Research Centre, University of Western Sydney.

Byrne, B. M., Shavelson, R. J., & Muthén, B. (1989). Testing for the equivalence of factor covariance and mean structures: The issue of partial measurement invariance. *Psychological Bulletin, 105*, 456–466.

Fox, K. R. (1990). *The Physical Self-Perception Profile manual*. DeKalb, IL: Office for Health Promotion, Northern Illinois University.

Fox, K. R., & Corbin, C. B. (1989). The Physical Self-Perception Profile: Development and preliminary validation. *Journal of Sport and Exercise Psychology, 11*, 408–430.

Ghorpade, J., Hattrup, K., & Lackritz, J. R. (1999). The use of personality measures in cross-cultural research: A test of three personality scales across two countries. *Journal of Applied Psychology, 84*(5), 670–679.

Hambleton, R. K., & Kanjee, A. (1995). Increasing the validity of cross-cultural assessments: Use of improved methods for test adaptations. *European Journal of Psychological Assessment, 11*(3), 147–157.

Harter, S. (1982). The Perceived Competence Scale for Children. *Child Development, 53*, 87–97.

Harter, S. (1985). *Self-Perception Profile for Children*. Denver, CO: University of Denver Press.

Hattie, J. (1992). *Self-concept*. Hillsdale, NJ: Erlbaum.

Jöreskog, K. G. (1993). Testing structural equation models. In K. A. Bollen & J. S. Long (Eds.), *Testing structural equation models* (pp. 294–316). Newbury Park, CA: Sage.

Jöreskog, K. G., & Sörbom, D. (1989). *LISREL 7: User's reference guide.* Mooresville, IN: Scientific Software.

Jöreskog, K. G., & Sörbom, D. (1993). *LISREL VIII: User's reference guide.* Mooresville, IN: Scientific Software.

Keith, L. K., & Bracken, B. A. (1996). Self-concept instrumentation: A historical and evaluative review. In B. A. Bracken (Eds.), *Handbook of self-concept* (pp. 91–170). New York: Wiley.

La Du, T. J., & Tanaka, J. S. (1995). Incremental fit index changes for nested structural equation models. *Multivariate Behavioral Research, 30*(3), 289–316.

MacCallum, R. C., & Hong, S. (1997). Power analysis in covariance structure modeling using GFI and AGFI. *Multivariate Behavioral Research, 32*(2), 193–210.

Marsh, H. W. (1987a). The factorial invariance of responses by males and females to a multidimensional self-concept instrument: Substantive and methodological issues. *Multivariate Behavioral Research, 22,* 457–480.

Marsh, H. W. (1987b). The hierarchical structure of self-concept and the application of confirmatory hierarchical factors analysis. *Journal of Educational Measurement, 24,* 17–39.

Marsh, H. W. (1988). *Self-Description Questionnaire, I.* San Antonio, TX: The Psychological Corporation.

Marsh, H. W. (1990a). A multidimensional, hierarchical self-concept: Theoretical and empirical justification. *Educational Psychology Review, 2,* 77–172.

Marsh, H. W. (1990b). *Self-Description Questionnaire, II.* San Antonio, TX: the Psychological Corporation.

Marsh, H. W. (1990c). The structure of academic self-concept: The Marsh/Shavelson model. *Journal of Educational Psychology, 82,* 623–636.

Marsh, H. W. (1992a). *Self-Description Questionnaire (SDQ) III: A theoretical and empirical basis for the measurement of multiple dimensions of late adolescent self-concept: A test manual and a research monograph.* Sydney: Faculty of Education, University of Western Sydney.

Marsh, H. W. (1992b). The content specificity of relations between academic achievement and academic self-concept. *Journal of Educational Psychology, 84,* 43–50.

Marsh, H. W. (1994a). The importance of being important: Theoretical models of relations between specific and global components of physical self-concept. *Journal of Sport and Exercise Psychology, 16,* 306–325.

Marsh, H. W. (1994b). Confirmatory factor analysis models of factorial invariance: A multifaceted approach. *Structural Equation Modeling, 1,* 5–34.

Marsh, H. W. (1996). Construct validity of Physical Self-Description Questionnaire responses: Relations to external criteria. *Journal of Sport and Exercise Psychology, 18,* 111–131.

Marsh, H. W., & Byrne, B. M. (1993a). Do we see ourselves as others infer: A comparison of self-other agreement on multiple dimensions of self-concept from two continents. *Australian Journal of Psychology, 45*(1), 49–58.

Marsh, H. W., & Byrne, B. M. (1993b). Confirmatory factor analysis of multitrait-multimethod self-concept data: Between-group and within-group invariance constraints. *Multivariate Behavioral Research, 28*(3), 313–349.

Marsh, H. W., & Hattie, J. (1996). Theoretical perspectives on the structure of self-concept. In B.A. Bracken (Eds.), *Handbook of self-concept* (pp. 38–90). New York: Wiley.

Marsh, H. W., Hey, J., Johnson, S., & Perry, C. (1997). Elite Athlete Self Description Questionnaire: Hierarchical confirmatory factor analysis of responses by two distinct groups of elite athletes. *International Journal of Sport Psychology, 28*(3), 237–258.

Marsh, H. W., Hey, J., Roche, L., & Perry, C. (1997). Structure of physical self-concept: Elite athletes and physical education students. *Journal of Educational Psychology, 89*(2), 369–380.

Marsh, H. W., & Hocevar, D. (1985). The application of confirmatory factor analysis to the study of self-concept: First and higher order factor structures and their invariance across age groups. *Psychological Bulletin, 97,* 562–582.

Marsh, H. W., & Redmayne, R. S. (1994). A multidimensional physical self-concept and its relation to multiple components of physical fitness. *Journal of Sport and Exercise Psychology, 16,* 45–55.

Marsh, H. W., Richards, G. E., Johnson, S., Roche, L., & Tremayne, P. (1994). Physical Self-Description Questionnaire: Psychometric properties and a multitrait-multimethod analysis of relations to existing instruments. *Journal of Sport and Exercise Psychology, 16,* 270–305.

Marsh, H. W., & Shavelson, R. J. (1985). Self-concept: Its multifaceted, hierarchical structure. *Educational Psychologist, 20,* 107–125.

Offer, D., Ostrov, E., Howard, K. I., & Dolan, S. (1992). *Offer Self-Image Questionnaire, Revised.* Los Angeles, CA: Western Psychological Services.

Pallas, A. M., Entwisle, D. R., Alexander, K. L., & Weinstein, P. (1990). Social structure and the development of self-esteem in young children. *Social Psychology Quarterly, 53*(4), 302–315.

Reise, S. P., Widaman, K. F., & Pugh, R. H. (1993). Confirmatory factor analysis and item response theory: Two approaches for exploring measurement invariance. *Psychological Bulletin, 114*(3), 552–566.

Richards, G. E. (1988). *Physical Self-Concept Scale.* Sydney: Australian Outward Bound Foundation.

Rosenberg, M. (1965). *Society and the adolescent self-image.* Princeton, NJ: Princeton University Press.

Rosenberg, M. (1979). *Conceiving the self.* New York: Basic Books.

Shavelson, R. J., & Bolus, R. (1982). Self-concept: The interplay of theory and methods. *Journal of Educational Psychology, 74,* 3–17.

Shavelson, R. J., Hubner, J. J., & Stanton, G. C. (1976). Validation of construct interpretations. *Review of Educational Research, 46,* 407–441.

Shavelson, R. J., & Marsh, H. W. (1986). On the structure of self-concept. In R. Schwarzer (Ed.), *Anxiety and cognitions.* Hillsdale, NJ: Erlbaum.

Song, I. S., & Hattie, J. A. (1984). Home environment, self-concept, and academic achievement: A causal modeling approach. *Journal of Educational Psychology, 76,* 1269–1281.

Steiger, J. H. (1990). Structural model evaluation and modification: An interval estimation approach. *Multivariate Behavioral Research, 25,* 173–180.

Tanaka, J. S. (1993). Multifaceted conceptions of fit in structural equation models. In K.A. Bollen & J. S. Long (Eds.), *Testing structural equation models* (pp. 10–39). Newbury Park, CA: Sage.

Tomás, I. (1998). Equivalencia psicométrica de una traducción del cuestionario de autoconcepto físico PSDQ (Physical Self-Description Questionnaire) al castellano. *Psychometric equivalence of a translation of the PSDQ (Physical Self-Description Questionnaire) into Spanish.* Doctoral dissertation, University of Valencia, Spain.

Tucker, L. R., & Lewis, C. (1973). A reliability coefficient for maximum likelihood factor analysis. *Psychometrika, 38,* 1–10.

Van de Vijver, F., & Leung, K. (1996). Methods and data analysis of comparative research. In J. W. Berry, Y. H. Poortinga, & J. Pandey (Eds.), *Handbook of cross-cultural psychology* (2nd Ed., Vol. 3, pp. 257–300). Needham, MA: Allyn & Bacon.

Vispoel, W. P. (1995). Self-concept in the arts: An extension of the Shavelson model. *Journal of Educational Psychology, 87,* 134–145.

Widaman, K. F. (1985). Hierarchically nested covariance structure models for multitrait-multimethod data. *Applied Psychological Measurement, 9*(1), 1–26.

part IV

**APPLIED STUDIES:
FOCUS ON SPECIAL EDUCATION**

CHAPTER 9

SELF-CONCEPTS OF PREADOLESCENTS WITH MILD INTELLECTUAL DISABILITIES

Issues of Measurement and Educational Placement

Danielle K. Tracey, Herbert W. Marsh and Rhonda Craven

The impetus for the current investigation stemmed from one of the most fervently disputed debates in education—whether students with disabilities should be educated in segregated special classes with other students with similar disabilities or in regular classes with their peers without disabilities. This placement debate is indeed alive and well in New South Wales, Australia, as illustrated by a visit to any school or discussions with teachers, parents, policy makers, and even students themselves. However, an evaluation of the literature suggests that this debate has been based primarily on philosophy and presumptions rather than empirical research evidence. Within the existing empirical research, methodological flaws substantially weaken many studies.

International Advances in Self Research, pages 203–229
Copyright © 2003 by Information Age Publishing
All rights of reproduction in any form reserved.

Particularly contentious in this area of research, is the role of self-concept. Facilitating students' positive self-concepts is a central goal of education internationally. A positive self-concept is valued for its own sake, but also because it is an important facilitator of other desirable educational outcomes, as well as emotional and social benefits (Boersma & Chapman, 1991; Branden, 1994; Harter, 1990; Marsh & Yeung, 1997). Arguments for educational placement of students with disabilities are often based on the anticipated impact on self-concept. There currently exist two diametrically opposed perspectives—labeling theory and social comparison theory— about the impacts of placement in segregated and regular classes. Labeling theory suggests that placing these students in special classes with other students with disabilities will lead to lower self-concepts, while the big fish little pond effect based on social comparison theory predicts that this very same placement will enhance the self-concepts of students with disabilities. Hence, the purpose of this chapter is to review existing literature and theoretical models and present new empirical results that contribute to the resolution of this debate.

THE MOVEMENT TOWARDS INCLUSION

A significant shift has occurred in both the philosophies and policies regarding the education of students with disabilities throughout the world. Education systems throughout Australia and the world are moving towards the placement of students with special needs in regular classes (Dempsey & Foreman, 1997). Significant catalysts have fueled this progression. The premise of social justice, reflected in the civil rights movement of the 1960s, questioned "separate but equal" class assignment for all students. It was argued that students with disabilities have just as much right to access educational services as other students. Importantly, the argument away from segregated settings was partly based on the assumption that identifying children as special and isolating them from their peers without disability resulted in a decrease in self-concept because of the stigmatizing effect of being labeled as having a disability (Budoff & Gottlieb, 1976; Coleman, 1983; Dunn, 1968; Wang & Birch, 1984).

In 1968 two influential pieces of educational research were published (Dunn, 1968; Rosenthal & Jacobson, 1968) which questioned the role of special education and its excessive use of segregated learning environments for students with disabilities. Dunn (1968) recommended that many disability labels be abolished and students with mild intellectual disabilities be maintained in regular classes with special educators serving them within this environment. As such, he called for a moratorium on the continuance of self-contained special classes for students with mild intellectual disabilities. The results of such studies, termed the "efficacy studies," were used by both researchers and educators to support the premise of Dunn (1968) that it was time to reevaluate current special education practices. Since that time, however, the validity of these studies has been questioned with regard to the appropriateness of instruments employed, the degree of experimental control and the inability to replicate results (e.g. Elashoff & Snow, 1971; Gottlieb, 1981; Kaufman, Agard, & Semmel, 1985).

The normalization principle, or social role valorization (Wolfensberg, 1972), argued for the "physical and social inclusion of developmentally delayed individuals into the mainstream of community" (Thurman & Fiorelli, 1979, p. 340). The Least Restrictive Environment Clause of the United States Education of All Handicapped Children Act (1975) (also known as Public Law 94-142) and subsequent amendments to that act (now known as the Individuals with Disability Education Act of 1990, IDEA) extended the right to a free public education to all children, regardless of disability, in the least restrictive environment possible. In 1986, the U.S. Department of Education Office of Special Education and Rehabilitative Services issued the Regular Education Initiative (Will, 1986) as a result of the normalization principle. Proponents of the Regular Education Initiative argued that there was no place for segregated settings, particularly for students with mild disabilities, and that these students had a right to be educated not just in a regular school, but in a regular class with other students. Students were assessed on the basis of their needs and supported as far as possible in the regular classroom.

Since the late 1980s, special educators, academics, and advocacy groups have argued that the concept of integration, the Least Restrictive Environment and the Regular Education Initiative do not go far enough and that a fully inclusive educational approach was required (Lipsky & Gartner, 1987; Stainback, Stainback, & Forest, 1989). They claimed that to continue to maintain some students, in special schools and special classes, was discriminatory and inequitable. They argued for a full-inclusion initiative. The inclusive schooling policy was given increased momentum with the publication of the recommendations made at the World Conference on Special Education: Access and Quality held in Salamanca in 1994 (UNESCO, 1994). What has become known as the Salamanca Statement is now a powerful document guiding policy making on the placement of students with disabilities. The primary aim of the statement is to make the regular class the only option for the placement of students with disabilities, regardless of the students' level of need or educational history (UNESCO, 1994).

Australian Provision for Educating Students with Disabilities

Inclusive educational practices in Australia have developed from international legislation that is based on ensuring the rights of all students to receive an equitable education. The Disability Services Act (Australian Commonwealth Government, 1986) and The Disability Discrimination Act (Australian Commonwealth Government, 1992) are federal legislation that indirectly cover the area of education and ensure that educational services are provided to students with disabilities. The Disability Services Act (1986) was designed to ensure that the services provided "further the integration of persons with disability in the community and complement services available generally to persons in the community" (p. 2). The Australian Federal Government retains limited central power over the education of students with disabilities. Although these acts effectively guarantee the provision of educational services to all students, they do not specify the way in which these services should be delivered. These services are provided at the discretion of these states and territories (Foreman, 2000). Although all agree that students should be placed in the least restrictive environment, not surprisingly, the interpretation of what constitutes the least restrictive environment varies (Forlin, 1998).

Defining Mild Intellectual Disability

Research in this area faces the dilemma that terminology and definitions of disabilities vary between countries, and within the states and territories in Australia. In addition, these definitions change over time. For example, the criterion for intellectual disability published by the American Association on Mental Deficiency has witnessed five amendments, between 1959 and 1992 (Grossman, 1983). Currently the most widely accepted definition of intellectual disability is that proposed by the American Association on Mental Retardation (AAMR): "Mental retardation refers to substantial limitation in present functioning. It is characterized by significantly subaverage intellectual functioning, existing concurrently with related limitations in two or more of the following applicable adaptive skill areas: communication, self-care, home living, social skills, community use, self-direction, health and safety, functional academics, leisure and work. Mental retardation manifests before age 18" (AAMR Ad Hoc Committee on Terminology and Classification, 1992, p. 5).

The New South Wales Department of Education and Training (1998) define a student with mild intellectual disability (mental retardation is the American equivalent of intellectual disability in Australia) as a student achieving an IQ score within the range of 56–75 (inclusive of a 5 point standard error) on a standardized, individually administered test of intelligence; accompanied by impairments in adaptive functioning and school achievement.

Educational Placement Options for Preadolescents with Mild Intellectual Disabilities in New South Wales

The range of placement options in New South Wales schools for preadolescents diagnosed with mild intellectual disabilities include: regular class, early school support program, IM (mild intellectual disability) support unit, and schools for specific purposes (New South Wales Department of Education and Training, 1998). Placement in a school for specific purposes is a rare placement for students with mild intellectual disabilities, and thus was not discussed.

Students with mild intellectual disabilities may be enrolled in a regular class with their peers of various abilities. These students receive funding from the New South Wales Department of Education and Training to support the students' placement. An IM Support Unit is a special education class for students with mild intellectual disabilities located within a regular school. These units provide for a maximum enrolment of 18 students, within an expected band of 15–18. In New South Wales the minimum age for admission to an IM Support Unit is eight years, or approximately at the commencement of grade 3 (New South Wales Department of Education and Training, 1998).

The Early School Support Program supports students identified as having mild intellectual disability enrolled in kindergarten, grade 1 and grade 2 classes. All students placed in the Early School Support Program remain enrolled in and class members of their regular class. The early school support teacher works with an identified group of up to 15 students (across one, two or more than two schools). The early school support teacher assists class teachers to develop and implement individualized learning programs.

Self-Concept: Labeling Theory versus the Big Fish Little Pond Effect

Self-concept has played a critical role in the placement debate about whether students should be taught in special, segregated classrooms or in regular, mainstream classes. Opponents of special class placement typically argue that the identification, isolation and segregation of these students tend to foster a negative self-concept (known as labeling theory). Labeling theory was very influential in the 1950s and 1960s and was one of the arguments used against segregation (Dixon & Gow, 1993). As a consequence, in the past decade, there has been a strong movement towards the inclusion of students with disabilities into more heterogeneous educational environments, based on the belief that the inclusion of students with disabilities will enhance their self-concept as they become more involved with the mainstream activities of the school (Szivos-Bach, 1993). References to well-established research findings, however, are often absent from education policy rationales (Idol, 1997). Research does not support the assumption that placing students with disabilities in regular classes with nondisabled peers results in enhanced self-concept (Chapman, 1988; Renick & Harter, 1989; Silon & Harter, 1985; Strang, Smith, & Rogers, 1978).

Proponents of special class placement argue that the environment of the special class, which is generally less competitive and consists of students with similar difficulties, reduces the anxieties and frustrations of students with disabilities, and as a consequence, fosters the development of a positive self-concept. The role of social comparison (Festinger, 1954) processes in determining self-concepts has been a particular focus in self-concept research as exemplified by Marsh and his colleagues and the development of the big fish little pond effect (e.g., Marsh & Craven, 2001). This research has focused on students at the most able end of the ability spectrum, showing that attending academically selective schools has a significant negative effect on academic self-concept and little systematic effect on nonacademic self-concept (Marsh, Chessor, Craven, & Roche, 1995; Marsh & Craven, 1997). Marsh and Johnston (1993) expanded this theoretical basis to include the effects of special class placement on children with learning difficulties. According to their expansion of the big fish little pond effect, the academic self-concepts of students with mild intellectual disability should increase when placed in segregated educational environments as their reference group experience similar difficulties, and when these students make social comparisons they evaluate themselves more favorably. Marsh and Johnston (1993) did not, however, actually pursue any empirical tests of their theoretical predictions based on the social comparison theory and the big fish little pond effect.

Measurement of Self-Concepts in Preadolescents with Mild Intellectual Disabilities

Sound empirical investigation of the merit of these competing theories has been scant and among the studies that have been conducted, weak methodologies have been employed. The two major limitations of past research include the predominant use of a unidimensional measure of self-concept, and the use of measures that have not been validated for the specific population.

Unidimensional versus Multidimensional Perspectives

In self-concept research there is an ongoing debate about the relative usefulness of unidimensional perspectives that emphasize a single, relatively unidimensional, global domain of self-concept (sometimes referred to as self-esteem) and multidimensional perspectives based on multiple, relatively distinct components of self-concept. Based primarily on educational psychology research, Marsh and Craven (1997, p. 191) argued that: "If the role of self-concept research is to better understand the complexity of self in different contexts, to predict a wide variety of behaviors, to provide outcome measures for diverse interventions, and to relate self-concept to other constructs, then the specific domains of self-concept are more useful than a general domain."

Historically, special education research has treated self-concept as a unidimensional, global construct represented by a single score (e.g. Beltempo & Achille, 1990; Coleman, 1983; Strang, Smith & Rogers, 1978). In 1985, Silon and Harter assessed the factor structure of the Perceived Competence Scale for Children for students with mild intellectual disability and concluded "retarded children do not make distinctions about specific competence domains but rather simply make judgments about one's competence at activities in general, regardless of the nature. Thus they think one is either competent or not" (p. 223). Recent self-concept research and theory, however, informs us that self-concept is indeed a multidimensional construct and children make clear distinctions between specific domains of their lives when evaluating themselves (Marsh, Craven, & Debus, 1991). Utilizing a unidimensional perspective of self-concept does not take account of the fact that children may evaluate themselves differently in different domains of their lives. A total score that indiscriminately confounds academic and various nonacademic components of self-concept will fail to capture the impact on different aspects of the self-concept. Given the possible differential impact that educational placement has on academic and nonacademic self-concept, as suggested by big fish little pond effect, the administration of a multidimensional instrument is vital.

Suitability of Existing Instruments

Relative to the abundant philosophical debates and educational policy that permeate this field, there has been a dearth of empirical investigation. Failure to pursue sound research with this population is due, in part, to problems associated with measuring the self-concepts of students with mild intellectual disability. Byrne (1996) in her definitive review of self-concept measurement instruments bemoaned this problem and noted "a search of the literature revealed such instrumentation to be disappointingly sparse and serves to highlight this critical void in the availability of self-concept measures for special populations" (p. 221).

Given this critical void, studies that have sought to examine self-concepts among this group have simply used measures standardized on groups of children with average cognitive ability, assuming these instruments would be appropriate (e.g. Cardona, 1997; Chiu, 1990; Coleman, 1985). However, this assumption is unfounded. As a result, any interpretation of existing findings for this population is "murky" at best, given the inadequacies of instrumentation (Byrne, 1996).

The Self Description Questionnaire-I (SDQ-I) (Marsh, 1988) is internationally regarded as the strongest multidimensional self-concept instrument for school-age students (Boyle, 1994; Byrne, 1996; Hattie, 1992). Recent advances in self-concept theory and research have resulted in the successful measurement of self-concept for children younger than previously thought possible. The development of the SDQ-I individualized administration, SDQI-IA, has meant that the self-concept of children as young as five years of age has been successfully measured (Marsh, Craven & Debus, 1991; Marsh & Craven, 1997). Given these recent findings, we proposed that the SDQI-IA might be suitable for measuring the multidimensional self-concept of preadolescents with mild intellectual disabilities.

THE PRESENT INVESTIGATION

The two overarching objectives of the present investigation are to:

1. Evaluate whether the SDQI-IA has sound reliability and construct validity when used to measure the self-concepts of preadolescent students aged 7 to 13 years with mild intellectual disability, and whether self-concepts for this group are multidimensional;

2. Evaluate the impact of educational placement in either regular classes or special education classes on the self-concepts, comparing and contrasting predictions by labeling theory and the big-fish-little-pond effect.

We address these questions through a combination of cross-sectional and longitudinal analyses, using both quantitative and qualitative data.

METHOD

Participants

Participants were 211 students (120 males and 91 females) enrolled in grades 2–6. The age of the participants ranged from 7 years 5 months to 13 years ($M = 10.25$ years, $SD = 1.48$). Students had been identified as having a mild intellectual disability according to the NSW Department of Education and Training criteria, (IQ score within the range of 56–75 on a standardized, individually administered test of intelligence; accompanied by impairments in adaptive functioning and school achievement). The sample was culturally heterogeneous.

On the basis of the students' current educational placement, two separate groups of students were identified: 98 students were enrolled full-time in a regular class (58 males, 40 females), and 113 students were enrolled full-time in a special class—termed an IM Support Unit (62 males, 51 females). Parents of the students completed informed consent forms, and all students were instructed that their participation was voluntary.

Thirty-nine of the students participating in Study 1 also participated in a 12-month, 3-wave longitudinal study. Students were selected to partake in Study 2 on the basis that they were enrolled in Grade 2 and would be experiencing a possible change in educational placement the following school year. The average age of the students at Time 1 was 8 years 3 months. At the commencement of the study, all 39 students (22 males, 17 females) were enrolled full-time in grade 2 regular classes. At time 2 and 3, however, 21 students were enrolled in regular classes whereas 18 were enrolled in IM Support Units. Eight of the participants were chosen at random to partake in a brief semistructured interview at Time 3 (four in regular classes and four in IM Support Units).

Measures

Self-concept

The Self Description Questionnaire I—Individual Administration (SDQI-IA) assesses three areas of academic self-concept (reading, mathematics, and general school self-concept scales), four areas of nonacademic self-concept (physical ability, physical appearance, peer relationships, and parent relationships self-concept scales), and general self self-concept. Three total scores can also be measured on the basis of these scales: Academic self-concept (the average of reading, mathematics, and general school self-concept scales), Nonacademic self-concept (the average of Physical ability, physical appearance, peer relationships, and parent relationships self-concept scales), and Total self-concept (the average of academic and nonacademic self-concept scales). 64 items are presented as declarative statements and the respondent is asked to determine how this statement describes them (measured on a Likert-type scale ranging from 1 to 5).

Qualitative Interview Questions

Semistructured interviews were conducted to elucidate student perceptions of stigmatization and student preference for placement in either regular classes or IM Support Units. Questions were asked to ascertain whether students: perceived themselves as different to other students and whether this varied depending on their educational placement; experienced positive and/or negative peer relationships in their current educational placement; felt that their class was different to other classes in the school; experienced stigmatization and whether this varied according to their educational placement; and identified a preferred educational placement.

Procedure

As a prerequisite to this study, permission to conduct the research was granted from the NSW Department of Education and Training, and from principals at participating schools. Additionally, all students had returned written parental permission to participate and had given verbal consent at the commencement of each session. Students were tested individually, and testing was conducted in a location on the school grounds chosen to ensure that responses from other students would not be heard. The administration of the SDQI-IA took approximately 30 minutes for each student. Administration procedures outlined by Marsh, Craven, and Debus (1991) and Marsh and Craven (1997) were strictly adhered to. Demographic and educational information about students was gathered from their teacher on the same day of testing. The length of the qualitative interviews ranged from 5 to 15 minutes. The first author conducted all qualitative interviews.

The SDQI-IA was administered by the first author, a PhD student psychologist and a third year university student, all of whom had experience working with young children. Research assistants received training and practice sessions prior to the testing phase of the study. An individually administered interview procedure was used (see Tracey, 2002). In the actual administration of the SDQI-IA, six example items were read to the student. After reading each example item the interviewer asked the student whether he or she understood the sentence. If the student did not understand the sentence, the interviewer explained the sentence further, ascertained whether the student understood the sentence, reread the sentence, and requested a response. After ascertaining that the student understood the example item, the interviewer initially asked the student to respond "yes" or "no" to the sentence to indicate whether the sentence was a true or false description of the student. If the student initially responded "yes" the interviewer then asked the student whether he or she meant, "yes always" or "yes sometimes." If the student responded "no" the interviewer then asked the student whether she or he meant "no always" or "no sometimes." After the student successfully responded to sample items and questions raised were answered, the interviewer then read aloud each of the 64 positively worded items using the same procedure. Students were periodically asked if they understood subsequent items during the remainder of the administration to encourage them to seek clarification if needed. If the student indicated that she or he understood the sentence but could not decide whether to respond yes or no, the interviewer recorded a response of 3, halfway between the responses of "no sometimes," and "yes sometimes." This middle category was rarely selected, as this occurred infrequently and students were not told of this option. The response options were based on a 5 point response scale: 1 = "no always," 2 = "no sometimes," 3 = student understands sentence but does not state yes or no, 4 = "yes sometimes," and 5 = "yes always." Halfway through the administration of the SDQI-IA items the interviewer asked the student to do some physical activities for a brief period before the interviewer proceeded to administer the remaining 32 items.

Statistical Analyses

To determine internal consistency of the SDQI-IA, one-factor congeneric estimates of reliability were calculated for all 8 subscales and the 3 total scores. Analyses for measurement structure for the SDQI-IA were conducted with LISREL 8 (Joreskog & Sorbom, 1993) using maximum likelihood estimation. As in other SDQ research and recommended in the test manual (e.g., Marsh, 1988, 1990; Marsh & Hocevar, 1985), factor analyses were conducted on item-pair scores in which the first two items in each scale are averaged to form the first item pair, the next two items are used to form the second pair, and so forth. Educational placement was represented as a single-item construct and therefore, assumed measured without error. For the cross-sectional analyses, educational placement was included in the confirmatory factor analysis as a single-item construct to ascertain its relationship with students' self-concepts. For the longitudinal analyses, the effect of educational placement on students' self-concepts was ascertained with the application of repeated measures factorial analyses of covariance, using Time 1 responses as covariates. Transcripts of the qualitative interviews were analyzed manually using content analysis (Miles & Huberman, 1994). Once this process was complete two research psychologists were asked to "expert check" that the generated themes were agreed on (Strauss & Corbin, 1994).

RESULTS

Psychometric Properties Of SDQI-IA Responses by Students with Mild Intellectual Disability (Study 1)

Reliability Estimates

For the total sample of participants, internal consistency estimates for the subscales (see Table 9.1) were generally high with a mean omega of 0.88, and a range of 0.72 to 0.95. For the younger cohort (Year 2–4), the mean reliability estimate was 0.89 (0.72–0.96). For the older cohort (Year 5–6), the mean reliability estimate was 0.88 (0.77 to 0.95). Hence, the reliability estimates were similar for younger and older students. The internal consistency estimates for the three total scores were consistently high (i.e., mean for the total participants = 0.94). The high reliabilities for the total scores, however, were based partly on the larger number of items incorporated into these scales as the average correlation among the items was somewhat smaller than for the specific scales. The results indicated that the SDQI-IA was a reliable measure of the self-concepts of preadolescents with mild intellectual disabilities.

Table 9.1.   Summary of One Factor Congeneric Coefficient Estimates of Reliabilities

Scale	Year 2–4 (n = 121)	Year 5–6 (n = 90)	Total (n = 211)
	ω	ω	ω
Physical ability	.93	.85	.90
Physical appearance	.94	.93	.93
Peer relationships	.90	.89	.90
Parent relationships	.83	.89	.86
Reading	.93	.90	.90
Mathematics	.95	.93	.94
General-school	.88	.85	.86
General-self	.72	.77	.72
Total nonacademic	.93.	.93	.92
Total academic	.95	.94	.94
Total score	.96	.95	.95

Factor Structure and Multidimensionality

The confirmatory factor analysis based on the 8-factor model clearly identified all eight factors that the SDQI-IA was designed to measure. The factor loading for each variable (Table 9.2) was consistently high on the factor that it was designed to measure (average factor loading = 0.80). The goodness of fit values (TLI = .909 and RNI = .920) indicated that the model provided a reasonable fit to the data. Correlations among factors (see Table 9.2) varied from .10 to .80 (mean = 0.42). These correlations clearly demonstrate that preadolescent students with mild intellectual disability are successfully able to differentiate between multiple dimensions of self-concept.

These confirmatory factor analyses results offer strong support for a multidimensional model of self-concept for students with mild intellectual disability aged 7 to 13 years and provide further support for the Marsh/Shavelson model of self-concept on which the SDQI-IA was based. This finding substantiates the multidimensionality of self-concept for this population, a finding that has been questioned by past researchers (e.g. Silon & Harter, 1985). The current study with preadolescent students with mild intellectual disability produced similar findings to that of Little and colleagues' (1990) study of adolescents with mild intellectual disability and the SDQII.

These confirmatory factor analyses provide an exciting and unique set of results about the structure and nature of the self-concept of students with mild intellectual disability. It demonstrated that theory and instrument construction are inextricably entwined. From both a theoretical and practical perspective, the most important finding was the clearly differentiated factor structure of the SDQI-IA for preadolescents with mild intellectual disability and the good psychometric properties obtained for the SDQI-IA with this population.

Impact of Educational Placement on Preadolescents' Self-Concepts: Cross-sectional Analyses (Study 2)

The purpose of these analyses in Study 2 was to determine if there was a significant difference in the multiple dimensions of self-concept reported by students with mild intellectual disability placed in regular classes and those placed in IM Support Units. This evaluation tested empirically the competing predictions based on labeling theory and the big fish little pond effect. The cross-sectional results were based on responses of 211 students with mild intellectual disability placed in either regular classes ($n = 98$) or IM Support Units ($n = 113$).

A structural equation path model was constructed in which the main effects of age, gender, placement, and interactions among these variables were related to the eight SDQI-IA self-concept factors (see Figure 9.1). The effects of gender and age were small. Females reported significantly lower physical ability self-concept than did their male counterparts. As students grew older, there were statistically significant declines in physical appear-

Table 9.2. Factor Loadings and Correlations among Factors

Item parcel	PHYS	APPR	PEER	PRNT	READ	MATH	SCHL	GENL
Phys1	.69							
Phys2	.60							
Phys3	.85							
Phys4	.87							
Appr1		.89						
Appr2		.93						
Appr3		.72						
Appr4		.78						
Peer1			.80					
Peer2			.60					
Peer3			.90					
Peer4			.77					
Prnt1				.66				
Prnt2				.70				
Prnt3				.68				
Prnt4				.83				
Read1					.82			
Read2					.88			
Read3					.87			
Read4					.83			
Math1						.87		
Math2						.92		
Math3						.89		
Math4						.95		
Schl1							.75	
Schl2							.73	
Schl3							.72	
Schl4							.81	
Genl1								.41
Genl2								.66
Genl3								.68
Genl4								.67
Phys	1.00							
Appr	.27	1.00						
Peer	.41	.30	1.00					
Prnt	.31	.40	.31	1.00				

Table 9.2.   Factor Loadings and Correlations among Factors (Cont.)

Item parcel	PHYS	APPR	PEER	PRNT	READ	MATH	SCHL	GENL
Read	.24	.27	.46	.29	1.00			
Math	.32	.10	.28	.14	.31	1.00		
Schl	.36	.45	.48	.31	.69	.65	1.00	
Genl	.53	.59	.68	.57	.64	.47	.80	1.00

Note. PHYS = Physical ability APPR = Physical appearance PEER = Peer relationships
PRNT = Parent relationships READ = Reading MATH = Mathematics SCHL = General-
school GENL = General self-concept. All parameter estimates are presented in completely
standardized form.

ance and general school self-concept. There were no other significant
main effects of age, gender or age-by-gender on the self-concepts of students with a mild intellectual disability.

Path coefficients for placement demonstrated that students with mild
intellectual disability placed in an IM Support Unit reported significantly
higher peer relationships, reading, mathematics, general-school and general self-concept scores than students with mild intellectual disability
placed in regular classes. The effects of placement did not interact significantly with age or gender, but there was a significant three-way age-by-gen-
der-by-placement effect for parent relationships self-concept. Further
exploration of this three-way interaction suggests that as males with mild
intellectual disability grow older, those placed in regular classes report a
decline in parent relationships self-concept.

Predictions that there would be significantly negative effects of placement in regular classes for the three academic self-concept scales were
clearly supported. However, predictions that there would be no significant
difference between the two groups in terms of nonacademic self-concepts,
was only partially supported. Although there was no significant difference
between the physical ability, physical appearance and parent relationships
self-concepts of preadolescents with mild intellectual disability in regular
classes and IM Support Units, those in IM Support Units reported significantly higher peer relationships self-concept than did their regular class
counterparts.

Current educational policy and procedures are based, in part, on the
assumptions made by labeling theory that inclusion in regular classes will
enhance the self-concepts of students with disability. However, the results
of Study 2 provide an impressive endorsement of the big fish little pond
effect, and contradict labeling theory. Students with mild intellectual disability placed in IM Support Units report significantly higher peer relationship, mathematics, reading, general-school and general self-concept than

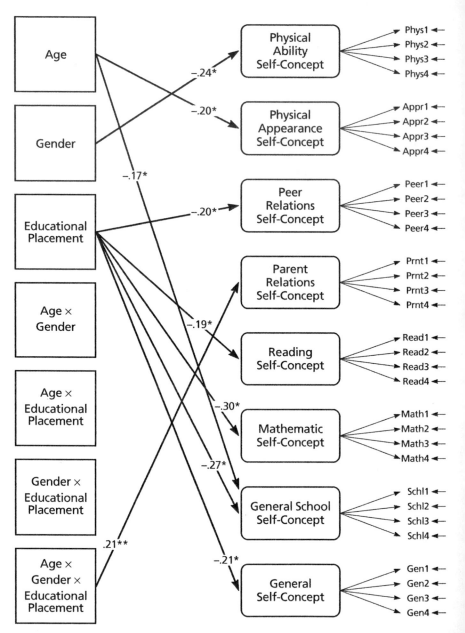

Figure 9.1.   Path Model Relating the main effects of Placement (2 = regular class, 1 = special class), age, gender (2 = female, 1 = male) and their interactions to eight self-concept factors. For purposes of presentations, only statistically significant path coefficients are presented (see Tracey, 2002, for full results). Goodness of fit statistics were **TLI = .887, RNI = .908, and RMSEA = .0570.**

students with mild intellectual disability placed in regular classes. The lack of interaction effects show that the placement effects generalize over gender and age, for the ages considered here. Indeed, these results refute the presumed benefits of inclusion advocated by proponents of labeling theory, and have significant policy implications for the worldwide inclusion movement.

These findings highlight that educational placement has a different effect on the academic and nonacademic self-concepts of students with mild intellectual disability. Indeed, it is argued that only a multidimensional measure of self-concept is capable of successfully capturing this differential effect. Measures of general self-concept, previously prominent in this area of research, are unable to detect differential impacts on specific dimensions of self-concept that underlie the predictions of the competing theories of labeling theory and the big fish little pond effect. As a result, the potency of arguments based on outdated unidimensional models of self-concept in testing these competing theories and the validity of findings emanating from such studies are dubious.

Impact of Educational Placement on Preadolescents' Self-Concepts: Longitudinal Analyses (Study 3)

The purpose of Study 3 was to evaluate the impact of placement in regular classes versus placement in IM Support Units on multiple dimensions of self-concept. The results were based on a cohort of 39 students with mild intellectual disability and were individually tested on three separate occasions over a period of twelve months. Time 1 was at the end of Year 2 when all students were in the same program (Early School Support Program) while enrolled full-time in regular classes. Time 2 was six months later, five academic months into Year 3 when 21 of these 39 students were enrolled in regular classes and 18 were in IM Support Units. Time 3 occurred at the end of Year 3, when students had been in their respective placements for ten academic months. This chapter reports the results of data analyses applied repeated measures, where time (2 occasions after initial baseline data) and educational placement (2 types—regular class and IM Support Unit) were cast as independent variables and responses gathered at Time 1, prior to differential educational placement, were used as covariates for the corresponding measure.

In preliminary analyses, for the total self-concept score (averaged across all eight self-concept scales) there was no significant main effect of educational placement, or time-by-educational placement interaction effect. However, there was a significant educational placement-by-scale-by-time interaction effect. Of central importance, the effect of educational placement-by-time varied significantly depending on the self-concept scale. To determine the nature of this interaction, separate analyses for the three academic self-concept scales, and the four nonacademic self-concept scales, and general self-concept were pursued to test a priori predictions.

For total academic self-concept (averaged across the three academic self-concept scales), there was no significant main effect of educational placement, time, or scale. However, there was a significant educational placement-by-time interaction effect, suggesting that over time students in the two educational placements differed. Results indicated (see Figure 9.2) that the difference in academic self-concept did not occur until Time 3, more than five months after being placed in either IM Support Units or regular classes. This change was a result of the relative increase in academic self-concept for students in IM Support Units, and a relative decrease in academic self-concept for students in regular classes. Furthermore, given that there were no significant interaction effects involving scale, this significant difference between placement groups was consistent for all three academic self-concept scales: reading, mathematics, and general-school. These finding support the big fish little pond effect in that students with mild intellectual disability placed in IM Support Units experienced higher academic self-concepts than their counterparts in regular classes.

For total nonacademic self-concept (averaged across the four nonacademic scales) there were no significant main effects of educational placement, time, or scale, and no significant interaction effects. These results support the predictions based on the big fish little pond effect that nonacademic self-concept is not affected by educational placement. The nonsignificant main effect of scale demonstrates that this pattern is consistent for

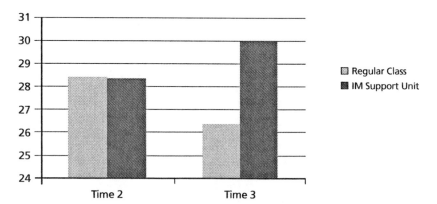

Figure 9.2.   Adjusted means of total academic self-concept for students with mild intellectual disability placed in regular classes or IM support units after five and ten months in their respective placement.

all four nonacademic self-concept scales: physical ability, physical appearance, peer relationships and parent relationships. Similarly, for general self-concept, there were no significant effects for educational placement, time, or the placement-by-time interaction. To confirm that the impact of educational placement-by-time was significantly different for total nonacademic and total academic self-concept, a further multiple factorial analyses was conducted to directly compare total nonacademic self-concept with total academic self-concept.

In summary, the results of the longitudinal analyses (Study 3) support the big fish little pond effect—and consequently contradict labeling theory. The nonacademic and general self-concepts of students with mild intellectual disability did not significantly differ according to educational placement. Students with mild intellectual disability in IM Support Units, however, reported significantly higher academic self-concepts than did students with mild intellectual disability in regular classes.

Qualitative Analyses (Study 4)

In Study 4 we summarize a qualitative investigation of the inclusion of students with mild intellectual disabilities—as reported by the students themselves. Interviews were conducted with eight students with mild intellectual disability in both regular classes ($n = 4$) and IM Support Units ($n = 4$) in an attempt to give a voice to these students and explore their experience and preference for educational placement. Through a process of "pattern coding" (Miles & Huberman, 1994), the following broad themes or constructs emerged.

Being Different to Other Students
The majority of students demonstrated an awareness of being different to other students because of their special learning needs. Five of the eight students identified that they were different because of their poor learning skills and their need for more help with school work than other students (2 in regular classes and 3 in IM Support Units).

- "I'm different. I'm different because some people get their work right, and I can get it wrong. We are different people. I've got a different brain" (Alex, regular class) (Please note: Fictitious names were used to ensure the confidentiality of participants).
- "Sometimes I'm not very good at reading and that. I do things different. They do different work. I do easier work cause they can do the work. Sometimes I can do it" (Bradley, IM Support Unit).

Peer Relationships

Interestingly, both students in regular classes and IM Support Units experienced a similar amount of negative peer relationships, however, students' difficulties originated from different educational placements. Students in regular classes reported negative interactions with students within their own class, whereas students in IM Support Units reported negative interactions with students from other classes. Students in regular classes appeared to be neglected, or worse, by their peers within their own class, whereas those in IM Support Units were actively rejected through teasing by students from different classes. It appears that students with mild intellectual disability in IM Support Units had their own class as a safe haven but were ridiculed by students in other classes (e.g. at recess). The students with mild intellectual disability in regular classes, on the other hand, did not feel really accepted in any school context. The quantitative peer relationships self-concept scores gathered through the SDQI-IA supported this finding. The following quotes are characteristic of the comments made by students in regular classes about being neglected by students in regular classes because of their placement:

- I don't fight with anyone or nothing, but like no-one in here talks to me in the playground (Veu, regular class).
- There are three boys in my class who call me dumb and won't sit next to me, but I tell the teacher and I stay next to the teacher (Mohamed, regular class).
- I play with my sister at lunch. She is in Year 5. I don't play with Samantha *(a girl in her class)* and them, they tell me not to (Clair, regular class).

My Class Being Different to Other Classes

Students with mild intellectual disabilities placed in regular classes and IM Support Units appeared to differ most in terms of this theme. Two of four students in regular classes reported that their class was no different to other classes and two reported that their class was different to other classes because of factual reasons not founded on differing learning needs. In contrast, all four students with mild intellectual disabilities placed in IM Support Units believed that their class was different to other classes. All respondents identified the unique features of the IM Support Unit as reasons for this difference; however, these differences were perceived as positive, negative and neutral.

- "Because we've got a small class. There is 11 people and normally there is 21 in other classes" (Candice, IM Support Unit).
- "Our class is different to other classes. Other classes do harder work and we do easy work" (Sarah, IM Support Unit).
- "It means you're like a dumb class" (Veu, IM Support Unit).

Preference for Educational Placement

Interviews with students with mild intellectual disabilities in regular classes did not reveal preference for educational placement. This may be directly related to the fact that they did not perceive any substantive difference between their class and others. In a powerful declaration, which embodies the premise of the big fish little pond effect, Clair (regular class) stated;

- "I want to be in a different class. It has too many people learning and I don't. It makes me feel sad."

Students in IM Support Units, however, verbalized quite clearly their opinion on being placed in IM Support Units. They perceived this placement as beneficial for learning, but expressed concern over the teasing they received as a result of this same placement.

- "I'd rather be in a small class cause then the teacher can learn more and they concentrate on me then if there is 22 and the teacher can do more stuff with us. I am happy here. I do pretty good work in here than the other class. I can do good work here and not in the other class. I can do better work in this class than the other class. I probably can't do spelling good in their class" (Lee, IM Support Unit).

DISCUSSION

Research summarized in this chapter provides a wealth of information for understanding self-concept for this population as well as for the inclusion debate. We now have new evidence of a multidimensional self-concept for preadolescents with mild intellectual disabilities, which to date, has been rejected (e.g. Silon & Harter, 1985). This finding has significant ramifications for all professionals working with these students and should influence their beliefs about mild intellectual disabilities and the nature of their interactions with these students. It is especially important to consider various domains of the self-concept as this study has clearly demonstrated that educational placement has a different impact on academic self-concept and nonacademic self-concept.

The present study reports on the first application of the SDQI-IA for preadolescents with mild intellectual disabilities. We now have a reliable and valid measure of the self-concepts of this population. The SDQI-IA may now be employed in future research and by practitioners and educators working with these students in order to both gage their self-concept, and measure the impact of interventions designed to enhance their self-concepts.

Students in regular classes and special classes differed significantly on several dimensions of self-concept. Students in regular classes had significantly lower self-concepts for all three academic scales (reading, mathematics, general school) in terms of the cross-sectional and longitudinal analyses. The cross-sectional analysis—based on a larger sample size—also revealed that those in special classes reported significantly higher peer relationships and general-self self-concepts.

The current results demonstrate that the predictions of the big fish little pond effect were also relevant for students with mild intellectual disability (as well as gifted and talented students which has been well documented). Results support the big fish little pond effect's prediction that special class placement enhances the academic self-concepts of students with mild intellectual disabilities. At the same time these findings contradict labeling theory—the basis of much current special education philosophy. In particular, proponents of labeling theory advocate that one of the substantial benefits of placing students with disabilities with students without disabilities, is the increased peer relationships experienced by those with disabilities. Conversely, both the quantitative and qualitative results emanating from this study, suggest that placing students with mild intellectual disabilities in IM Support Units may enhance their peer relationship self-concept. This finding suggests that proponents of labeling theory may need to reassess their argument, however, future research is required to confirm these findings.

Implications for Research and Theory

The present investigation clearly supports a multidimensional perspective of self-concept over the unidimensional perspective that still prevails in this area of research. A multidimensional model of self-concept was the key theoretical basis guiding this investigation. Current models and theories were critically assessed and the Shavelson, Hubner, and Stanton (1976) model and the subsequent Marsh and Shavelson (1985) revisions to this model were judged to be the best available theoretical model of the structure of self-concept. The results of the present investigation clearly attest to the multifaceted structure of self-concept for preadolescents with mild intellectual disability that has been rejected in previous studies in this area (e.g. Silon & Harter, 1985). In support of the construct validity of the multidimensional self-concept responses and consistent with predictions from the big fish little pond effect, the negative effects of regular class placement were largely limited to academic areas of self-concept. There were no significant effects of placement for self-concepts of physical ability, physical appearance, and parent relationships—although Study 2 suggested that there might be negative effects of regular class placement for peer relationship self-concepts. Furthermore, the present investigation has advanced this field of research by identifying the SDQI-IA as a reliable and valid self-concept instrument for assessing multiple dimensions of self-concept with preadolescents with mild intellectual disabilities. The identification of an appropriate instrument for this population also ensures that researchers may utilize the SDQI-IA to address substantive issues based on between-construct studies within this population.

These results lend substantial support to the value of social comparison theory (Festinger, 1954) and the big fish little pond effect (Marsh, 1984) in understanding the influence of special education placement on the self-concepts of preadolescents with mild intellectual disability. In turn, results suggest the re-evaluation of the predictions made by labeling theory (Goffman, 1963) that has dominated special education philosophy and policy. Evidence from the qualitative interviews suggest that students with mild intellectual disability in IM support units experience stigmatization as a result of their placement, however, it is likely (as proposed by Marsh & Johnston, 1993) that these labeling effects are off-set by the concomitant social comparison effects and therefore academic self-concept is bolstered. This calls for the refinement of labeling theory to embody predictions of the big fish little pond effect and the incorporation of labeling effects into explanations of assimilation and contrast effects predicted by the big fish little pond effect in relation to students with mild intellectual disability.

Implications for Educational Practice

The current findings call into question current international educational policy and philosophy. For instance, the NSW Department of Education and Training reports that "it has been moving and will continue to move from the provision of predominantly segregated educational settings to the provision of services in the regular neighborhood school for students with disabilities" (New South Wales Department of School Education, 1992, p. 4). The current policy of placing students with mild intellectual disabilities into regular classes forces the individual into a situation where the majority of comparisons he or she makes with others are negative, resulting in adverse effects on his or her academic self concept. This is problematic given that a positive self-concept is highly related to one's academic achievement, academic behavior, and social and emotional adjustment (Boersma & Chapman, 1991; Branden, 1994; Harter, 1990; Marsh & Yeung, 1997).

The results of this study challenge special educators and policy makers to recognize the detrimental impact of inclusion on students' self-concepts and devise appropriate strategies to counter this negative effect, rather than accepting the largely unsupported inference from labeling theory that the effects of inclusion on self-concept are positive. To place a child in an educational environment in which he or she cannot maintain feelings of self worth, may actually increase rather than decrease the restrictiveness of the school environment which is in discord with the Individuals with Disabilities Education Act of 1990.

These findings are particularly important if there is a continuation of the current inclusion movement, which seems highly likely. Educational policy needs to be determined by educational research. It does not follow that positive self-concept will flow automatically from physical inclusion in the regular class, as predicted by labeling theory and further research is needed. However, given the saliency of the external frame of reference in determining one's self-concept, such resources may do little to bolster the self-concepts of students with disabilities who remain in regular classes. Therefore, if this is the case, the inclusion policy must be challenged.

The present study promotes the need to look at educational alternatives in terms of student outcomes rather than on the basis of unsupported theoretical models. The most important criterion must be, which placement is superior for each individual. This decision should not be based solely on philosophical considerations, but on empirical evidence. The current study provides an important tool for gathering such empirical evidence—the SDQI-IA. These findings imply that one should take another look at policy trends to include students with mild intellectual disabilities in regular classes. Clearly, major policy decision can not and should not rest on the results of any single study, especially one that addresses the effects of educational placement on a single variable in one country alone. These results, however, should serve as a catalyst for future research to adequately and empirically assess the merits of the inclusion movement.

REFERENCES

American Association on Mental Retardation Ad Hoc Committee on Terminology and Classification. (1992). *Mental retardation: Definition, classification and systems of support* (9th Ed). Washington, DC: American Association on Mental Retardation.

Australian Commonwealth Government. (1986). *Disability Services Act.* Canberra: Australian Government Publishing Service.

Australian Commonwealth Government. (1992). *Disability Discrimination Act.* Canberra: Australian Government Publishing Service.

Beltempo, J., & Achille, P. (1990). The effect of special class placement on the self-concept of children with learning disabilities. *Child Study Journal, 20*(2), 81–103.

Boersma, F., & Chapman, J. (1991). Assessment of learning disabled students' academic self-concepts with the past findings from 15 years of research. *Developmental Disability Bulletin, 19*, 81–104.

Boyle, G. (1994). Self-Description Questionnaire: A review. *Test Critiques, 10*, 632–643.

Branden, N. (1994). *Six pillars of self-esteem.* New York: Bantam.

Budoff, M., & Gottlieb, J. (1976). Special-class EMR children mainstreamed: A study of an aptitude (learning potential) × treatment interaction. *American Journal of Mental Deficiency, 81,* 1–11.

Byrne, B. (1996). *Measuring self-concept across the lifespan: Issues in instrumentation.* Washington, DC: American Psychological Association.

Cardona, C. (1997, March). *Including students with learning disabilities in mainstream classes: A 2-year Spanish study using a collaborative approach to intervention.* Paper presented at the Annual Meeting of the American Educational Research Association, Chicago, IL.

Chapman, J. (1988). Learning disabled children's self-concepts. *Review of Educational Research, 58,* 347–371.

Chiu, L. (1990). Self-esteem of gifted, normal and mild mentally handicapped children. *Psychology in the Schools, 27,* 263–268.

Coleman, J. (1983). Handicapped labels and instructional segregation: influences on children's self-concepts versus the perceptions of others. *Learning Disability Quarterly, 6,* 3–11.

Coleman, J. M. (1985). Achievement level, social class, and the self-concepts of mildly handicapped children. *Journal of Learning Disabilities, 18*(1), 26–30.

Dempsey, I., & Foreman, P. (1997). Trends in the educational placement of students with disabilities in New South Wales. *International Journal of Disability, Development and Education, 44*(3), 207–216.

Dixon, R., & Gow, L. (1993, November). *The self concept of developmentally delayed students at a vocational college: A preliminary report.* Paper presented at the ASSID National Conference, Newcastle.

Dunn, L. (1968). Special education for the mildly retarded: Is much of it justifiable? *Exceptional Children, 34,* 5–22.

Elashoff, J., & Snow, R. (1971). *Pygmalion reconsidered.* Worthington, OH: Jones.

Festinger, L. (1954). A theory of social comparison processes. *Human Relations, 7,* 117–140.

Foreman, P. (2000). *Integration and inclusion in action* (2nd ed.). New South Wales, Australia: Harcourt Brace & Company.

Forlin, C. (1998, September). *Teachers' perceptions of the stress associated with inclusive education and their methods of coping.* Paper presented at the 21st National Conference of the Australasian Association of Special Education, Brisbane, Australia.

Goffman, E. (1963). *Stigma: Notes on the management of a spoiled identity.* Englewood Cliffs, NJ: Prentice-Hall.

Gottlieb, J. (1981). Mainstreaming: Fulfiling the promise? *American Journal of Mental Deficiency, 86,* 115–126.

Grossman, H. (Ed.). (1983). *Classification in mental retardation.* Washington, DC: American Association on Mental Deficiency.

Harter, S. (1990). Issues in the assessment of self-concept of children and adolescents. In A. La Greca (Ed.), *Through the eyes of the child: Obtaining self-reports from children and adolescents.* Boston: Allyn & Bacon.

Hattie, J. (1992). *Self-concept.* Hillsdale, NJ: Erlbaum.

Idol, L. (1997). Key questions related to building collaborative and inclusive schools. *Journal of Learning Disabilities, 30*(4), 384–394.

Joreskog, K., & Sorbom, D. (1993). *LISREL 8: Structural equation modeling with the SIMPLIS command language.* Chicago: Scientific Software International.

Kaufman, M., Agard, T., & Semmel, M. (1985). *Mainstreaming: Learners and their environment.* Cambridge, MA: Brookline Books.

Lipsky, D., & Gartner, A. (1987). Capable of achievement and worthy of respect: Education for handicapped students as if they were full-fledged human beings. *Exceptional Children, 54,* 69–74.

Little, T., Widaman, K., Farren, A., MacMillan, A., Hemsley, R., & MacMillan, D. (1990). *The factor structure and reliability of the Self Description Questionnaire (SDQII) in an early adolescent populations, stratified by academic level, ethnicity and gender.* Riverside, CA: University of California, School of Education.

Marsh, H. (1984). Self-concept, social comparison and ability grouping: A reply to Kulik and Kulik. *American Educational Research Journal, 21,* 799–806.

Marsh, H. (1988). Self-description-Questionnaire 1. *SDQ-1 manual and research monograph.* San Antonio: The Psychological Corporation.

Marsh, H. (1990). A multidimensional, hierarchical model of self-concept: Theoretical and empirical justification. *Educational Psychology Review, 2,* 77–172.

Marsh, H., Chessor, D., Craven, R., & Roche, L. (1995). The effects of gifted and talented programs on academic self-concept: The big fish strikes again. *American Educational Research Journal, 32,* 285–319.

Marsh, H., & Craven. R. (1997). Academic self-concept: Beyond the dustbowl. In G. Phye (Ed.) *Handbook of classroom assessment: Learning, achievement and adjustment* (pp. 131–198). Orlando, FL: Academic Press.

Marsh, H. W., & Craven, R. (2001). The pivotal role of frames of reference in academic self-concept formation: The big fish little pond effect. In F. Pajares & T. Urdan (Eds.), *Adolescence and education* (Vol. 2, pp. 83–123).

Marsh, H., Craven, R., & Debus, R. (1991). Self-concepts of young children aged 5 to 8: Their measurement and multidimensional structure. *Journal of Educational Psychology, 83,* 377–392.

Marsh, H., & Hocevar, D. (1985). The application of confirmatory factor analysis to the study of self-concept: First and higher order factor structures and their invariance across age groups. *Psychological Bulletin, 97,* 562–582.

Marsh, H., & Johnston, C. (1993). Multidimensional self-concepts and frames of reference: Relevance to the exceptional learner. In F. E. Obiakor & S. Stile (Eds.), *Self-concept of exceptional learners: Current perspectives for educators.* Duduque, IA: Kendall/Hunt.

Marsh, H., & Shavelson, R. (1985). Self-concept: Its multifaceted, hierarchical structure. *Educational Psychologist, 20,* 107–125.

Marsh, H., & Yeung, A. (1997). Causal effects of academic self-concept on academic achievement: Structural equation models of longitudinal data. *Journal of Educational Psychology, 89,* 41–54.

Miles, M., & Huberman, A. (1994). *Qualitative data analysis: A expanded sourcebook* (2nd ed.). Newbury Park, CA: Sage.

New South Wales Department of Education and Training. (1998). *Special education handbook for schools.* New South Wales: Author.

New South Wales Department of School Education. (1992). *Integration statement.* Sydney: New South Wales Government Printer.

Renick, M., & Harter, S. (1989). Impact of social comparisons on the developing self-perceptions of learning disabled students. *Journal of Educational Psychology*, *81*, 631–638.

Rosenthal, R., & Jacobson, L. (1968). *Pygmalion in the classroom: Teacher expectation and pupils' intellectual development*. New York: Holt, Rinehart and Winston.

Shavelson, R., Hubner, J., & Stanton, G. (1976). Self-concept: Validation of construct interpretations. *Review of Educational Research, 46*, 407–441.

Silon, E., & Harter, S. (1985). Assessment of perceived competence, motivational orientation, and anxiety in segregated and mainstreamed educable mentally retarded children. *Journal of Educational Psychology, 77*(2), 217–230.

Stainback, W., Stainback, S., & Forest, M. (1989). *Educating all students in the mainstream of regular education*. Baltimore: Paul H. Brookes.

Strang, L., Smith, M., & Rogers, C. (1978). Social comparison, multiple reference groups, and the self-concepts of academically handicapped children before and after mainstreaming. *Journal of Educational Psychology, 70*, 487–497.

Strauss, A., & Corbin, J. (1994). Grounded theory methodology. In N. Denzin & Y. Lincoln (Eds.), *Handbook of qualitative research* (pp. 273–285). Newbury Park, CA: Sage.

Szivos-Bach, S. (1993). Social comparisons, stigma and mainstreaming: The self-esteem of young adults with a mild mental handicap. *Mental Handicap Research, 6*, 217–236.

Tracey, D. K. (2002). Self-Concepts of preadolescents with mild intellectual disabilities: Issues of measurement and educational placement. Doctoral thesis, SELF Research Centre, University of Western Sydney. [http://edweb.uws.edu.au/self/Theses/Tracey/Thesis.htm]

Thurman, S., & Fiorelli, J. (1979). Perspectives on normalization. *The Journal of Special Education, 13*, 339–345.

UNESCO. (1994). *The Salamanca statement and framework for action on special needs education*. New York: Author.

United States Education of All Handicapped Children Act. (1975). *Public Law 94–142. 94th Congress of United States of America, S.6* Education for all handicapped children Act of 1975.

Wang, M., & Birch, J. (1984). Comparison of a full-time mainstreaming and a resource room approach. *Exceptional Children, 50*, 33–40.

Will, M. (1986). *Educating students with learning problems—a shared responsibility*. Washington, DC: U.S. Department of Education, Office of Special Education and Rehabilitative Services.

Wolfensberger, W. (1972). *The principle of human services*. Toronto, Canada: National Institute on Mental Retardation.

CHAPTER 10

SELF-CONCEPT ENHANCEMENT FOR STUDENTS WITH LEARNING DIFFICULTIES WITH AND WITHOUT ATTENTION DEFICIT HYPERACTIVITY DISORDER

Waheeda Tabassam and Jessica Grainger

Often parents and teachers of students with learning disabilities point out that these students have negative self-concept or low self-esteem. Self-perception of students with learning disabilities (LD) has been a focus of research during the last three decades (Harter, Whitesell, & Junkin, 1998). There is mounting research evidence that students with LD have lower self-estimations compared to normally achieving peers (Bender, 1986, 1994; Bender & Wall, 1994; Chapman, 1988a, Chapman & Boersma, 1979; Mercer, 1997; McInerney, 1999; Rogers & Saklofske, 1985). A significant number of students with LD have negative self-estimations and research shows that a negative self-concept can be quite problematic in adulthood and may tremendously affect the lives of these adults (Bender, 1994). Researchers (Mercer, 1997; Smith, 1994) have, therefore, stressed that the self-con-

International Advances in Self Research, pages 231–260
Copyright © 2003 by Information Age Publishing
All rights of reproduction in any form reserved.

cept concerns of students with LD should be addressed in just as intense a manner as their academic concerns, to ensure that these children grow up with enough personal strengths to undertake the challenges of life.

This chapter provides an overview of the issues related to self-perceptions of students with LD and identifies some useful strategies for the enhancement of self-perceptions of students with learning and attention difficulties. The Australian Council for Specific Learning Difficulties (AUS-PELD) suggests the use of the term "learning difficulties" (instead of learning disabilities), arguing that most of the children who experienced problems in school were not demonstrably impaired or disabled. Therefore the term *learning difficulties* (LD) has been used in Australia and New Zealand (Ashman & Elkins, 1998) and will be used in this chapter, however it will be necessary to use the term learning disabilities when referring to American research.

Definition of Learning Disability

Students with academic learning disabilities (LD) are those children or adolescents who are not achieving in one or more academic areas in school when compared with their peers. These students have normal intelligence but are not achieving at a level either anticipated in relation to their intellectual ability or commensurate with their typical peers (O'Shea, O'Shea, & Algozzine, 1998). The Association for Children with Learning Disability (ACLD) (ACLD Newsbriefs, 1986) wrote the following definition of learning disability:

> Specific Learning Disability is a chronic condition of presumed neurological origin, which selectively interferes with the development, integration, and/or demonstration of verbal and/or nonverbal abilities. Specific Learning Disabilities exist as a distinct handicapping condition and varies in its manifestation and in degree of severity. Throughout life, the condition can affect self-esteem, education, vocation, specialization, and/or daily living activities. (p. 15)

This definition stresses the lifelong nature of a learning disability and it also places emphasis on the social and emotional aspects. The definition reflects the fact that in view of the complications there is also a specific need to address issues of self-esteem and self-concept in this population.

Prevalence of Learning Difficulties

Prevalence estimates of LD ranges from 1% to 30% (Ashman & Elkins, 1998). According to O'Shea and colleagues (1998), the prevalence of learning disabled students relative to all students with disabilities has ranged from 28% to 64%. In Australia, the prevalence of LD ranges from 11% to 20% in primary schools and 6.25% to 11% at secondary level (Ashman & Elkins, 1998). Learning difficulties have been reported more among males than females. Smith (1994) reports a 2:1 to 6:1 male to female ratio in the LD population.

Types of Learning Difficulties

Academic difficulties of students with LD are usually noted in reading, mathematics, written language and oral language. However, reading and mathematics difficulties are the most common learning difficulties. Almost 10 to 15% of a school population experience difficulty in reading (Harris & Sipay, 1990). Reading experiences strongly influence a student's self-image and feeling of competency, and reading failure may lead to poor self-concept, anxiety and lack of motivation (Clever, Bear, & Juvonen, 1992; Heyman, 1990).

The mathematics difficulties, which usually emerge in the early years and continue throughout secondary school (Mercer, 1997), may stem from slowness in operation execution (Kirby & Becker, 1988), developmental delays (Cawley, Fitzmaurice-Hayes, & Shaw, 1988), memory deficiencies (Bley & Thornton, 1995), language problems (Cawley, 1985), lack of effective cognitive and metacognitive strategies (Cherkes-Julkowski, 1985) and procedural error (Russell & Ginsburg, 1984). These difficulties can interfere with the successful acquisition of mathematical concepts and skills in areas such as computations, problem solving and mental calculations.

In some circumstances the social and emotional characteristics of students with LD predispose them for reading and/or mathematics disabilities. For example, the emotional reaction of some individuals to mathematics is so negative that they develop a specific anxiety related to mathematics. This condition is believed to stem from a fear of school failure and low self-esteem and causes students to become so tense that their ability to solve, learn or apply mathematical concepts is impaired (Slavin, 1991). Therefore, Mercer (1997) suggests that the noncognitive aspects of learning difficulties such as social and emotional aspects deserve more attention.

Social and Emotional Problems of Students with LD

Most common social and emotional problems of students with learning difficulties may include low self-esteem, poor peer-relations, negative self-concept, poor self-efficacy beliefs, maladaptive attributional style and even depression (Ashman & Elkins, 1998; Mercer, 1997). These complications are closely related to each other and may have a severe impact on a student's overall adjustment and achievement behavior. Many students with learning difficulties experience problems with social acceptance (Bender, 1994), social skills (Bender, 1994; Smith, 1994) and social competence (Bender & Wall, 1994). However, poor self-concept of students with LD is the most common problem that has been identified by a number of researchers (Bender, 1994; Chapman, 1988a, 1988b; Mercer, 1997, 1991; Rogers & Saklofske, 1985; Smith, 1994). As self-concept plays a significant role in the learning processes, the development of a positive self-concept has been one of the recognized goals of education (Marsh & Craven, 1997).

Self-concept of Students with LD

Research over the last two decades has clearly evidenced that students with learning difficulties (LD) have lower self-estimations compared to normally achieving peers (Bender, 1986, 1994; Bender & Wall, 1994; Chapman, 1988a, Chapman & Boersma, 1979; Mercer, 1997; McInerney, 1999; Rogers & Saklofske, 1985). Several possible causes have been presented for the lower self-perceptions of students with learning difficulties. Research shows that students with learning difficulties generally experience prolonged failure in academic and social situations, and therefore may hold lowered self-worth and negative self-concept. According to Mercer (1997) social rejection or social isolation and academic problems may be associated with poor self-concept in students with LD. However, research over the last decade has clearly shown that most students with learning difficulties hold a lower self-concept regarding their academic skills, whereas their nonacademic self-concept is almost equivalent to that of typically achieving peers (Chapman, 1988a; Harter, Whitesell, & Junkin, 1998; Kloomok & Cosden, 1994). Bender and Wall (1994), after reviewing 27 studies on self-concept, reported that students with LD exhibited lower academic self-concept and lower perceived academic competence than their peers without disabilities. Pearl (1992) suggests that lower self-concept can be both a cause and a result of social, emotional, and academic problems. However there is limited empirical support for a cause-effect relationship between academic problems and poor self-perceptions. Mercer (1997) suggests that it is reasonable to consider that academic problems result in social and emotional problems and vice versa and that clearly there is an interactive model in which both primary and secondary factors impinge on each other in a reciprocal and interactive manner.

Attributional Style of Students with LD

Attributional style is a specific way to explain and attribute the causes of one's successes and failures (Seligman, 1991). Studies report students with LD often display a negative attributional style whereby failure is attributed to internal causes (lack of ability and efforts) and success attributed to external causes (luck and chance) (Bryan, 1986; Cooley & Ayres, 1988; Pearl, 1982, 1992; McInerney, 1999; Rogers & Saklofske, 1985). Researchers (Peterson, Buchanan, & Seligman, 1995) identified three dimensions of attributional style or explanatory style: internal/external, stable/unstable and global/specific. According to Peterson and colleagues (1995), individuals who possess internal, stable and global attributions for their successes, and/or possess external, unstable, and specific attributions for their failures, will demonstrate a positive attributional style. In contrast the individuals with external, unstable, and specific attributions for success outcomes and/or internal, stable and global attributions for failure outcomes would demonstrate a negative attributional style. In other words an individual with a positive attributional style tends to internalize responsibility in success situations and externalize responsibility in failure situations, whereas an individual with a negative attributional style usually internalizes responsibility in failure situations and externalizes responsibility in success situations.

An individual's attributional style may be associated with his/her self-concept. McInerney, (1999) suggests that children with high academic self-concept attribute their success to internal and stable factors (ability and efforts). These feelings contribute to further satisfaction with their performance and therefore lead to higher academic self-concept and further striving for achievement. In contrast, children with lowered academic self-concept attribute their success to external and unstable factors and they do not feel the pride associated with their success. McInerney (1999) further suggests that a child's sense of self and self-worth, which includes beliefs about personal ability or self-efficacy, and the child's interpretation of prior successful and unsuccessful experiences influence his/her motivation to learn. Thus a negative attributional style may reduce the individual's motivation to strive for further achievement.

Self-efficacy Beliefs of Students with LD

Self-efficacy is a personal belief about one's capabilities to organize and implement actions, necessary to attain designated levels of performance (Bandura, 1982, 1997). Perceived self-efficacy or efficacy beliefs play an influential role in academic attainment. Bandura (1997) has reported that regardless of ability levels students with higher self-efficacy beliefs perform well in all situations. Research indicates that students with learning difficulties generally have poor beliefs about their efficacy for achieving academic success (Schunk, 1985; Schunk & Hanson, 1985; Schunk & Swartz, 1993). Bandura (1997) suggests that students may perform poorly either because they lack the skills or because they have the skills but lack the perceived self-efficacy to complete the task successfully. Thus a strong sense of self-efficacy plays a positive role in the achievement process.

Relationship Between Self-concept, Self-attributions and Self-efficacy Beliefs

Back in 1988, Cooley and Ayres demonstrated a positive correlation between self-concept scores and ability/effort attributions of preadolescents with learning disabilities. Specifically they reported that the lower the self-concept of students with LD, the more likely they were to attribute their failure to lack of ability. Other researchers have also demonstrated a close relationship between academic self-concept and attributions for academic success and failure (e.g., Craven, Marsh, & Debus, 1991; Marsh, 1988; Marsh, 1984). Marsh (1988) demonstrated a consistent pattern of relationship between multidimensional self-concept and multidimensional attributions for the causes of success and failures. However, these studies do not assume that lower academic self-concept leads to negative attributions or vice versa.

Attributions are also related to self-efficacy beliefs. Schunk (1984, 1990) and Schunk and Cox (1986), in a series of experiments have shown that students' self-efficacy about a particular task is influenced by the type of attributions used by the students to explain success and failure. Attributions and self-efficacy beliefs also influence self-concept. Recent studies that compared self-concept and self-efficacy beliefs in academic context suggested that perception of one's academic self-concept was strongly influenced by one's efficacy beliefs (Bong & Clark, 1999; Pajares, 1996). The self-perception of personal efficacy was said to be a core aspect of an individual's self-concept (Brandtstadter, 1999). Individuals with enhanced self-efficacy usually exhibit increased intrinsic motivation, more favorable self-perceptions and more adaptive attributional patterns (Bong & Clark, 1999; Pajares, 1996). These findings indicate that self-concept, self-efficacy beliefs and self-attribution are closely related to each other and in order to get a complete picture of self-perceptions of students with learning difficulties it is important to consider all of these variables.

COMORBIDITY BETWEEN LEARNING DIFFICULTIES AND ATTENTION DEFICIT HYPERACTIVITY DISORDER

Many studies have demonstrated the presence of attention and behavioral problems in children with LD (Bender, 1986; McKinney & Feagans, 1983, 1984). Attention Deficit/Hyperactivity Disorder (ADHD) is a diagnostic label employed by the American Psychiatric Association in the Diagnostic and Statistical Manual of Mental Disorder DSM-III-R (1987) and DSM-IV (1994). Children with this disorder may fail to give close attention to details; their work is often messy and is performed carelessly. They may find it hard to persist with tasks until completion and often move on to other tasks before the completion of a previous task. They experience difficulty in following instructions and organizing tasks and activities. These children are easily distracted, have poor concentration and frequently do not seem to be listening (Green & Chee, 1994).

There is a significant co-occurrence of learning difficulties (LD) and Attention Deficit/Hyperactivity Disorder (ADHD). A considerable comorbidity (40% to 80%) has been reported between LD and ADHD and almost one-third of the students with LD are thought to have Attention Deficit/ Hyperactivity Disorder (ADHD) (Hallahan, 1989; Robins, 1992). The National Health and Medical Research Council Report (Carmichael et al., 1997) reviewed studies in which coexisting learning difficulties were reported in 10% to 90% of students diagnosed with ADHD. The incidence of learning problems within the population of children with ADHD has been estimated as ranging from 43% to 92% (Biederman, Newcom, & Sprich, 1991). According to DeLong (1995) ADHD prevalence rates for students labeled as having learning disabilities range from 41% to 80%, and estimates of learning disabilities in the ADHD population range from 9% to 80%. Perhaps the most reliable data, concerning the comorbidity issue, emerged from the review of McKinney, Montangue, and Hocutt (1993). When stringent identification criteria were applied for both ADHD and LD, McKinney and colleagues found that comorbidity occurred in at least 10% to 20% of cases, although the prevalence of co-occurrence varied from 9% to 63% across the studies reviewed. However, if even the most conservative of these figures is accepted, there are many students with LD who are experiencing ADHD.

Social and Emotional Problems of Students with Comorbid LD/ADHD

Many social, emotional and educational difficulties are associated with attention deficit hyperactivity disorder (Hoza, Pelham, Milich, Pillow, &

McBride, 1993). Research indicates that children with ADHD, due to their inattention and impulsive activities, experience frequent exposure to failures, receive negative feedback from parents, teachers and peers, and have to experience significant problems with peer rejection and popularity (Bender, 1997; Cunningham, Siegal, & Offord, 1985; Cantwell & Baker, 1991; Hinshaw & Melnick, 1995; Mercer, 1997; Milich, Loney & Landau, 1982). Studies have also reported that students with ADHD hold poor self-concept and negative attributional patterns (Hoza et al., 1993; Hoza, Waschbusch, Pelham, Molina, & Milich, 2000; Huntington & Bender, 1993). Biederman and Steingard (1989) suggest that the assessment of self-perception of children and intervention at elementary school level is very important since 30% to 50% of children with LD and ADHD appear to face continued difficulties throughout adolescence and adulthood. In addition, the risk of diminished self-esteem increases as attentional symptoms persist throughout the life span. Research provides evidence that negative self-concept and/or low self-esteem is a typical problem for adolescents whose ADHD symptoms endure. Weiss and Hechtman (1993) reported that adults with ADHD scored significantly lower than controls on two of the three measures administered to assess self-esteem. Adults who still had problems with concentration, social interactions, emotional disturbance and impulsivity also exhibited poor self-concept. It seems possible that the social, emotional and academic difficulties would be intensified for the students who have both problems, LD and ADHD, rather than just LD. The risk factors associated with LD may increase markedly when there is co-occurrence of ADHD, and the interaction between LD and ADHD may, in consequence, cause further decrements in the self-perceptions of individuals with comorbid LD/ADHD.

Although a significant number of children with LD have an associated ADHD, little research has been undertaken to explore the self-concept and related constructs like attributional style and self-efficacy beliefs of students with comorbid LD/ADHD. In particular, most of the previous studies on the self-perceptions of students with LD have not specifically identified or broken down their samples into subgroups such as learning difficulties with ADHD and learning difficulties without ADHD. Given a high comorbidity between LD and ADHD and the nature of problems associated with both disorders it seems possible that students with comorbid LD/ADHD would experience more severe social and emotional problems than either group alone. An investigation of self-perceptions of students with comorbid LD/ADHD may provide a better understanding of the problems arising from the interaction of learning difficulties and ADHD. In view of the issues surrounding the psychological and emotional well being of children with LD and LD/ADHD, it is clearly important to examine the factors that influence their self-concept and also to develop interventions for the enhancement of self-concept.

SELF-CONCEPT ENHANCEMENT-SIGNIFICANCE AND APPROACHES

It is widely believed that a positive self-concept always plays a significant role in social and learning processes. Students with a positive self-concept usually are academically successful and socially well adjusted, whereas students who hold negative self-perceptions feel inadequate and give up when the task is difficult (Bandura, 1982; Chapman, 1988a; Marsh & Craven, 1997). Self-concept enhancement interventions help students feel good about themselves and their abilities. Therefore the development of positive self-concepts is considered to be one of the most important goals of education (Marsh & Craven, 1997).

Significance of Enhancing Self-concept for Students with LD and LD/ADHD

It is generally held that students who hold a positive self concept tend to be academically successful, socially well adjusted, more readily accepted by their peers and usually try harder and persist longer when faced with difficult tasks. On the other hand, students who hold negative self-perceptions feel personally and socially inadequate and tend to reduce their efforts or give up altogether when a task is difficult (Bong & Clark, 1999; Bryan, 1986; Chapman, 1988; Craven et al., 1991). Children with LD and ADHD usually experience repeated social and academic failures and they gradually develop an identity or self-image linked to failure. This negative self-image persists into adolescence and even into adulthood and does not appear to change over time (Chapman, 1988; Magg & Behrens, 1989; Ritter, 1989). Studies have indicated that adolescents with learning disabilities are much more likely to be victims of depression and suicide than normally achieving students (Bender, Rosenkrans, & Crane, 1999; Harter, 1993, 1998; Huntington & Bender, 1993). Thus, it is very important to develop interventions for the enhancement of self-concept for students with a handicapping condition such as LD and LD/ADHD.

Self-concept Enhancement Approaches

Self-concept enhancement studies typically use two approaches to change self-concept, either direct enhancement or indirect enhancement approaches. The direct enhancement approach targets self-concept by providing direct praise and performance feedback. The indirect enhancement approach seeks to enhance self-concept indirectly by targeting a related construct, such as attributional style or the self-efficacy beliefs of the participants (Marsh & Craven, 1997). The individual's attributional style impacts on his/her self-concept such that individuals with a positive attributional style generally have a positive self-concept. Researchers have also verified a consistent relationship between self-concept, self-attributions and achievement outcomes (Marsh, 1984; Marsh, Cairns, Relich, Barnes, & Debus, 1984). These findings seem to suggest that self-concept can be changed indirectly by changing the individual's attributional patterns.

Attributional Retraining

Attributional retraining strategies attempt to teach participants desirable causal attributions about behavioral outcomes (i.e., success and failure) and attempt to reduce undesirable or maladaptive causal attributions. According to Weiner's (1986) attribution theory individuals high in achievement motivation attribute their success to internal causes (ability and efforts) and their failure to external causes (task difficulty and luck). Weiner (1986) claimed that in self-concept enhancement programs the perceived causes of performance (attributions) must be changed in order to change self-concept. Self-efficacy theory (Bandura, 1982, 1997) assumes that success attributed to ability and effort can enhance efficacy and when success is attributed to ability or effort, pride is experienced. This experience of pride enhances self-concept. The learned helplessness model (Abramson, Seligman, & Teasdale, 1978) assumes that an internal global and stable attributional style for failure is associated with low self-concept while an internal stable and global attributional style for success enhances positive self-concept. All three models emphasize the importance of attributing success to ability and effort, and failure to lack of effort and task difficulty. Marsh (1984), however, has demonstrated a negative relation between high self-concept scores and lack of effort attributions, and has recommended that strategy attributions in failure situations may be an important alternative to attributing failure to lack of effort. Students with LD may have a low ability therefore it is not desirable to teach them to attribute failure to a lack of ability or effort. Attributing failure to incorrect strategies, rather than lack of ability or effort, seems more suitable for enhancing academic self-concept of students with learning difficulties.

Research on Self-concept Enhancement

Craven, Marsh, and Debus (1991) and Craven (1996) implemented a self-concept enhancement intervention for students with low academic self-concept, which was based on both direct and indirect enhancement approaches. The intervention employed a combination of performance feedback and attributional retraining. In order to enable students to generate an appropriate system of self-reinforcement that would assist the enhancement of academic self-concept by a direct means, ability attributional statements (Schunk, 1983, 1985) were coupled with performance feedback. Researchers named this type of feedback "internally focused performance feedback." Craven and colleagues (1991) and Craven (1996) explain that internally focused feedback encourages students to perceive that they are competent in specific subject areas, which leads to the development of positive self-perception in those specific subject areas (e.g., reading and mathematics). The studies assumed the relationship between self-concept and self-attributions was reciprocal; therefore, a change in attributions would be associated with changes in academic self-concept. The results indicated that the intervention techniques focused on the enhancement of academic self-concept had substantial effects on academic self-concept (i.e., reading self-concept or maths self-concept) but little effect on nonacademic components (physical ability self-concept or physical appearance self-concept). These studies provide some guidelines for developing successful self-concept enhancement intervention.

According to Craven and colleagues (Craven et al., 1991; Marsh & Craven, 1997; Craven & Marsh, in press) a self-concept enhancement intervention would be more successful if: specific facets, rather than global aspects, of self-concept are targeted, the targeted areas of self-concept are logically related to the goals of the intervention, the instruments that specifically tap the constructs that are the targets of the intervention are used, and the measures of the actual processes thought to be responsible for self-concept change are included. The Craven and colleagues (1991) and Craven (1996) studies indicate the success of attributional retraining in enhancing the academic self-concept of normally achieving students. It might be possible that similar techniques would also be effective in enhancing the academic self-concept of students with learning difficulties. Although a number of studies have been conducted with normally achieving students, there is a paucity of self-concept enhancement intervention studies for students with LD and comorbid LD/ADHD. The major concern of this chapter, which flows from the awareness of literature on self-perceptions of LD and ADHD, is the identification of the need to implement interventions for the enhancement of self-perceptions of students with LD and LD/ADHD. An early identification and intervention program may be warranted for the overall emotional well being of this population. Previous studies have indicated that self-attributions and self-efficacy beliefs are closely linked to each other and to self-concept. It is, therefore, possible to improve the self-perception of students by improving their self-efficacy beliefs and/or by changing their maladaptive attributional patterns.

THE PRESENT INVESTIGATION

Based on Craven's guidelines the present investigation sought to assess the effectiveness of an intervention designed to enhance the academic self-concept of students with LD and students with comorbid LD/ADHD. The intervention utilized attributional retraining focused on changing self-concept through changing participant's attributional patterns. It was expected that a positive change would occur in academic attributional style, and this in turn would impact on academic self-concept and also academic self-efficacy beliefs. Parallel to the results obtained in previous studies on self-concept enhancement (Craven et al., 1991; Craven, 1996), it was predicted that, as a result of this intervention, a significant positive change would occur in the targeted areas of self-concept (i.e. reading self-concept and maths self-concept), a smaller positive change might occur in the related areas of self-concept (school self-concept), however, no significant change was anticipated for areas of self-concept unrelated to the intervention (nonacademic self-concept). It was also expected that LD students, in comparison to LD/ADHD students, would experience more gains in the targeted areas of self-concept.

METHOD

Procedure

The participants in this study were students with LD and with comorbid LD/ADHD who reported significantly lower scores on academic self-concept but whose nonacademic self-concept was not significantly different from that of normally achieving peers. Thus the intervention was focused to enhance academic self-concept. A total of 36 participants, comprising 18 participants with LD and 18 participants with comorbid LD/ADHD, age from 8 years to 11.6 years, in grade 3 to 6, drawn from nine public schools in the eastern suburbs of Sydney, Australia, participated in this study. These students were previously identified by a larger study on self-perceptions of students with LD and LD/ADHD, conducted by the authors (Tabassam & Grainger, 2002). The participants exhibited a low academic self-concept score that fell into the bottom quartile of the academic self-concept score measured by the Self-Description Questionnaire SDQ-1 (Marsh, 1990). Each student in LD and LD/ADHD groups demonstrated a full-scale intelligence score greater than 79 on the Wechsler Intelligence Scale for Children (Wechsler, 1991). The students with comorbid LD/ADHD also demonstrated a score greater than 1.5 standard deviations above the mean for their respective age and gender on the ADHD-Teacher Rating Scale and the ADHD-Parent Rating Scale (DuPaul, 1991).

All participants with LD and LD/ADHD were students of regular classes and were placed in a special education withdrawal class for reading and mathematics at their schools. Students with a learning disability due to physical or sensory handicap were excluded from the sample. No significant difference in socioeconomic status, age or intellectual ability was found between the two groups.

Instruments

In order to assess the self-concept of the participants the Self-Description Questionnaire SDQ-1 (Marsh, 1990) was used. The SDQ-1 was designed to measure specific facets of the self-concept of preadolescents from Grades 2 to 6 and has sound psychometric properties. The SDQ-1 consists of eight scales. On the basis of these scales the instrument provides scores for academic, nonacademic and general self-concepts.

The Academic Attributional Style Questionnaire (AASQ) was utilized to assess the attributional style of the participants. This instrument was developed and standardized by the authors in a previous study (Tabassam & Grainger, 2002). The AASQ measures the attributional style for academic success and failure and it was patterned after the Children's Attributional Styles Questionnaire (CASQ) (Kaslow, Tannenbaum, & Seligman, 1978). The items of the AASQ consist of hypothetical events related to a child's success or failure in reading, mathematics and general class work. The 20-item AASQ comprised two scales: a 10-item scale measures negative attributional style and a 10-item scale measures positive attributional style. Internal consistency for the total 20-item scale was .79.

The Academic Self-efficacy Beliefs Scale (ASES) (Tabassam & Grainger, 2002) assessed academic self-efficacy of the participants. This is a 14-item instrument designed to assess students' self-efficacy beliefs for achieving success in reading and mathematics. The ASES comprised two subscales: a reading efficacy subscale and a mathematics efficacy subscale with 7 items comprising each subscale. Scores for reading efficacy, maths efficacy and for composite academic self-efficacy can be obtained. Reliability coefficients of .83 for the maths self-efficacy scale, .85 for the reading self-efficacy scale and .87 for the total 14-item scale were obtained (Tabassam & Grainger, 2002).

Research Design

A waitlist control, pretest posttest design was employed in order to test whether the given intervention was effective. Self-concept, academic attributional style and academic self-efficacy beliefs were assessed on four different occasions: T1—at the beginning of the waitlist control period, T2—after an eight-week interval from the first assessment, to identify if any changes in self-concept, attributional style and self-efficacy beliefs had occurred during the waitlist period, T3—after implementation of a seven week intervention, and T4—10 weeks following the intervention. The first 8-weeks interval (T1–T2) was a waitlist control period, the second 8-weeks period (T2–T3) was an intervention period and the third 10-weeks interval (T3–T4) was the follow-up period. It was predicted that the changes in self-concept scores, during the experimental period, would be significantly larger than the changes during the control period and these changes would be maintained during follow-up period. Further, it was expected that the changes would be larger for the targeted areas of self-concept (academic self-concept) than nontargeted areas (nonacademic self-concept), and changes would be higher for the LD group as compared to LD/ADHD group.

Intervention

The intervention employed in this study was designed to enhance academic self-concept by utilizing an indirect self-concept enhancement approach. Attributional retraining was the main component of the intervention whereby students were trained to attribute success (in reading and mathematics) to internal causes (their own ability and effort) and to attribute failure to external causes (task difficulty and/or not using the right strategy to successfully complete the task). The attributional training was delivered for reading and mathematics tasks. These tasks were prepared with the help of the participants' teachers and were set according to the participants' grades and ability levels. The tasks were arranged into low and high difficulty level so that feedback could be provided appropriately for each level. For each reading and mathematics task, attributional feedback was given separately and individually, as soon as the student completed the given task. Attributional feedback involved attributing the child's success to internal causes such as the child's effort, ability and using the correct strategy, and attributing the child's failure to external causes such as chance and lack of adequate strategy. Consistent with the previous studies (Craven, 1996; Craven et al., 1991) the attributional training involved the following key elements:

1. Identifying that the child had competently completed the task ("you have done your maths problem well");
2. Attributing success on the task to the child's ability in the subject area ("you obviously have the ability to do well in mathematics");
3. Attributing success on the task to the child's efforts in using the right strategy (you have done that maths task well as you put in effort and used the right strategy");
4. Attributing failure on the task to the task difficulty and the need to learn the correct strategy coupled with ability attributional statements ("It is a bit of a difficult task but as you have the ability you will be able to work it out by using the correct method").

The intervention was administered to groups of five students at a time. Each group received 14 sessions on attributional retraining, comprising seven sessions for reading and seven for mathematics. During each session attributional feedback was delivered to each of the students individually on each reading and mathematics activity. Posttest assessments were taken at the end of the 7-weeks intervention program and the follow up assessment was conducted ten weeks after the completion of the intervention program.

RESULTS

In order to test the hypotheses regarding the intervention's effects on the dependent variables Repeated Measures Multivariate Analysis of Variance (MANOVA) were computed with the scores obtained on four assessments (T1, T2, T3 and T4) of the dependent variables, for the two groups. Mean scores and standard deviations for the dimensions of self-concept, academic attributional styles and academic self-efficacy beliefs for the two groups (LD and LD/ADHD) and for the combined sample at T1, T2, T3, and T4 are presented in Table 10.1 and Table 10.2 respectively.

It appears from the mean scores given in Table 10.1 and Table 10.2 that there are no changes in the dependent variables during the waitlist control period (T1–T2) but there appears to be changes during the intervention period (T2–T3), which although relatively small, do suggest that the inter-

Table 10.1. Means and Standard Deviations for Self-concept, Academic Attributional Styles and Academic Self-efficacy Beliefs assessed at Prewaitlist, Preintervention, Postintervention and Follow-up for LD and LD/ADHD Subjects

The dependent variables	Subjects with LD (n = 18)				Subjects with LD/ADHD (n = 18)			
	Time 1 Prewaitlist	Time 2 Pre-intervention	Time 3 Post-intervention	Time 4 10 weeks Follow-up	Time 1 Prewaitlist	Time 2 Pre-intervention	Time 3 Post-intervention	Time 4 10 weeks Follow-up
	Mean (SD)	Mean (SD)	Mean (SD)	Mean (SD)	Mean (SD)	Mean (SD)	Mean (SD)	Mean (SD)
Academic self-concept	23.18 (4.18)	22.81 (4.10)	25.29 (4.07)	24.76 (4.15)	21.91 (6.98)	21.74 (6.96)	23.89 (8.13)	23.74 (7.95)
Nonacademic self-concept	31.16 (4.58)	31.19 (4.57)	31.08 (3.85)	31.13 (4.23)	29.96 (5.69)	30.14 (5.95)	30.88 (5.93)	30.68 (5.71)
Positive Attributions	5.33 (1.90)	5.44 (1.97)	6.42 (2.00)	6.77 (1.86)	5.16 (1.79)	5.33 (1.78)	6.50 (1.81)	6.21 (1.92)
Negative Attributions	6.33 (2.27)	6.61 (2.20)	4.94 (1.58)	5.16 (1.72)	6.61 (1.75)	6.88 (1.71)	4.77 (1.55)	5.05 (1.73)
Reading Self-efficacy	20.05 (4.20)	20.33 (4.18)	22.22 (3.73)	22.50 (3.69)	20.50 (4.69)	20.50 (4.55)	21.83 (4.23)	22.33 (4.41)
Maths Self-efficacy	19.61 (4.04)	19.55 (4.00)	20.66 (4.13)	20.72 (4.32)	19.00 (4.04)	19.22 (4.15)	20.21 (4.16)	20.22 (4.26)

Note. Negative attributions show a decrease in scores at T3, which should be noted as a positive trend whereas all the other scales show increase in scores at T3 as indicative of a positive change. LD = students with learning difficulties, LD/ADHD = students with learning difficulties and co-morbid attention deficit hyperactivity disorder.

Table 10.2.   Means and Standard Deviations for the Dimensions of Self-Concept, Academic Attributional Style and Academic Self-efficacy Beliefs, Assessed at Prewaitlist, Preintervention, Postintervention and Follow-up for the Combined Sample (*n* = 36)

Dimensions of self-concept, academic attributional style and academic self-efficacy beliefs	Time 1 Prewaitlist Mean (SD)	Time 2 End waitlist and Pre-intervention Mean (SD)	Time 3 Post-intervention Mean (SD)	Time 4 10-weeks follow up Mean (SD)
Academic self-concept	22.47 (5.77)	22.27 (5.73)	24.59 (6.44)	24.25 (6.27)
Nonacademic self-concept	30.52 (5.23)	30.63 (5.37)	31.04 (5.00)	30.90 (4.95)
Positive Attributions	5.25 (1.82)	5.38 (1.85)	6.47 (1.88)	6.86 (1.86)
Negative Attributions	6.47 (2.00)	6.75 (1.94)	4.86 (1.55)	5.11 (1.70)
Reading Self-efficacy	20.27 (4.39)	20.41 (4.31)	22.02 (3.92)	22.41 (4.01)
Maths Self-efficacy	19.30 (3.99)	19.38 (4.02)	20.44 (4.09)	20.47 (4.23)

vention has had an impact. It also appears that once these changes had occurred they were maintained during the follow-up period (T3–T4). In order to test if these observed changes in the dependent variables were significant, a Repeated Measures Multivariate Analyses of Variance (MANOVA) was computed with the scores of the six dependent variables (see Table 10.2) over the four assessments as the within-subject factor and the two groups (LD and LD/ADHD) as the between-subject factor. The Wilks' criterion yielded a significant within-subject effect for the combination of all the dependent variables, $F(18, 266) = 13.68$, $p < .001$, whereas the between-subject effect was not significant. Univariate statistics indicated an overall significant positive change for the participant's academic self-concept, $F(3, 99) = 24.96$, $p < .001$, but no significant change for nonacademic self-concept.

The results indicated, after intervention, a significant increase in participants' scores for positive attributions, $F(3, 99) = 38.92$, $p < .001$, reading self-efficacy, $F(3, 99) = 43.22$, $p < .001$, and for mathematics self-efficacy, $F(3, 99) = 41.62$, $p < .001$. These results suggest that the intervention had produced significant changes in the dependent variables. The between-subject effect was not significant and this indicates that the two groups (LD and LD/ADHD) did not differ significantly on the dependent variables after intervention. Thus the intervention has had a similar impact on the participants with LD and those with comorbid LD/ADHD. The assumptions about the changes in the dependent variables during the waitlist control period, experimental period and follow-up period were examined using the tests of repeated measures of within-subjects contrast over the three periods. The results are described for each period.

Changes in the Dependent Variables during Waitlist Control Period

As no intervention was administered during the waitlist control period it was assumed that there would be no significant changes in the dependent variables during this period. A Repeated Measures MANOVA, conducted for the scores on all six dependent variables for the complete sample, indicated that during the waitlist control period there were no significant changes in the participants' academic self-concept, $F(1, 33) = 3.55$, $p > .05$, nonacademic self-concept, $F(1, 33) = 1.59$, $p > .05$, positive attributions, $F(1, 33) = 2.27$, $p > .05$, negative attributions, $F(1, 33) = 3.49$, $p > .05$, reading self-efficacy beliefs, $F(1, 33) = 1.06$, $p > .05$, and maths self-efficacy beliefs, $F(1, 33) = 0.63$, $p > .05$.

Changes in the Dependent Variables during the Experimental Period

It was assumed that there would be significant changes in the dependent variables during the experimental period. The results from within-subjects contrast revealed during the experimental period there was a significant change for the participants' academic self-concept, $F(1, 33) = 34.70$, $p < .001$, while no significant change was found for the nonacademic self-concept, $F(1, 33) = 3.61$, $p > .05$. The results also indicated that during the experimental period there was a significant increase in the scores for positive attributions, $F(1, 33) = 38.33$, $p < .001$, reading self-efficacy beliefs, $F(1, 33) = 46.88$, $p < .001$, and maths self-efficacy beliefs, $F(1, 33) = 49.44$, $p < .001$.

Changes in the Dependent Variables during the Follow-up Period

It was expected that, as a result of the intervention, the gains in the dependent variables would be maintained over time. It was assumed that no significant changes would occur in the dependent variables during the follow-up period. The results from the repeated measures contrasts of within-subjects indicated that during the follow-up period no significant change was found for the participants' academic self-concept The results also revealed that during the follow-up period a small increase was present for positive attributions, $F(1, 33) = 6.08$, $p < .01$, whereas no significant change was present for negative attributions. During the follow-up period there was also a small but statistically significant increase in the scores for reading self-efficacy, $F(1, 33) = 6.17$, $p < .01$, but no significant change was present for maths self-efficacy. These results suggest that the gains in the dependent variables as a result of this intervention were maintained during the follow-up period.

The Intervention's Effects on the Targeted and Nontargeted Areas of Self-Concept

Table 10.3 presents mean scores and standard deviations over four assessments for the eight scales of self-concept for the combined sample. The intervention's effects on the targeted and nontargeted areas of self-concept were identified by the Repeated Measures ANOVA, computed over the four assessments of the eight dimensions of self-concept for the total sample ($n = 36$). The results revealed a significant within-subject main effect for the combination of all dimensions of self-concept ($F(24, 276) = 3.70$, $p < .001$). Univariate F values were significant for the targeted areas of self-concept (i.e., reading self-concept ($F(3, 102) = 15.19$, $p < .001$), mathematics self-concept ($F(3, 102) = 15.73$, $p < .001$), and school self-concept ($F(3, 102) = 10.58$, $p < .001$). The significant results in relation to school self-concept perhaps indicate a transfer effect of the intervention to related areas of academic self concept. There was no significant change for nontargeted areas of self-concept, (physical ability, physical appearance, parent relation self-concept) offering further support for the validity of the intervention.

Table 10.3. Means and Standard Deviations for the Dimensions of Self-concept, Assessed at Pre waitlist, Pre-intervention, Post-intervention and Follow-up for the Combined Sample ($n = 36$)

Self-concept Scales on the SDQ-1	Time 1 Pre waitlist Mean (SD)	Time 2 End waitlist and Pre-intervention Mean (SD)	Time 3 Post-intervention Mean (SD)	Time 4 10-weeks follow up Mean (SD)
Academic self-concept				
Reading self-concept	22.08 (6.50)	21.97 (6.60)	24.50 (8.15)	24.02 (8.05)
Mathematics self-concept	21.11 (5.75)	20.88 (5.59)	23.19 (6.46)	22.97 (6.29)
School self-concept	24.22 (6.74)	23.97 (6.71)	26.08 (7.33)	25.75 (7.23)
Non-academic self-concept				
Parent-relation self-concept	33.55 (5.38)	33.91 (5.59)	33.86 (6.58)	33.50 (6.39)
Peer-relations self-concept	29.52 (7.08)	29.41 (7.14)	31.27 (5.79)	31.36 (5.91)
Phys. Ability self-concept	30.88 (6.11)	31.02 (6.18)	31.13 (6.52)	30.80 (6.21)
Appearance self-concept	28.11 (7.18)	28.16 (7.23)	27.91 (6.22)	27.86 (6.04)
General self-concept	31.63 (6.36)	31.52 (6.89)	32.63 (6.50)	32.25 (6.43)

However, a small but significant increase was observed for the scores regarding peer-relation self-concept ($F(3, 102) = 5.98$, $p < .01$). Moderate effect sizes (.1 to .3) were established for the targeted areas of self-concept (academic self-concept), whereas no significant impact was found on the general self-concept of the participants. These results provide support for the hypotheses predicting that significant changes would occur in the targeted areas of self-concept, smaller changes would occur in the related areas of self-concept and no significant change would occur in nontargeted areas of self-concept.

The Intervention's Effects for Students with LD and Students with LD/ADHD

The mean scores and standard deviations for different subscales of self-concept, for the two groups (LD and LD/ADHD), over four assessments are presented in Table 10.4. It was assumed that, as a result of this intervention, students with comorbid LD/ADHD, as compared to the students with LD, would experience fewer positive changes in their academic self-concept. As mentioned earlier, a comparison of students with LD and with comorbid LD/ADHD, before intervention, indicated no preexisting differences between the two groups on the dependent variables. The results obtained from the Repeated Measures MANOVA for between-subject differences revealed that after the intervention the two groups (LD and LD/ADHD) did not differ significantly on any of the dependent variables. These results suggested the intervention was almost equally effective for LD and LD/ADHD students and the participants with LD and with comorbid LD/ADHD had benefited similarly from the intervention.

DISCUSSION

This study was designed to test the effectiveness of attributional retraining for self-concept enhancement of LD and LD/ADHD students. The participants had learning difficulties in reading and mathematics and they reported significantly lower scores on academic self-concept, academic attributional style and academic self-efficacy beliefs when compared to normally achieving peers. The intervention program was, therefore, specifically designed to enhance their academic self-concept indirectly, utilizing an attributional retraining technique.

A number of researchers have hypothesized a reciprocal link between self-concept and self-attributions (Cooley & Ayres, 1988; Craven et al., 1991; Marsh et al., 1984; Pearl, 1982; Weiner, 1986). Based on this sug-

Table 10.4. Means and Standard Deviations for the Dimensions of Self-concept Assessed at Prewaitlist, Preintervention, Postintervention and Follow-up for Subjects with LD and with LD/ADHD

Subscales on the SDQ-1	Subjects with LD (n = 18)				Subjects with LD/ADHD (n = 18)			
	Time 1 Prewaitlist	Time 2 Pre-intervention	Time 3 Post-intervention	Time 4 10 weeks Follow-up	Time 1 Prewaitlist	Time 2 Pre-intervention	Time 3 Post-intervention	Time 4 10 weeks Follow-up
	Mean (SD)	Mean (SD)	Mean (SD)	Mean (SD)	Mean (SD)	Mean (SD)	Mean (SD)	Mean (SD)
Reading	23.05 (5.15)	22.88 (5.38)	25.38 (6.43)	24.66 (6.12)	21.33 (7.70)	21.05 (7.67)	23.61 (8.67)	23.38 (8.97)
Maths.	21.27 (5.09)	21.00 (4.75)	23.66 (5.16)	23.44 (5.59)	20.94 (6.49)	20.77 (6.47)	22.72 (7.66)	22.50 (7.06)
School	25.00 (4.67)	24.55 (4.48)	26.83 (4.90)	26.16 (4.68)	23.44 (8.40)	23.38 (8.47)	25.33 (9.20)	25.33 (9.24)
Parent	34.05 (5.06)	34.27 (5.09)	33.88 (5.31)	33.27 (5.17)	33.05 (5.78)	33.55 (6.17)	33.83 (7.81)	33.72 (7.57)
Peer	29.66 (5.57)	29.55 (5.85)	31.33 (5.02)	31.22 (5.05)	29.38 (8.49)	29.27 (8.41)	31.22 (6.62)	31.50 (6.81)
Physical Ability	32.16 (6.79)	32.05 (6.67)	32.44 (5.03)	32.61 (5.29)	29.61 (5.23)	30.00 (5.64)	29.83 (7.65)	29.16 (6.73)
Physical Appearance	28.44 (6.17)	28.61 (6.37)	27.22 (5.10)	27.33 (5.31)	27.77 (8.24)	27.72 (8.16)	28.61 (7.25)	28.33 (6.82)
General self-concept	30.77 (5.24)	30.55 (4.48)	31.16 (6.33)	31.25 (6.23)	29.50 (6.80)	29.16 (7.27)	31.00 (8.15)	31.38 (7.91)

Note. Reading = Reading Self-concept, Maths = Mathematics self-concept, School = School self-concept, Parent = Parent-relation self-concept, Peer = Peer-relation self-concept, Physical Ability = Physical Ability self-concept, Physical Appearance = Physical Appearance self-concept, LD = students with learning difficulties, LD/ADHD = students with learning difficulties and comorbid attention deficit hyperactivity disorder.

gested link between self-concept and self-attributions, the intervention utilized an indirect self-concept enhancement approach that targeted attributional training. More specifically the intervention was employed to increase participants' self-attributions in success situations, in the targeted areas (reading self-concept and mathematics self-concept), to internal causes (their own efforts and ability), and in failure situations to external causes (task difficulty or not using the right strategy to complete the task successfully). It was expected that as a result of this intervention a positive change would occur in participants' academic attributional beliefs and this positive change would be associated with positive changes in academic self-concept.

The effectiveness of the intervention was verified by the results, which indicated that there were significant changes in the participants' academic attributions, academic self-efficacy beliefs and academic self-concept, during the experimental period. No significant changes were found during the waitlist control period and follow up period. The results also revealed a significant increase in the scores of the targeted areas of self-concept (reading and mathematics self-concepts) and no significant change in the non-targeted areas (nonacademic self-concept). These results confirmed the validity of the intervention (attributional retraining) in enhancing academic self-concept. The intervention also had an effect on the related areas of academic self-concept. The results indicated that during the experimental period a small positive change had occurred in the subjects' school self-concept. The school self-concept of the participants was not targeted in the intervention program; however, the enhanced level of school self-concept that occurred as a result of the intervention suggests the possibility of a transfer effect of the intervention to a related academic area.

An important aspect of the intervention was that it focused on some specific dimensions of self-concept rather than on overall self-perceptions. The importance and logic of targeting specific dimensions of self-concept instead of targeting global self-concept has been suggested in previous studies (Harter, 1998; Harter et al., 1998; Craven & Marsh, in press; Craven et al., 1991; Marsh & Craven, 1997). Dietz (1998) suggests that the self-concept enhancement studies which do not focus on specific dimensions of self-concept, generally produce less significant changes in self-concept. Marsh and Craven (1997) suggest that "if a child has a low reading self-concept the most direct mean of enhancing this facet of self-concept is by directly targeting it rather than general self-concept" (p. 192). The results obtained from the present study have confirmed that targeting specific dimensions of self-concept is an effective procedure for enhancing academic self-concept. Academic self-perception is usually considered to be an important factor for successful learning. A positive change in academic self-concept may eventually help LD students to become more productive and active learners. The findings that students with LD display significantly lower academic self-concept scores (and not nonacademic self-concept) compared to normally achieving peers suggests there is a need for interventions focusing on the enhancement of LD students' academic self-perceptions.

Previous research has suggested that people with high self-esteem evaluate their performance more positively than those with low self-esteem even when their performance is equivalent (Taylor & Brown, 1988). It was also suggested that children with a high self-concept reinforce themselves more than children with a low self-concept (Ames, 1978; Marsh & Craven, 1997) and they maintain their high self-concept through this self-reinforcement process. Consistent with this view, Marsh and Craven (1997) suggest that intervention techniques that focus on generating a self-reinforcement process in children would be more successful in raising self-concept than techniques which do not focus on generating a self reinforcement process. The present intervention was aimed to enhance academic self-concept through targeting the academic attributional beliefs of the participants. As the individuals with a positive attributional style attribute their success to their own abilities and efforts, they usually feel good about their abilities and they utilize a self-reinforcement process to enhance their self-perceptions (Marsh & Craven, 1997; McInerney, 1999). A program similar to the present intervention could instill a self-reinforcement system in the participants by changing their attributional patterns. The results have demonstrated that the intervention was effective in changing participants' academic attributional beliefs, which impacted positively on their self-efficacy beliefs and academic self-concept.

An important feature of the present investigation is that it utilizes uni-model approach. Some previous studies on the enhancement of self-perception have used a combination of different treatment approaches in a single program. For example, Craven and colleagues (1991) utilized a combination of attributional retraining and internally focused performance feedback to enhance the academic self-concept of normally achieving students. Miranda, Villaescusa, and Vidal-Abarca (1997) used a combination of attributional retraining and self-regulation procedures with students with learning disabilities. Similarly in 1995, Rawson and Cassady utilized a combination of behavior modification and group interactions to improve the self-perceptions of students with learning disabilities. However, a combination of different intervention techniques in one program compounds the effects of different interventions, making it not possible to distinguish the impact of specific components of any. In contrast, the present study utilized a single technique (attributional retraining only) to enhance academic self-concept. Thus the uni-model intervention approach in this study has provided important data that suggests attributional retraining is an effective intervention for enhancing LD students' self-concept.

Overall the findings suggest that academic self-concept can be enhanced indirectly through attributional retraining techniques by targeting specific facets of academic self-concept. The results support the effectiveness of a cognitive model in changing maladaptive attributions, which assume that maladaptive behavioral and emotional reactions can be modified by changing intervening cognitions or beliefs (Forsterling, 1985). The findings of this study have shown that as a result of the intervention a significant positive change occurred in the academic attributional style and the academic self-efficacy beliefs of the participants. The attributional modification techniques utilized in this study appear to have had an impact on the individual's beliefs of efficacy, which in turn appears linked to positive feelings of self-perception in the participants. Thus a mediating process of change in the self-efficacy beliefs seems to be a plausible explanation, which has apparently led to positive changes in the academic self-perceptions of the participants. These results provide further support for the argument presented by researchers (Marsh, 1984, 1986; Marsh et al., 1984; Pajares, 1996; Schunk, 1984) in relation to close links between self-concept, self-attributions and self-efficacy beliefs.

An important feature of attributional change can be linked to enhanced achievement level. Many studies have shown that altered academic attributional beliefs influence academic achievement directly (Marsh, 1984; Pearl, 1982; Schunk, 1981, 1983, 1984) and also indirectly through the mediating variable of self-efficacy beliefs (Schunk, 1984, 1990). Although exploring the effects of attributional change and enhanced academic self-concept on participants' achievement level was not the focus of the present study, it does appear possible that the positive changes in academic attributions and academic self-efficacy beliefs of the participants, that occurred as a result of the intervention, may have the potential to positively influence academic achievement. Craven and colleagues (1991) have suggested that after the completion of a self-concept enhancement intervention a time lag is necessary to allow the changes in self-concept to increase desirable academic striving behavior and subsequent achievement. Hence, it is possible to surmise that enhanced academic self-concepts, as a result of a promising intervention, may be associated with a positive impact on academic achievement. Further research is needed to explore the effects of enhanced self-concept on academic achievement and to ascertain the role of important mediating variables.

SUMMARY

This study has evaluated a promising intervention for enhancing academic self-concept for students with LD and with LD/ADHD. The findings indicated the effectiveness of attributional retraining technique in producing positive changes in the targeted areas of academic self-concept. The results also offer further support for a relation between academic attributional beliefs and academic self-perceptions. The results offer support for the validity of attributional retraining as an effective intervention for enhancing self-concept and self-efficacy and demonstrate that attributional retraining is a viable technique for the population investigated.

REFERENCES

Abramson, L. L., Seligman, M. E. P., & Teasdale, J. D. (1978). Learned helplessness in humans: Critique and reformulation. *Journal of Abnormal Psychology, 87,* 49–74.

American Psychiatric Association. (1987). *Diagnostic and Statistical Manual of Mental Disorders* (3rd ed. revised). Washington, DC: Author.

American Psychiatric Association. (1994). *Diagnostic and Statistical Manual of Mental Disorders* (4th ed.). Washington, DC: Author.

Ames, C. (1978). Children's achievement attributions and self-reinforcement: Effects of self-concept and competitive reward structure. *Journal of Educational Psychology, 70,* 345–355.

Ashman, A., & Elkins, J. (1998). *Educating children with special needs.* Australia: Prentice-Hall.

Association for Children with Learning Disabilities. (1986, September-October). ACLD description: Specific learning disabilities. *ACLD Newsbriefs,* pp. 15–16.

Bandura, A. (1982). Self-efficacy mechanism in human agency. *American Psychologist, 37,* 122–147.

Bandura, A. (1997). *The exercise of control.* New York: W. H. Freeman.

Bender, W. N. (1986). Teachability and behavior of learning disabled children. *Psychological Reports, 59,* 471–476.

Bender, W. N. (1994). Social-emotional development; the task and the challenge. *Learning Disability Quarterly. 17,* 250–252.

Bender, W. N. (1997). *Understanding ADHD: A practical guide for teachers and parents.* Englewood Cliffs, NJ: Prentice-Hall.

Bender, W. N., Rosenkrans, C. B., & Crane, M. (1999). Stress, depression and suicide among students with learning disabilities: Assessing the risk. *Learning Disability Quarterly, 22,* 143–155.

Bender, W. N., & Wall, M. E. (1994). Social-emotional development of students with learning disabilities. *Learning Disability Quarterly, 17,* 323–341.

Biederman, J., & Steingard, R. (1989). Attention-deficit hyperactivity disorder in adolescents. *Psychiatric Annals, 19*(11), 587–596.

Biederman, J., Newcom, J., & Sprich, S. (1991). Co-morbidity of attention deficit hyperactivity disorder with conduct, depressive, anxiety, and other disorders. *American Journal of Psychiatry, 148*, 564–577.

Bley, N. S., & Thornton, C. A. (1995). *Teaching mathematics to students with learning disabilities* (3rd ed.). Austin, TX: PRO-ED.

Bong, M., & Clark, R. E. (1999). Comparison between self-concept and self-efficacy in academic motivation research. *Educational Psychologist, 34*(3), 139–153.

Brandtstadter, J. (1999). The self in action and development. In J. Brandtstadter & R. M. Learner (Ed.), *Action and self-development* (pp. 37–65). Thousands Oaks, CA: Sage.

Bryan, T. (1986). Self-concept and attributions of the learning disabled. *Learning Disabilities Focus, 1*(2), 82–89.

Cantwell, D. P., & Baker, L. (1991). Association between attention deficit hyperactivity disorder and learning disorder. *Journal of Learning Disabilities, 24*, 88–95.

Carmichael, P., Adkins, L., Gaal, I., Hutchins, P., Levey, F., McCormack, J., Oberklaid, F., Pearson, C., & Storm, V. (1997). *Attention deficit hyperactivity disorder.* Australia: National Health and Medical Research Council.

Cawley, J. (1985). *Cognitive strategies and mathematics for the learning disabled.* Austin, TX: PRO-ED.

Cawley, J., Fitzmaurice-Hayes, A., & Shaw, R. (1988). *Mathematics for the mildly handicapped—A guide to curriculum and instruction.* Boston: Allyn and Bacon.

Chapman, J. W. (1988a). Learning disabled children's self-concepts. *Review of Educational Research, 58*(93), 347–371.

Chapman, J. W. (1988b). Cognitive motivational characteristics and academic achievement of learning disabled children: A longitudinal study. *Journal of Educational Psychology, 80*(3), 357–365.

Chapman, J. W., & Boersma, F. J. (1979). Learning disabilities, locus of control and mother attitudes. *Journal of Educational Psychology, 71*, 250–258.

Cherkes-Julkowski, M. (1985). Information processing: A cognitive view. In J. Cawley (Ed.), *Cognitive strategies and mathematics for the learning disabled* (pp. 117–138). Austin, TX: PRO-ED.

Clever, A., Bear, G., & Juvonen, J. (1992). Discrepancies between competence and importance in self-perception of children in integrated classes. *The Journal of Special Education, 26*(2), 125–138.

Cooley, E. J., & Ayres, R. R. (1988). Self-concept and success-failure attributions of non-handicapped students and students with learning disabilities. *Journal of Learning Disabilities, 21,* 174–178.

Craven, R. G. (1996). *Enhancing self-concept: A large scale longitudinal study in an educational setting.* Unpublished doctoral thesis, University of Sydney, Australia.

Craven, R. G., & Marsh, H. W. (in press). The enigma of understanding and enhancing self-concept: Historical developments, recent advances and new directions for going boldly beyond the frontier. *International perspectives on the self.*

Craven, R. G., Marsh, H. W., & Debus, R. L. (1991). Effects of internally focused feedback and attributional feedback on enhancement of academic self-concept. *Journal of Educational Psychology, 83*(1), 17–27.

Cunningham, C. E., Siegal, L. S., & Offord, D. R. (1985). A developmental dose response analysis of the effects of methylphenidate on the peer interactions of attention deficit disordered boys. *Journal of Child Psychology and Psychiatry, 26.* 955–971.

DeLong, R. (1995). Medical and pharmacological treatment of learning disabilities. *Journal of Child Neurology, 10*(Suppl. 1). 92–95.

Dietz, D. J. (1998). A test of a multi-session model of an attributional retraining program. *Dissertation Abstracts International, 58*(10-A), 3844.

DuPaul, G. J. (1991). *The ADHD Rating Scale: Normative data, reliability and validity.* Unpublished manuscript, University of Massachusetts Medical Center, Worcester, MA.

Forsterling, F. (1985). Attributional retraining: A review. *Psychological Bulletin, 98,* 495–512.

Green, C., & Chee, K. (1994). Management of attention-deficit disorder: A personal perspective. *A Modern Medicine Reprint, 37,* 38–53.

Hallahan, D. P. (1989). Attention disorders: specific learning disabilities. In T. Husen & T. N. Postlethwait (Eds.), *The international encyclopedia of education: Research and studies* (Vol. 1, pp. 98–99). New York: Pergamon.

Harris, A. J., & Sipay, E. R. (1990). *How to increase reading ability: A guide to developmental and remedial methods* (9th ed.). New York: Longman.

Harter, S. (1993). Causes and consequences of low self-esteem in children and adolescents. In R. F. Baumeister (Eds.), *Self-esteem: The puzzle of low self-regard* (pp. 87–116). New York: Plenum Press.

Harter, S. (1998). The development of self-representations. In W. Damon (Ed.), *Handbook of child psychology* (Vol. 3, pp. 553–617). John Wiley & Sons.

Harter, S., Whitesell, N. R., & Junkin, L. J. (1998). Similarities and differences in domain specific and global self-evaluations of learning disabled, behaviorally disordered, and normally achieving adolescents. *American Educational Research Journal, 35*(4), 653–680.

Heyman, W. B. (1990). The self-perception of a learning disability and its relationship to academic self-concept and self-esteem. *Journal of Learning Disabilities, 23*(8), 472–475.

Hinshaw, S. P., & Melnick, S. M. (1995). Peer relationships in boys with attention-deficit hyperactivity disorder with and without co-morbid aggression. *Development and Psychopathology, 7,* 627–647.

Hoza, B., Pelham, W. E. Milich, R., Pillow, D., & McBride, K. (1993). The self-perception and attributions of attention deficit hyperactivity disordered boys. *Journal of Abnormal Child Psychology, 21*(3), 271–284.

Hoza, B., Waschbusch, D. A., Pelham, W. E., Molina, B. S. G., & Milich, R. (2000). Attention-Deficit/Hyperactivity Disorder and control boys' responses to social success and failure. *Child Development, 71*(2), 432–446.

Huntington, D. D., & Bender, W. N. (1993). Adolescents with learning disabilities at risk? Emotional well-being, depression, suicide. *Journal of Learning Disabilities. 26,* 159–166.

Kaslow, N. J., Tannenbaum, R. L., & Seligman, M. E. P. (1978). *The KASTAN: A children's attributional style questionnaire.* Unpublished manuscript, University of Pennsylvania.

Kirby, J. R., & Becker, L. D. (1988). Cognitive components of learning problems in arithmetic. *Remedial and Special Education, 9*(5), 7–15, 27.

Kloomok, S., & Cosden, S. (1994). Self-concept in children with learning disabilities: The relationship between global self-concept, academic "discounting" non-academic self-concept and perceived social support. *Learning Disability Quarterly, 17,* 140–153.

Magg, J. W., & Behrens, J. T. (1989). Depression and cognitive self-statements of learning disabled and seriously emotionally disturbed adolescents. *The Journal of Special Education, 23,* 17–27.

Marsh, H. W. (1984). Relationships among dimensions of self-attributions, dimensions of self-concept, and academic achievements. *Journal of Educational Psychology, 76,* 1291–1308.

Marsh, H. W. (1986). Self-serving effect (bias?) in academic attributions: its relation to academic achievement and self-concept. *Journal of Educational Psychology, 78,* 190–200.

Marsh, H. W. (1988). *Self-Description Questionnaire. A theoretical and empirical basis for the measurement of multiple dimensions of preadolescent self-concept: A test manual and a research monograph.* San Antonio, TX: The Psychological Corporation.

Marsh, H. W. (1990). *The Self-Description Questionnaire-I: SDQ-1 Manual.* Sydney, Australia: University of Western Sydney.

Marsh, H. W., Cairns, L., Relich, J., Barnes, J., & Debus, R. L. (1984). The relationship between dimensions of self-attribution and dimensions of self-concept. *Journal of Educational Psychology, 76,* 3–32.

Marsh, H. W., & Craven, R. G. (1997). Academic Self-concept: Beyond the dustbowl. In G. Phye (Ed.), *Handbook of classroom assessment: Learning, achievement and adjustment* (pp. 131–198). Orlando, FL: Academic Press.

McInerney, D. M. (1999). What should teachers do to get children to want to read and write? Motivation for literacy acquisition. In A. J. Watson & L. R. Giorcelli (Eds.), *Accepting the literacy challenge* (pp. 95–115). Sydney, Australia: Scholastic.

McKinney, J. D., & Feagans, L. (1983). Adaptive classroom behavior of learning disabled students. *Journal of Learning Disabilities, 16,* 360–367.

McKinney, J. D., & Feagans, L. (1984). Academic and behavioral characteristics: Longitudinal studies of learning disabled children and average achievers. *Learning Disability Quarterly, 7,* 251–265.

McKinney, J. D., Montague, M., & Hocutt, A. M. (1993). Educational assessment of students with attention deficit disorder. *Exceptional Children, 60*(2), 125–131.

Mercer, C. D. (1991). *Students with learning disabilities* (4th ed.). New York: Merrill.

Mercer, C. D. (1997). *Students with learning disabilities* (5th ed.). Englewood Cliffs, NJ: Prentice-Hall.

Milich, R., Loney, J., & Landau, S. (1982). Independent dimensions of hyperactivity and aggression: A validation with playroom observation data. *Journal of Abnormal Child Psychology, 19,* 607–623.

Miranda, A., Villaescusa, I. M., & Vidal-Abarca, E. (1997). Is attribution retraining necessary? Use of self-regulation procedures for enhancing the comprehension strategies of children with learning disabilities. *Journal of Learning Disabilities, 30*(5), 503–512.

O'Shea, L. J., O'Shea, D. J., & Algozzine, B. (1998). *Learning disabilities: From theory towards practice.* Englewood Cliffs, NJ: Prentice-Hall.

Pajares, F. (1996). Self-efficacy beliefs in academic settings. *Review of Educational Research, 66,* 543–578.

Pearl. R. (1982). LD children's attributions for success and failure. A replication with a labeled LD sample. *Learning Disability Quarterly, 5,* 173–176.

Pearl. R. (1992). Psychosocial characteristics of learning disabled students. In N. N. Singh & I. L. Beale (Eds.), *Learning disabilities: Nature, theory and treatment* (pp. 96–125). New York: Springer-Verlag.

Peterson, C., Buchanan, G. M., & Seligman, M. E. P. (1995). Explanatory style: History and evolution of the field. In G. M. Buchanan & M. E. P. Seligman (Eds.), *Explanatory style* (pp. 3–24). Hillsdale, NJ: Erlbaum.

Rawson, E. H., & Cassady, C. J. (1995). Effects of therapeutic intervention on self-concepts of children with learning disabilities. *Child and Adolescents Social Work Journal, 12*(1), 19–31.

Ritter, D. R. (1989). Social competence and problem behaviour of adolescent girls with learning disabilities. *Journal of Learning Disabilities, 22,* 460–461.

Robins, P. M. (1992). A comparison of behavioural and attentional functioning in children diagnosed as hyperactive or learning disabled. *Journal of Abnormal Child Psychology, 20,* 65–82.

Rogers, H., & Saklofske, D. E. (1985). Self-concept, locus of control and performance expectations of learning disabled children. *Journal of Learning Disabilities, 18,* 273–278.

Russell, R., & Ginsburg, H. (1984). Cognitive analysis of children's mathematical difficulties. *Cognitive and Instructions, 1,* 217–244.

Schunk, D. H. (1981). Modeling and attributional effects on children's achievement: A self-efficacy analysis. *Journal of Educational Psychology, 73,* 93–105.

Schunk, D. H. (1983). Ability versus effort attributional feedback on children's perceived efficacy and achievement. *Journal of Educational Psychology, 75,* 848–856.

Schunk, D. H. (1984). Self-efficacy perspective on achievement behavior. *Educational Psychologist, 19,* 48–58.

Schunk, D. H. (1985). Self-efficacy and classroom learning. *Psychology in the Schools, 22,* 208–223.

Schunk, D. H. (1990). Self-efficacy and cognitive achievement: Implications for students with learning problems. In K. J. Torgesen (Ed.), *Cognitive and behavioural characteristics of children with learning disabilities* (pp. 139–158). Austin, TX: PRO-ED.

Schunk, D. H., & Cox, P. D. (1986). Strategy training and attributional feedback with learning disabled students. *Journal of Educational Psychology, 78,* 201–209.

Schunk, D. H., & Hanson, A. R. (1985). Peer models: Influence on children's self-efficacy and achievement. *Journal of Educational Psychology, 77,* 313–322.

Schunk, D. H., & Swartz, C. W. (1993). Goals and progress feedback: effects on self-efficacy and writing achievement. *Contemporary Educational Psychology, 18,* 337–354.

Seligman, M. E. P. (1991). *Learned optimism.* Australia: Random House.

Slavin, R. (1991). *Educational psychology.* Englewood Cliffs, NJ: Prentice-Hall.

Smith, C. R. (1994). *Learning disabilities: The interaction of learner, task, and setting* (3rd ed.). Boston: Allyn and Bacon.

Tabassam, W., & Grainger, J. (2002). Self-concept, attributional style and self-efficacy beliefs of students with learning disabilities with and without attention deficit hyperactivity disorder. *Learning Disability Quarterly, 25,* 141–151.

Taylor, S. E., & Brown, J. D. (1988). Illusion and well being: A social psychological perspective on mental health. *Psychological Bulletin, 103,* 193–210.

Wechsler, D. (1991). *Manual for the Wechsler Intelligent Scale for Children* (3rd ed.). New York: Psychological Corp.

Weiner, B. (1986). *An attributional theory of motivation and emotion.* New York: Springer-Verlag.

Weiss, G., & Hechtman, L. (1993). *Hyperactive children grown-up: Empirical findings and theoretical considerations.* New York: Guilford Press.

CHAPTER 11

MAINTAINING POSITIVE SELF-CONCEPT

Social Comparisons in Secondary School Students with Mild Learning Disabilities Attending Mainstream and Special Schools

Jason W. Crabtree

The education of students in England with mild learning disabilities (MLD) (IQ ranging between 55 and 75) is currently undergoing major revision, with an increasing number of these students being included in mainstream schools rather than in special MLD schools. Inclusion policy is not just limited to England but is in fact being adopted internationally. It would seem important that such a rethinking of educational policy is supported by research that acknowledges the benefits of inclusion. Despite this, little research exists that confirms the supposed benefits of inclusion such as improvements in academic achievement or the reduction of stigma, fostering a more positive self-concept. As previous research has suggested that positive self-concept is a precursor of higher academic achievement, it would appear that considering the impact of inclusion on self-concept is of primary importance when assessing the benefits of inclusion policy.

Existing research that has examined the impact of inclusion policy on MLD students and similar groups of students with learning disabilities has

International Advances in Self Research, pages 261–287
Copyright © 2003 by Information Age Publishing
All rights of reproduction in any form reserved.

primarily focused on the academic and social benefits of inclusion policies for these students. The conclusions drawn from the majority of this research have been tentative regarding the benefits of inclusion. Furthermore, the impact of educational change on the self-concept of MLD students has been the focus of even less research. The neglect of this particular area of research is surprising, as an individual's perception of themselves, their self-concept, is not an autonomous construct. Self-concept has been shown to influence and be influenced by many different aspects of life, including behavior, personality and mood. Enhancing self-concept has been considered to be a desirable goal in itself, furthermore, as previously mentioned it has been argued that a positive self-concept is an antecedent of higher academic achievement. If this is the case then research designed to investigate the benefits of inclusion should also focus on self-concept as a possible determinant of academic achievement.

An equally important reason for researching the self-concept of MLD students with reference to inclusion is to provide insight into the formation of self-concept. The educational transition that this group of students is currently undergoing means that they will encounter not only different school placements but also different social comparison groups. Theories of self-concept formation fall into three broad perspectives, the internalization of others' perceptions (Mead, 1934; Gergen, 1977), the ratio of one's successes to pretensions or maintaining consistency of self (James, 1892; Rogers, 1959), and social comparison of one's own abilities with those of one's peers (Festinger, 1954). The inclusion of MLD students in mainstream schooling provides a unique opportunity to investigate the extent to which an individual's social comparison group underlies the formation of their self-concept. Social comparison theory would predict that MLD students attending MLD special schools would have more positive self-concepts than MLD students attending mainstream schools. This is because special school MLD students have greater accessibility to a social comparison group closer to their own level of ability with which to compare when evaluating their self-concept, than MLD students attending mainstream schools. A further aim therefore of the current research is to examine the influence of the social comparison group on the self-concept of MLD students by comparing the self-concept of both MLD students attending special MLD schools and mainstream schools who select different social comparison groups when assessing their self concept.

This chapter addresses the impact of inclusive education policy on the self-concept of students with mild learning disabilities. Specifically, the research presented examines and compares the self-concept of MLD students attending special MLD schools and mainstream schools. Furthermore, consideration is given to the formation of self-concept in this group, with particular reference to social comparison processes.

BACKGROUND

The Move Towards Inclusion

Special education policy in the United Kingdom has undergone a major change in direction in the last decade. It is now general policy, not just in the United Kingdom but in the majority of countries around the world, to aim for inclusion of pupils with special educational needs (SEN) into mainstream schooling. The United Nations Educational, Scientific and Cultural Organization (UNESCO) Salamanca World Statement on Special Educational Needs Education (1994), called on all governments to adopt the principle of inclusive education. It was proposed that all children should be enrolled into mainstream education, unless there are compelling reasons for not doing so (UNESCO, 1994). UNESCO gave the following reasons for the proposed move towards inclusive education:

> Regular schools with this inclusive orientation are the most effective means of combating discriminatory attitudes, creating welcoming communities, building an inclusive society and achieving education for all; moreover, they provide effective education to the majority of children and improve the efficiency and ultimately the cost-effectiveness of the entire education system (UNESCO, 1994).

In response to the UNESCO Salamanca World Statement the U.K. government produced a parliamentary paper titled "Excellence for All Children, Meeting Special Education Needs" (Department for Education and Employment, 1997). This paper highlights the promotion of inclusion of children with SEN within mainstream schooling wherever possible. By 2002 the government aims that "a growing number of mainstream schools will be willing and able to accept children with a range of special educational needs: as a consequence, an increasing proportion of those children with statements of SEN who would currently be placed in special schools will be educated in mainstream schools" (Department for Education and Employment, 1997, p.9). It is also intended that "national and local programmes will be in place to support increased inclusion" (Department for Education and Employment, 1997, p. 9).

Self-concept: Comparisons Between Students With and Without Learning Difficulties

One of the key points of recent educational policy (e.g., Department for Education and Employment, 1997) is that inclusion into mainstream schooling of children with special educational needs is likely to reduce the stigma that is associated with attending a special school. For example, Purkey (1970) suggested that ability grouping might be more humiliating for students than remaining in the regular classroom. If children who attend special schools experience the stigma that educational policy makers perceive them to experience, then it is likely that this stigma will have a negative effect on their self-concept. Indeed, psychologists (e.g. Allport, 1954; Cartwight, 1950; Erikson, 1956) and the lay public have generally assumed that members of stigmatized groups, such as people with learning disabilities, should have low self-esteem and a poor sense of self-worth.

Various social psychological theories (e.g. social constructivist theory; social identity theory; symbolic interactionist theory) have predicted that members of stigmatized groups should have lower levels of self-concept than nonstigmatized individuals. For example, Gergen's social constructivist theory (1977) postulates that an individual's self-concept is formed through the internalization of the views that others hold regarding that individual. Hence if an individual is stigmatized, the individual will internalize the stigmatized views resulting in a negative self-concept. Nevertheless, research comparing the self-concept of stigmatized and nonstigmatized groups has rarely found great differences between these groups. It would therefore appear that objective levels of disadvantage and discrimination are often poor predictors of self-concept. Alternatively, the lack of observed difference between the self-concept of stigmatized and nonstigmatized groups in previous research may be due to the methodological weaknesses of the research, such as viewing self-concept as a unidimensional construct and employing poor measurement instruments.

Research examining and comparing the self-concept of students with learning disabilities (LD) against students without LD has provided somewhat conflicting and inconclusive results. A number of studies have revealed LD children to have lower levels of self-concept than normally achieving students (e.g., Alley, Deshlar, & Warner, 1979; Black, 1974; Griffiths, 1970; Rogers & Saklofske, 1985; Rosenthal, 1973). While other studies have not found such differences to exist (e.g. Donnell, 1975; Endler & Minden, 1971; Ribner, 1978). Several explanations have been given for these contradictions, including a lack of consistency in the definition of both learning disability populations and the construct of self-concept. Also, methodological differences between studies and methodological weaknesses, as well as a lack of equivalence between self-concept measures, have all contributed to the mixed findings (Silverman & Zigmond, 1983).

Other studies that have directly compared the self-concept of individuals with and without learning disabilities have found smaller than expected differences in levels of self-concept (Johnson, Johnson, & Rynders, 1981; Chapman, 1988; Lincon & Chazan, 1979). For example, Lincoln and Chazan (1979) studied LD and non-LD children aged between 10 and 13 and found a significant difference between the two groups of children only on the cognitive subscales of the Harter (1979) Perceived Competence Scale for Children (PCSC). In contrast, on the other three subscales of the measure (social competence, physical competence and self-esteem), no significant differences were found between individuals with learning disabilities and those without learning disabilities.

More recent research on the self-concept of children with LD has generally found these children display relatively positive feelings of general self-concept that differ little from that displayed by children without LD (Bear & Minke, 1996; Chapman, 1988; Cooley & Ayres, 1988; Gronlick & Ryan, 1990; Renick & Harter, 1988, 1989; Sabornie, 1994; Winne, Woodlands, & Wong, 1982). Differences have been found to emerge between children with LD and those without LD when using multidimensional measures of self-concept, primarily on cognitive/academic self-concept subscales (Baarstad, 1978; Gronlick & Ryan, 1990; Kistner & Osbourne, 1987; Lincoln & Chazan, 1979; Renick & Harter, 1988, 1989).

Thus, although early research relating to children with LD using unidimensional measures of self-concept suggested that they had lower self-concept than their peers without disabilities, there appears to be as much variation in self-concept among students with LD as there is between students with and without LD. These findings have implications for both theories of self-concept formation and theories relating to self-concept structure. First, LD students cannot be simply internalizing others' stigmatized views of them, as their self-concept is not generally negative. This indicates that other processes are important in the formation of their self-concept. Second, self-concept would appear to be best described as being multidimensional as LD students have been found to have differing perceptions of themselves in different domains, their self-concept is not generally negative or positive across all domains.

The previous research discussed here would suggest that it is not correct to assume that individuals with learning difficulties suffer from poor self-concept as a result of being labeled or by receiving special educational treatment. Although their labels may be seen to be stigmatizing and special school attendance may be stigmatized, research shows this to have little negative effect on special school students' perceptions of their school or themselves. These findings could arise if LD students are not aware of the stigma attached to their learning problem or attending a special school. However, it would appear that this is not the case as previous research suggests that individuals with learning difficulties are very aware of the stigma attached to their learning problems and also aware of the stigma attached to their special schooling.

Awareness of Stigma

Norwich (1997) interviewed 19 pupils with MLD attending special schools on what they thought other people might think about going to a special school, to see if they were aware of the stigma associated with special schooling. Specifically, pupils were asked what their parents, mainstream school pupils, other special school pupils and their siblings' views would be about attending a special school. They were found to perceive both parents and siblings as having mainly positive views about attending special schooling, while they saw both special school peers and mainstream school peers as having a higher proportion of negative views regarding attendance of special schools. It would therefore seem that these pupils were aware of the stigmatization attached to attending a special school, as they were able to express the negative views of special schooling held by both their special and mainstream school peers.

Correspondingly, in a study conducted by Jahoda, Markova, and Cattermole (1988), individuals with a "mild mental handicap" displayed an insight into being stigmatized and had experienced both abuse and rejection from others. While these individuals appeared very aware of their stigmatization and had experienced its effects, only a very small number saw themselves as being essentially different. They had not internalized a handicapped view of themselves. This finding, as with that of Norwich (1997), offers evidence to the contrary of social constructivist theories (Gergen, 1977) of the development of self-concept. The individuals included in these studies have not simply assimilated the views of important others in the formation of their self-concept. It would appear that individuals with learning disabilities employ other mechanisms in the development of their self-concept that function to maintain a relatively positive self-concept despite the stigmatized views others hold about them.

Self-Concept and Social Comparisons

It has been proposed that students with learning disabilities are vulnerable to poor self-concepts due to their academic failure, the stigmatizing nature of their learning problems, and the segregation from mainstream schooling that many learning disabled students experience (e.g. Calhoun & Elliot, 1977; Gorlow, Butler, & Guthrie, 1963; Meyerowitz, 1962; Piers & Harris, 1964). In contrast more recent research that has investigated the self-concept of students with learning disabilities attending special schools compared to students without learning disabilities has often found fewer differences than expected (e.g. Chapman, 1988; Crabtree & Rutland, 2001). The lack of any major difference in self-evaluation between adolescents with learning disabilities and nondisabled individuals suggests that adolescents with learning disabilities may develop strategies to maintain positive self-evaluations. Indeed, Crocker and Major (1989) outlined three mechanisms or processes by which stigmatized individuals may protect their self-concept: (a) attributing negative feedback to discrimination against the group; (b) selectively comparing outcomes with those of the in-group, rather than with a relatively advantaged out-group, and (c) strategically devaluing those dimensions of comparison on which their group typically performs poorly and valuing those attributes on which their group excels.

The selective comparison of outcomes with in-group members rather than with members of relatively advantaged out-groups is the mechanism identified by Crocker and Major (1989) that is the main focus of this current investigation. The tendency of individuals to make in-group social comparison as a means of buffering the self-concept has been noted by various psychologists (e.g., Festinger, 1954, Gibbons, 1986, Tajfel & Turner, 1986). Previous research has indicated that the reference group used by children with learning disabilities affects self-esteem (Gibbons, 1981, 1985; Harter, 1986). For example, Harter (1986) found that "mainstreamed" children with a mental handicap perceived their scholastic ability as equal to that of "normal-IQ" children, whereas "mainstreamed" children with a learning disability (but "normal-IQ") perceived their scholastic competence as lower than that of "normal-IQ," nonlearning-disabled children. Harter explained this paradox by examining the comparison groups that each group reported using when making their self-perceptions. Children with a mental handicap regularly compared themselves with their mentally handicapped peers, whereas children with a learning disability reported comparing themselves consistently with "normal-IQ" children without a learning disability.

It has been suggested by Veroff and Veroff (1980) that the school environment emphasizes social comparison. It would appear that from the very start of their school career, children experience some form of evaluation with reference to the ability of other children that surround them. This is initiated through practices such as the grading of students, ability-level class grouping and the various forms of praise that are given to students. Therefore, this is a particularly pertinent issue for children with learning disabilities, as they are a minority group who generally have low levels of academic achievement amongst a majority group of children without learning disabilities who generally display higher levels of academic achievement.

Research Investigating Self-Concept and
Social Comparison Processes in Stigmatized Groups

Research which has specifically investigated the social comparisons used by individuals who belong to stigmatized groups, such as individuals with learning disabilities, has had mixed findings. The proposition that a special classroom environment provides the opportunity to engage in positive social comparisons has been demonstrated in two related studies conducted by Towne and Joiner (1966) and Schurr (1967). In the first study, conducted by Towne and Joiner, 62 students placed in special classes were given the General Self-Concept of Ability (GSCA) measure to complete. It was found that their GSCA scores increased over the period of a year. In the second study, Schurr found that if the students remained in the special classes for a second year their GSCA scores continued to rise, whereas if they were placed back in mainstream classes their GSCA scores were reduced.

Coleman (1983) also found that part-time and full-time special class placement had the effect of enhancing the self-esteem of children with learning disabilities compared to those who were placed in mainstream classes. This was despite the prediction made by the students' mothers that special class placement would reduce their self-esteem. In the three studies conducted by Towne and Joiner (1966), Schurr (1967) and Coleman, the assumption is made that the students in special class placement must be making different social comparisons to those who are placed in mainstream classrooms. The social comparisons made by the students are not directly assessed in any of the studies, leaving the possibility open for other factors to account for the observed differences in self-esteem. For example, in all three studies, all those students with higher levels of self-esteem attended special classes. Therefore, it may have been some supportive element of these special classes that promoted a positive self-esteem, rather than the opportunity for them to make social comparisons with students of similar ability.

In a study by Strang, Smith, and Rogers (1978) an attempt was made to directly manipulate the social comparison group used by academically handicapped children (aged between 8 years and 3 months and 11 years) when completing a measure of self-concept. The children either had to compare their abilities with normally achieving peers or complete the measure without any explicit reference to a comparison group. It was found that those children asked to compare themselves with normally achieving peers had significantly lower perceptions of themselves than those children who had not been specifically told to compare themselves with another group. While this study appears to clearly show that social comparison with a more able group reduces self-perceptions, it is not without problems. A criticism of this study is that it is unclear against whom the group that was given no explicit instructions regarding social comparison group were comparing themselves. This is particularly significant because in other research it has been found that learning disabled children do not necessarily spontaneously choose other learning disabled children as a social comparison group (Renick & Harter, 1989).

Both Coleman (1983) and Strang and colleagues (1978) used the Piers-Harris scale to measure the self-perceptions of the children involved in their studies. A criticism of this measure made by Renick and Harter (1989) is that, although this scale includes items from a diverse range of areas, it provides only a global measure of self-esteem. Harter (1982, 1983, 1985) and others (Shavelson, Hubner, & Stanton, 1976; Marsh & Shavelson, 1985) have found, though, that children make clear distinctions between specific domains of their lives when evaluating themselves. Therefore, studies that have used the Piers-Harris scale suffer a limitation in that they cannot take account of the fact that children may evaluate themselves differently in different domains of their lives.

Renick and Harter (1989) conducted a study investigating the effect of altering the social comparison groups used by learning disabled students on their self-concept. The learning disabled students were placed in mainstream schools but attended learning disabilities resource rooms for a certain period of time each day. This provided the students with two possible social comparison groups: other learning disabled students and mainstream students without learning disabilities. The students completed the Harter Self-Perception Profile for Children (SPPC), initially spontaneously choosing one of the available comparison groups. The students then completed the SPPC again, this time using the comparison group they had not used previously. It was found that the LD students perceived themselves to be more academically able in the learning disabled classroom compared to the regular classroom.

Unexpectedly, 84% of the learning disabled students spontaneously compared themselves with their regular classroom peers. This result is contrary to Festinger's (1954) social comparison framework, which theorizes that individuals are more likely to make comparisons with similar rather than dissimilar others, which in turn should result in more positive self-evaluations than comparisons with more able out-groups. If this were the case then the vast majority of learning disabled students should have spontaneously chosen their learning disabled peers in the resource facility they attended as their social comparison group.

Regardless of these findings, Renick and Harter's study clearly demonstrates that the use of different social comparison groups can have an impact on the self-perceptions of students with learning disabilities. Whether the study would apply to naturalistic settings is somewhat questionable, since the students were artificially made to make social comparisons with a group they did not spontaneously choose to make social comparisons with. Renick and Harter (1989) also suggested that the SPPC might not be an appropriate measure of self-perceptions for students with learning disabilities. In fact, they have developed a measure of self-perceptions specifically designed for students with learning disabilities, known as the Self-Perception Profile for Learning Disabled Students (SPPLD) (Renick & Harter, 1988). It could also be argued that the explicit instructions given to participants in studies, such as with Renick and Harter (1989) and Strang and colleagues (1978), may have focussed the participants attention on the social comparison process, highlighting the idea that differing social comparison groups can result in a difference in rating one's competence.

Smith and Nagle (1995) conducted a study investigating the self-perceptions and social comparisons made by US LD students in grades 3 and 4. All students attended "regular" elementary schools in which they received special educational services in a resource setting for 1 to 2 hours a day. The SPPLD was used to measure the students' self-perceptions and a scale relating to social comparison choice was used to assess the social comparison group used when evaluating their self-perceptions. Students' self-perceptions were not found to be affected by their choice of reference group. This finding is contrary to social comparison theory, which proposes that making social comparisons with similar others is likely to protect or enhance an individual's self-perceptions. Smith and Nagle (1995) suggest that their findings may be influenced by the relatively young age of their sample (mean age 117 months). Previous research by Renick and Harter (1989) has also suggested that older children are more likely to make use of social comparisons than younger students.

AIMS

The purpose of this study was to investigate the multidimensional facets of self-concept using the Self-Perception Profile for Learning Disabled Students (Renick & Harter, 1988) with students with MLD attending special schools and mainstream schools and students without MLD attending mainstream schools, aged 11 to 16 years. The social comparison group used by the two groups of MLD students was also explicitly examined by asking with whom they compared themselves when evaluating their competencies. It was expected that the two groups of students would use different social comparison groups due to the differing social groups that are accessible to them.

Previous research suggests that students attending special schools should make social comparisons with other MLD pupils, as this is the most accessible comparison group to them. According to the social comparison approach this will result in positive self-evaluations, as levels of competence amongst MLD students are likely to be equivalent. In contrast, it was expected that students with MLD included in mainstream schools would be more likely to use students without MLD as their social comparison group, as this group is more accessible than other students with MLD. It was predicted that this may result in more negative self-evaluations, since students without MLD are likely to have higher levels of competence than students with MLD. Since this study investigated multidimensional facets of self-concept, it was expected that any differences observed between the two groups of MLD students would be limited to academic domains, as these are the domains in which MLD students primarily differ from students without MLD.

METHOD

Participants

In total, there were 514 participants involved in this study, 111 of which were secondary school students with MLD who attended one of two special schools. Sixty-nine of the participants were secondary school pupils with MLD who attended special education units in one of five mainstream schools. These students attended the school's special education units when their non-MLD peers had English and maths lessons. The MLD students were included in all other classes (e.g. art, PE, religious education, history, geography and science) and general registration and assemblies. All of the MLD students in this study had received statements of special educational needs. MLD traditionally refers to individuals with learning difficulties with, in IQ terms, scores in the 55–70 range. The remaining 334 participants were secondary school students without learning disabilities attending one of four mainstream schools. All of the participants came from schools within one local education authority (LEA) in the South of England.

The number of male and female participants in each group for the two MLD groups and the mainstream group can be seen in Table 11.1. In both of the MLD groups the proportion of males to females is higher than in the mainstream group, this reflects the make up of the special school population with a greater proportion of males receiving statements of moderate learning difficulties (Male, 1996). The mean age of the MLD participants who attended special schools was 13.3 years ($SD = 1.6$), the mean age of MLD participants attending MLD units in mainstream schools was 13.4 years ($SD = 1.6$) while the mean age of the mainstream students was 13.4 years ($SD = 1.4$). All pupils completed the questionnaire in either the spring or the summer terms of 1999.

Table 11.1. Number of Participants by School Placement, Age, and Gender

Age	MLD Special Schools		MLD Mainstream Schools		Non-MLD Mainstream Schools[1]	
	Males	Females	Males	Females	Males	Females
11	11	5	5	5	14	9
12	20	6	14	2	45	40
13	15	5	7	3	35	45
14	15	2	4	4	34	28
15	20	3	14	8	30	28
16	8	1	2	1	16	7
Total	89	22	46	23	174	157

Note. Three of the non-MLD mainstream school students failed to indicate their gender, therefore their data was excluded in any analyses that included gender as a variable.

Instruments

A modified version of the Self-Perception Profile for Learning Disabled Students (SPPLD) (Renick & Harter, 1988) prepared for English MLD samples was used to measure the self-concept of the participants. This instrument was designed to measure the self-perceptions of LD students in ten domains, of which five domains are academic (general intellectual ability, reading competence, spelling competence, writing competence and maths competence), four are nonacademic (physical appearance, social competence, behavioral conduct and athletic competence) and one assesses global self-worth. Crabtree (2002) has shown the SPPLD to have sound psychometric properties with regard to U.K. samples of students identified as having MLD and students without MLD aged between 11 and 16. Results of factor analyses were found to provide an interpretable solution for both samples of students. Internal consistency reliability levels were found to be acceptable for all subscales in the non-MLD sample and all but two subscales in the MLD sample, these being the social acceptance and global self-worth subscales with reliability levels of .57, just below the prescribed acceptable level of .70 (Nunnally, 1978). Correlations between subscales, mean subscale item scores and standard deviations for both samples of students were found to closely replicate those found by Renick and Harter (1988) in their standardization of the measure on U.S. LD students. In addition, Crabtree (2002) found gender and age trends across both samples that followed similar patterns to those predicted from previous research, thus providing construct validity for the SPPLD.

In total the SPPLD is comprised of 46 items, the reading, spelling, writing and maths competency subscales each comprising 4 items, while the general intellectual ability, social acceptance, athletic competence, behavioral conduct, physical appearance and global self-worth subscales comprise 5 items each. Items within each subscale are counter balanced so that two or three items start with positive statements and two or three start with negative statements. Counter balancing of items is designed to avoid acquiescence as suggested by Paulhus (1991).

The SPPLD uses a structured alternative format (see Figure 11.1). This format is designed to reduce the amount of socially desirable responses made by the students as they are identifying with other kids rather than having to identify with individualistic statements such as "I am a slow reader." For each item, the students have to decide which of the two statements is most like them; those on the right side or those on the left side. Once they have decided which statement is most like them, they have to decide if that statement is really true for them, or sort of true for them. The response can then be scored on a four-point scale with a score of 1 for the lowest competence ratings and 4 for the highest competence ratings.

The social comparison groups used by the participants when evaluating their self-perceptions in the nine domain specific subscales of the SPPLD was assessed using the "Who I Am Like" questionnaire. This questionnaire enabled the assessment of whether the MLD students chose other MLD students with whom to make social comparisons or whether they chose students without MLD. The "Who I Am Like" questionnaire used in this study was based on the questionnaire designed by Renick and Harter (1988) for assessing comparison groups. Both groups of students were provided with several alternative social comparison groups that they might use when evaluating their self-competencies. These social comparison groups reflected two general comparison groups: in-groups (others with MLD) and out-groups (others without MLD). This study employed several versions of the "Who I Am Like" questionnaire to ensure that the questionnaire was relevant to the participants who completed it. For instance, each of the mainstream schools from which MLD students were sampled had different names for their educational resource unit that the MLD students attended for certain classes. Each school therefore received a specific version of the

Q. 33

Figure 11.1.   Example of SPPLD reading competence subscale item.

questionnaire that included the particular name given to their educational resource unit as one source of individuals with which social comparisons could have been made.

Procedure

In the special schools involved in the study, the researcher supervised the administration of the questionnaires. This was done with the help of class teachers and classroom support assistants. The instructions for completion of the questionnaires and the questions were read out to students by the researcher, due to the possibility that some of the students may have encountered difficulties in reading the questionnaire if they were left to complete it by themselves. In some cases, further explanation of questions had to be given, but at no point was any attempt made to answer the questions for the students. The SPPLD and "Who I Am Like" questionnaire were administered to a whole class at once (i.e., to groups of 6 to 12 students) at a convenient time during the school day.

In the mainstream schools, the researcher again supervised the administration of the questionnaires with help from the class teacher and classroom assistants. The questionnaire administration took place at a time during the school day when all of the MLD students were time tabled to be taught in the educational resource unit. Administration was conducted for groups of between 10 and 15 students. As with the MLD students attending MLD schools, the instructions for completion of the questionnaire and questions on both questionnaires were read out to the students in order to aid completion. In both samples the students first completed the SPPLD and only then did they complete the "Who I am like" questionnaire to assess which social comparison group they used when evaluating their self-perceptions.

RESULTS

Group Comparisons of Subscale Scores

The mean subscale item scores on the Self-Perception Profile for Learning Disabled Students for each of the three groups, MLD school students, MLD students attending mainstream schools and mainstream school students without MLD, can be seen in Table 11.2, along with standard deviations and the number of students in each group. Comparisons were made amongst the mean subscale item scores on the SPPLD of the three groups of students using one-way ANOVA.

Table 11.2.   Mean Subscale Item Scores for the Three Samples, Standard Deviations and Number of Subjects

Subscale	MLD MLD School	MLD Mainstream School	Non-MLD Mainstream School
General Intellectual Ability	3.103 SD = 0.605 n = 107	2.400 SD = 0.503 n = 65	2.753 SD = 0.574 n = 314
Reading Competence	2.544 SD = 0.790 n = 108	2.638 SD – 0.802 n = 67	3.049 SD = 0.696 n = 317
Writing Competence	2.593 SD = 0.783 n = 107	2.519 SD = 0.693 n = 67	2.760 SD = 1.064 n = 318
Spelling Competence	2.549 SD = 0.837 n = 108	2.525 SD = 0.745 n = 69	2.888 SD = 0.724 n = 319
Maths Competence	2.702 SD = 0.826 n = 105	2.413 SD = 0.712 n = 69	2.757 SD = 0.777 n = 320
Social Acceptance	2.957 SD – 0.089 n = 106	3.036 SD = 0.715 n = 66	2.999 SD = 0.571 n = 309
Athletic Competence	2.850 SD = 0.743 n – 109	2.691 SD = 0.763 n = 66	2.742 SD = 0.747 n = 313
Behavioural Conduct	2.947 SD = 0.733 n = 106	2.883 SD = 0.704 n = 63	2.785 SD = 0.801 n = 314
Physical Appearance	2.899 SD = 0.805 n = 105	2.761 SD = 0.787 n = 67	2.490 SD = 0.702 n = 312
Global Self-Worth	3.015 SD = 0.668 n = 108	3.021 SD = 0.712 n = 68	2.948 SD = 0.571 n = 314

Note.   SD = standard deviation; n = number of participants

Significant differences were found between the groups on several subscales. On the general intellectual ability subscale a significant difference was found between the three groups $F(2,483) = 10.25$, $p < .001$. Post hoc tests showed students attending MLD schools and students without MLD attending mainstream schools to have significantly higher scores than students with moderate learning difficulties attending mainstream schools (Tukey HSD, $p < .05$). Similarly, on the maths competence subscale, a significant difference was found between the three groups $F(2,491) = 5.54$, $p =$

.0042. Post hoc tests showed students attending MLD schools and students without MLD attending mainstream schools to have significantly higher scores than students with moderate learning difficulties attending mainstream schools (Tukey HSD, $p < .05$).

On the physical appearance subscale the analysis showed a significant difference between the mean subscale scores of the three groups, $F(2,481) = 13.57$, $p < .001$. Post-hoc tests showed that both of the MLD groups, those attending special schools and those attending mainstream schools, had significantly higher scores on this subscale than mainstream students without MLD (Tukeys HSD, p < .05).

Finally, on both the Reading and Spelling Competence subscales, significant differences were found between the groups $F(2,489) = 23.46$, $p < .001$; $F(2,493) = 12.21$, $p < .001$, respectively. Post-hoc tests showed that on both subscales mainstream students without MLD scored significantly higher than MLD school students and MLD students attending mainstream schools (Tukeys HSD, $p < .05$). No other significant differences were found between the groups on the other subscales of the SPPLD.

Social Comparison Groups Chosen by Integrated and Special School LD Students

There was a trend for students attending special schools to make social comparisons with other individuals in their social group, while for MLD students attending mainstream schools there was a trend for them to make social comparisons with individuals in their out-group (see Table 11.3). Chi-square analyses revealed a significant association between school placement and selected social comparison group on each of the nine domain-specific subscales of the SPPLD (shown in Table 11.3). The results from the chi-square analyses provide statistical support for the frequency trends observed in Table 11.3.

Table 11.3.   Frequencies of Selected Social Comparison Group on Each Subscale for LD Students Attending Special Schools and Mainstream Schools, and Chi-square Results

	Special Schools		Mainstream Schools			
Subscale	In-group	Out-group	In-group	Out-group	$X\Sigma$	P
General Intellectual Ability	81	29	17	46	35.5	< 0.001
Reading Competence	94	16	26	37	36.8	< 0.001
Writing Competence	86	24	15	49	49.7	< 0.001
Spelling Competence	85	25	25	36	22.5	< 0.001

Table 11.3.   Frequencies of Selected Social Comparison Group on Each Subscale for LD Students Attending Special Schools and Mainstream Schools, and Chi-square Results (Cont.)

| Subscale | Special Schools | | Mainstream Schools | | | |
	In-group	Out-group	In-group	Out-group	X^2	P
Maths Competence	88	22	19	42	39.9	< 0.001
Athletic Competence	82	26	9	53	59.7	< 0.001
Social Acceptance	71	39	14	48	27.9	< 0.001
Behavioural Conduct	89	20	10	52	69.6	< 0.001
Physical Appearance	79	30	10	50	48.3	< 0.001

Comparison of Subscale Scores by Social Comparison Group for MLD School Students

For each subscale of the SPPLD, the mean scores of those students who made in-group comparisons were compared with those students who made out-group comparisons using *t*-tests (see Table 11.4).

A significant difference was found between those students who made in-group comparisons and out-group comparisons on the general intellectual ability subscale, $t(105) = 2.40$, $p = .018$ with those students making in-group comparisons having significantly higher scores on the general intellectual ability subscale than those students who made out-group comparisons. A second significant difference was observed between the two groups on the spelling competence subscale, $t(106) = 3.66$, $p < .001$. As with the general intellectual ability subscale, those students making in-group comparisons had significantly higher scores on the spelling competence subscale than those students who made out-group social comparisons.

No significant differences were found between students who made in-group comparisons and students who made out-group comparisons on the other seven domain-specific subscales, these being: reading competence, writing competence, maths competence, social acceptance, athletic competence, behavioral conduct, and physical appearance. However, on the social acceptance, physical appearance, maths competence and writing competence subscales the students who had made in-group comparisons had a higher mean subscale score than those who had made out-group comparisons. Only on the reading competence, athletic competence and behavioral conduct subscales were the students who made out-group comparisons found to have higher mean scores than those who made in-group comparisons, though in each case the difference between the two groups was negligible (see Table 11.4).

Table 11.4.   Mean Subscale Item Scores for those MLD Students in Special Schools who made In-group Comparisons and Those Who Made Out-group Comparisons, and T-test Results

Domain	In-group comparisons	Out-group comparisons	t-value	Degrees of freedom	Sig.
General Intellectual Ability	2.783 SD = 0.637 n = 80	2.467 SD = 0.426 n = 27	2.91	67.35	.005[a]
Reading Competence	2.546 SD = 0.780 n = 92	2.583 SD = 0.875 n = 15	−0.17	105	.867
Writing Competence	2.636 SD = 0.754 n = 83	2.413 SD = 0.878 n = 23	1.21	104	.230
Spelling Competence	2.702 SD = 0.777 n = 83	2.040 SD = 0.844 n = 25	3.66	106	< .001
Maths Competence	2.747 SD = 0.826 n = 84	2.488 SD = 0.825 n = 20	1.26	102	.209
Social Acceptance	2.987 SD = 0.676 n = 78	2.900 SD = 0.705 n = 26	0.56	102	.574
Athletic Competence	2.845 SD = 0.705 n = 71	2.858 SD = 0.819 n = 38	−0.09	107	.932
Behavioural Conduct	2.944 SD = 0.735 n = 86	2.960 SD = 0.742 n = 20	−0.09	104	.931
Physical Appearance	2.966 SD = 0.784 n = 76	2.736 SD = 0.859 n = 28	1.29	102	.199

Note.   SD = standard deviation, n = number of participants. [a] Levene's test for equality of variances found the two groups to have significantly different variances, $F = 6.280$, $p = .014$. The t-value, degrees of freedom and significance level are given for unequal variances.

Comparison of Subscale Scores by Social Comparison Group for MLD Students Attending Mainstream Schools

As with the MLD students attending MLD schools, the MLD students attending mainstream schools were divided into two groups on the basis of their answers to the "Who I Am Like" questionnaire. Those who made social comparisons with other students in the MLD unit were labelled as making in-group comparisons, while those students making comparisons with other kids in their class/form or school were labeled as making out-group comparisons. This division of the students into the two groups was conducted for each of the nine domain specific subscales of the SPPLD, because when completing the "Who I Am Like" questionnaire, they had the opportunity to chose a different social comparison group for each of the subscales of the SPPLD. On each subscale, the mean scores of those students who made in-group comparisons were compared with those of the students who made out-group comparisons using t-tests. The mean subscale item scores, standard deviations, and numbers for each group can be seen in Table 11.5, along with t-test results.

One significant difference in mean subscale scores was found between MLD students attending mainstream schools who made in-group comparisons and out-group comparisons, this being on the athletic competence subscale $t(57) = -2.32$, $p = .024$. Those students who made in-group social comparisons had significantly lower levels of Athletic Competence than those students who made out-group social comparisons. No other significant differences were found in SPPLD subscale scores between mainstream school MLD pupils who made in-group comparisons and out-group comparisons.

Inspection of mean subscale scores for the two groups shows that on all subscales excluding general intellectual ability and spelling competence, those students making out-group social comparisons had higher mean scores than those making in-group social comparisons. In the case of general intellectual ability and spelling competence, those students making in-group social comparisons had a negligibly higher mean score than those making out-group comparisons.

DISCUSSION

Comparing the Self-Concept of MLD and non-MLD Students

The results of the current research replicated those of previous research that had compared the self-concept of LD students with non-LD students using multidimensional measures of self-concept (Baarstad, 1978; Gronlick & Ryan, 1990; Kistner & Osbourne, 1987; Lincoln & Chazan, 1979; Renick & Harter, 1988, 1989). Specifically, non-MLD students were only observed to have higher self-concepts than MLD students on academic domains of the SPPLD. On nonacademic domains of the SPPLD there was either no difference between MLD and non-MLD students or as on the Physical Appearance domain MLD students had significantly more positive self-concepts than non-MLD students. Negative self-concept in MLD students would therefore appear to be limited to the domains in which they face particular difficulties. These findings also clearly demonstrate the multifaceted nature of self-concept. Different areas of self-concept are clearly separate and low self-concept in one area does not mean that self-concept will generally be low.

Table 11.5.   Mean Subscale Item Scores for Those MLD Students in Mainstream Schools Who Made In-group Comparisons and Out-group Comparisons, and T-test Results

Domain	In-group comparisons	Out-group comparisons	t-value	Degrees of freedom	Sig.
General Intellectual Ability	2.388 SD = 0.422 n = 16	2.386 SD = 0.545 n = 44	0.01	58	.994
Reading Competence	2.540 SD = 0.717 n = 25	2.701 SD = 0.868 n = 36	−0.77	59	.447
Writing Competence	2.367 SD = 0.687 n = 15	2.543 SD = 0.719 n = 47	−0.83	60	.408
Spelling Competence	2.570 SD = 0.631 n = 25	2.535 SD = 0.843 n = 36	0.18	59	.860
Maths Competence	2.355 SD = 0.738 n = 19	2.435 SD = 0.710 n = 42	−0.40	59	.691
Social Acceptance	2.800 SD = 0.819 n = 9	3.047 SD = 0.711 n = 51	−0.94	58	.351
Athletic Competence	2.292 SD = 0.710 n = 13	2.848 SD = 0.775 n = 46	−2.32	57	.024
Behavioural Conduct	2.660 SD = 0.766 n = 10	2.954 SD = 0.697 n = 48	−1.19	56	.237
Physical Appearance	2.300 SD = 0.807 n = 10	2.783 SD = 0.749 n = 48	−1.83	56	.072

Note. SD = standard deviation, *n* = number of participants

Self-Concept and Social Comparisons in MLD Students

The findings offer support for the social comparison approach to self-concept formation. MLD students attending special schools were found to have positive general intellectual ability and maths self-concepts, scoring significantly higher than did integrated MLD students. It was found on all nine domain specific subscales of the SPPLD that there was a significant association between school placement and the social comparison group selected by students when evaluating their self-concept. As expected, the majority of students with MLD attending special schools chose other MLD peers within their school as their social comparison group. In contrast, the majority of MLD students in mainstream schools chose students in regular classes as their social comparison group rather than other students with MLD in the educational resource units they attended (Table 11.3).

According to the social comparison approach the higher self-perceptions on the academic domains of general intellectual ability and maths competence observed in MLD students attending special schools in this study may be due to them selecting other MLD students as their social comparison group. As their performance in these domains is similar to that of their selected social comparison group their perceptions of competence in these domains is also positive. In contrast, MLD students attending mainstream schools were shown to use students without MLD as a social comparison group since in mainstream schools there is a smaller population of MLD students to use as a social comparison group. As the students without MLD generally display higher levels of academic ability than students with MLD, social comparison theory predicts that the MLD students attending mainstream schools would display poorer self-perceptions.

Further evidence for the impact of social comparison groups on self-concept can be seen from the comparison of SPPLD subscale scores by social comparison group for both the MLD school students and MLD students attending mainstream schools. MLD students attending special schools who made in-group social comparisons were found to have significantly higher scores on the general intellectual ability and spelling competence subscales of the SPPLD than MLD school students who made out-group social comparisons. Whereas MLD students attending mainstream schools making out-group social comparisons were found to have more positive athletic competence than MLD students attending mainstream schools who made in-group comparisons.

Interestingly on the reading, writing and spelling competence subscales no significant differences were observed between the two groups of MLD students. This finding is contrary to the social comparison approach, which would predict that special school MLD students would display higher self-perceptions in these areas due to making social comparisons with other individuals of similar ability, while LD students attending mainstream schools would have lower self-perceptions due to making social comparisons with individuals who have higher levels of ability. It was also found on the reading and spelling domains that both groups of MLD students had significantly lower scores than the non-MLD students. The domains of spelling, writing and reading are particularly salient to students with MLD, as these are the academic areas in which their learning disability tends to have greatest impact. In the case of special school MLD students, it would appear that making social comparisons with similar others does not promote a positive self-concept in the reading, writing and spelling competence domains. It is possible that students with MLD are too aware of their difficulties in these particular areas of their lives to engage in social comparisons that enhance their perceptions of competence.

While social comparisons have clearly been shown to influence self-concept, the findings of the current research also suggest that social comparisons cannot solely account for the formation of MLD students' self-concept. It is possible that in the mainstream school setting MLD students may face more stigmatization than in special schools because of their more obvious difference from their non-MLD peers. Therefore rather than in-group social comparisons providing a source of positive self-evaluation, in-group social comparisons may become a source of negative self-evaluations due to the association with a stigmatised group. This would also account for why mainstream MLD students more frequently made social comparisons with out-groups rather than with their in-group even though an in-group of others with MLD was available to them. It would appear that the relative value within an individual's local environment of the group that they choose to make social comparisons with has an influence on their self-concept.

Overall, the results of the comparison of domain scores between the MLD special school group and MLD mainstream school groups suggest that MLD special school students have higher academic self-perceptions than MLD mainstream school students. In terms of nonacademic self-perceptions and global self-worth the results suggest that MLD students differed little with respect to school placement. The results also provide some evidence for the social comparison approach to self-concept formation, with special school MLD students scoring higher than MLD students attending mainstream schools on the general intellectual ability and maths competence subscales. The social comparison approach could not account for all of the results since the two groups of MLD students were not found to significantly differ in their perceptions of reading, writing and spelling competence. Perhaps other mechanisms besides that of social comparisons are involved in the formation of these domains of self-concept for students with MLD.

Limitations and Future Research

The results of this study need to be interpreted cautiously for several reasons. It was not possible to match the two groups of MLD students in the different school settings. This gave rise to the possibility that other differences exist between the two groups that may account for the findings discussed. It is possible that the two groups of MLD students may significantly differ in their academic abilities, thus accounting for the observed differences in their academic self-evaluations. However, this would appear to be somewhat unlikely since it was the integrated MLD pupils who displayed lower academic self-evaluations rather than the MLD students attending special schools. If a significant difference were to exist between integrated and special school MLD students, it would most likely occur in the opposite direction, with integrated MLD students displaying higher academic self-evaluations than special school MLD students. This is because MLD students who are academically more able are also more likely to be considered for integration into mainstream schooling.

Another reason why the results of this study should be treated with some caution relates to the instrument used to measure self-concept. The use of inadequate self-concept measures is a problem that has long plagued self-concept research. More research is needed to assess the Self-Perception Profile for Learning Disabled Students' validity and reliability on MLD samples outside the United States. Although it may appear to be the best measure available at present, it does not mean that improvements could not be made in the measurement of self-concept in MLD samples.

It would be of additional benefit to this area of research if future studies focus on the development of improved measures of self-concept designed for use with minority groups. Furthermore, future research could examine the effect of integration on self-concept amongst groups of students moving from special schools to integrated placements in mainstream schools. Although one of the aims of this study was to examine the effect of integration on MLD students, confounding variables could account for this study's findings because two independent groups of MLD students were used. Future research might consider studying just one group of students measuring self-concepts while initially in special schools and after integration into mainstream schools. This would provide clearer evidence of the effects of integration on self-concept and social comparison group choice.

CONCLUSION

This study has shown that MLD students attending special schools generally have more positive academic self-perceptions than MLD students integrated into mainstream schools. One possible explanation for this is that MLD students attending special schools are more likely to make social comparisons with other MLD students, whereas integrated MLD students are more likely to make social comparisons with students who do not have MLD. It would appear that social comparison group selection is not the only determinant of MLD students' self-concept, because expected differences on three of the academic domains were not found. Despite the observed difference in academic self-perceptions, the two groups were not found to significantly differ in their perceptions of global self-worth, suggesting that academic self-perceptions in integrated MLD students have less impact on this domain. Interestingly, these findings have mixed implications for policies of inclusive education, which warrant further investigation. In terms of current U.K. integration policy it would appear from the findings of this study, that integration does not have its expected positive benefits on self-concept. Thus it appears that integration policy is not meeting one of its central aims of combating discriminatory attitudes. Instead the results of this study imply that MLD students who have been integrated into mainstream schools may face greater levels of stigmatization than those attending special schools, leading them to refrain from making social comparisons with other MLD students.

ACKNOWLEDGMENTS

The author would like to thank the students and staff involved in this study.

REFERENCES

Alley, G. R., Deshler, D. D., & Warner, M. M. (1979). Identification of learning disabled adolescents: A Bayesian approach. *Learning Disability Quarterly, 2,* 76–83.

Allport G. W. (1954). *The nature of prejudice.* Cambridge, MA: Addison-Wesley.

Baarstad, J. (1978). *Perceived competence and motivational orientation in normal and learning disabled children.* Unpublished masters thesis, University of Denver, Colorado.

Bear, G., & Minke, K. (1996). Positive bias in maintenance of self-worth among children with learning difficulties. *Learning Disability Quarterly, 19,* 23–32.

Black, F. W. (1974). Self-concept as related to achievement and age in learning disabled children. *Child Development, 45,* 1137–1140.

Calhoun, G., & Elliot, R. N. (1977). Self-concept and academic achievement of educable retarded and emotionally disturbed pupils. *Exceptional Children, 43,* 379–380

Cartwright, D. (1950). Emotional dimensions of group life. In M. L. Raymert (Ed.), *Feelings and emotions.* New York: McGraw-Hill.

Chapman, J. W. (1988). Learning disabled children self-concepts. *Review of Educational Research, 58*, 347–371.

Coleman, J. M. (1983). Handicapped labels and instructional segregation: Influence on children's self-concepts versus the perceptions of others. *Learning Disability Quarterly, 6*, 3–11.

Cooley, E. J., & Ayres, R. R. (1988). Self-concept and success failure attributions of nonhandicapped students and students with learning disabilities. *Journal of Learning Disabilities, 31,* 174–178.

Crabtree, J. W. (2002) *The self-concept of students with moderate learning difficulties.* Unpublished doctoral dissertation, Buckinghamshire Chilterns University College.

Crabtree, J. W., & Rutland, A. (2001). Self-concept and social comparisons amongst adolescent with learning disabilities. *Journal of Community and Applied Social Psychology, 11,* 247–259.

Crocker, J., & Major, B. (1989). Social stigma and self-esteem: The self-protective properties of stigma. *Psychological Review, 96,* 608–630.

Department for Education and Employment. (1997). *Excellence for all children: Meeting special educational needs.* London: The Stationary Office.

Donnell, M. K. (1975). The comparative effects of teacher reinforcement on self-esteem and of achievement on affective variables and achievement in LD children. *Dissertation Abstracts International, 35,* 4287.

Endler, N. S., & Minden, H.A. (1971). *Anxiety, conformity, and self-perception as related to learning disabilities* (ERIC # ED 033 537). York University, Downsview, Ontario.

Erickson, R. J. (1956). The adolescent within the family. *Journal of Child Psychiatry, 3,* 115–136.

Festinger, L. (1954). A theory of social comparison processes. *Human Relations, 7,* 117–40.

Gergen, K.J. (1977). The social construction of self-knowledge. In T. Mischel (Ed.), *The self: Psychological and philosophical issues.* Oxford: Basil Blackwell.

Gibbons, F. X. (1981). The social psychology of mental retardation: What's in a label? In S. S. Brehm, S. M. Kassin, & F. X. Gibbons (Eds.), *Developmental social psychology.* New York: Oxford University Press.

Gibbons, F. X. (1985). A social-psychological perspective on developmental disabilities. *Journal of Social and Clinical Psychology, 3,* 391–404.

Gibbons, F. X. (1986). Stigma and interpersonal relationships. In S. C. Ainlay, G. Becker, & L. M. Coleman (Eds.), *The dilemma of difference* (pp. 123–144). New York: Plenum Press.

Gorlow, L., Butler, A., & Guthrie, G. (1963). Correlates of self-attitudes of retardates. *American Journal of Mental Deficiency, 67,* 549–554.

Griffiths, A. N. (1970). Self-concept in remedial work with dyslexic children. *Academic Therapy, 6,* 125–133.

Gronlick, W. S., & Ryan, R. M. (1990). Self perceptions, motivation, and adjustment in children with learning disabilities: A multiple group comparison study. *Journal of Learning Disabilities, 23,* 177–184.

Harter, S. (1979). *The perceived competence scale for children.* Unpublished manual, University of Denver, Colorado.

Harter, S. (1982). The perceived competence scale for children. *Child Development, 53,* 87–97.

Harter, S. (1983) Developmental perspectives on the self-system. In E. M. Hetherington (Ed.), *Handbook of child psychology: Vol. 4. Socialisation, personality and social development* (275–385). New York: Wiley.

Harter, S. (1985). *Manual for the self-perception profile for children.* Denver, CO: University of Denver.

Harter, S. (1986). Processes underlying the construction, maintenance and enhancement of the self-concept in children. In J. Suls & A. G. Greenwald (Eds.), *Psychological perspectives on the self* (Vol. 3, pp. 136–182). Hillsdale, NJ: Erlbaum.

Jahoda, A., Markova, I., & Cattermole, M. (1988). Stigma and the self-concept of people with a mild mental handicap. *Journal of Mental Deficiency Research, 32,* 103–115.

James, W. (1892). *Psychology: The briefer course.* New York: Holt, Rinehart & Winston.

Johnson, R. T., Johnson, D. W., & Rynders, J. (1981). Effect of co-operative, competitive, and individualistic experiences on self-esteem of handicapped and nonhandicapped students. *The Journal of Psychology, 108,* 31–34.

Kistner, J., & Osbourne, M. (1987). A longitudinal study of LD children's self-evaluations. *Learning Disability Quarterly, 10,* 258–266.

Licoln, A., & Chazan, S. (1979). Perceived competence and intrinsic motivation in learning disability children. *Journal of Clinical Child Psychology, 8,* 213–216.

Male, D. (1996). Who goes to MLD schools? *British Journal of Special Education, 23,* 35–41.

Marsh, H. W., & Shavelson, R. J. (1985). Self-concept: Its multifaceted, hierarchical structure. *Educational Psychologist, 20,* 107–125.

Mead, G. H. (1934). *Mind, self and society.* Chicago: University of Chicago Press.

Meyerowitz, J. H. (1962). Self-derogations in young retardates and special class placement. *Child Development, 33,* 443–451.

Norwich, B. (1997). Exploring the perspectives of adolescents with moderate learning difficulties on their special schooling and themselves: Stigma and self-perceptions. *European Journal of Special Needs Education, 12,* 38–53.

Nunnally, J. C. (1978). *Psychometric theory.* New York: McGraw-Hill.

Paulhus, D. L. (1991). Measurement control of response bias. In J. P. Robinson, P. R. Shaver, & L. S. Wrightsman (Eds.), *Measures of social psychological attitudes, Vol. 1. Measures of personality and social psychological attitudes* (pp. 17–59). San Diego, CA: Academic Press.

Piers, E. B., & Harris, D. B. (1964). Age and other correlates of self-concept in children. *Journal of Educational Psychology, 55,* 91–95.

Purkey, W. W. (1970). *Self-concept and school achievement.* New York: Prentice-Hall.

Renick, M. J., & Harter, S. (1988). *Manual for the self-perception profile for learning disabled students.* Denver, CO: University of Denver.

Renick, M. J., & Harter, S. (1989). Impact of social comparisons on the developing self-perceptions of learning disabled students. *Journal of Educational Psychology, 81,* 631–638.

Ribner, S. (1978). The effects of special class placement on the self-concept of exceptional children. *Journal of Learning Disabilities, 11,* 319–323.

Rogers, C. R. (1959). A theory of therapy, personality and interpersonal relationships as developed in the client-centered framework. In S. Koch (Ed.), *Psychology: A study of a science*, (Vol. 3, pp. 184–256). New York: McGraw-Hill.

Rogers, H., & Saklofske D. H. (1985). Self-concepts, locus of control, and performance expectations of learning disabled children. *Journal of Learning Disabilities, 18*, 273–278.

Rosenthal, J. H. (1973). Self-esteem in dyslexic children. *Academic Therapy, 9*, 27–39.

Sabornie, E. J. (1994). Social-affective characteristics in early adolescents identified as learning disabled and nondisabled. *Learning Disabilities Quarterly, 17*, 268–279.

Schurr, S. (1967). *The effect of special class placement on the self-concept of the educable mentally retarded child, part II.* Unpublished doctoral dissertation, Michigan State University.

Shavelson, R. J., Hubner, J. J., & Stanton, G. C. (1976). Self-concept: Validation of construct interpretations. *Review of Educational Research, 46*, 407–441.

Silverman, R., & Zigmond, N. (1983). Self concept in learning disabled adolescents. *Journal of Learning Disabilities, 16*, 478–482.

Smith, D., & Nagle, R. (1995). Self-perceptions and social comparisons among children with LD. *Journal of Learning Disabilities, 28*, 364–371.

Strang, L., Smith, M. D., & Rogers, C. M. (1978). Social comparison, multiple reference groups, and the self-concepts of academically handicapped children before and after mainstreaming. *Journal of Educational Psychology, 70*, 187–197

Tajfel, H., & Turner, J. C. (1986). The social identity theory of intergroup behaviour. In S. Worchel & W. G. Austin (Eds.), *The psychology of intergroup relations* (pp. 7–24). Chicago: Nelson-Hall.

Towne, R. C., & Joiner, L. M. (1966). *The effect of special class placement on the self-concept of ability of the educable mentally retarded child.* Washington, DC: U.S Government Printing Office.

United Nations Educational, Scientific and Cultural Organisation. (1994). *Salamanca World Statement on Special Educational Needs.* Paris, France: Author.

Veroff, J., & Veroff, J. B. (1980) *Social incentives.* New York: Academic Press.

Winne, P. H., Woodlands, M. J., & Wong, B. Y. L. (1982). Comparability of self-concept among learning disabled, normal and gifted students. *Journal of Learning Disabilities, 15*, 470–475.

part V

CROSS-CULTURAL RESEARCH

CHAPTER 12

TESTING FOR EQUIVALENT SELF-CONCEPT MEASUREMENT ACROSS CULTURE

Issues, Caveats, and Application

Barbara M. Byrne

Although mean group differences in self-concept scores across culturally diverse groups have been of interest for many decades, investigation into the extent to which self-concept *measures* are equivalent across such groups is a relatively recent phenomenon. Of important concern is the use of self-concept instruments that have been developed and normed in one culture and then used in another culture, either in their original linguistic form, or as a translated version of the original instrument. Both testing approaches carry very strong, and likely unrealistic assumptions of instrument equivalence across culture, because comparison of mean cultural group scores represent the primary substance of most cross-cultural research, the extent to which the instrument is measuring the *same* construct(s) in exactly the *same* way within each group is clearly critical; should this assumption not hold, then the issues of bias and/or adequate test translation is of primary concern.

International Advances in Self Research, pages 291–313
Copyright © 2003 by Information Age Publishing
291

This chapter addresses these measurement issues within the framework of self-concept research and has four primary purposes: (a) to identify and elaborate on the issue of bias in cross-cultural research; (b) to explore the issue of equivalence in cross-cultural research; (c) to examine criteria bearing on the adequate translation of an instrument from one language to another, for purposes of use in a culture which differs from the one in which it was developed; and (d) to outline procedures used in testing for the equivalence of self-concept measurements across culture.

Typically, cross-cultural research embraces one of two perspectives in measuring a construct of interest: (a) use of the same measuring instrument, in its original linguistic form, across cultural groups, and (b) use of a translated version of an instrument for populations whose culture differs from the one in which the instrument was originally developed and normed. In both instances, researchers and clinicians have no grounds for assuming, either that the instrument operates equivalently, or that the norms are equally relevant across groups. Although most research concerned with these methodological issues, to date, has focused on achievement tests, the issues are particularly potent for psychological assessment in general, and self-concept measurement in particular. In this regard, Oyserman and Markus (1993, p. 212) have noted, "Though individuals worldwide all appear to have a sense of self, its content, processes, and structures are bound to sociocultural context and thus are likely to differ."

In general, problems indigenous to the measurement of self-concept across culture relate to two primary issues: instrument equivalence and adequate test translation. As a result of rapidly increasing interest in the ways by which perceptions of self can differ across culture, research bearing on these two aspects of self-concept measurement would appear to hold center stage. We turn now to a review of the primary issues.

The Issue of Bias in Cross-cultural Research

Bias refers to the validity of scores from an assessment measure, albeit with a specific focus on *differential validity* between two or more groups. Essentially, there are two aspects of the bias issue: (a) the question of fairness, and (b) the idea of measuring different things for different groups. Likely, as a consequence of their very different orientations, the operational definition of bias, has tended to differ for cognitive and for affective instruments of measurement. Typically, bias associated with cognitive measures is interpreted as meaning that equally able individuals, from different groups, have unequal opportunities of success. Bias related to affective measures, on the other hand, conveys the notion that test scores based on the same items measure different traits and characteristics for each group.

Indeed, given the less concrete nature of psychological constructs, and the fact that their structure is so strongly influenced by cultural factors, affective measures such as attitude scales, require very strong evidence that the test items tap the underlying constructs in exactly the same way for all groups.

In terms of cross-cultural research, van de Vijver and Tanzer (1997) emphasize that the issue of bias does not relate to the intrinsic properties of an assessment instrument per se, but rather, to the characteristics of the respondents from each cultural group. Furthermore, statements regarding bias always refer to the use of an instrument within the framework of a particular cross-cultural comparison. For example, whereas an instrument may reveal evidence of bias in a comparison of Canadians and Germans, such evidence may not be present in a comparison of Canadians and Australians.

In general, problems of bias in cross-cultural research can be linked to three primary sources: (a) the construct of interest, (b) the methodological procedures, and (c) the item content. We turn now, to a brief description of each of these types of bias.

Construct Bias

Construct bias conveys the notion that the construct being measured holds some degree of differential meaningfulness across the cultural groups under study. This type of bias can arise as a consequence of three important factors. First, the behaviors being tapped as behavioral indicators of a construct can be differentially appropriate across cultural groups. A good example here can be drawn from the work on filial piety, the concept of being a "good" son or daughter. Given the widely discrepant structure of this concept for Western and non-Western societies, it is commonplace to find comparisons made between cultures embracing each of these social structures. For example, children in China are expected to fulfill substantially more and different obligations towards parents and grandparents, than are children say, in the United States or Canada. As a consequence, then, it seems logical to assume that perceptions of self relative to one's parents would be based on a differential set of criteria; these criteria, in turn, generating a differential set of behaviors considered to tap the underlying construct of filial piety.

Second, the extent to which all relevant dimensions of the construct have been included in the formulation of item content varies across groups. Take, for example, a self-concept instrument that has been structured in accordance with a theoretical perspective that includes the facet of emotional self-concept. Pertinent to some cultures, the concept of emotional self-concept may be totally meaningless or irrelevant. As a consequence, all items designed to measure emotional self-concept will be rendered inappropriate for the cultural group in question.

Finally, the sampling of behaviors considered to represent the constructs being measured, may be inadequate for a particular cultural group. For example, in cultures where one's ties involve large extended families, it seems reasonable to assume that perceptions of self within the social context (i.e., social self-concept) would be based on a much broader range of social interactive behaviors than would be the case for cultures such as Canada and the United States in which the extended family is rapidly becoming an historical artifact.

Method Bias

A second major source of bias, *method bias*, can derive from one of three aspects of the methodology used in making comparisons across cultures. The first of these is termed *sample bias* and relates to the incomparability of samples on phenomena other than the target factors under study. A case in point can be made in the measurement of academic self-concepts. Despite the fact that selected groups of children from different cultures might be categorized as belonging to the same grade level, it is nonetheless very easy for their educational experiences to be dramatically different. As a consequence, the criteria on which they formulate their self-perceptions of academic ability in particular subject areas may be vastly different. Take, for example, the case of verbal self-concept. Historically, it has been customary to link this dimension of academic self-concept to English as a school subject. However, this is one academic area for which the curriculum can vary widely even within the same culture. Without question, then, it seems reasonable to assume that this curriculum will likely differ across culture as well. For example, one curriculum of study might emphasize acquired skills related to literature, grammar, reading ability, and writing ability; in another culture, only reading and writing ability may be considered of primary importance.

A second type of method bias derives from problems associated with the assessment measure used and is therefore termed *instrument* bias. More specifically, it relates to the differential response, by comparative groups, to the structured format of the assessment instrument. One recognized source of instrument bias is that of *stimulus familiarity*. An example can be found in the work of Deregowski and Serpel (1971) in which Scottish and Zimbabwean children were asked to sort models of animals and cars, and then asked to do so again based on photographs of these models. Although the authors reported no cultural differences when the actual models were sorted, the Scottish children attained significantly higher scores when the sorting was based on the photographs. Given that most self-concept instruments are based on paper-pencil tests that are structured around a multiple-choice, Likert scaling format, it is indeed possible that this type of stimulus response may be unfamiliar to some cultural groups thereby reflecting itself in a biasing of item scores. A second type of *instrument* bias can be found with respect to *patterns of response*. These patterns can reflect evidence of response bias in one of two ways: (a) by consistently selecting one of the two extreme scale points (high, low), and with such selection being completely independent of the item content. This type of response bias is termed a *response style*, and (b) by selecting scale points, either consciously, or unconsciously, in such a way as to convey a favorable impression of oneself (e.g., social desirability, acquiescence). This type of response bias is termed a *response set*.

Response bias, whether it is in the form of a response style or a response set, is certainly not uncommon to cross-cultural research in general, nor to self-concept research, in particular. (For a more extensive discussion of response bias relative to self-concept, see Byrne, 1996.) Early work in this area, for example, has shown a clear tendency for Hispanics, as opposed to non-Hispanics, to choose the extreme response option of multicategory Likert scales (see e.g., Hui & Triandis, 1989; Marín, Gamba, & Marín, 1992). More recently, in a comparison of factor analytic structure related to the Beck Depression Inventory for Canadian, Bulgarian, and Swedish adolescents, Byrne and Campbell (1999) reported a substantially different pattern of response for the latter. Although all three nonclinical adolescent groups typically assigned a large percentage of their responses to the lowest category (no indication of depression) as might be expected, this assignment was dramatically higher and more consistent for Swedish adolescents. This discrepant responding pattern by the Swedes was attributed to the highly salient and important cultural value of self-disclosure.

Two recent cross-cultural studies have specifically addressed the issue of differential response bias (Watkins & Cheung, 1995; Cheung & Rensvold, 2000). The first of these focused on patterns of response related to subscale scores from the Self Description Questionnaire for Australian, Chinese, Nepalese, Nigerian, and Filipino children 12–14 years of age (Watkins & Cheung, 1995). Although findings from this study revealed no evidence of response set bias (e.g., socially desirable responding), substantial differences in response styles (e.g., acquiescent/ extreme responding) across culture were reported. These differences were attributed to possible linguistic difficulties for non-Australian children, and to differential patterns of cognitive style and self-disclosure. Arguing that both acquiescent and extreme response styles may constitute important sources of cross-cultural differences with respect to survey-type instruments, the second study (Cheung & Rensvold, 2000) used confirmatory factor analysis to test the extent to which these response styles differed across eleven countries for scores from the "Work Orientation" subscale of the International Social Survey Program (ISSP, 1989). Findings from this study provided further evidence that failure to take into account the differential styles of response patterning relative to each cultural group under study can seriously bias resulting assessment scores. Cheung and Rensvold (p. 209) concluded that, unless cross-cultural researchers test first for the invariance of acquiescent and extreme response styles across groups, "valid inferences concerning cross-cultural differences and similarities will be hard to discover and equally difficult to recognize once discovered."

The final source of method bias is that of *administration bias*. Although this type of bias can distort all modes of testing, the interview format would appear to be particularly vulnerable. Indeed, van de Vijver and Tanzer (1997) have noted that communication problems between interviewers and interviewees can easily occur, particularly when their first languages and cultural backgrounds are different. These authors further posit that, given an interviewee's insufficient knowledge of the testing language, and/or an interviewer's mode of address is in violation of the cultural norms of the interviewees, the collection of appropriate data can be seriously jeopardized.

Item Bias

A final category of bias is that of *item bias*. As its name implies and in contrast to construct and method bias, item bias refers to distortions at the item level. As such, items are said to be biased if they elicit a differential meaning of their content across cultural groups. Differential interpretation of item content by members of culturally-different groups derives largely from a diversity of sociocultural contexts that include the family, the school, the peer group, and society at large. For example, Oyserman and Markus (1993) noted that whereas American families urge children to stand up for themselves and not be pushed around, Japanese families, stress the value of working in cooperation with others. In contrast to Americans, they do not perceive the yielding of personal autonomy as a depression of one's self-esteem. Thus, from this example, it seems evident that differing socialization practices cannot help but lead to different sets of criteria against which to judge one's perception of self.

The above family-oriented example epitomizes the contrasting values and philosophic tenets held by individualistic Western societies versus collectivist Eastern societies. Whereas Western societies place high value on *independence* and individual freedom, Eastern societies neither assume nor value such individualism; in contrast, these societies seek to maintain *interdependence* among individuals (Markus & Kitayama, 1991). Regardless of independent/interdependent orientation, however, it is important to note that perceptions of self do not exist merely as cognitive representations, but also, as social representations (e.g., emotional, motivational, and interpersonal behaviors) that are collectively shared by others in the same culture. Indeed, Kitayama, Markus, and Lieberman (1995, pp. 526–527) have shown, via a taxonomic progression of cultural shaping, that one's individual characterization is "crafted within specific social settings (e.g., home, school, work) which, in turn, are made up of and shaped by a variety of sociopsychological processes such as linguistic conventions, socialization practices, scripts for everyday behavior, as well as educational, religious, and media practices." As a consequence, one's perception of self will always be formulated within the framework of his or her immediate culture.

The basic principle of individualistic versus collectivist thought can lead to differential assessments of self in at least two other ways. First, response to self-concept items often involves the process of social comparison. However, because perspectives of others is rooted in widely discrepant philosophies within Western and Eastern societies, this comparative process will be influenced by a cultural bias that ultimately leads to differential perceptions of self. For example, Oyserman and Markus (1993) noted that whereas Japanese, Korean, and Thai respondents tend to view others as better, smarter, more sociable, and more in control than *themselves*, Americans tend to perceive themselves as better than others in a number of different domains. This perception of others on the part of Eastern respondents has been termed the self-efficacy bias which is consistent with the tendency to be other-serving, rather than self-serving, in the attempt to submerge the self (Oyserman & Markus, 1993). Second, response to self-concept items will also be governed by the importance of one's self-representations relative to other society members. For example, in Western societies, these representations tend to be located *within the individual* and are tied to particular desires, preferences, and attributes (Markus & Kitayama, 1991). As a consequence, they stimulate concerns associated with the development of one's potential. Thus, although others in society are important to the individual, they are only so, in the sense of providing a benchmark against which to evaluate one's own inner attributes of self (Markus & Kitayama, 1991). In contrast, for individuals from Eastern societies, self-representations are determined by perceptions of the self *in relation to others*. Given this emphasis on the individual's connectedness or interdependence to others (Markus & Kitayama, 1991), self-evaluations by these individuals will be based on their relationships with others, rather than on their own unique attributes. Because most measures of self-concept are structured in the form of self-report inventories that require respondents to invoke social comparison processes and to assess one's self in relation to others, these instruments are particularly prone to item bias.

Having presented examples of how the individualism/collectivism dichotomy might possibly account for cross-cultural discrepancies in perceptions of self, it is important that I now present an alternate perspective on this popular typology. Despite its wide acceptance among cross-cultural researchers in accounting for cultural differences in the self-construal of individuals across the lifespan, there are some who remain skeptical of its purported explanatory powers. While Bond (1996) has questioned the hasty embrace of the dichotomy in light of quite insufficient empirical support, Watkins (this volume), and McInerney (this volume) and colleagues (McInerney, Roche, McInerney, & Marsh, 1997; McInerney, Hinkley, Dowson, & Van Etten, 1998) have clearly demonstrated little to no empirical evidence to substantiate such claims. Based on data comprising responses to self-concept instruments for high school students, college students, and adults from 24 countries, Watkins concluded that, although there are definite differences in perceptions of self across cultures, these differences cannot be explained in terms of Western versus non-Western or individualism/collectivism orientations.

From a somewhat different cross-cultural perspective, the work of McInerney and colleagues has been equally compelling in casting doubt on the legitimacy of the individualism/collectivism dichotomy. Based on a series of studies designed to tap differences in goals and values associated with motivation and mastery orientations between children from majority Western societies (Australia, Canada, United States) and minority indigenous cultural groups within these societies (Aborigine, Betsiamite Indian, Navajo Indian, respectively) findings have consistently shown little to no support for this typology. Indeed, such emerging, albeit consistent results have led McInerney (see this volume) to suggest that predicted differences between cultural groups, based on the individualism/collectivism notion, may be more complex than originally posited by Markus and Kitayama (1991).

Other important factors that can contribute to the differential interpretation of item content are the impact of cultural norms (e.g., legality of drug use), ambiguous item content, use of colloquialisms (idiomatic expressions unique to a particular culture), and poor item translation. These latter issues are addressed below under the rubric of "Adequacy of Instrument Translation."

The Issue of Equivalence in Cross-cultural Research

As noted earlier, a common, albeit incorrect assumption in research that tests for mean differences across groups, is that the measuring instrument is operating in exactly the same way for each group under study. Such assumptions imply equivalence across populations with respect to both its measurement and its theoretical structure. Most typically, when we speak of *measurement equivalence*, we refer to two issues: (a) the extent to which the factor pattern and weighting of loadings is invariant (i.e., group-equivalent interpretation of item content; and (b) the extent to which errors of measurement are equivalent (i.e., group-equivalent reliability of the instrument). Adherence to the latter equivalence constraint, however, is considered to be excessively stringent and is typically not tested in determining evidence of invariance. *Structural equivalence* refers to the extent to which the theoretical structure of the instrument is invariant across groups. In other words, those correlations among multidimensional facets of the underlying construct are group-equivalent. Finally, of additional concern in cross-cultural research, as noted earlier, is the presence of systematic error in the form of response bias for one group, albeit not for the other; or in the event that it exists for both groups, that it is of an equivalent form (see e.g., Cheung & Rensvold, 2000).

To the extent that an instrument of measurement is not equivalent across groups, any comparison of test and normative scores will be impaired. There are two approaches to testing for the group-equivalence of measuring instruments—one rooted in item response theory (differential item functioning) and the other, rooted in the analysis of covariance structures (structural equation modeling within the framework of a confirmatory factor analytic model). Whereas the differential item functioning approach, to date, has been applied almost solely to achievement data that are unidimensional in structure, the confirmatory factor analytic approach has been used largely with psychological data that are multidimensionally structured. As a consequence, virtually all tests for the equivalence of self-concept measures have been based on the application of confirmatory factor analysis.

As noted above, it seems evident that when an instrument is developed and normed in one culture and then used in another culture—either in its original form, or as a translated version of the original instrument, the risk of bias, and ultimately, equivalence, is extremely high. It is important, then, that we now review issues related to the translation/adaption of measuring instruments.

The Issue of Adequate Instrument Translation

Needless to say, the rigor with which an instrument is translated into another language bears critically on its construct validity. In this regard, Sperber, Devellis, and Boehlecke (1994), and others (Spielberger, 1992; Tanzer & Sim, 2000; van de Vijver & Hambleton, 1996), have argued that it is not sufficient merely to demonstrate the adequacy of translation and back translation, but also, that the psychometric properties of the test in the second language are as adequate as those in the original language. Thus, in adapting a measuring instrument to another language, it is essential to consider a balanced treatment of psychological, linguistic, and cultural phenomena. Once the newly translated instrument has been formulated, the next logical step is to test the extent to which the factorial measurements (i.e., factor loadings), as well as the factorial structure (i.e., relations among the underlying constructs or factors) of the instrument are consistent with the original instrument (van de Vijver & Poortinga, 1992). Because the conversion of a measuring instrument from one language to another involves more than just linguistic translation, then, these modified instruments are more appropriately termed "adapted," rather than "translated" tests.

One of the major difficulties in translating psychological instruments of measurement is the accurate transmission of meaning associated with idioms that may be unique to a particular culture (Spielberger, 1992). For example the expression "I am usually calm, cool, and collected" which is often used in item content related to emotional self-concept is an American colloquialism that does not translate smoothly into other languages. Thus, in adapting any instrument into another language, it is important to seek out metaphors in the target language that most closely tap the essence of the construct being measured. For items containing culture-specific content which cannot be translated, Poortinga (1995) suggests that they be either modified prior to being translated, or that they be removed entirely.

Because cultural and linguistic differences are a function of traditional customs, norms and values, it is possible for a construct to be interpreted and conceptualized within a completely different framework by two culturally different groups. For example, based on a translated version of the "How I See Myself Questionnaire" (Juhasz, 1985), Watkins and Regmi (1993) found the appropriateness of self-concept dimensions related to friends, family, and physical appearance to be somewhat dubious for Nepalese adolescents; in sharp contrast, these dimensions are highly salient for adolescents in Western societies. Clearly, then, it is essential that the researcher determine the extent to which a construct is meaningful in a particular culture before translating an instrument into the language of the target culture.

It is evident that the use of adapted tests is a complex process that encompasses a number of underlying assumptions concerning the equivalency of the original and adapted versions of a measuring instrument. Given the rapid growth of cross-cultural research in recent years, together with the resulting translation of many psychological tests into other languages, the International Test Commission (ITC) recognized the need for a standardized set of guidelines regarding the development and use of translated tests. The first of these, entitled "Guidelines for the Translation and Adaptation of Tests" (see Hambleton, in press), comprises 22 guidelines that are organized into four categories: context, instrument development and adaptation, administration, and documentation/ interpretation. In turn, each guideline is described by a rationale for inclusion, steps to its achievement, a list of common errors, and references for follow-up research. A critical review and field-test of these new and important guidelines can be found in Tanzer and Sim (2000) and Hambleton, Yu, and Slater (2000), respectively.

Having emphasized the importance of testing for the equivalence of an instrument across cultural groups within the framework of two scenarios: (a) when the instrument is used in its original form with a group whose culture differs from the one within which it was developed, and (b) when the instrument is translated and adapted for use with a group whose culture differs from the one within which it was developed, the question arises as to how one should proceed when confronted with findings of *nonequivalent* factorial measurement and structures. Indeed, such findings need not be the cause of despair. Rather, researchers are advised to identify the theoretical elements or processes that possibly account for the cultural differences (Markus & Kitayama, 1991); these differential features, in themselves, can provide a rich and informative insight into important cultural differences related to psychometric phenomena. For an example of differential factorial structure related to a self-concept instrument used across different cultural groups, readers are referred to Watkins, Hattie, and Regmi (1994).

Having identified both the sources of bias that may impact the measurement of self-concept across culture, together with the primary issues related to the equivalence of measuring instruments across culture, we turn now to a paradigmatic application.

MEASURING SELF-CONCEPT ACROSS CULTURE: TESTING FOR INSTRUMENT EQUIVALENCE

For didactic purposes, the example application to be presented here focuses on four of eight subscales comprising a widely known and used self-concept instrument. Specifically, we test for equivalence of the four subscales measuring nonacademic self-concepts as derived from the Self Description Questionnaire I (SDQ-I; Marsh, 1992) across Australian and Nigerian preadolescents; these include physical self-concepts related to ability (PSCAb) and appearance (PSCAp), as well as social self-concepts related to peers (SSCPe) and parents (SSCPa). The model of self-concept to be tested is shown schematically in Figure 12.1. All analyses are based on the analysis of covariance structures within the framework of a confirmatory factor analytic model, using the EQS program (Bentler & Wu, 2000). (For further details related to applications of structural equation modeling in general, and confirmatory factor analysis in particular, readers are referred to Byrne, 1994, 1998, 2001.)

The Measuring Instrument

The SDQ-I is a 76-item self-report inventory based on a 5-point Likert-scale format designed for use with children ranging in age from 8 through 12 years. The respondent is presented with a series of short statements (e.g., I am good looking), and then asked to select the option, which most appropriately reflects his or her level of agreement; choices range from "false" (1) to "true" (5). The SDQ-I has been shown to be one of the most psychometrically sound measures of self-concept available (see Byrne, 1996).

Based on research that has shown the ability of young children to respond inappropriately to negatively worded items (Marsh, 1986), Marsh has recommended that these item scores not be included in the tallying of subscale total scores. Accordingly, then, no negative items were used in structuring and testing the model shown in Figure 12.1. As a consequence, eight items measured each facet of nonacademic self-concept. Consistent with symbolic convention associated with structural equation modeling, these items (i.e., observed variables) are shown enclosed within rectangles, and their underlying self-concept facets (i.e., unobserved constructs) represented by ellipses. In addition, consistent with theory, the four nonacademic self-concept facets are shown to be intercorrelated as represented by the double-headed arrows.

The Samples

The Australian sample consisted of 497 preadolescents; these data were complete (i.e., no missing values). The original sample of Nigerian preadolescents was 465, albeit with missing scores on some variables. In addressing the issue of incomplete data, all cases having > 8% missing data were deleted from the analyses. For the remaining sample of 439, the randomly missing data were imputed with values derived from a multiple regression in which three item scores from the same congeneric set of indicators (i.e., items measuring the same facet of self-concept) were used as the predictor variables.

The Procedure

As a prerequisite to testing for factorial invariance, it is customary to consider a baseline model, which is estimated for each group separately. This model represents the one that best fits the data from the perspectives of both parsimony and substantive meaningfulness. Given that the χ^2 statistic and its degrees of freedom are additive, the sum of the χ^2 values derived

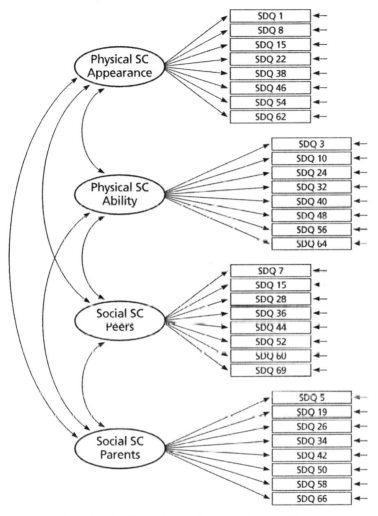

Figure 12.1.   Model of hypothesized nonacademic self-concept structure based on the Self Description Questionnaire-I.

from the model-fitting process for each group separately, reflects the extent to which the underlying structure fits the data across groups when no cross-group constraints are imposed. Nonetheless, because measuring instruments are often group-specific in the way they operate, baseline models are not expected to be completely identical across groups. For example, whereas the baseline model for one group might include cross-loadings (i.e., loading of an item on a nontarget factor), and/or error covariances, this may not be so for other groups under study (see e.g., Byrne & Campbell, 1999). A priori knowledge of such group differences is critical to the application of invariance-testing procedures (see Byrne, Shavelson, & Muthén, 1989).

Because the estimation of baseline models involves no between-group constraints, the data can be analyzed separately for each group. However, in testing for invariance, equality constraints are imposed on particular parameters and, thus, the data for all groups must be analyzed simultaneously to obtain efficient estimates (Bentler, 1995; Jöreskog & Sörbom, 1996); the pattern of fixed and free parameters nonetheless remains consistent with the baseline model specification for each group. Overall, tests for invariance, using covariance structure analysis, can involve both measurement and structural components of a model, the particular combination varying in accordance with the model under study. In the case of our 1st-order CFA model to be tested here (see Figure 12.1), the pattern of factor loadings and structural relations among the factors are of primary interest.

RESULTS

Baseline Models

Australians

Testing for the validity of hypothesized nonacademic self-concept structure for Australian adolescents, based on the SDQ-I, yielded a marginally well-fitting model as indicated by the goodness-of-fit values reported in Table 12.1. The key indicators here are the Satorra-Bentler χ^2 statistic (S-Bχ^2; Satorra & Bentler, 1988), the related Robust CFI index (CFI*; Bentler, 1990), and the Root Mean Square Error of Approximation (RMSEA; Steiger, 1998).

The S-Bχ^2 serves as a correction for the χ^2 statistic when distributional assumptions are violated. It has been shown to be the most reliable test statistic for evaluating covariance structure models under various distributions and sample sizes (Hu, Bentler, & Kano, 1992). The CFI ranges in value from zero to 1.00. A CFI value of .90 has served as the rule-of-thumb lower limit cutpoint of acceptable fit. Computation of the Robust CFI (CFI*) is based on S-B χ^2 values, rather than on uncorrected χ^2 values. Because evaluation of model fit was based on the S-B χ^2 statistic in the present study, the CFI*, rather than the CFI, was used as the index of practical fit. Finally, the RMSEA takes into account the error of approximation in the population and asks the question "How well would the model, with unknown but optimally chosen parameter values, fit the population covariance matrix if it were available?" (Browne & Cudeck, 1993, pp. 137–138). This discrepancy, as measured by the RMSEA, is expressed per degree of freedom, thus making it sensitive to model complexity; values less than .05 indicate good fit, and values as high as .08 represent reasonable errors of approximation in the population.

Table 12.1.   Models of Nonacademic Self-concept Structure: Goodness of Fit Statistics

Model	χ^2	df	$S\text{-}B\chi^2$	CFI^*	RMSEA	Difference in $S\text{-}B\chi^2$	df
Australian ($N = 497$)							
Initial	1436.48	458	1059.28	.90	.07		
Final[a]	1203.21	455	903.88	.92	.06	155.40	3
Nigerian ($N = 439$)							
Initial	936.11	458	739.94	.92	.05		
Final[b]	895.11	457	702.49	.93	.05	30.45	1

Note. [a] Error covariances between: Items 24 and 40; Items 19 and 26 Cross-loading of Item 38 on the Social Self-concept (Peers) factor.
[b] Error covariance between Items 19 and 26.

For analyses based on the EQS program, the Lagrange Multiplier Test (LMTest) statistics serve in pinpointing sources of model misfit. More specifically, these modification indices identify which fixed parameters, if freely estimated in a subsequent analysis, would yield the largest drop in χ^2 value. In the case of the present model, a review of the multivariate LMTest χ^2 statistics revealed two error covariances and two cross-loadings as being the major impediments to a better-fitting model. The two error covariances were between Items 40 and 24 from the Physical Self-concept of Ability subscale, and between Items 26 and 19 from the Social Self-concept of Parent Relations subscale. Scrutiny of the content for each of these item pairs revealed evidence of possible content overlap (e.g., "I like my parents" [Item 19]; "My parents like me" [Item 26]). The two cross-loadings involved (a) the regression of Item 38 (measuring PSC-Appearance) on the Social Self-concept of Peer Relations factor, and (b) the regression of Item 32 (PSC-Ability) on the Physical Self-concept of Appearance factor. The fact that Item 38 ("other kids think I am good looking") loaded on the nontarget factor of Peer Relations would appear to be substantively reasonable. On the other hand, the loading of Item 32 ("I have good muscles") on the nontarget factor of physical appearance would seem to be male-specific; estimation of this parameter was therefore not considered in any respecification for the full sample. Given the substantive meaningfulness of the two error covariances, and the cross-loading of Item 38 on SSC-Peers factor, the model was respecified to include these additional parameters and then reestimated.

Because these three parameters represent the only difference between the initial (Model 1) and the respecified (Model 2) models (i.e., whereas they are fixed to 0.0 in Model 1, they are freely estimated in Model 2), Model 1 is said to be "nested" in Model 2. As such, we can compare the fit of Model 2 with that of Model 1 in determining the extent to which the additionally estimated parameters improved goodness-of-fit between the specified model and the data. This comparison is based on the difference in χ^2 values (symbolized as $\Delta\chi^2$), which is distributed as a χ^2 statistic with degrees of freedom equivalent to the difference in degrees of freedom between the two models. In the present case, however, because we have chosen to interpret the S-Bχ^2, rather the regular χ^2 statistic, this comparison is based on the S-Bχ^2. Statistical significance related to this ΔS-Bχ^2 is determined by checking the chi-square table in any statistics textbook. Results of the comparison between Model 1 and Model 2, for Australians, yielded a statistically better-fitting model (ΔS-B$\chi^2_{(3)}$ = 155.4; CFI* = .92) that was subsequently retained as the baseline model for Australian preadolescents.

Nigerians

As shown in Table 12.1, testing of the hypothesized model, for Nigerian preadolescents, yielded a S-B$\chi^2_{(458)}$ value of 732.94, a CFI* value of .92, and an RMSEA value of .05. Interestingly, consistent with partial findings from the Australian data, a review of the LMTest statistics attributed substantial misfit to the misspecification of an error covariance between Items 26 and 19, from the Social Self-concept-Parents subscale. In contrast to the Australian findings, however, the LMTest χ^2 value was clearly demarcated from lesser values representing the other fixed parameters in the model, thereby indicating no further need for the estimation of additional parameters. (For a more extensive explanation and illustration of this criterion, within the context of the EQS program, readers are referred to Byrne, 1994.) Respecification of this model to include the error covariance between Items 26 and 19 yielded a S-B$\chi^2_{(457)}$ value of 702.49, a CFI* value of .93, and an RMSEA value of .05; it served as the baseline model for Nigerian preadolescents.

Beyond the assessment of overall fit, all parameter estimates in both baseline models were found to be both feasible and statistically significant; all standard errors were within normal range. In summary, the baseline models for Australian and Nigerian preadolescents differed only with respect to (a) the additional error covariance between Items 40 and 24, and (b) the cross-loading of Item 38 on the Social SC-Peers factor for the Australians; the other covariance between items 26 and 19 was common to both cultural groups. The similarity of factor structure, notwithstanding, it is important to emphasize that just because the revised model was similarly specified for both groups, offers no guarantee of the equivalence of item measurements and underlying theoretical structure across the preadolescent groups; these hypotheses must be tested statistically. For example, despite an identically specified factor loading, it is possible that, with the imposition of equality constraints across groups, the tenability of invariance does not hold; that is, the link between the item and its target factor differs across the groups (see e.g., Byrne & Campbell, 1999). Such postulated equivalencies, then, must be tested statistically. We turn now to these tests for invariance.

Tests for Invariance Across Groups

When analyses focus on multigroup comparisons, with constraints specified between groups (i.e., particular parameters are constrained equal across groups), it is imperative that parameters for all groups be estimated simultaneously. In the case of our application here, constraints were imposed on all estimated factor loadings and factor correlations. More specifically, these parameter values, for the Nigerian group, were constrained to equal those estimated for the Australian group. It is worth noting that, given the cross-loading specific only to the Australian group, this parameter was not constrained equal for the Nigerian group (see Byrne, 1994, 1998, 2001). Therefore, it is also important to note that, because the multigroup equivalence of random measurement error is now widely acknowledged as being an excessively stringent constraint, and of little utility, these parameters, together with the common error covariance, were not tested for their invariance across groups. Results from these analyses are summarized in Table 12.2.

As can be seen in Table 12.2, testing for the invariance of measurement and structural parameters yielded evidence of several inequalities across the two cultural groups. In particular, these related to seven factor loadings, three factor variances and three factor covariances. In general, these findings reveal statistically significant differences between Australian and Nigerian adolescents with respect to variances, and associated covariances related to Physical SC-Appearance, Physical SC-Ability, and Social SC-Peers; no group differences were found for the variance related to Social SC-Parents, and related covariances with the other three factors. These findings of discordant structure suggest that Australians and Nigerian preadolescents differ in what they perceive as important influences on their social relationships with peers. For the Australians, it would appear that one's physical ability is the critical factor; for the Nigerians, on the other hand, it is physical appearance. Given these findings of structural inequality, it is interesting to note that findings of measurement inequality pertained only to items measuring Physical SC-Ability (Items 24, 40, 56), Social SC-Peers (Items 52, 60), and Social SC-Parents (Items 19, 26).

Table 12.2.   Nonequivalent Parameters Across Australian and Nigerian Preadolescents

Parameter	Content	Related Factor(s)
Factor Loadings		
Item 24	enjoy sports and games	PSC (Ability)
Item 40	good at sports	PSC (Ability)
Item 56	good athlete	PSC (Ability)
Item 52	more friends than most kids	SSC (Peers)
Item 60	popular with kids of same age	SSC (Peers)
Item 19	I like my parents	SSC (Parents)
Item 26	my parents like me	SSC (Parents)
Variances		
Factor 1	PSC (Appearance)	
Factor 3	SSC (Peers)	
Factor 4	SSC (Parents)	
Covariances		
Factors 1 & 2	PSC (Appearance/Ability)	
Factors 1 & 3	PSC (Appearance)/SSC (Peers)	
Factors 2 & 3	PSC (Ability)/SSC (Peers)	

Note.   PSC = physical self-concept; SSC = social self-concept

DISCUSSION

The focus of this chapter was to emphasize the importance of knowing that an assessment instrument is measuring the *same* psychological constructs in exactly the *same* way for each group in a study of cross-group comparisons. To this end, I demonstrated one approach to testing for measurement and structural equivalence across cultural groups using analysis of covariance structures. For examples of alternative approaches, readers are referred to Little (1997), Marsh, Hey, Roche, and Perry (1997), and McInerney, Yeung, and McInerney (2001).

Based on an instrument that, except for one cross-loading for the Australian sample, the factorial structure was identical, results revealed evidence of noninvariance related to 13 of the 70 estimated parameters in the model (7 factor loadings, 3 factor variances, and 3 factor covariances). Having determined these noninvariant findings, the question is whether the differences represent "true" differences in the measurement and structure of nonacademic SC for Australian and Nigerians preadolescents—or, whether the differences are a function of particular biasing effects in the data. Given that the instrument was administered in its original language (English) to both the Australian and Nigerian samples, it is highly possible that the noninvariant findings may be related directly to problems of method, and/or item bias. While construct bias may also have been a contending factor here, it is important to recognize that, in fact, the language in which the SDQ-I was administered, may be totally irrelevant.

Overall, the only way to adequately answer questions bearing on findings of "true" versus "spurious" differences is to reexamine each nonequivalent parameter in light of possible sources of bias. In the interest of space here, however, I limit my post hoc reexamination to only one of the noninvariant parameters reported (the loading of Item 24 on the Physical SC - Ability factor), and suggest possible sources of bias as contributing factors. As an initial step in trying to account for the nonequivalence of parameters, its is helpful to review the patterns of response, as well as the skewness and kurtosis values related to the items in question. Graphs of these values, as they relate to Item 24 for Australians and Nigerians, are presented in Figure 12.2.

Inspection of the graphs shown in Figure 12.2 reveals a vivid difference in the way Australian and Nigerian preadolescents responded to Item 24 ("I enjoy sports and games"). Now, why should this be? Quite possibly, con-

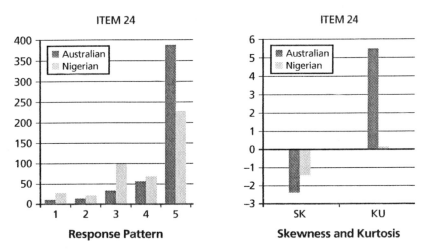

Figure 12.2.   (a) Pattern of Response to ITEM 24 by Australians and Nigerians; (b) Skewness and Kurtosis related to ITEM 24 for Australians and Nigerians.

struct bias may play a role in this discrepancy of responses, in the sense that the behavior being tapped by the item differs across the two cultures. In other words, "enjoying sports and games" conveys a different meaning for Australian, than it does for Nigerian preadolescents. For example, whereas the Australians may interpret the item content as implying that "I enjoy *playing* sports and games," the Nigerians may interpret it as "I enjoy *viewing* sports and games (as a spectator only)." Hence, the behavior tapped, in this instance, would be clearly diverse.

Given the ambiguity of its content, as noted above, item bias may also be a factor in explaining the noninvariance of Item 24. Such incertitude can lead to quite dissimilar interpretations of the statement to which respondents are asked to react. Further complicating the issue is the possibility that responses may also be colored by particular cultural norms. For example, it may be that sports represent a highly valued component of Australian society, whereas in Nigeria, its status may be of a lower rank, or somewhat equivocal at best.

Finally, it is possible that sample bias may also have been a contributing factor in triggering the noninvariance of Item 24. However, considering the relatively small number of nonequivalent parameters, overall, this possibility would seem to be somewhat unlikely,

CONCLUSION

In this chapter, I have addressed many of the important issues that researchers should consider when their research endeavors include testing for differences between cultural groups. Typically, the primary focus of substantive research is to determine the extent to which there is evidence of differences between the means of selected variables across groups. However, as emphasized in this chapter, such inquiry assumes that the measuring instrument is operating equivalently for both groups, an assumption that is not always tenable. To the extent that the assessment measure is not operating in exactly the same way across samples, any interpretation of mean difference findings will be dubious, at best.

Although the condition of instrument equivalence is always a critically important consideration in multigroup comparisons, it is particularly so when the comparative groups are drawn from different cultures. Indeed, as noted in this chapter, many aspects of the measurement process can serve to weaken the assumed equivalence of the instrument through the introduction of bias, a condition that renders scores to be differentially valid across groups. Of primary importance, are the effects of construct bias, method bias, and item bias, all of which have been detailed in this chapter.

Given the many assumptions held in conducting research involving cross-group comparisons, together with the many pitfalls that can impact such research, it seems evident that researchers need to validate the equivalence of the measuring instrument before embarking on any tests for mean differences. As a means to illustrating how, and to what extent, a measuring instrument can vary across cultural groups, I considered it instructive to include a practical application to data. Accordingly, I outlined procedures that could be used in testing for the equivalence of the SDQ-I across Australian and Nigerian preadolescents. Presented with a detailed discussion of issues and caveats related to cross-cultural research, together with this paradigmatic example, it is hoped that this chapter has served in heightening the sensitivity of researchers to the equivalency issue related to multigroup comparisons in general, and cross-cultural comparisons, in particular.

REFERENCES

Bentler, P. M. (1990). Comparative fit indexes in structural models. *Psychological Bulletin, 107,* 238–246.

Bentler, P. M. (1995). *EQS: Structural equations program manual.* Encino, CA: Multivariate Software.

Bentler, P. M., & Wu, E. J. C. (2000). *EQS for Windows: User's guide.* Encino CA: Multivariate Software.

Bond, M. H. (1996). *Social psychology across cultures: Two ways forward.* Keynote address at the International Congress of Psychology, Montreal.

Browne, M. W., & Cudeck, R. (1993). Alternative ways of assessing model fit. In K. A. Bollen & J. S. Long (Eds.), *Testing structural equation models* (pp. 445–455). Newbury Park, CA: Sage.

Byrne, B. M. (1994). *Structural equation modeling with EQS and EQS/Windows: Basic concepts, applications, and programming.* Thousand Oaks, CA: Sage.

Byrne, B. M. (1996). *Measuring self-concept across the lifespan: Issues and instrumentation.* Washington, DC: American Psychological Association.

Byrne, B. M. (1998). *Structural equation modeling with LISREL, PRELIS, and SIMPLIS: Basic concepts, applications, and programming.* Mahwah, NJ: Erlbaum.

Byrne, B. M. (2001). *Structural equation modeling with AMOS: Basic concepts, applications, and programming.* Mahwah, NJ: Erlbaum.

Byrne, B. M., & Campbell, T. L. (1999). Cross-cultural comparisons and the presumption of equivalent measurement and theoretical structure: A look beneath the surface. *Journal of Cross-cultural Psychology, 30,* 557–576.

Byrne, B. M., Shavelson, R. J., & Muthén, B. (1989). Testing for the equivalence of factor covariance and mean structures: The issue of partial measurement invariance. *Psychological Bulletin, 105,* 456–466.

Cheung, G. W., & Rensvold, R .B. (2000). Assessing extreme and acquiescence response sets in cross-cultural research using structural equation modeling. *Journal of Cross-cultural Research, 31,* 187–212.

Deregowski, J. B., & Serpell, R. (1971). Performance on a sorting task: A cross-cultural experiment. *International Journal of Psychology, 6,* 273–281.

Hambleton, R. K. (in press). Issues, designs, and technical guidelines for adapting tests into multiple languages and cultures. In R. K. Hambleton, P. Merenda, & C. Spielberger (Eds.), *Adapting educational and psychological tests for cross-cultural assessment.* Mahwah, NJ: Erlbaum.

Hambleton, R. K., Yu, J., & Slater, S. C. (2000). Fieldtest of the ITC Guidelines for adapting educational and psychological tests. *European Journal of Psychological Assessment, 15,* 270–276.

Hu, L. T., Bentler, P. M., & Kano, Y. (1992). Can test statistics in covariance structure analysis be trusted? *Psychological Bulletin, 112,* 351–362.

Hui, C. H., & Triandis, H. C. (1989). Effects of culture and response format on extreme response style. *Journal of Cross-cultural Psychology, 20,* 296–309.

International Social Survey Program. (1989). *International social science program: Work orientations, 1989* [Computer file]. Ann Arbor, MI: Inter-university Consortium for Political and Social Research [Distributors].

Jöreskog, K. G., & Sörbom, D. (1996). *LISREL 8: User's reference guide.* Chicago, IL: Scientific Software International.

Juhasz, A. M. (1985). Measuring self-esteem in early adolescents. *Adolescence, 20,* 877–887.

Kitayama, S., Markus, H. R., & Lieberman, C. (1995). The collective construction of self-esteem. In J. A. Russell, J-M. Fernandez-Dels, A. S. R. Mansteed, & J. C. Wellenkamp (Eds.), *Everyday conceptions of emotion: An introduction to the psychology, anthropology, and linguistics of emotion* (pp. 000–000). Boston: Kluwer.

Little, T. D. (1997). Mean and covariance structures (MACS) analyses of cross-cultural data: Practical and theoretical issues. *Multivariate Behavioral Research, 32,* 53–76.

Marín, G., Gamba, R. J., & Marín, B. V. (1992). Extreme response style and acquiescence among hispanics. *Journal of Cross-cultural Psychology, 23,* 498–509.

Markus, H. R., & Kitayama, S. (1991). Cultural variation in the self-concept. In J. Strauss & G. R. Goethals (Eds.), *The self: Interdisciplinary approaches.* New York: Springer-Verlag.

Marsh , H. W. (1986). The negative item bias in rating scales for preadolescent children: A cognitive-developmental perspective. *Developmental Psychology, 22,* 37–49.

Marsh, H. W. (1992). *Self Description Questionnaire (SDQ) I: A theoretical and empirical basis for the measurement of multiple dimensions of preadolescent self-concept: A test manual and research monograph.* Macarthur, New South Wales, Australia: Faculty of Education, University of Western Sydney.

Marsh, H. W., Hey, J., Roche, L. A., & Perry, C. (1997). Structure of physical self-concept: Elite athletes and physical education students. *Journal of Educational Psychology, 89,* 369–380.

McInerney, D. M., Roche, L. A., McInerney, V., & Marsh, H. W. (1995). Cultural perspectives on school motivation: The relevance and application of goal theory. *American Educational Research Journal, 34,* 207–236.

McInerney, D. M., Hinkley, J., Dowson, M., & Van Etten, S. (1998). Aboriginal, Anglo, and immigrant Australian students' motivational beliefs about personal academic success: Are there cultural differences? *Journal of Educational Psychology, 90,* 621–629.

McInerney, D. M., Yeung, S. Y., & McInerney, V. (2001). Cross-cultural validation of the Inventory of School Motivation (ISM). *Journal of Applied Measurement, 2,* 134–152.

Oyserman, D., & Markus, H. R. (1993). The sociocultural self. In J. Suls (Ed.), *Psychological perspectives on the self: The self in social perspective* (pp. 187–220). Hillsdale NJ: Erlbaum.

Poortinga, Y. H. (1995). Use of tests across cultures. In T. Oakland & R. K. Hambleton (Eds.), *International perspectives on academic assessment* (pp. 187–206). Boston: Kluwer.

Satorra, A. & Bentler, P. M. (1988). Scaling corrections for chi-square statistics in covariance structure analysis. *American Statistical Association 1988 proceedings of the business and economics section* (pp. 308–313). Alexandria, VA: American Statistical Association.

Sperber, A. D., Devellis, R. F., & Boehlecke, B. (1994). Cross-cultural translation: Methodology and validation. *Journal of Cross-cultural Psychology, 25,* 501–524.

Spielberger, C. D. (1992). Critical issues in psychological assessment. *Bulletin of the International Test Commission, 19,* 59–64.

Steiger, J. H. (1998). A note on multiple sample extensions of the RMSEA fit index. *Structural Equation Modeling: A Multidisciplinary Journal, 5,* 411–419.

Tanzer, N. K., & Sim, C. Q. E. (2000). Adapting instruments for use in multiple languages and cultures: A review of the ITC Guidelines for Test Adaptations. *European Journal of Psychological Assessment, 15,* 258–269.

Van de Vijver, F. J. R., & Hambleton, R. K. (1996). Translating tests: Some practical guidelines. *European Psychologist, 1,* 89–99.

Van de Vijver, F. J. R., & Poortinga, Y. H. (1992). Testing culturally heterogeneous populations: When are cultural loadings undesirable? *Bulletin of the International Test Commission, 19,* 37–39.

Van de Vijver, F., & Tanzer, N. K. (1997). Bias and equivalence in cross-cultural assessment: An overview. *European Review of Applied Psychology, 47,* 263–279.

Watkins, D., & Cheung, S. (1995). Culture, gender, and response bias: An analysis of responses to the Self Description Questionnaire. *Journal of Cross-cultural Psychology, 26,* 490–504.

Watkins, D., Hattie, J., & Regmi, M. (1994). *The structure of self-esteem of Nepalese children. Psychological Reports, 74,* 832–834.

Watkins, D., & Regmi, M. (1993). The basis of self-esteem of urban and rural Nepalese children. *The Journal of Social Psychology, 2,* 255–257.

CHAPTER 13

MOTIVATIONAL GOALS, SELF-CONCEPT, AND SENSE OF SELF—WHAT PREDICTS ACADEMIC ACHIEVEMENT?

Similarities and Differences between Aboriginal and Anglo Australians in High School Settings

Dennis M. McInerney

School motivation and achievement for an individual are the products of a complex set of interacting motivational goals, sense of self and self-concept variables. Motivational goals may be differentially salient to individuals from different cultural backgrounds, and sense of self, including academic self-concept, may vary across cultural groups. This chapter describes a project that examines the nature of motivational goals held by Aboriginal students; the nature of their academic self-concepts, and the nature of their sense of self within school settings. In particular, I examine the similarities and differences between the Aboriginal group ($N = 270$) and a comparator Anglo Australian group ($N = 833$) on these variables, and the comparative ability of these variables to predict valued school outcomes:

International Advances in Self Research, pages 315–346

315

intention to complete further education, liking and valuing school, student achievement and school attendance for both groups.

Australian Aboriginal students are the most educationally disadvantaged group and have the highest dropout rate of any racial or ethnic group in Australia. For example, the National Review of Education for Aboriginal and Torres Strait Islander People found that: "Indigenous people remain the most educationally disadvantaged group in Australia. From preschool to higher education, Aboriginal and Torres Strait people still participate and attend significantly less in education than the rest of the population" (Commonwealth of Australia, 1995; see also Eckermann, 1999; Fogarty & White, 1994; Hewitt, 2000). In some cases, retention rates appear to be worsening (see, for example, Dingman, Mroczka & Brady, 1995; Purdie & McCrindle, nd; Purdie, Tripcony, Boulton-Lewis, Fanshawe & Gunstone, 2000). A survey conducted in 1994 by the Australian Council for Educational Research (ACER) found that approximately 45% of Aboriginal and Torres Strait Islander primary students have significantly lower literacy and numeracy achievement compared to approximately 16% of other Australian primary students (Commonwealth of Australia, 1994). Statistics (Commonwealth of Australia, 1993: p.3) show 10 per cent of all Aboriginal and Torres Strait Islander people aged 15 years and over have post-school educational qualifications, compared with a national proportion of 31%.

Many factors are implicated in the relatively poor school achievement of Aboriginal students (see for example, McInerney, 1989, 1990, 1991; Purdie & McCrindle, nd; Purdie, Tripcony, Boulton-Lewis, Fanshaw & Gunstone, 2000). Socio-economic factors such as ill health, poverty, high unemployment, poor job prospects and racial prejudice are no doubt involved. Geographic and locale factors such as the placement of poorly prepared and inexperienced teachers in remote areas, high teacher turnover, isolation from mainstream experiences and lack of resources also have an impact on the quality of education presented to these children. Home background factors such as the relatively recent introduction of compulsory education for Aboriginal people, level of parental understanding of the importance and function of education, and level of parental encouragement and appropriate support for children to continue schooling, substandard housing and overcrowding giving poor facilities for home study, and relatively few Aboriginal models of success in a school environment may also be implicated. Other causes posited from time to time include socio-cultural factors such as: language skills deficits, cognitive, motivational and learning style differences, socialization practices within Aboriginal communities at variance to mainstream culture, peer group influences antipathetic to formal schooling, shyness, and poor attendance.

It is also commonly thought that a cultural conflict between the values and goals of schooling and the values and goals of the Aboriginal children predispose these children to poor school achievement and to drop-out (see, for example, Purdie et al, 2000; Fogarty & White, 1994; Ledlow, 1992). Authors discussing this issue suggest that while mainstream schools and teachers value mastery, future time orientation, competition and individual success, their Aboriginal pupils, in contrast, value harmony, present time orientation, maintenance of the status quo, anonymity, submissiveness, group orientation and non competitiveness. Australian Aboriginal children are often stereotyped, therefore, as lacking the motivation to achieve and the cognitive processes needed to achieve at school. It is also believed that they come from homes that lack the socialization practices needed to inculcate "appropriate" achievement values in children.

While the above factors may have an impact on the motivation and performance of Aboriginal students in mainstream school settings, and on their desire to complete schooling, there are inadequate research data available on many of these variables. Indeed, many of these beliefs about the lack of achievement of Aboriginal children in school settings are based upon little more than folk-loric tradition passed on from teacher to teacher, or academic to academic. Furthermore, many of these posited causes, such as socio-economic factors, lie outside the influence of the school and so remain intractable unless more effective social equality policies are introduced at a national level. Nevertheless, some of the above factors, particularly those dealing with motivational factors lie within the influence of schools, and if appropriate data are available on which to make decisions, schools may modify their programs to more effectively suit indigenous students.

In this study I concentrate on motivational and self-concept variables and their impact on school achievement of Australian Aboriginal children. I examine, through a large-scale psychometric study, the nature of their motivational goals, sense of self and self-concept in school settings. I then compare these attributes to those of Anglo students in order to ascertain whether there are differences between these groups. Furthermore, I examine whether Western groups are, thereby, better prepared to "survive" within school systems than Aboriginal children because of the compatability of their motivational attributes with those fostered within the school system. In order to study this latter contention I examine the relationship of motivational goals, self-concept and sense of self to a range of school related achievement measures such as school academic achievement, attendance at school, and intention to go on to further education as well as how much students like and value school.

ACHIEVEMENT GOAL THEORY AND
SELF-CONCEPT THEORY

The study is grounded in achievement goal theory and self-concept theory. Achievement Goals are presumed to guide students' behaviour, cognition, and affect as they become involved in academic work (Ames, 1992; Dweck & Elliott, 1983; Pintrich, Marx & Boyle, 1993; Wentzel, 1991). Two goals have received considerable attention from researchers: mastery goals and performance goals. Central to a mastery goal is the belief that effort leads to success, and the focus of attention is on the intrinsic value of learning. Mastery goals and their achievement are "self-referenced." In contrast, central to a performance goal is a focus on one's ability and sense of self-worth. Ability is shown by doing better than others, by surpassing norms, or by achieving success with little effort. Public recognition for doing better than others through grades, rewards and approval from others, is an important element of performance goal orientation. Performance goals and achievement are, therefore, "other referenced." In more recent theorising the performance goal construct has been partitioned into performance approach and performance avoidance goals to help interpret previous inconsistent findings regarding the relationship of this goal to valued achievement outcomes (Elliott, 1997; Urdan, 1997). Implicit in both mastery and performance goals is a focus on individualism where priority is given to the goals and values of individuals. There is little attention paid to goals and values such as working to preserve in-group integrity, interdependence of members and harmonious relationships, sometimes referred to as collectivist values, which may be more salient to students from non-Western cultural backgrounds (Kagitcibasi & Berry, 1989; Triandis, 1995; Triandis et al, 1993; Schwartz, 1990). Furthermore, the bipolar mastery versus performance continuum, while giving us valuable insights into some aspects of the motivational process and the ways in which schools may emphasize one or other of these two goal structures, suggests that these goals are mutually exclusive. Recent theorizing and research, however, suggest that these are not dichotomous and that individuals may hold both mastery and performance goals, varying in salience, depending on the nature of the task, the school environment and the broader social and educational context of the institution (see e.g., Blumenfeld, 1992; Meece, 1991; Pintrich & Garcia, 1991; Wentzel, 1991). Students may also hold multiple goals such as a desire to please one's parents, to be important in the peer group, or to preserve one's cultural identity, each of which may impact upon their level of motivation for particular tasks in school settings. Indeed, these multiple goals interact providing a complex framework of motivational determinants of action (see Blumenfeld, 1992; Dowson & McInerney, 2002; McInerney, 1989ab, 1990, 1991, 1994, 1995; McInerney & Sinclair, 1992;

McInerney & Swisher, 1995; Pintrich & Schrauben, 1992). In this study the range of goals has been expanded to reflect a multiple goal approach based on the Personal Investment Model developed by Maehr (1984; Maehr and Braskamp, 1986) and include: Task, Effort, Competition, Social Power, Affiliation, Social Concern, Praise and Token. To these I added five general motivation scales, viz, Mastery General, Performance General, Social General, Valuing Motivation and Global Motivation. Major foci of this study are, therefore, to examine the relevance of these goals to Aboriginal children, which are the important and not so important ones, and how these patterns are similar to, or different from, those of the Anglo Australian group included in the study.

Self-concept

It is also widely accepted that an individual's Self-concept is related to school adjustment, satisfaction and achievement (Marsh, 1990, 1992, 1993; Marsh & Craven, 1997; see also Graham, 1994; Sanders, 1987). International research suggests, paradoxically, that the self-concept of indigenous and minority groups often surpasses that of their White peers, while their achievement rates are, in general, lower. It is also widely accepted that academic achievement is more strongly related to academic self-concept than to non-academic and general components of self-concept. In general, research indicates that specific academic Self-concepts, such as Mathematics and Verbal are strongly positively correlated to their respective academic achievements, but are nearly uncorrelated with each other. In contrast, academic achievement in various areas is moderately to highly correlated (Marsh, 1992). In order to examine the nature and importance of Self-concept to the Aboriginal students participating in this study three academic self-concept scales, drawn from Marsh's ASDQ (Marsh, 1992) were included, viz, English Self-concept, Maths Self-concept and General Academic Self-concept. To these scales were added four other Sense of Self scales namely, Positive and Negative Self-esteem, Self Reliance and Sense of Purpose (see McInerney, Roche, McInerney & Marsh, 1997 and Maehr and Braskamp 1986) to examine whether academic self-concept measures taken from the ASDQ related more strongly to achievement that these more general measures. Major foci of the study, are therefore, to examine the nature of sense of self and academic self-concept for Aboriginal children; how these relate to their salient motivational goals and valued educational outcomes, and how these patterns are similar to, or different from the Anglo group included in the study.

Hypotheses

Based upon assumptions about Aboriginal students and literature related to individualism and collectivism (see Triandis 1995; Triandis et al, 1993), and to guide analyses I hypothesized that the Aboriginal students would be significantly stronger on the social (collectivist) goals (viz, Affiliation, Social Concern, Social General) and significantly weaker on the mastery and performance (individualist) goals (viz, Task, Effort, Competition, Social Power, Mastery General, and Performance General). Because traditional societies are thought to value the present more than the future and to seek immediate rewards for effort I also hypothesised that Aboriginal students would be higher on the extrinsic motivators Praise and Token. I hypothesised no difference for Valuing Motivation and Global Motivation. In line with much literature examining the self-concept of indigenous and minority groups I also hypothesized that there would be no differences between the Aboriginal and Anglo students on the academic Self-concept scales or Positive and Negative Self-esteem (see Marsh, 1987). However, again in line with stereotypes and assumptions I hypothesised that the Aboriginal students would be significantly weaker on the Sense of Self scales viz, Sense of Purpose and Self Reliance. Finally, in line with achievement and attendance levels of Aboriginal students in Australian schools I hypothesised that the Aboriginal students would be significantly weaker on Intention to Complete Further Education, Affect to School, Valuing School, Maths Achievement, English Achievement, and significantly higher on days absences. Table 13.1 presents a summary of these hypotheses.

Table 13.1.   Hypothesised Differences between Aboriginal and Anglo-Australian Groups on ISM, GAGOS, Sense of Self Scale, Academic Self-concept, and Outcomes Measures

Goals	Aboriginal	Anglo-Australian
ISM		
Task		* (ND)
Effort		* (ND)
Competition	(*)	*
Social Power	(*)	*
Affiliation	* (✓)	
Social Concern	* (ND)	
Praise	* (✓)	
Token	* (✓)	

Table 13.1.   Hypothesised Differences between Aboriginal and Anglo-Australian Groups on ISM, GAGOS, Sense of Self Scale, Academic Self-concept, and Outcomes Measures (Cont.)

Goals	Aboriginal	Anglo-Australian
GAGOS		
Mastery General		* (ND)
Performance General	(*)	*
Social General	* (✓)	
Motivation Value	ND	(*)
Global Motivation	ND (SD)	
Sense of Self		
Sense of Purpose		* (ND)
Sense of Reliance		* (ND)
Negative Self Esteem	ND(SD)	
Positive Self Esteem	ND (✓)	
ASDQ		
English	ND (✓)	
Mathematics	ND (✓)	
General Academic	ND (✓)	
Outcomes		
Further Education		* (ND)
Affect	(*)	*
Value		* (ND)
Math Rank		* (✓)
English Rank		* (✓)
Attendance of School		* (✓)

Notes:
* indicates that it is hypothesised that this group will be significantly stronger on this scale; ND indicates no significant difference hypothesised between groups; (✓) indicates hypothesis confirmed; (*) indicates significant difference in opposite direction to hypothesis; (ND) indicates no significant difference between groups; (SD) indicates significant difference between groups with Aboriginal group higher.

METHODOLOGY

Participants

Participants were from Grades 7, 8, and 9 at five rural and six urban high schools in NSW (N = 1,103). There were 561 males and 542 females and their average age was 13 years. There were 270 Aboriginal children (129 males and 141 females). There were 833 Anglo-Australian students (432 males and 401 females). Permission was obtained from the Department of Education and Training (DET) and the University's Human Ethics Committee to conduct the study. Parents of the students completed informed consent forms, and all students were told that their completion of the survey was voluntary. Details of the purpose of the study were repeated at the beginning of each survey session. Survey sessions were conducted with intact class groups, or where the numbers were small, as in the rural centres, in full school groups. No teachers were involved in the administration of the survey.

Instruments

The Inventory of School Motivation (ISM), (see McInerney & Sinclair, 1991, 1992; McInerney, Roche, McInerney & Marsh, 1997 and McInerney & Yeung, 2000) consists of twelve scales relating to the following motivational goals and sense of self values presumed to influence learning:

Task: (4 items) Interest in the task and wanting to improve understanding. Examples of this dimension are "I like to see that I am improving in my schoolwork" and "I need to know I am getting somewhere with my schoolwork."

Effort: (7 items) Willingness to expend effort to improve schoolwork. Examples of this dimension are "When I am improving in my schoolwork I try even harder" and "I am always trying to do better in my schoolwork."

Competition: (7 items) Competitiveness in learning. Examples of this dimension are "I like to compete with others at school" and "I work harder if I am trying to be better than others."

Social Power: (6 items) Seeking social power and status. Examples of this dimension are "I work hard at school to be put in charge of a group" and "I work hard at school because I want the class notice me."

Affiliation: (3 items) Interest in belonging to a group when doing schoolwork. Examples of this dimension are "I can do my best work at school when I work with others" and "I prefer to work with other people at school rather than work alone."

Social Concern: (5 items) Concern for other students and a willingness to help them with their school work. Examples of this dimension are "It is very important for students to help each other at school" and "I like to help other students do well at school."

Praise: (5 items) Seeking praise and recognition for schoolwork. Examples of this dimension are "At school I work best when I am praised" and "I want to be praised for my good schoolwork."

Token: (7) Seeking tangible rewards for schoolwork. Examples of this dimension are "I work best in class when I get some kind of rewards" and "I work hard in school for rewards from the teacher."

Sense of Purpose: (6 items) Valuing school for the future. Examples of this dimension are "I aim my schooling towards getting a good job" and "I want to do well at school to have a good future."

Self Reliance: (8 items) Self-reliance and confidence within academic settings. Examples of this dimension are "I often try new things on my own" and "I don't need anyone to tell me to work hard at school."

Negative Self-esteem: (7 items) Negative feelings about general academic ability at school. Examples of this dimension are "I often worry that I am not very good at school" and "I often think that there are things I can't do at school."

Positive Self-esteem: (5 items) Positive feelings about general academic ability at school. Examples of this dimension are "I succeed at whatever I do at school" and "I think I'm as good as everybody else at school."

General Motivation Scales

The General Achievement Goal Orientation Scale (GAGOS) (see McInerney & Yeung, 2000) consists of five general motivation scales:

Mastery General (5 items) measures the student's perception of how mastery oriented they are. Examples of this dimension are: "I am most motivated when I see my work improving" and " I am most motivated when I am becoming better at my work."

Performance General (8 items) measures the student's perception of how performance oriented they are. Examples of this dimension are: "I am most motivated when I am doing better than others" and "I am most motivated when I receive good marks."

Social General (5 items) measures the student's perception of how socially oriented they are. Examples of this dimension are: " I am most motivated when I work with others" and "I am most motivated when I am in a group."

Global Motivation (5 items) measures the student's perception of how motivated they are at school. Examples of this dimension are: "I feel motivated at school a lot of the time" and "I am often motivated in my schoolwork."

Valuing Motivation (3 items) measures how much students value motivation at school. Examples of this dimension are: "Motivation is important to do well at school" and "Students who are motivated do well at school."

Academic Self-concepts

Academic self-concepts are concerned with how students see their abilities generally, and specifically in terms of English and Mathematics. Items were selected from Marsh's ASDQ (1992) instrument namely:

General Academic Self-concept (5 items) Self-conceptions regarding student's overall abilities. Examples of this dimension are "I get good marks in most school subjects" and "I learn things quickly in most school subjects."

English Self-concept (5 items) Student's self-conceptions of their English abilities. Examples of this dimension are "I am good at English" and "Work in English is easy for me."

Mathematics Self-concept (5 items) Student's self-conceptions of their Mathematics abilities. Examples of this dimension are "I have always done well in Mathematics" and "I learn things quickly in Mathematics."

Outcome Measures

Three self-report outcome measures were used in the study, namely, intention to complete further education (Furthed), affect to school (Affect), and valuing school (Value). Items were answered using a Likert-type scale from strongly agree (5) to strongly disagree (1). Three objective outcome measures were also included in the study, namely, Mathematics Rank and English Rank, taken from the mid-year assessments at each school, and days absent in Term Two of the year the study was conducted.

ANALYSES AND RESULTS

From a psychometric perspective, exploratory and confirmatory factor analyses of the Inventory of School Motivation, GAGOS, and the Academic Self Description Questionnaire have offered considerable empirical support for the validity and utility of these instruments in cross cultural contexts (reported in McInerney, 1995; McInerney & Swisher, 1995; McInerney, McInerney & Roche, 1995; McInerney & Sinclair, 1991, 1992; McInerney, Roche, McInerney & Marsh, 1997; McInerney & Yeung & McInerney, 2000; Marsh 1992). Table 13.2 presents the reliability estimates on each scale for the Aboriginal and Anglo groups as well as the descriptive statistics.

To examine differences between groups on each of these instruments analyses were conducted in sets, namely, ISM, Sense of Self, GAGOS and ASDQ using multivariate analysis of variance with cultural background (Aboriginal and Anglo) as the independent variables. Levene's Test indicated that of the twenty-three Likert scales used in the study there was homogeneity of variance (the exceptions being Task, Social Power, Affiliation, Sense of Purpose, English Self-concept and Maths Self-concept). It is accepted that the use of multivariate analysis of variance is a conservative measure of true significant differences. Wilks Lambda was used to examine overall main effects. Oneway analyses of variance were conducted with Math Rank, English Rank and Days Absent to examine differences between the two groups as MANOVA was not considered appropriate.

Significant differences were found for the ISM (see Figure 13.1). Follow-up univariate F-test with 1,086 degrees of freedom indicated significant differences on Competition, Social Power, Affiliation, Praise and Token. An examination of the means indicated that Aboriginal students were significantly higher on each of these scales. There were no significant differences on Task, Effort and Social Concern.

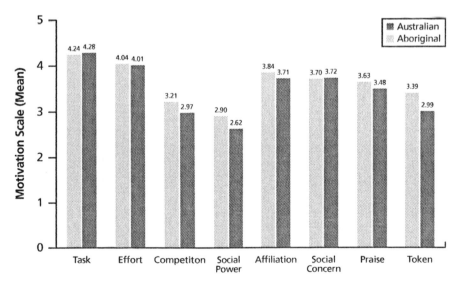

Figure 13.1.   Motivation profile of students by cultural background (Aboriginal and Anglo-Australian).

Table 13.2.   Descriptive Statistics, Reliability Estimates and Significant Differences (MANOVA) on Scales and Outcome Measures for Aboriginal and Anglo Groups

Scales	Aboriginal			Anglo-Australian			Significant Differences F ratio, df (MANOVA)
	Mean	Standard Deviation	Reliability	Mean	Standard Deviation	Reliability	
ISM							F = 7.657, df = 8, 1079
Task	4.24	0.59	0.65	4.28	0.53	0.58	.402
Effort	4.04	0.65	0.79	4.01	0.64	0.80	.496
Competition	3.21	0.85	0.80	2.97	0.85	0.82	F = 17.825, .000
Social Power	2.90	0.91	0.83	2.62	0.80	0.81	F = 22.463, .000
Affiliation	3.84	0.80	0.59	3.71	0.90	0.72	F = 5.669, .017
Social Concern	3.70	0.72	0.66	3.72	0.66	0.68	.804
Praise	3.63	0.80	0.76	3.48	0.86	0.82	F = 7.846, .005
Token	3.39	0.90	0.84	2.99	0.84	0.81	F = 49.404, .000
Sense of Self							F = 14.973, df = 4, 1083
Sense of Purpose	4.25	0.69	0.84	4.31	0.59	0.83	.155
Sense of Reliance	3.83	0.56	0.65	3.84	0.52	0.68	.664
Negative Self Esteem	3.11	0.66	0.62	2.77	0.68	0.71	F = 51.702, .000
Positive Self Esteem	3.66	0.69	0.59	3.70	0.71	0.75	.647
GAGOS							F = 5.845, df = 5, 1080
Mastery General	4.01	0.68	0.78	4.01	0.62	0.74	.668
Performance General	3.28	0.77	0.81	3.13	0.78	0.82	F = 8.187, .004
Social General	3.65	0.78	0.73	3.51	0.78	0.76	F = 10.641, .001
Motivation Value	4.05	0.72	0.66	4.16	0.66	0.69	F = 4.867, .028
Global Motivation	3.57	0.76	0.75	3.48	0.80	0.83	F = 3.597, .058

Table 13.2.   Descriptive Statistics, Reliability Estimates and Significant Differences (MANOVA) on Scales and Outcome Measures for Aboriginal and Anglo Groups (Cont.)

Scales	Aboriginal			Anglo-Australian			Significant Differences F ratio, df (MANOVA)
	Mean	Standard Deviation	Reliability	Mean	Standard Deviation	Reliability	
ASDQ							
English	3.49	0.92	0.89	3.49	0.80	0.86	.961
Mathematics	3.17	1.07	0.93	3.30	0.98	0.91	.088
General	3.72	0.76	0.84	3.67	0.73	0.87	.380
Outcomes							
Further Education	3.63	0.97	0.89	3.65	1.06	0.93	.770
Affect	3.25	1.06	0.59	2.83	1.04	0.71	.000
Value	4.26	0.59	0.81	4.25	0.59	0.83	.773
Math Rank	2.77	1.05		3.12	0.95		.000
English Rank	2.64	0.95		3.24	0.93		.000
Attendance at School	2.13	1.38		1.39	0.74		.000

Significant differences were found for the Sense of Self Scale (Figure 13.2). Follow-up univariate *F*-test with 1,086 degrees of freedom indicated significant differences on Negative Self-esteem. An examination of the means indicated that Aboriginal students were significantly higher than Anglo-Australian students. There were no significant differences on any of the other scales.

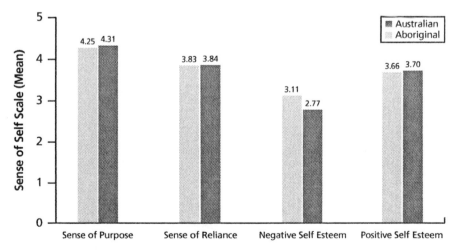

Figure 13.2.   Sense of Self Scale by cultural background of students (Aboriginal and Anglo-Australian).

Significant differences were found for the GAGOS (Figure 13.3). Follow-up univariate F-tests with 1084 degrees of freedom indicated significant differences on Performance General, Social General, Motivation Value and Global Motivation. An examination of the means indicate that Aboriginal students are significantly higher on each of these scales except Motivation Value. There was no significant difference on Mastery General.

There were no significant differences on any of the ASDQ scales (Figure 13.4).

Significant differences were found for the Outcome Scales (Figure 13.5). An examination of the means indicated that Aboriginal students were signifi-

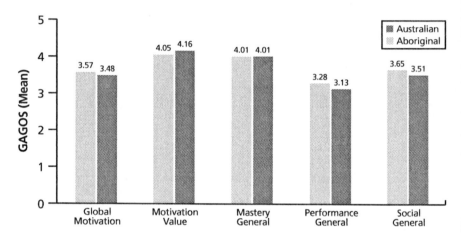

Figure 13.3.   General Achievement Goal Orientation by Cultural Background (Aboriginal and Anglo-Australian)

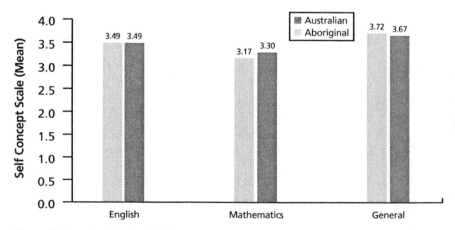

Figure 13.4.   Academic Self Concept scales by cultural background of students (Aboriginal and Anglo-Australian).

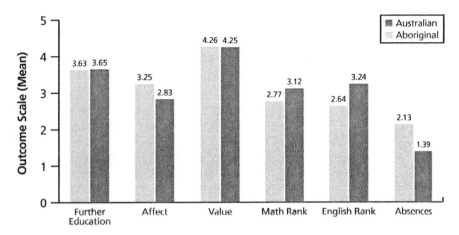

Figure 13.5.   Outcome scales by cultural background of students (Aboriginal and Anglo-Australian)

cantly higher than Anglo-Australian on Affect, and significantly lower on Mathematics Rank, English Rank and missed significantly more days at school. These were no significant differences on Further Education or Valuing Education.

Table 13.1 presents an analysis of confirmed and disconfirmed hypotheses. Contrary to my hypothesised differences between the two groups based upon individualism/collectivism there were no significant differences between the groups on the Individualist oriented mastery scales Task and Effort, however, the Aboriginal group was stronger on the Individualist oriented performance scales, Competition and Social Power. They were also significantly higher on Performance General. In line with my hypotheses on social orientation Aboriginal students were more Affiliation oriented and significantly higher on Social General, but there was no significant difference on Social Concern. In line with my hypotheses based on traditional societies being more extrinsically oriented the Aboriginal students were significantly higher on Praise and Token. Aboriginal students were significantly higher on Global Motivation, while the Anglo students were significantly higher on Motivation Value.

Only one of the Sense of Self hypotheses was supported with there being no significant difference in Positive Self-esteem. In contrast to my hypotheses Aboriginal students were higher on Negative Self-esteem, and there were no significant differences on Self Reliance and Sense of Purpose. All three hypotheses for the ASDQ were supported with no significant differences on any of these scales. Finally, in contrast to my hypotheses, Aboriginal students were higher on Affect and there were no differences on Furthed or Value. The three hypotheses on Math Rank, English Rank and attendance were supported. These results are summarised in Table 13.1 and means and standard deviations for each of these scales are presented in Table 13.2.

In order to examine whether these findings were confounded by locale (more Aboriginal students attended rural schools, while more Anglo students attended urban schools) I selected only schools with Aboriginal students and compared the Aboriginal and Anglo students at these schools. There were virtually no differences in the results to the MANOVA conducted with the full group of Anglos at all schools. Hence, the significant differences appear to represent true differences between Aboriginal students and Anglos, not differences confounded by locale.

Summary

A number of these findings are quite notable. The Aboriginal students in this sample appear to be more highly motivated by performance orientation (Competition and Social Power) than the Anglo students. This does not support the contention that students coming from more collectivist oriented societies should be less performance oriented. Furthermore, my expectation that these students would be less mastery oriented, based on the individualism/collectivism typology was not supported, there were no differences between the groups on mastery orientation (Task and Effort). The further expectation that the Aboriginal students would be more socially oriented was only partially supported. In line with expectations Aboriginal students appear more extrinsically oriented (Praise and Token). Convergent validity evidence for this is provided by the GAGOS results where the Aboriginal students were, surprisingly, significantly more Performance General oriented. Again, there were no differences between the two groups on Mastery General. It is also interesting to note that the Aboriginal students were significantly stronger on Global Motivation, while the Anglos were significantly stronger on Value Motivation.

It should also be noted that there were no significant differences on the three positive Sense of Self scales, however, it is worrying that the Aboriginal students were higher on Negative Self-esteem. In line with much research, there were no differences between the groups on academic self-concept, and in contrast to expectations, Aboriginal students expressed the desire to go on to further education and valued schooling as much as the Anglo students, and liked school more, a very interesting set of results given the relatively poor school achievement and retention of Aboriginal students in schools. In fact, in line with expectations the Aboriginal students were significantly poorer in mathematics and English and missed more days at school than the Anglo group.

These results call into question assumptions about Aboriginal students that they are less mastery or performance oriented than Anglos. Indeed, the findings run quite counter to these assumptions. There is, however, support for the belief that Aboriginal students are more socially oriented. The results also call into question the belief that Aboriginal students lack the internal belief in themselves to do well at school. Indeed, on all of the Sense of Self, ASDQ, Furthed and Value scales there were no significant differences, the exception being on Negative Self-esteem, where the Aboriginal students were higher, and Affect, were they were also significantly stronger than the Anglos.

The Significant Predictors and Self-report Outcomes

In order to ascertain the importance of these variables to valued school outcomes a series of multiple regression analyses were conducted. Each of the sets of predictor variables, namely, motivational goal orientations taken from the ISM and the GAGOS, sense of self variables, and academic self-concept variables were entered as single sets into separate multiple regression analyses for each group with the following criterion variables: intention to complete further education, valuing of schooling and affect towards school. These analyses were conducted separately for each group (Aboriginal and Anglo) to evaluate the capacity of the variables to predict the outcome variables, the relative importance of each predictor variable to explaining variance in the outcome variables, and finally to examine differences in the patterns of significant predictor variables across the two groups. The comparisons referred to in the following sections are non-statistical but give the flavour of the differences and similarities in patterns across the two groups. A finding of significant positive or negative relationship for a particular variable for one group and a non-significant relationship for the second group does not mean that there are significant differences between the two groups as significance is effected by the number of participants in each group. For example, it would be possible for a smaller non-Aboriginal relationship to be significant, whereas a larger Aboriginal relationship to be non-significant. Given this caveat, the following results still tell an interesting tale regarding the strong similarities between the two groups across the scales.

Table 13.3 indicates that for both the Aboriginal and Anglo groups the combined ISM scales were able to explain a significant amount of variance across the three self-report outcome variables, intention to complete further education (Furthed), valuing education (Value), and liking schooling (Affect) and the proportion of variance explained was similar for both groups (the one exception being Furthed for the Anglo group). Of particular note is the finding that the most important predictor for each of these outcomes for both groups was Effort. The more effort oriented individuals from both the Aboriginal and Anglo groups had stronger intentions to complete further education, valued education more, and liked school more. A narrower band of goal orientations were significant predictors for the Aboriginal group than the Anglo group, however, this could be an arte-fact of the larger sample size of Anglos. Token reinforcement was a nega-tive predictor for Furthed for both groups while Social Power was a positive predictor for the Aboriginal group. Task orientation was a positive predic-tor for both groups for valuing education. Affiliation was a significant nega-tive predictor for both groups on Affect, while Praise was a significant positive predictor for the Aboriginal group.

Table 13.3 indicates that the Sense of Self Scales were able to explain a significant amount of variance on the three outcome variables, with the proportion of variance explained very similar for the two groups. Clearly the most important predictor for both groups was Sense of Purpose. Stu-dents from both groups that were high on Sense of Purpose were also stronger on Furthed, Value and Affect. Sense of Reliance was the strongest predictor for Affect for both groups. Again, a broader range of predictors was significant for the Anglo group although the overall level of variance explained was very similar to that of the Aboriginal group.

The General Achievement Goal Orientation Scales (GAGOS) also explained a significant level of variance across the three outcome measures for both groups (an exception being Value for the Anglo group). Global Motivation was the strongest predictor for both groups for Furthed and Affect. Mastery General was the strongest predictor for both groups for Value. Refer to Table 13.3.

Finally, Table 13.3 also indicates that the Academic Self Description Scales were able to explain a significant level of variance in the three out-come measures. Clearly, General Academic self-concept is an important predictor for both groups for each outcome. English self-concept is also a significant predictor for both groups. However, Maths self-concept does not appear as important a predictor for the Aboriginal group.

Table 13.4 indicates the important predictors across the groups. It is apparent from this and Table 13.3 that whatever motivational dynamics were working they were much the same for both groups. In other words, all motivational models (ISM, Sense of Self, GAGOS and ASDQ) were able to explain similar amounts of variance for both groups. The various models appear to be equally applicable to explaining variance in outcomes for both Aboriginal and Anglo students. It is also quite apparent that the most significant predictors are almost identical for both groups. In other words, Effort, Sense of Purpose, Global Motivation, English Self-concept, and General Academic Self-concept appear equally salient to Aboriginal and

Table 13.3.   Model Summary and Standardized Coefficients (Beta) of Multiple Regressions across Aboriginal and Anglo-Australian Groups on Valued Academic Outcomes

Scales	Furthed		Value		Affect	
	Aboriginal	Anglo-Australian	Aboriginal	Anglo-Australian	Aboriginal	Anglo-Australian
ISM	R=0.55 R^2=0.30 *	R=0.43 R^2=0.18*	R=0.63 R^2=0.39*	R=0.59 R^2=0.34*	R=0.57 R^2=0.32*	R=0.62 R^2=0.38*
Task	.092	.042	.252*	.153*	−.018	−.038
Effort	.331*	.279*	.352*	.363*	.366*	.527*
Competition	−.034	.038	.053	.199*	−.092	.008
Social Power	.162*	.017	−.012	−.081*	.037	.089*
Affiliation	−.078	−.104*	.052	.060*	−.164*	−.169*
Social Concern	.137	.118*	.024	.016	.125	.105*
Praise	.128	.102*	.014	.109*	.186*	.054
Token	−.154*	−.136*	.037	−.062	.097	−.052
Sense of Self	R=0.52 R^2=0.27*	R=0.51 R^2=0.26*	R=0.68 R^2=0.47*	R=0.69 R^2=0.48*	R=0.47 R^2=0.22*	R=0.54 R^2=0.29*
Sense of Purpose	.358*	.323*	.546*	.630*	.125	.262*
Sense of Reliance	.145	.082	.115	.040	.271*	.297*
Negative Self Esteem	−.026	−.151*	−.013	.026	−.042	−.072*
Positive Self Esteem	.080	.094*	.086	.085*	.133	.034
GAGOS	R=0.46 R^2=0.21*	R=0.38 R^2=0.15*	R=0.59 R^2=0.35*	R=0.54 R^2=0.29	R=0.52 R^2=0.27*	R=0.56 R^2=0.32*
Mastery General	.052	.153*	.340*	.334*	−.045	.136*
Performance General	.058	−.022	.032	.089*	.002	.033
Social General	.130	−.067	.073	.006	.069	−.082*
Motivation Value	.016	.058	.086	.147*	−.005	−.039
Global Motivation	.291*	.255*	.176*	.095*	.507*	.494*
ASDQ	R=0.44 R^2=0.19*	R=0.43 R^2=0.18*	R=0.44 R^2=0.20	R=0.40 R^2=0.16*	R=0.47 R^2=0.22*	R=0.44 R^2=0.20*
English	.233*	.165*	.150*	.178*	.161*	.153*
Mathematics	.106	.171*	.041	.141*	.204*	.103*
General Academic	.186*	.220*	.309*	.201*	.219*	.287*

Note.   * indicates a significant R^2 and significant predictor.

Table 13.4.   Summary of Significant Positive and Negative Predictors across Aboriginal and Anglo-Australian Groups on Valued Academic Outcomes

Scales	*Furthed*		*Value*		*Affect*	
	Aboriginal	*Anglo-Australian*	*Aboriginal*	*Anglo-Australian*	*Aboriginal*	*Anglo-Australian*
ISM						
Task			+ (+)	+		
Effort	+ (+)	+	+	+	+ (+)	+ (+)
Competition				+ (+)		
Social Power	+ (+)			−		+ (+)
Affiliation		− (−)		+	− (−)	− (−)
Social Concern		+ (+)				+ (+)
Praise		+		+	+ (+)	
Token	−	− (−)				
Sense of Self						
Sense of Purpose	+ (+)	+ (+)	+ (+)	+ (+)		+
Sense of Reliance					+	+ (+)
Negative Self Esteem		− (−)				−
Positive Self Esteem		+		+		
GAGOS						
Mastery General		+	+ (+)	+ (+)		+ (+)
Performance General				+		
Social General						−
Motivation Value				+		
Global Motivation	+	+	+	+ (+)	+ (+)	+ (+)
ASDQ						
English	+ (+)	+	+	+ (+)	+	+
Mathematics		+		+ (+)	+ (+)	+
General Academic	+	+	+	+	+	+ (+)

Note. + indicates a positive predictor, − indicates a negative predictor. (+) indicates a positive predictor when the combined significant predictors are included for each group. (−) indicates a negative predictor when the combined significant predictors are included for each group.

Anglo students. It is also apparent that each of the models individually appear to explain similar levels of variance, with the ASDQ explaining slightly less variance than the other models.

In order to evaluate the relative importance of the significant predictors from each model for each group a final multiple regression analysis was conducted for each group separately which included only the significant predictors from each previous analysis entered as a single block of variables. Table 13.5 presents the results. This combined set of 'significant' predictor variables was able to explain a similar and significant amount of variance in the outcome measures for both the Aboriginal and Anglo groups. Some important patterns emerged. First, Sense of Purpose for schooling is clearly the strongest relative predictor of Furthed and Value for both groups. Effort and Global Motivation were also relatively strong predictors for both groups on Affect (and for the Aboriginal group Effort on Furthed). Finally, Mastery General was a relatively strong predictor for both groups on Value. Otherwise most of the other predictors in the relevant equations only contributed in a minor way to explaining variance in the outcomes.

Summary

There are a number of important features of these analyses to reiterate. First, broadly the various scales used seemed to work in a similar fashion in predicting outcomes for the two groups. Second, the pattern of relatively important significant predictors was very similar for both groups. Third, internal motivators such as Sense of Purpose, Effort, Mastery orientation, and Global Motivation seem much more salient to both groups than external performance oriented motivators such as Competition, Social Power, and Praise, and the social oriented motivators such as Affiliation, Social Concern and Social General. In other words mastery oriented goals and Sense of Purpose appear to 'swamp' the influence of performance, social and extrinsic goals for both Aboriginal and Anglo groups. When combined in this way the ASDQ contributed little to variance explained across the three self report outcomes, although in the separate multiple regressions the ASDQ scales were significant predictors, which suggests that the effect of the academic self-concept scales was taken-up by one of the other variables. Indeed, when only the significant predictors were analysed for each group Sense of Purpose clearly emerged as the dominant motivator for both groups followed by Effort and Global Motivation. Clearly the dynamics of motivation of both Aboriginal and Anglo students in our sample are

Table 13.5.   Model Summary and Standardized Coefficients (Beta) of Multiple Regressions across Aboriginal and Anglo-Australian Groups on Valued Academic Outcomes (Significant Predictors Variables from Table 13.3)

Scales	Furthed		Value		Affect	
	Aboriginal	Anglo-Australian	Aboriginal	Anglo-Australian	Aboriginal	Anglo-Australian
ISM	R=0.56 R^2=0.31*	R=0.55 R^2=0.30*	R=0.70 R^2=0.49*	R=0.73 R^2=0.53*	R=0.61 R^2=0.37*	R=0.65 R^2=0.43*
Task			.140*	.028		
Effort	.217*	−.029	.023	.007	.181*	.314*
Competition				.115*		
Social Power	.163*			−.047		.076*
Affiliation		−.075*		.042	−.123*	−.133*
Social Concern		.091*				.076*
Praise		.076		.059	.156*	
Token	−.116	−.083*				
Sense of Self						
Sense of Purpose	.229*	.295*	.403*	.563*		.047
Sense of Reliance					.005	.055*
Negative Self Esteem		−.085*				−.013
Positive Self Esteem		.037		.008		
GAGOS						
Mastery General		−.012	.154*	.111*		−.081*
Performance General				−.025		
Social General						−.011
Motivation Value				.037		
Global Motivation	.047	.018	.016	−.104*	.194*	.219*
ASDQ						
English	.136*	.075	−.007	.063*	.059	.018
Mathematics		.118		.075*	.158*	.018
General Academic		.093	.093	.014	.091	.090*

Note. * indicates a significant predictor

broadly very similar. In order to check whether location confounded the results (i.e., more Aboriginal students lived in rural locations and Anglos in urban locations) I selected only Anglos at the schools attended by Aboriginal students. The results replicated very closely those reported above, hence, location does not seem to be a factor influencing the results.

Objective Outcome Variables

The analyses reported above indicate that a relatively large proportion of variance is explained by each of the instruments on the self-report outcomes. There is always some doubt about the usefulness of such information as self-report predictors correlated with self-report outcomes could inflate the variance explained due to inherent response bias characterising self-report measures. In order to ascertain whether the instruments could predict outcome measures, and whether the patterns would be the same between the Aboriginal and Anglo groups I performed a series of multiple regression analyses using three 'objective' outcome measures taken from school records, namely, mathematics ranks, English ranks and days absence. The maths and English ranks were taken from the mid year school assessment and are presented as a five point normally distributed scale (5 = excellent, 4 = good, 3 = average, 2 = poor, 1 = very poor). Days absence was a continuous scale indicating the number of days absence students had in Term Two of the study. While these are objective measures they are also limited as outcome measures. First, ranks constrain variance hence the chance of large amounts of variance being explained is constrained. Second, while motivation and academic self-concept are important in students' achievement, achievement levels are also influenced by many other variables such as the quality of teaching, and the nature of the evaluation of achievement used. Consequently, it is always expected that considerable variance will be left unexplained by self-report motivation scales. Third, days absence is not always the most accurate outcome measure, in the sense that schools record the upper levels of this in various ways, for example, some schools will continue counting, while others set a ceiling on the absolute number of days absent and then stop counting. There were also outliers in the absence data. To alleviate these problems I recoded absence data as five ranks, knowing that this constrained the variance. Nevertheless, given these caveats on the usefulness of the objective data there were some promising results. Table 13.6 indicates that each of the scales were able to explain a significant (albeit small) amount of variance in English Rank for both groups. What is striking from the Table is that it is Task, Effort, Sense of Purpose and Global Motivation that appear to be relatively important predictors for the Aboriginal group. Effort, and

Table 13.6.   Summary and Standardized Coefficients (Beta) of Multiple Regressions across Aboriginal and Anglo-Australian Groups on Valued Academic Outcomes (Grouped Days Missed— and Math and English Ranks)

	Attendance		Math Rank		English Rank	
Scales	Aboriginal	Anglo-Australian	Aboriginal	Anglo-Australian	Aboriginal	Anglo-Australian
ISM	$R=0.24$ $R^2=0.06$	$R=0.13$ $R^2=0.02$	$R=0.29$ $R^2=0.08$	$R=0.26$ $R^2=0.07*$	$R=0.41$ $R^2=0.17*$	$R=0.27$ $R^2=0.07*$
Task	−.036	−.006	−.053	−.094	.203	.025
Effort	−.004	−.104*	.066	.161*	.176	.135*
Competition	.147	.042	−.152	.100	−.138	.005
Social Power	−.038	.015	−.110	−.110	.097	−.065
Affiliation	−.104	.061	−.119	−.155*	−.133	−.105*
Social Concern	−.188*	.006	.105	.085	.185	.093
Praise	.053	.005	.218	.002	−.053	.021
Token	.000	−.058	.024	−.059	−.153	−.120*
Sense of Self	$R=0.29$ $R^2=0.08*$	$R=0.15$ $R^2=0.02*$	$R=0.27$ $R^2=0.07*$	$R=0.33$ $R^2=0.11*$	$R=0.40$ $R^2=0.16*$	$R=0.31$ $R^2=0.10*$
Sense of Purpose	−.091	−.010	.095	.013	.341*	.111*
Sense of Reliance	−.071	−.003	−.085	.122*	.163	.063
Negative Self Esteem	.243*	.100*	−.192*	−.277*	−.144	−.275*
Positive Self Esteem	.008	−.064	.128	−.031	−.120	−.074
GAGOS	$R=0.13$ $R^2=0.02$	$R=0.12$ $R^2=0.02*$	$R=0.18$ $R^2=0.03$	$R=0.22$ $R^2=0.05*$	$R=0.29$ $R^2=0.09*$	$R=0.24$ $R^2=0.06*$
Mastery General	−.026	−.078	−.025	.005	.062	−.018
Performance General	.093	−.016	−.105	−.007	−.105	−.022
Social General	−.060	.061	−.031	−.171*	−.178	−.118*
Motivation Value	−.063	.030	.013	.032	.106	.190*
Global Motivation	−.054	−.070	.206	.149*	.233*	.095
ASDQ	$R=0.17$ $R^2=0.03$	$R=0.11$ $R^2=0.01*$	$R=0.32$ $R^2=0.10*$	$R=0.37$ $R^2=0.14$	$R=0.17$ $R^2=0.03$	$R=0.30$ $R^2=0.09*$
English	−.018	.030	−.012	.085	.160	.270*
Mathematics	−.054	−.025	.345*	.372*	−.106	.018
General Academic	−.127	−.113*	−.074	−.058	.017	.039
Approximate N[a]	224	760	140	500	140	500

Note. * indicates a significant predictor

Sense of Purpose are also relatively important to the Anglo group. Negative Self-esteem appears important to both groups across the three outcome measures with students with high levels of Negative Self-esteem missing more school days, and obtaining lower ranks in maths and English. This pattern was the same for both groups. While not significant, General Academic Self-concept was the strongest predictor of Attendance for the two groups, Mathematics Self-concept was the strongest predictor of Maths Rank for both groups, and English Self-concept was the strongest predictor of English rank for both groups. Table 13.6 presents these results.

Correlations

Finally, I wanted to investigate the interrelationships between the various scales for the Aboriginal group. In order to do this I scrutinised the zero-order correlations. This examination indicates that the mastery oriented scales are strongly correlated (>.5) with low correlations with the performance, extrinsic and social oriented scales. Performance and extrinsic oriented scales are strongly inter correlated (>.5) with quite low correlations with most other variables, although Praise is strongly correlated with Effort, Self-reliance, Social Concern, Mastery General, and Global Motivation, suggesting that Praise relates to both mastery and performance orientations. Affiliation is not strongly correlated with other scales except Social General, while Social Concern has strong correlations with Effort, Praise, Sense of Purpose, Mastery General, Social General and Global Motivation, suggesting that concern for others is strongly linked with a mastery orientation at school. The three positive Sense of Self variables (Sense of Purpose, Self Reliance, and Positive Self-esteem) are strongly inter-correlated, and also strongly correlated with the mastery oriented scales as well as Social Concern. In general, there are low correlations between the Sense of Self variables and the performance and extrinsic oriented scales suggesting that there are strong links between feeling good about oneself at school and a mastery orientation.

English Self-concept was strongly correlated (>.5) with Effort, Self-Reliance, Positive Self-Esteem and General Academic Self-concept. It has a weak relationship with Mathematics Self-concept. Mathematics Self-concept is poorly correlated with most other scales with the strongest correlation being with General Academic Self-concept. While Mathematics and English Ranks were highly correlated (>.7) there were weak correlations with their respective Mathematics and English Self-concepts, although, in line with theory, the correlation with the matched Self-concept was stronger than the unmatched. The weak correlations were a surprising finding as I expected strong correlations between the academic Self-concepts and their matched academic achievement. The overall pattern of correlations for Mathematics was weaker than for English. General Academic Self-concept was strongly correlated with Effort, Sense of Purpose, Self Reliance, Positive Self-esteem, Global Motivation and English Self-concept. Depending on the direction in which one views this, it is quite apparent again that very positive Self-concepts are related strongly to a mastery orientation rather than to either a performance, extrinsic or social orientation.

The three outcomes, intention to go on to further education, liking school, and valuing school are relatively strongly correlated (>.4) with the mastery oriented scales, positive sense of self scales, Global Motivation, and General Academic Self-concept scale.

These results give convergent and divergent validity evidence for the scales, with like scales being more highly correlated than unlike scales. Furthermore, they clearly give further evidence that a mastery orientation and positive Sense of Self values appear consistently more salient than performance and extrinsic orientations for the Aboriginal students in this study. Tables 13.7 and 13.8 report the bivariate correlations for both the Aboriginal and full groups for comparison.

DISCUSSION

There were no significant mean differences on the mastery oriented scales, and these scales, together with Sense of Purpose and Global Motivation were significant predictors for the Aboriginal and Anglo groups. On most significant predictors in the multiple regression analyses, such as mastery orientation (Task and Effort), sense of self (Sense of Purpose), general motivation scales (Mastery General, Global Motivation) and academic self-concept (Maths, English and General), there were few differences in patterns of prediction, or the relative salience of predictors to the groups. On a broader level these results emphasise the importance of a mastery orientation over performance, extrinsic and social orientations in the school setting. Where significant mean differences did occur on performance orientation (Competition and Power), extrinsic orientation (Praise and Token) and social orientation (Affiliation and Social General) these were not, by-and-large, significant predictor variables in the multiple regression analyses. In a number of cases the mean differences ran counter to expectations with the Aboriginal group being more performance oriented than the Anglos.

These results suggest first, that, far from lacking the motivation to achieve, as was suggested as a possible reason for their lack of success at school in the earlier part of this chapter, Aboriginal students are more or less motivated in the same ways as the Anglo group, and their achievement

Table 13.7. Bivariate Correlations between All Scales (Aboriginal Group)

Goals	Task	Effort	Compet	Socpower	Affil	Socialcn	Praise	Token	Sop	Sr	Negsc	Passc	Furthed	Affect	Value	Masteryg	Performg	Socialg	Motval	Globmot1	Engsc	Mathsc	Gensc1
Task	1	.683	.208	.236	.267	.453	.445	.274	.597	.563	.035	.475	.404	.339	.540	.636	.308	.420	.548	.545	.388	.164	.370
Effort	.683	1	.280	.269	.333	.582	.571	.405	.758	.724	.014	.677	.489	.503	.589	.694	.445	.508	.611	.753	.496	.276	.521
Compet	.208	.280	1	.719	.290	.293	.462	.561	.261	.396	.243	.379	.188	.159	.243	.321	.701	.384	.219	.327	.266	.149	.258
Socpower	.236	.269	.719	1	.313	.387	.512	.529	.230	.388	.261	.377	.259	.208	.256	.266	.781	.450	.232	.385	.305	.101	.312
Affil	.267	.333	.290	.313	1	.375	.367	.376	.342	.256	.158	.320	.133	.084	.271	.453	.408	.591	.301	.511	.181	.078	.216
Socialcn	.453	.582	.293	.387	.375	1	.553	.431	.551	.480	.116	.457	.401	.407	.404	.495	.421	.528	.454	.511	.381	.278	.422
Praise	.445	.571	.462	.512	.367	.553	1	.618	.475	.514	.183	.486	.377	.435	.393	.578	.650	.527	.440	.597	.410	.302	.448
Token	.274	.405	.561	.529	.376	.431	.618	1	.296	.353	.264	.415	.184	.325	.311	.394	.611	.463	.304	.401	.227	.174	.295
Sop	.597	.758	.261	.230	.342	.551	.475	.296	1	.606	-.019	.636	.496	.373	.670	.633	.364	.469	.470	.573	.438	.220	.508
Sr	.563	.724	.396	.388	.256	.480	.514	.353	.606	1	.029	.682	.412	.437	.497	.567	.502	.410	.419	.617	.528	.308	.533
Negsc	.035	.014	.243	.261	.158	.116	.183	.264	-.019	.029	1	-.057	-.047	-.055	-.044	.118	.224	.188	.080	.003	-.080	-.066	-.039
Passc	.475	.677	.379	.377	.320	.457	.486	.415	.636	.682	-.057	1	.414	.412	.516	.516	.453	.415	.371	.607	.532	.335	.565
Furthed	.404	.489	.188	.259	.133	.401	.377	.184	.496	.412	-.047	.414	1	.441	.437	.337	.311	.346	.269	.428	.386	.260	.385
Affect	.339	.503	.159	.208	.084	.407	.435	.325	.373	.437	-.055	.412	.441	1	.317	.306	.281	.309	.262	.512	.365	.351	.415
Value	.540	.589	.243	.226	.271	.404	.393	.311	.670	.497	-.044	.516	.437	.317	1	.551	.339	.395	.413	.437	.363	.225	.425
Masteryg	.636	.694	.321	.266	.453	.495	.578	.394	.633	.567	.118	.516	.337	.306	.551	1	.431	.557	.557	.639	.364	.203	.359
Performg	.308	.445	.701	.781	.408	.421	.650	.611	.364	.502	.224	.453	.311	.281	.339	.431	1	.579	.322	.511	.389	.196	.385
Socialg	.420	.508	.384	.450	.591	.528	.527	.463	.469	.410	.188	.415	.346	.309	.395	.557	.579	1	.398	.540	.362	.172	.376
Motval	.548	.611	.219	.232	.301	.454	.440	.304	.470	.419	.080	.371	.269	.262	.413	.557	.322	.398	1	.513	.321	.145	.355
Globmot1	.545	.753	.327	.385	.289	.511	.597	.401	.573	.617	.003	.607	.428	.512	.437	.639	.511	.540	.513	1	.465	.347	.519
Engsc	.388	.496	.266	.305	.181	.381	.410	.227	.438	.528	-.080	.532	.386	.365	.363	.364	.389	.362	.321	.465	1	.302	.519
Mathsc	.164	.276	.149	.101	.078	.278	.302	.174	.220	.308	-.066	.335	.260	.351	.225	.203	.196	.172	.145	.347	.302	1	.444
Gensc1	.370	.521	.258	.312	.216	.422	.448	.295	.508	.533	-.039	.565	.385	.415	.425	.359	.385	.376	.355	.519	.519	.444	1

Table 13.8. Bivariate Correlations between All Scales (Full Group)

Goals	Task	Effort	Compet	Socpower	Affil	Socialcn	Praise	Token	Sop	Sr	Negsc	Possc	Furthed	Affect	Value	Masteryg	Performg	Socialg	Motival	Globmot1	Engsc	Mathsc	Gensc1
Task	1	.630	.210	.164	.120	.414	.439	.249	.552	.484	-.097	.405	.304	.330	.475	.629	.301	.259	.520	.467	.321	.149	.324
Effort	.630	1	.232	.212	.083	.506	.495	.295	.712	.652	-.195	.579	.408	.561	.542	.688	.361	.304	.505	.714	.423	.265	.492
Compet	.210	.232	1	.641	.203	.076	.424	.544	.220	.288	.161	.264	.094	.156	.272	.294	.688	.274	.149	.180	.201	.164	.214
Socpower	.164	.212	.641	1	.262	.212	.462	.535	.163	.241	.216	.199	.110	.192	.178	.258	.768	.368	.117	.226	.196	.075	.195
Affil	.120	.083	.203	.262	1	.205	.259	.291	.119	.024	.190	.040	-.040	-.072	.136	.195	.290	.673	.142	.054	.196	-.012	.015
Socialcn	.414	.506	.076	.212	.205	1	.425	.242	.443	.366	-.058	.317	.300	.354	.311	.435	.287	.453	.372	.468	.265	.149	.308
Praise	.439	.495	.424	.462	.259	.425	1	.595	.417	.384	.049	.359	.249	.339	.381	.514	.646	.415	.355	.460	.301	.122	.313
Token	.249	.295	.544	.535	.291	.242	.595	1	.218	.272	.236	.258	.061	.207	.234	.332	.631	.409	.200	.270	.115	.088	.187
Sop	.552	.712	.220	.163	.119	.443	.417	.218	1	.542	-.168	.544	.457	.415	.682	.593	.303	.272	.453	.551	.362	.226	.436
Sr	.484	.652	.288	.241	.024	.366	.384	.272	.542	1	-.250	.685	.376	.461	.435	.535	.347	.193	.384	.604	.482	.383	.559
Negsc	-.097	-.195	.161	.216	.190	-.058	.049	.236	-.168	-.250	1	-.354	-.236	-.155	-.130	-.090	.128	.203	-.089	-.216	-.249	-.246	-.276
Possc	.405	.579	.264	.199	.040	.317	.359	.258	.544	.685	-.354	1	.391	.398	.446	.487	.315	.160	.357	.536	.468	.409	.570
Furthed	.304	.408	.094	.110	-.040	.300	.249	.061	.457	.376	-.236	.391	1	.397	.469	.314	.150	.101	.234	.364	.332	.274	.385
Affect	.330	.561	.156	.192	-.072	.354	.339	.207	.415	.461	-.155	.398	.397	1	.357	.373	.224	.140	.217	.542	.337	.250	.414
Value	.475	.542	.272	.178	.136	.311	.381	.234	.682	.435	-.130	.446	.469	.357	1	.520	.307	.235	.392	.404	.327	.237	.376
Masteryg	.629	.688	.294	.258	.195	.435	.514	.332	.593	.535	-.090	.487	.314	.373	.520	1	.428	.359	.544	.610	.364	.199	.384
Performg	.301	.361	.688	.768	.290	.287	.646	.631	.303	.347	.128	.315	.150	.224	.307	.428	1	.435	.257	.344	.278	.144	.289
Socialg	.259	.304	.274	.368	.673	.453	.415	.409	.272	.193	.203	.160	.101	.140	.235	.359	.435	1	.232	.292	.119	.049	.138
Motival	.520	.505	.149	.117	.142	.372	.355	.200	.453	.384	-.089	.357	.234	.217	.392	.544	.257	.232	1	.423	.309	.135	.292
Globmot1	.467	.714	.180	.226	.054	.468	.460	.270	.551	.604	-.216	.536	.364	.542	.404	.610	.344	.292	.423	1	.405	.275	.464
Engsc	.321	.423	.201	.196	-.006	.149	.301	.115	.362	.482	-.249	.468	.332	.337	.327	.364	.278	.119	.309	.405	1	.181	.610
Mathsc	.149	.265	.164	.075	-.012	.149	.122	.088	.226	.383	-.246	.409	.274	.250	.237	.199	.144	.049	.135	.275	.181	1	.402
Gensc1	.324	.492	.214	.195	.015	.308	.313	.187	.436	.559	-.276	.570	.385	.414	.376	.384	.289	.138	.292	.464	.610	.402	1

Note. (Coefficient / (Cases) / 2-tailed Significance). "." Is printed if a coefficient cannot be computed

342

values are very similar to Anglo children. Second, the academic Self-concept of the Aboriginal students is very similar to that of the other students. This is in contrast to a number of other studies, which suggest that the self-concept of minorities is, paradoxically, higher than that of the mainstream group despite poorer school performance. Third, there are no significant differences on Sense of Self except with Negative Self-esteem. Paradoxically, while the Aboriginal students are as positive to education as measured by Furthed, Affect and Value as the Anglo students, they are achieving significantly more poorly. Fourth, the simple dichotomising of groups as individualist or collectivist is not supported by this study. A group commonly categorised as collectivist (the Aboriginal group) was no more collectivist or individualist than the Anglo group on the measures used in this study.

What does all the above tell us about Aboriginal children and their motivation at school? The first and most important finding is that, across the broad range of scales used in this study, the similarities between the Aboriginal and non-Aboriginal groups far outweigh any differences. It would appear from these results that Aboriginal children, even in remote locations, are motivated by the same motives and self beliefs that influence children from Anglo backgrounds. These results tell a positive story regarding the capacity of Aboriginal children to do well at school given the right sort of motivational school environment. The findings also suggest that key variables used to distinguish Western and indigenous groups do not appear to be salient in the school contexts studied. These results, replicated on a number of occasions with other diverse groups, suggest two paradoxes. First, if the motivational profiles of the Aboriginal and Anglo groups are so similar, why is there a difference in educational outcomes? Second, within the Aboriginal group there are always some who achieve well, despite the relatively poor achievement levels of the group as a whole. What is it that the successful indigenous students "have" or "do" that distinguishes them from their unsuccessful peers? These paradoxes suggest that at least five elements need to be considered in order to further our understanding of the motivational dynamics that influence achievement for this disadvantaged group. First, there is a need to examine the nature of the future goals that students' hold; their development over time, and their relationship to day-to-day achievement goals and learning processes. It is plausible that Aboriginal students do not do well at school because they have a different sense of the future and its relationship to their schooling and do not perceive the instrumental value of schooling in the same way as other students. Second, the motivational goals examined in this research may have failed to uncover goals that are more salient to Aboriginal students', goals that, if reflected in school settings, might better facilitate learning. Third, Aboriginal students may lack or fail to use the learning and self-regulatory strategies needed to coordinate their learning or may have different learning and self-regulatory modes of behaviour. Fourth, the historical experiences of Aboriginal people within assimilationist and often-racist educational institutions may moderate the future goals, achievement goals and perceived utility of schooling for Aboriginal students. Finally, the quality of schooling Aboriginal students receive may be inferior for a variety of reasons (e.g., isolation, poor teachers, poor school facilities, perceived irrelevance of the curriculum) predisposing these students to achieve poorly relative to more advantaged groups. Further research is required to examine these possibilities.

REFERENCES

Ames, C. (1984). Competitive, cooperative, and individualistic goal structures: a cognitive-motivational analysis. In R. Ames, & C. Ames (Eds.), *Research on motivation in education: Vol. 1. Student motivation.* Orlando: Academic Press.

Ames, C. (1992). Classrooms: Goals, structures, and student motivation. *Journal of Educational Psychology, 84,* 261–271.

Blumenfeld, P. C. (1992). Classroom learning and motivation: Clarifying and expanding goal theory. *Journal of Educational Psychology, 84,* 272–281.

Commonwealth of Australia (1993). *Joint policy statement: National Aboriginal and Torres Strait Islander education policy.* Canberra. DEET.

Commonwealth of Australia. (1994). *National review of education for Aboriginal and Torres Strait Islander peoples.* Canberra: Australian Government Publishing Service.

Commonwealth of Australia (1995). *The commonwealth Government's response to the review of education for Aboriginal and Torres Strait Islander peoples.* Canberra: Australian Government Publishing Service.

Dowson, M., & McInerney, D. M. (2002). What do students say about their motivational goals? Towards a more complex and dynamic perspective on student motivation. *Contemporary Educational Psychology, 28,* 91–113.

Dweck, C. S., & Elliott, E. S. (1983). Achievement motivation. In P. Mussen (Ed.), *Handbook of child psychology* (pp. 643–691). New York: Wiley.

Eckermann, A-K. (1999). Aboriginal education in rural Australia: A case study in frustration and hope. *Australian Journal of Education, 43,* 5–23.

Elliott, A. J. 1997. Integrating the "classic" and "contemporary" approaches to achievement motivation: A hierarchical model of approach and avoidance achievement motivation. In M. L. Maehr & P. Pintrich (Eds.), *Advances in motivation and achievement.* (Vol. 10, pp143–179). Greenwich, CT: JAI.

Fogarty, G. J., & White, C. (1994). Differences between values of Australian Aboriginal and non-Aboriginal students. *Journal of Cross-Cultural Psychology, 25,* 394–408.

Graham, S. (1994). Motivation in African Americans. *Review of Educational Research, 64,* 55–117.

Hewitt, D. (2000) A clash of world views: Experiences form teaching Aboriginal students. *Theory into Practice, 39,* 111–118.

Kagitcibasi, C., & Berry, J. W. (1989). Cross-cultural psychology: Current research and trends. *Annual Review of Psychology, 40*, 493–531.

Ledlow, S. (1992). Is cultural discontinuity an adequate explanation for dropping out? *Journal of American Indian Education, 31*, 21–36.

Maehr, M. L. (1984). Meaning and motivation. Toward a theory of personal investment. In R. Ames and C. Ames (Eds.), *Research on motivation in education: Vol.1. Student motivation*. Orlando: Academic Press.

Maehr, M. L., & Braskamp, L.A. (1986). *The motivation factor: A theory of personal investment*. Lexington, MA: Lexington.

Marsh, H. W. (1987). The Big-Fish-Little-Pond Effect on Academic Self-concept. *Journal of Educational Psychology, 79*, 280–295.

Marsh, H. W. (1990). A multidimensional, hierarchical self-concept: Theoretical and empirical justification. *Educational Psychology Review, 2*, 77–171.

Marsh, H W, (1992). Content specificity of relations between academic achievement and academic self-concept. *Journal of Educational Psychology, 84*, 35–42.

Marsh, H. W. (1993). Academic self-concept: Theory measurement and research. In J Suls (Ed.), *Psychological perspectives on the self* (Vol. 4, pp. 59–98). Hillsdale, NJ: Erlbaum.

Marsh, H. W., & Craven, R. (1997). Academic self-concept: Beyond the dustbowl. In G. Phye (Ed.), *Handbook of classroom assessment: Learning, achievement, and adjustment* (pp. 131–198). Orlando, FL : Academic Press.

McInerney, D. M. (1989). Urban Aboriginals parents' views on education: A comparative analysis. *Journal of Intercultural Studies. 10*, 43–65.

McInerney, D. M. (1990). The determinants of motivation for urban Aboriginal students: A cross-cultural analysis. *Journal of Cross-Cultural Psychology, 21*, 474–495.

McInerney, D. M. (1991). Key determinants of motivation of urban and rural non-traditional Aboriginal students in school settings: Recommendations for educational change. *Australian Journal of Education, 35*. 154–174

McInerney, D. M. (1995). Goal theory and indigenous minority school motivation: Relevance and application. In P. R. Pintrich & M. L. Maehr (Eds.), *Advances in motivation and achievement.* (Vol. 9. pp. 153–181). Greenwich, CT: JAI Press.

McInerney, D. M., McInerney, V., & Roche, L. (1995). The relevance and application of goal theory to interpreting indigenous minority group motivation and achievement in school settings. Paper presented at the annual meeting of the American Educational Research Association, San Francisco, April 18–22.

McInerney, D. M., Roche, L., McInerney, V., & Marsh, H. W. (1997). Cultural perspectives on school motivation: The relevance and application of goal theory. *American Educational Research Journal 34.*, 207–236.

McInerney, D. M., & Sinclair, K. E. (1991). Cross cultural model testing: Inventory of School Motivation. *Educational and Psychological Measurement, 51*, 123–133.

McInerney, D. M., & Sinclair, K. E. (1992). Dimensions of school motivation. A cross-cultural validation study. *Journal of Cross-Cultural Psychology, 23*, 389–406.

McInerney, D. M., & Swisher, K. (1995). Exploring Navajo motivation in school settings. *Journal of American Indian Education, 33*,28–51.

McInerney, D. M., Yeung, A, S., & McInerney V. (2000). The meaning of school motivation. Multidimensional and hierarchical perspectives and impacts on schooling. Paper presented at the annual meeting of the American Educational Research Association, New Orleans, April 24–29.

Meece, J. L. (1991). The classroom context and students' motivational goals. In Maehr, M. L., & Pintrich, P. R. (Eds.), *Advances in motivation and achievement. A research annual.* (Vol. 7. pp. 261–285). Greenwhich, CT: JAI Press.

Pintrich, P. R., & Garcia, T. (1991). Student goal orientation and self-regulation in the college classroom. In Maehr, M. L., & Pintrich, P. R. (Eds.), *Advances in motivation and achievement. A research annual.* (Vol. 7. pp. 371–402). Greenwich, CT: JAI Press.

Pintrich, P. R., Marx, R. W., & Boyle, R. (1993). Beyond "cold" conceptual change: The role of motivational beliefs and classroom contextual factors in the process of conceptual change. *Review of Educational Research, 63,* 167–199.

Pintrich, P. R., & Schrauben, B. (1992). Students' motivational beliefs and their cognitive engagement in classroom academic tasks. In D. Schunk & J. Meece, (Eds.), *Student perceptions in the classroom* (pp. 149–183). Hillsdale, NJ: LEA.

Purdie, N. & McCrindle, A. (nd). Self-concept among indigenous and non-indigenous students. An unpublished article.

Purdie, N., Tripcony, P., Boulton-Lewis, G., Fanshawe, J., & Gunstone, A. (2000). Posaitive Self-identity for indigenous students and its relationship to school outcomes. A project funded by the Commonwealth Department of Education, Training and Youth Affairs. Canberra.

Schwartz, S. H. (1990). Individualism-Collectivism: Critique and proposed refinements. *Journal of Cross-Cultural Psychology, 21,* 139–157.

Triandis, H. (1995). Motivation and achievement in collectivist and individualist cultures. *Advances in Motivation and Achievement* (Vol. 9, pp. 1–30). Greenwich, CT: JAI Press.

Triandis, H. C. et al (1993). An etic-emic analysis of individualism and collectivism. *Journal of Cross-Cultural Psychology,* 24, 366–383.

Urdan, T. 1997. Achievement goal theory: Past results, future directions. In M. L. Maehr & P. Pintrich (Eds.), *Advances in Motivation and Achievement.* (Vol. 10, pp. 99–141). Greenwich, CT: JAI

Wentzel, K. R. (1991). Social and academic goals at school: Motivation and achievement in context. In Maehr, M. L., & Pintrich, P. R. (Eds.), *Advances in Motivation and Achievement. A Research Annual.* (Vol. 7.pp. 185–212). Greenwich, CT: JAI Press.

CHAPTER 14

SOCIAL GROUP IDENTITY AND ITS EFFECT ON THE SELF-ESTEEM OF ADOLESCENTS WITH IMMIGRANT BACKGROUND

David L. Sam and Erkki Virta

This chapter focuses on the self-esteem of adolescents with immigrant backgrounds with special emphasis on its relationship with ethnic identity. With respect to this relationship, Sam and Virta examined whether this is moderated or mediated by perceived discrimination and majority identity. In addition, they compared the level of reported self-esteem among these immigrant adolescents with that of their majority host counterparts. From social identity theory, it has been argued that identity and self-esteem are positively related. It is further argued that disparaged minority group members will have a lower self-esteem than their host majority counterparts because of prejudice, negative stereotypes and discrimination. However, these arguments have shown mixed findings. It is against this background that Sam and Virta developed this chapter. Initially, they identified the possible reasons for these mixed findings, and argued that perceived discrimination and degree of the minority group member's identification, with the majority group, i.e., majority identity, may either mediate or moderate the

International Advances in Self Research, pages 347–373

relationship between ethnic identity and self-esteem. They also suggested that the level of the minority group member's self-esteem might be related to the way they simultaneously identify with their own group and that of the majority group. These hypotheses are examined among three distinct ethnic groups with immigrant backgrounds in Norway and Sweden. While the mediating/moderating roles of the majority identify and perceived discrimination is rejected, the study suggested that a high identification with one's ethnic group as well as with the majority group might lead to higher self-esteem. On the other hand, a simultaneous low identification with both the ethnic and majority groups will lead to lower levels of self-esteem. These findings might be useful when planning strategies, in helping ethnic minority group members in their adjustment to settle in a new country.

THE PROBLEM

Do adolescents with ethnic minority status have lower self-esteem than their peers belonging to the majority group? What is the relationship between ethnic identity and majority identity on the one hand and self-esteem on the other, among ethnic minority adolescents? How is the relationship between ethnic identity and self-esteem influenced by perceived discrimination and by majority identity? With respect to the latter question, we were specifically interested in whether perceived discrimination and majority identity mediated or moderated the relationship between ethnic identity and self-esteem. These are the questions that we address in this chapter.

Self-esteem is an important dimension of the self-construct, because it is crucial to an individual's psychological well-being, including life satisfaction and mental health (Diener & Diener, 1995). In this chapter, we direct our attention to the self-esteem of adolescents with minority status in Western societies, an issue that has been both elusive and controversial. Our intention is to recast some of these controversies and verify our arguments with a comparative study on three distinct ethnic minority groups in Northern Europe, specifically Norway and Sweden.

Ethnic Identity and Psychological Well-being

The role of ethnic identity in the psychological well-being of ethnic minority adolescents is a burgeoning area of research on the acculturation of these adolescents (Crocker, Luhtanen, Blaine, & Broadnax, 1994; Liebkind, 1993; Phinney, 1990, 1991; Phinney & Chavira, 1992; Phinney & Devich-Navarro, 1997; Rosenthal & Feldman, 1992a, 1992b; Sanchez & Fernandez, 1993; Verkuyten, 1994, 1995; Yu & Berryman, 1996; Zak, 1993).

Following social identity theory (Tajfel, 1981; Tajfel & Turner, 1986), it has been postulated that being a member of a group and identifying with the group is an important determinant of a person's self-esteem. However, a low self-esteem is suggested to arise if the group the individual is a member of is the subject of negative stereotypes, prejudice and discrimination.

While a link between group identity in general and self-esteem has indeed been demonstrated (Crocker, Voelkl, Testa, & Major, 1991; Crocker, Cornwell & Major, 1993), this relationship with respect to racially and ethnically disparaged group members is unclear. Here, conflicting results have been found (Crocker & Major, 1989; Hughes & Demo, 1989; Richman, Clark, & Brown, 1985; Jensen, White, & Galliher, 1982; Rosenberg & Simmons, 1972; Verkuyten, 1994). Consequently, several reviewers of the literature (e.g., Cross, 1991; Phinney, 1990; 1991; Porter & Washington, 1979) have concluded that there is little consistent evidence for the postulated relationship.

Furthermore, there have been mixed findings concerning the hypothesis that members of racially and ethnically stigmatised groups would have lower self-esteem than their counterparts belonging to more esteemed groups. For example, in a review of 16 studies, Verkuyten (1994) identified eight studies where no differences were found between White majority members and ethnic group members presumed to be targets of racial discrimination. Of the remaining eight studies, four observed higher self-esteem among the White group members, whereas the remaining four found the exact opposite.

Reasons presented to account for these mixed findings have varied. One obvious reason has been the differences in the conceptualization of ethnic identity. It has also been suggested that studies have varied in the extent to which they have taken into consideration the individual's degree of identification with the larger society and the socio-cultural context under which the investigations have taken place. Furthermore, studies have not always taken into consideration the level of ethnic identity development and the stigmatised group members' own self-protective measures for resiliency (Crocker & Major, 1989; Phinney, 1990, 1991; Phinney & Chavira, 1992; Verkuyten, 1988, 1994).

The Moderator–Mediator Distinction

One of the questions dealt with in this chapter is whether the relationship between ethnic identity and self-esteem is influenced by other factors, specifically by perceived discrimination and majority identity. Within the psychological literature, two forms of relationships, mediator and moderator, have been identified, albeit the terms are often used synonymously and erroneously. A variable is said to be a *mediator* if it *accounts for* the relation between an independent and a dependent variable. A *moderator*, in turn, *effects the direction and/or strength* of that relationship. Baron and Kenny (1986) have suggested that while *mediating* variables "speak" to the underlying mechanisms by explaining how or why particular effects occur, *moderating* variables "speak" to specifying the conditions under which particular effects occur. Rogosch, Chassin, and Sher (1990) have also suggested that *moderating* variables can be thought of as protective or buffer variables that act to reduce the impact of a known vulnerability, or serve as magnifying variables that increase the impact of known vulnerability.

Some criteria and statistical procedures have been presented to test whether a variable can qualify as a mediator or moderator. Using perceived discrimination as an example, for it to qualify as a *mediator* between ethnic identity and self-esteem, Baron and Kenny (1986) argue that two conditions have to be met. (a) Ethnic identity must first be able to predict both self-esteem and perceived discrimination, and perceived discrimination must also be able to predict self-esteem; (b) the strength of the relationship between ethnic identity and self-esteem must be eliminated or greatly weakened when self-esteem is regressed on ethnic identity and perceived discrimination. For perceived discrimination to qualify as a *moderator* in the same relationship, it is important to demonstrate a significant interaction between perceived discrimination and ethnic identity. Although significant main effects for ethnic identity and perceived discrimination on self-esteem may be observed, these are not necessary prerequisites in order to demonstrate the *moderator* effect of perceived discrimination.

PREVIOUS RESEARCH

Ethnic Identity as a Multidimensional Concept

Ethnic identity has been suggested to be a multidimensional concept. In her review, Phinney (1991) identified at least five different dimensions: (1) Self-identification as a group member, (2) involvement in ethnic behaviors and practices, (3) knowledge about the group, (4) commitment to or sense of belonging to the group, and (5) positive evaluation of the group. These dimensions may have different relationships to one another, and to self-esteem. For instance, it is possible to have a strong commitment to the group, without knowledge about the group's history and values. This phenomenon is referred to as unexamined or pre-encounter ethnic identity (Cross, 1995; Helms, 1990; Marcia, 1980; Phinney, 1989). Group membership per se has not been found related to the level of self-esteem (Phinney, Cantu, & Kurtz, 1997).

Failure on the part of previous research to examine how the various dimensions of ethnic identity are related to self-esteem makes predictions about the relationship problematic. In the study presented in this chapter, two aspects of the concept are jointly examined, namely (1) ethnic identity as commitment to, or sense of belonging to the group, and (2) the positive evaluation of the group. A positive relationship was expected between these aspects of ethnic identity and self-esteem, because both ethnic identity and self-esteem focus on the affective component of self-concept.

Majority Identity

Identification with the larger society, that is, majority identity, has also been argued to be important for the psychological task of self-definition among ethnic minority members. It has been argued that a strong sense of ethnic identity devoid of positive identification to the larger society may trigger psychological conflict (Phinney, 1991). This argument suggests that majority identity could possibly serve as a mediator or a moderator in the relationship between ethnic identity and self-esteem. In other words, majority identity may either account for (mediate) the relationship between ethnic identity and self-esteem or effect (moderate) this relationship.

However, the mediating and moderating roles of majority identity in the relationship between ethnic identity and psychological well-being have received only a little attention. In a study among African-Americans, and Latino adolescents in Southern California, Phinney, Ferguson, and Tate (1997) found no significant relationship between identification with American identity (i.e., majority identity) and self-esteem. This suggests that majority identity could possibly not be a *mediator.* Majority identity as a *moderator* is, however, inconclusive from the study, because the authors did not check on the significance of the interaction between ethnic and majority identities on self-esteem. Sanchez and Fernandez (1993), on the other hand, have demonstrated the *moderator* role of majority identity on the relationship between acculturative stress and ethnic identity among a group of Latino adolescents in the Miami area.

It has been argued that majority identification on the part of disparaged group members may be problematic because of prejudice, discrimination and negative stereotypes from members of the larger society (Birman, 1994; Inman & Baron, 1996). A dissonance may arise if one identified with his or her "oppressors." In other words, the more one perceives discrimination from the larger society, the more difficulty the individual would have in identifying with the larger group (Birman, 1994; Pratto & Lemieux, 2001). Some studies have found support for this argument (e.g., Aguirre, Saenz, & Hwang, 1985; Floyd & Gramann, 1995), whereas others have found contradictory results (Portes, 1994; Portes, Parker, & Cobas, 1980). Thus, the precise relationship between perceived discrimination and majority identity still remains unclear.

Bicultural Identity and Psychological Well-being

Previously ethnic identity and majority identity were viewed as belonging to the opposite ends of a uni-dimensional construct where a high identification with one group necessarily meant a low identification with the other. Thus, it was deemed incompatible to have high or low identification with the two groups simultaneously. However, currently, ethnic identity and majority identity are viewed as two separate constructs, where it is possible to have high identification or low identification on both constructs (Phinney, 1990; Sanchez & Fernandez, 1993). It is also possible to have high identification on one construct, and a low on the other. These identifications have variously been referred to as integration or biculturalism, when the individual has high identification on both constructs, and marginalization when one has low identification on both constructs. A high identification with the ethnic group, and a low identification with the majority group as referred to as Separation, and the opposite, i.e., low identification with the ethnic group and a high identification with the majority group is referred to as Assimilation (Birman, 1994; Phinney, 1990).

Studies have suggested that integrated individuals or biculturals generally report better psychological well-being than marginalized, separated and assimilated individuals, and that marginalized individuals tend to be worse off than the others (Berry & Sam, 1997; LaFromboise, Coleman, & Gerton, 1993; Sam, 2000). It was therefore expected that in the current study presented in this chapter that integrated individuals would report the highest self-esteem compared to the other three forms of identifications. It was also expected that marginalized individuals would reported the lowest self-esteem scores.

Perceived Discrimination and Self-esteem

There is ample evidence to the effect that racial and ethnic discrimination either directly or indirectly causes psychological problems (Clark, Anderson, Clark, & Williams, 1999; Dion & Earn, 1975; Dion, Dion, & Pak, 1992; Pak, Dion, & Dion, 1991). A positive sense of ethnic identity however, is suggested to protect the individual from the potentially negative impact of prejudice and discrimination against the group (Phinney, 1990). In other words, a positive sense of ethnic belonging will moderate the relationship between perceived discrimination and psychological well-being. However, without explicitly testing for perceived discrimination as a moderator, Phinney, Madden, and Santos (1998) could not find support for the buffering effect of perceived discrimination on the relationship between ethnic identity and self-esteem.

Another question, particularly dealt with in this chapter, is whether *perceived discrimination* mediates (accounts for) or moderates (effects) the relationship between ethnic identity and self-esteem. Van Oudenhoven and Eisses (1998) have found that migrants who sought to maintain their ethnic identity felt that they received more stereotyping prejudice and discrimination from members of the larger Dutch society. Such a finding and the known relationship between perceived discrimination and self-esteem provide some of the prerequisites needed for perceived discrimination to qualify as a *mediator*. However, this is yet to be demonstrated.

In reiteration, we will report in this chapter some results from a study in which we tried to find some answers to the following questions:

1. Do adolescents with ethnic minority status have lower self-esteem than their peers belonging to the majority group?

2. How are ethnic minority identity and majority identity, and combinations of the two identities, relate to self-esteem among ethnic minority adolescents?

3. Do perceived discrimination and majority identity mediate (account for) or moderate (effect) the relationship between ethnic identity and self-esteem?

We examined these questions in a study of Chilean, Turkish, and Vietnamese adolescents with immigrant backgrounds in Norway ($n = 312$) and Sweden ($n = 528$) together with their host national peers from the two respective countries ($n = 436$).

The Cultural Context for the Study

It is important that the findings from the present study are understood within its proper context, consequently in the following section, we briefly describe the socio-cultural context of Norway and Sweden where the present study was undertaken. As countries, neither Norway nor Sweden are regarded as attractive countries for immigration. However, both countries have, over the past few decades attracted large numbers of migrants from the South either fleeing political and ethnic violence, or in search of labour and subsequent family reunification. Currently, approximately 6% and 18% of the national population of Norway and Sweden respectively are made up of persons with foreign background. About a third of these foreigners in both countries come from the developing countries of Asia, Central and South America, and Africa (Brochmann, 1999; Hammar, 1999).

In the present chapter, our interest has been on immigrants from Chile, Turkey, and Vietnam, who are also among the largest ethnic groups in both countries. These three ethnic groups in addition, share a similar immigration history to the two countries. Turks were recruited to the two countries as alien workers following the economic growth in Europe in the late 1960s. However, while permanent residency was offered to those arriving in Sweden, alien workers to Norway and the rest of Europe were regarded as temporary guest workers, who could be repatriated following the end of their work contract (Hammar, 1999). Vietnamese and Chileans, both with refugee background, migrated to the two countries following the fall of Saigon in 1975 in Vietnam and the rise of Pinochet to power in Chile in 1973.

Resettlement policies for foreign nationals in both Sweden and Norway are based on integration. That is, foreigners are expected to maintain their original cultural identity as well as to identify with the larger majority society). Other key elements in this integration policy are partnership in terms of equality between foreign nationals and host nationals, and freedom of choice where foreign nationals are free to choose which aspects of the two cultures (i.e., their original culture and the host culture) they will abide by (Westin, 1999). Sweden, however, is seen as being more liberal with their practice of freedom of choice compared to Norway. As such, we were not surprised to find in a recent study that Turks in Norway reported higher levels of perceived discrimination than their peers in Sweden (Virta, Sam, & Westin, in press)

Method

All together 1,276 adolescents (256 Vietnamese; 401 Turkish; 183 Chilean and 436 host nationals) participated in the study. These were recruited from junior and senior high schools in the Greater Stockholm area in Sweden, and five major Norwegian cities with relatively high concentrations of immigrant families. With a few exceptions (e.g., Vietnamese in Sweden), data collection involved completing a structured questionnaire during a school session. A team made up of the project leader in the respective countries and a team of student assistants who traveled to the cities and schools undertook data collection. The questionnaires were self-explanatory, but a standard instruction was given at the start of the session in which students were informed that participation was voluntary, and that responses were confidential. In both countries, about 15% of the students who were approached to participate in the study refused to do so. Table 14.1 gives a more detailed demographic description of the sample.

To assess the different issues we were interested in, a questionnaire was developed specifically for the study by a group of international scholars including the present authors as well as others such as John Berry (Canada), Jean Phinney (USA) and Colette Sabatier (France). The questionnaire covered issues such as school adjustment, ethnic and national language use and proficiency, attitudes towards acculturation, ethnic and minority identities, perceived discrimination, self-esteem, life satisfaction and mental health problems. Except for demographic questions, all the items were answered on a 5-point Likert scale ranging from 1 = "strongly disagree" or "never" to 5 = "strongly agree" or "very often." Below is a brief description of the variables that we focused on in this present study.

- *Demographics:*   Participants had to report on their gender, age, place of birth (whether Norwegian/Swedish or foreign born), age of arrival in the host country, ethnicity of themselves as well as that of their parents. Participants were asked to report on their mother's and father's current occupations.
- *Self-esteem:*   This was measured using Rosenberg's (1986) 10-item self-esteem inventory. A sample item was "On the whole I am satisfied with myself".
- *Perceived discrimination:* This scale consisted of nine items, five of which assessed direct experience of discrimination—negative or unfair treatment from others (e.g., I have been teased or insulted because of my ethnic background). The remaining four items assessed the sources of the negative treatment (e.g., teachers, pupils, etc.).
- *Social group identity:*   Two forms of these—ethnic identity and majority identity were separately assessed. *Ethnic identity* was assessed using seven items drawn from Phinney's Multigroup Ethnic Identity Measure (1992). It included statements such as "I feel I am part of the *Vietnamese/ Turkish/Chilean* culture," and "Being part of the *Vietnamese/Turkish/Chilean* culture is embarrassing to me" (reversed in scoring), that focused primarily on ethnic belonging and pride. *(Majority) Norwegian/Swedish identity* was assessed using three items adapted from Phinney and Devich-Navarro (1997). An example of item from this scale is: "I am proud of being Norwegian/Swedish."

All the scales used in the study had good internal reliability, that is, the questions of each scale measured the same concept, the alpha values ranged from .73 to .93 (Sam & Virta, 2001). Pan-cultural factor analyses also showed that the scales were comparable across countries and across ethnic groups. The pan-cultural factor analyses showed Tucker's phi values over .90 for all the items, suggesting good structural equivalence of the

Table 14.1. Demographic Description of the Sample

	Norway				Sweden			
	Norwegians $n = 209$	Vietnamese $n = 150$	Turks $n = 112$	Chileans $n = 50$	Norwegians $n = 227$	Vietnamese $n = 106$	Turks $n = 289$	Chileans $n = 133$
Age (in yr.)								
Mean (sd)[2]	15.13 (1.58)	15.52 (1.65)	15.36 (1.81)	14.98 (1.53)	16.06 (1.73)	16.25 (1.82)	15.11 (1.74)	15.51 (1.99)
Gender								
Girls (%)	99 (47.83)	80 (53.69)	52 (46.85)	24 (48.98)	118 (51.98)	76 (52.20)	139 (48.10)	61 (45.86)
Boys (%)	108 (52.17)	69 (46.31)	59 (53.15)	25 (51.02)	109 (48.02)	50 (47.80)	150 (51.90)	72 (54.14)
Birth place								
Host-born (%)	208 (99.5)	50 (33.56)	56 (50.00)	6 (12.24)	226 (99.60)	29 (27.365)	221 (77.00)	37 (28.03)
Foreign-born (%)	1 (0.50)	99 (66.44)	56 (50.00)	43 (87.76)	1 (0.40)	77 (72.64)	66 (23.00)	95 (71.97)
Length of stay (in yr.)[3]								
Mean (sd)		9.83 (3.98)	8.35 (3.90)	8.51 (2.66)		9.08 (4.79)	7.90 (4.15)	10.99 (2.25)
Occstat[4]								
Unskilled (%)	7 (4.12)	40 (52.63)	43 (81.13)	7 (17.95)	31 (15.74)	40 (64.51)	126 (66.97)	37 (35.92)
Skilled (%)	23 (13.53)	26 (34.21)	7 (13.21)	14 (35.90)	36 (18.27)	13 (20.97)	34 (17.80)	22 (21.36)
White collar (%)	68 (40.00)	4 (5.26)	1 (1.89)	8 (20.51)	79 (40.10)	4 (6.45)	19 (9.95)	34 (33.01)
Professional (%)	72 (42.35)	6 (7.89)	2 (3.77)	10 (25.64)	51 (25.89)	5 (8.06)	12 (6.28)	10 (9.71)

Notes. The group referred to as Vietnamese in Sweden was made up of 59% Chinese and 41% Vietnamese both of whom migrated to Sweden from Vietnam. The two groups in Sweden have been found not to differ on key demographic and psychological variables (Virta & Westin, 1999). The groups differed on their mean ages [$F(7, 1265) = 10.16, p < 0.001$]. Tukey's HSD post-hoc test indicated that the differences were as follows: NC < S & SV; ST < S & SV and N < S & ST. N = Norwegians, S = Swedes, NC = Chileans in Norway; ST = Turks in Sweden; SV = Vietnamese in Sweden. Of foreign-born adolescents in host country. OCCATAT = Occupational status is a rough estimation of SES, and is based on the highest occupation of both father's and mother's. The groups differed significantly on their SES $\chi^2 (21) = 363.29, p < 0.001$).

356

measures across the countries and ethnic groups (Van de Vijver, Liebkind, & Vedder, 2000).

In dealing with the research questions of the present study, we have relied on Pearson correlation, analysis of variance (ANOVA) and multiple regression analyses. ANOVA analyses were followed by post hoc test using Tukey's honestly significant difference. Mean values from ANOVA have been presented graphically in bar charts.

RESULTS

Initially, we examined the relationship of the age of the adolescents and also the parents' SES with the adolescent's self-esteem. Self-esteem was neither related to the adolescents' age nor to the SES of their parents. Therefore, these factors were ignored in subsequent analyses.

Self-esteem: Comparison Between Ethnic Minorities and their Majority Peers

Analysis of variance results indicated that although ethnic minority adolescents in Norway and Sweden differed from their majority peers with respect to level of self-esteem [$F(7, 1244) = 11.16$; $p < 0.01$] they did not always report lower self-esteem than their majority counterparts. As can be seen in Figure 14.1 which shows the means scores on self-esteem, Vietnam-

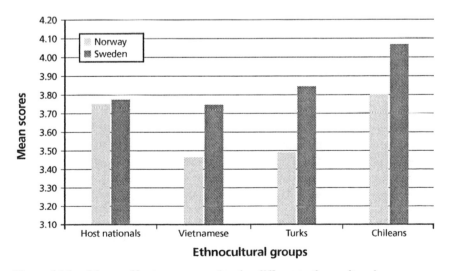

Figure 14.1.   Mean self-esteem scores for the different ethnocultural groups

ese in both countries reported the lowest self-esteem. However, Vietnamese in Sweden reported a higher self-esteem than their peers in Norway. Further more, Chileans in Sweden reported the highest level of self-esteem, which was significantly higher than both groups of host national adolescents.

Relations Between Social Group Identity, Perceived Discrimination and Self-esteem

Using Pearson correlation, ethnic identity was related to high self-esteem in all the ethnic groups in both countries. These relationships were statistically significant, except for the Chileans in Norway. Perceived discrimination, in turn, was significantly related to low self-esteem. The consistency of the relationships between self-esteem on the one hand, and perceived discrimination and ethnic identity on the other, suggest that perceived discrimination may be a mediator between ethnic identity and self-esteem. This issue however, is closely examined in the next section. Majority identity showed mixed relationships with ethic identity, perceived discrimination and self-esteem. However, in some cases, majority identity showed a positive and significant relationship with self-esteem, perceived discrimination and ethnic identity. In other cases, this relationship was negative and significant. In yet some cases, the relationship was not significant. A summary of the relationships among these variables is shown in Table 14.2. The mixed nature of the relationship between majority identity on the one hand, and self-esteem, perceived discrimination and ethnic identity on the other suggests that any evidence of the mediating role of majority identity may also be inconsistent.

Perceived Discrimination and Majority Identity as a Moderator/Mediator in the Relation Between Ethnic Identity and Self-esteem

To verify whether perceived discrimination and/or majority identity moderated the relationship between ethnic identity and self-esteem, we performed a series of multiple regression analyses. To begin with, ethnic identity and perceived discrimination (see Table 14.3) and ethnic identity and majority identity (see Table 14.4) were first entered into the regression model as predictors of self-esteem (Step 1). Then in Step 2, these same two predictor variables together with an interaction between them were entered into the model as a third variable. Thus in Step 1, only two predictors are used, and in Step 2, three predictors are used. Consequently under

Step 1 in Tables 3 and 4, two standard regression coefficients, beta, are indicated, and under Step 2, three beta coefficients are given. The Multiple R^2, (the explained variance) under Step 1, is for the two-predictor variables, and in Step 2, the Multiple R^2 is for all three factors. According to Baron and Kenny (1986), a variable may be a moderator if during Step 2, the explained variance increases significantly, that is, when the interaction between the two predictor variables are entered into the model.

Our analyses indicated that neither perceived discrimination nor majority identity might be acting as a moderator in the relationship between ethnic identity and self-esteem with the exception of one case—Vietnamese in Norway. Generally, the interaction effects either did not change the explained variance, or if it did, it increased it by just 0.01 in all the analyses (see Tables 14.3 & 14.4). The only exception was the interaction between ethnic identity and majority identity among Vietnamese in Norway (see Table 14.4) where the explained variance rose from 0.08 to 0.12.

Table 14.2.   Relationship between Self-esteem, Ethic Identity, Majority Identity and Perceived Discrimination among Vietnamese, Turks and Chileans in Norway and Sweden

Bivariate Pairs	Vietnamese		Chileans		Turks	
	Norway	Sweden	Norway	Sweden	Norway	Sweden
Self-esteem— Ethnic Identity	.20[*]	.34[***]	.10	.25[**]	.23[*]	.21[**]
Self-esteem— Majority Identity	.18[*]	13	.10	−.17[*]	.22[*]	−.01
Self-esteem— Perceive Discrimination	−.36	−.42[***]	−.52[***]	−.17[*]	−.28[*]	−.25[***]
Ethic Identity— Majority Identity	−.10	.07	−.31[*]	−.33[**]	−.14	−.27[**]
Ethnic Identity— Perceived Discrimination	−.06	−.15	−.12	−.05	.02	−.18[**]
Majority Identity— Perceived Discrimination	−.19[*]	−.19	.14	−.17[*]	−.14	−.01

Note. * $p > 0.05$; ** $p < 0.01$; *** $p < 0.001$

Multiple regression analyses were once again used to ascertain a mediating effect of perceived discrimination/majority identity in the relationship between ethnic identity and self-esteem. Here, ethnic identity must first be able to predict (i.e., significant beta co-efficient) separately majority identity, perceived discrimination and self-esteem. These are indicated in the first column under the dependent variables in Tables 14.5 and 14.6. In

Table 14.3.   Regressions Predicting Self-esteem from Perceived Discrimination, Ethnic Identity, and Their Interaction for Different Ethnic Groups in Norway and Sweden[a]

	Step I		Step II	
	Beta	*Multiple R^2*	*Beta*	*Multiple R^2*
Vietnamese in Norway				
Ethnic identity	.18*		.39	
Perceived discrimination	−.37***	.18***	−.02	
Interaction (EI*PD)			−.39	.19***
Turks in Norway				
Ethnic identity	.23*		−.15	
Perceived discrimination	−.29**	.13**	−1.00	
Interaction (EI*PD)			.82	.14**
Chileans in Norway				
Ethnic identity	.10		.33	
Perceived discrimination	−.52***	.30***	−.31	
Interaction (EI*PD)			−.43	.31**
Vietnamese in Sweden				
Ethnic identity	.29***		.55*	
Perceived discrimination	−.34***	.23***	.18	
Interaction (EI*PD)			−.56	.24***
Turks in Sweden				
Ethnic identity	.16***		−.01	
Perceived discrimination	−.21***	.08***	−.68	
Interaction (EI*PD)			.49	.08***
Chileans in Sweden				
Ethnic identity	.24**		.01	
Perceived discrimination	−.16[b]	.09**	−.82	
Interaction (EI*PD)			.69	.09**

Notes.   [a] Multiple R^2 reported under Step 1 is for both predictors (PD and EI), and that reported under Step II is for both predictors and the interaction effect.
[b] $p = 0.06$; * $p > 0.05$; ** $p < 0.01$; *** $p < 0.001$

Table 14.4.   Regressions Predicting Self-esteem from Ethnic Identity, Majority Identity, and Their Interaction for Different Ethnic Groups in Norway and Sweden

	Step I		Step II	
	Beta	Multiple R^2	Beta	Multiple R^2
Vietnamese in Norway				
Ethnic identity	.22**		.92**	
Perceived discrimination	.20*	.08**	1.25**	
Interaction (EI*MI)			−1.23*	.12***
Turks in Norway				
Ethnic identity	.26*		.23	
Perceived discrimination	.25*	.11**	.18	
Interaction (EI*MI)			.08	.11*
Chileans in Norway				
Ethnic identity	.15		.00	
Perceived discrimination	.15	.03	.20	
Interaction (EI*MI)			.34	.03
Vietnamese in Sweden				
Ethnic identity	.33***		.35	
Perceived discrimination	.10	.12**	.14	
Interaction (EI*MI)			−.05	.12**
Turks in Sweden				
Ethnic identity	.22***		.36*	
Perceived discrimination	.05	.05**	.61	
Interaction (EI*MI)			−.55	.05**
Chileans in Sweden				
Ethnic identity	.22*		.23	
Perceived discrimination	−.10	.07**	−.06	
Interaction (EI*MI)			−.04	.07*

Note.   Multiple R^2 reported under Step 1 is for both predictors (MI and EI), and that reported under Step II is for both predictors and the interaction effect. $p > 0.05$; ** $p < 0.01$; *** $p < 0.001$

addition, perceived discrimination/majority identity must also be able to separately predict self-esteem. These are indicated in the second column under dependent variables in Tables 14.5 and 14.6. Finally, the strength of the relationship between ethnic identity and self-esteem should be eliminated or greatly weakened if self-esteem was regressed on ethnic identity and perceived discrimination/majority identity. The final regression coefficients were indicated in the third column under the dependent variables in Tables 14.5 and 14.6.

Table 14.5.   Regressions of Perceived Discrimination on Ethnic Identity; Self-esteem on Ethnic Identity and Perceived Discrimination Separately, and Self-esteem on Ethnic Identity and Perceived Discrimination at the Same Time for Vietnamese, Turks and Chileans in Norway and Sweden

	Dependent variables		
	Perceived discrimination[a]	Self-esteem[b]	Self-esteem[c]
Vietnamese in Norway			
Ethic identity	Ns	$.19^*$	Ns
Perceived discrimination		$-.38^{***}$	Ns
Turks in Norway			
Ethic identity	Ns	$.22^*$	Ns
Perceived discrimination		$-.28^{**}$	Ns
Chileans in Norway			
Ethic identity	Ns	Ns	Ns
Perceived discrimination		$-.54^{***}$	Ns
Vietnamese in Sweden			
Ethic identity	Ns	$.34^{***}$	$.29^{**}$
Perceived discrimination		$-.38^{***}$	$-.34^{***}$
Turks in Sweden			
Ethic identity	$-.15^{**}$	$.19^{***}$	$.16^{***}$
Perceived discrimination		$-.24^{***}$	$-.21^{***}$
Chileans in Sweden			
Ethic identity	Ns	$.25^{**}$	$.24^{***}$
Perceived discrimination		$-.17^*$	.16Ns

Notes.   Only significant beta values are reported.
[a] Regression of Perceived discrimination on ethnic identity
[b] Regression of self-esteem on ethnic identity and perceived discrimination separately
[c] Regression of self-esteem on ethnic identity and perceived discrimination at the same time.
Ns = not significant; * $p > 0.05$; ** $p < 0.01$; *** $p < 0.001$

Table 14.6.   Regressions of Majority Identity on Ethnic Identity; Self-esteem on Ethnic Identity and Majority Identity Separately, and Self-esteem on Ethnic Identity and Majority Identity at the Same Time for Vietnamese, Turks and Chileans in Norway and Sweden

	Dependent variables		
	Perceived discrimination[a]	Self-esteem[b]	Self-esteem[c]
Vietnamese in Norway			
Ethic identity	Ns	.19[*]	.22[**]
Perceived discrimination		.18[*]	Ns
Turks in Norway			
Ethic identity	−.20[*]	.22[*]	.26[*]
Perceived discrimination		.22[*]	.25[**]
Chileans in Norway			
Ethic identity	−.31[*]	Ns	Ns
Perceived discrimination		Ns	Ns
Vietnamese in Sweden			
Ethic identity	Ns	.34[***]	.33[*]
Perceived discrimination		Ns	Ns
Turks in Sweden			
Ethic identity	−.28[*]	.19[**]	.22[**]
Perceived discrimination		Ns	Ns
Chileans in Sweden			
Ethic identity	−.33[***]	.25[**]	.22[**]
Perceived discrimination		−.17[*]	Ns

Notes.   Only significant beta values are reported. Regression of majority identity on ethnic identity.
[a] Regression of self-esteem on ethnic identity and majority identity separately.
[b] Regression of self-esteem on ethnic identity and majority identity at the same time.
[c] Regression of self-esteem on ethnic identity and perceived discrimination at the same time.
Ns = not significant; * $p > 0.05$; ** $p < 0.01$; *** $p < 0.001$.

Regarding the mediating roles of majority identity and perceived discrimination (see Tables 14.5 & 14.6), none of the two criteria suggested by Baron and Kenny (1986) were met among the three ethnic groups in Norway. Ethnic identity could neither predict perceived discrimination alone, nor could it predict self-esteem when it was together with perceived discrimination. Although some of the initial conditions regarding majority identity as a mediator were met for Turks and Chileans in Norway (see Table 14.6), not all of them were met at the same time in any of the three ethnic groups in Norway. Similarly in Sweden, some of the prerequisites were met, as indicated for instance by ethnic identity predicting majority identity among Turks and Chileans in Sweden (see Table 14.6). However, the final decisive condition (i.e., significantly lower beta co-efficient for ethnic identity indicated in the third column, self-esteem as dependent variable, compared with the beta-coefficient in the second column, self-esteem as dependent variable) was not met in any of the groups. The one case that was close to *mediation* was Turks in Sweden with respect to perceived discrimination (see Table 14.5). However, the effect of ethnic identity did not change dramatically (the beta coefficient dropped from .19 to .16) when perceived discrimination was introduced into the regression model. Both beta values were significant at $p < 0.001$. In the prediction of self-esteem, perceived discrimination was also found to consistently predict self-esteem in both countries and among all the ethnic groups.

Relation Between Group Identity and Self-Esteem

We categorized our respondents into the four categories of Assimilated, Integrated, Separated and Marginalized, using their scores on the measures of ethnic and majority identity. For example, people who scored on or over her/his group mean on the measure of majority identity and under the group mean on ethnic identity was categorized as Assimilated. A person who scored over or on her/his group mean on both ethnic and majority identity was categorized as Integrated, and so forth. In that manner, we created four categories in each ethnic group: Assimilated, Integrated, Separated and Marginalized. These four categories were then used as a single scale with four categories.

The various combinations of majority and ethnic identities appear to be related differently to self-esteem. Thus as can be seen in Figure 14.2, adolescents who strongly identified with both their ethnic group and with the majority group, that is, Integrated, generally reported higher self-esteem than those who reported low identification with both groups, that is, Marginalized. This was so for all the ethnic groups with the exception of Chileans in Norway. Similarly, adolescents who identified strongly with their own ethnic group and reported low identification with the majority group (Separation) also generally reported high self-esteem.

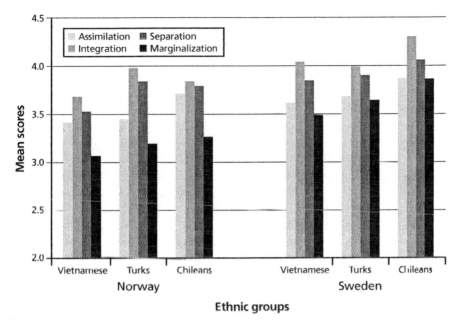

Figure 14.2.   Mean scores of self-esteem based on different combinations of ethnic and majority identities for 3 ethnic groups in Norway and Sweden.

DISCUSSION

Results from the present study suggest that, the three adolescents with immigrant background in Norway and Sweden do not necessarily report lower self-esteem than their majority peers. In some cases, and in particular for Chileans in Sweden, the reported self-esteem was higher than that of Norwegian and Swedish adolescents. Although ethnic identity was found to be positively related to self-esteem, and perceived discrimination negatively related to self-esteem, perceived discrimination does not appear to mediate or moderate the relationship between ethnic identity and self-esteem. Majority identity did not also appear to mediate or moderate the relationship between ethnic identity and self-esteem. However, it appears that the self-esteem of these adolescents with immigrant background is closely related to the degree to which they simultaneously identified with their ethnic group and the majority group. Specifically, adolescents who reported high identification with both groups, that is, Integrated adolescents reported higher self-esteem than those who reported low identification with both groups, that is, Marginalized adolescents. The finding that some adolescents with immigrant backgrounds do not necessarily report lower self-esteem compared to members of the majority group, and that some, actually have higher self-esteem scores is consistent with the conclusion reached by Verkuyten (1994). The finding that Chileans in Norway and Sweden reported self-esteem levels comparable to that of their majority peers, and did not differ from each other raises the view that self-esteem to some extent may be a function of one's ethnicity and the country of residence. This view perhaps gains further support by the fact that Vietnamese in both countries also reported the lowest self-esteem. While it is difficult to account for the relatively high self-esteem scores among Chileans in the two countries, the low self-esteem scores among the Vietnamese may be in line with their Confucian child upbringing (see Ho, 1994) where modesty may be deemed as a virtue. It may be worthwhile to add that low self-esteem among Vietnamese may not necessarily be related to other aspects of their adaptation. Virta and Westin (1999) for instance, found that Vietnamese adolescents in Sweden reported better school adjustment than their peers with Turkish, Swedish, and Finnish background.

Studies have also indicated that there is an acceptance hierarchy for immigrants and ethnic minority groups in various settlement countries where some groups are more preferred or accepted than others (Berry & Kalin, 1995). It is therefore possible that the relative self-esteem scores found among the three ethnic groups is a reflection of their relative positions on the acceptance hierarchy by the majority group members. In other words, Chileans are probably more preferred in the two countries than Vietnamese. This assertion however, is only a speculation.

Generally, the immigrant adolescents in Sweden reported higher self-esteem than their peers in Norway. This might be due to the fact that the Swedish integration policy fosters a strong ethnic identity, which in turn promotes good self-esteem. Although the study did not set out to examine the levels of ethnic identity among the immigrant groups in the two countries, our analyses indicated that the three immigrant adolescent groups in Sweden generally also reported higher ethnic identity than their peers in Norway.

As this study shows, highly perceived discrimination was consistently related to low self-esteem among the three ethnic groups in both countries suggesting that discrimination may be detrimental to a person's self-esteem. While this finding gains support from previous ones (e.g., Clark et al., 1999) it does not resolve the question of causality, namely, whether perceived discrimination causes poor self-esteem or the other way round as has been suggested by Phinney and her associates (1998). When it comes to the role of ethnic identity in the self-esteem of ethnic minority adolescents, it appears that it boosts one's self-esteem, due to the positive relationship between ethnic identity and self-esteem. However, it does not appear that negative effects of perceived discrimination either moderate or mediate the relationship between ethnic identity and self-esteem.

Just as ethnic identity was found to be positively related self-esteem, studies have also found positive relationship between majority identity and self-esteem (Phinney et al., 1997). However, in the present study, with few exceptions, the majority identity was not positively related to self-esteem. As a matter of fact, it even appears that for Chileans in Sweden, high majority identity might be detrimental to their self-esteem. There may be several reasons for the lack of consistent positive relationship between majority identity and self-esteem. First, the positive relationship found between majority identity and self-esteem is suggested to be applicable for White samples (Phinney et al., 1997). The samples of the present study were all members of ethnic minority groups. Furthermore, the settlement policies of both Norway and Sweden do not emphasize that ethnic minority members need to identify with the majority culture in order to be accepted. Thus, for many of these adolescents high majority identification was not required of them, in addition to the fact it may be unrealistic for many of them as a result of their visible external features making their ethnic minority status more salient in the daily discourse. Our analyses indicated that mean scores on majority identity were consistently lower than mean scores on ethnic identity.

Although majority identity alone does not appear to be related to one's self-esteem, together with ethnic identity, the two appear to be related to one's self-esteem. This finding is a further support to the view that a combination of one's old heritage culture and the new majority culture for adolescents with immigrant background may be good for the person's psychological well-being (Sam, 2000). The need for high dual identification and its importance for the psychological well-being is in line with Phinney's (1991) assertion that a strong sense of ethnic identity devoid of positive identification with the larger society may trigger psychological conflicts. Inability to find significant differences among Chileans in Norway opting for Integration, Marginalization, Separation, and Assimilation may be due to the smallness of sample size.

Limitations of the Study

Even though we contend that neither perceived discrimination nor majority identity either moderates or mediates the relationship between ethnic identity and self-esteem, we also acknowledge that our contention is based on multiple regression analyses which are not as robust as structural equation modeling (SEM). Thus, we recommend that future studies use an SEM approach to verify the possible moderating/mediating roles of majority identity and perceived discrimination in the relationship between ethnic identity and self-esteem.

Two other factors, which previous studies have speculated on with respect to the relationship between ethnic identity and self-esteem, but could not be examined in this study are the roles of sense of efficacy and the degree of ethnic identity development. For brevity, gender was also not included as a factor in the analyses, although there may be reasons to believe that boys and girls differ in their self-esteem (Alsaker, 1990). These issues require some examination in future studies if we are to fully unravel the relationship between ethnic identity and self-esteem.

The results of this study provide some insights into the self-concept of ethnic minority adolescents, and in particular the role of ethnic identity in their self-esteem. Social identity theory contends that ethnic minority adolescents may be vulnerable to poor self-esteem especially if the group to which they belong is the target of negative stereotypes, prejudice and ethnic discrimination. Accordingly, it is expected that ethnic minority group members would have a lower self-esteem when compared with more esteemed White majority group members. In addition, it is expected that the self-esteem of such ethnic minority members will be positively related to the level of their ethnic identification. In spite of the intuitive nature of the theory, findings from the research literature have been mixed and have given rise to a number of speculations.

A problem with many of the findings is that several of the studies have either focused on one or a few ethnic groups in one country (e.g., Rotheram-Borus, 1990; Verkuyten, 1995; Phinney, Ferguson, & Tate, 1997) or an ethnic group in two different countries (e.g., Rosenthal & Feldman, 1992b). From a cross-cultural psychological perspective, findings from such studies may be specific either to the ethnic group(s) in the study, or the country where the study was undertaken (Berry, Poortinga, Segall, & Dasen, 2002; Segall, Dasen, Berry, & Poortinga, 1999). One advantage of the present study is the fact that it involved two countries, and three ethnic groups in addition to the majority national group. As such, the stability and generality of the findings go a step beyond that of previous ones.

SUMMARY AND CONCLUSIONS

The present study indicates that adolescents with an ethnic minority status do not necessarily report lower self-esteem than their peers belonging to the majority group. While ethnic identity is positively related to self-esteem, and perceived discrimination was negatively related self-esteem, it appeared that perceived discrimination neither moderates nor mediates the relationship between ethnic identity and self-esteem. Similarly, majority identity does not appear to have a mediating or moderating role in the relationship. Reported self-esteem appears to arise against a background of one's ethnicity, degree of perceived discrimination and a combination of the person's dual identification with his/her own ethnic group and the majority host group. Importantly, poor self-esteem may arise as a result of low identification with both groups, (i.e., Marginalization) and high self-esteem may arise from high identification with both groups (i.e., Integration). Because Integrated adolescents also reported high self esteem, it may perhaps be a good idea for professionals who work with ethnic minority adolescents to help them develop dual positive identification with their own group and the majority group of the society of settlement.

{ack}*Acknowledgments.*   The empirical basis of this paper comes from the Norwegian and Swedish portions of the ICSEY project. All the collaborators of the project are gratefully acknowledged. These are (in alphabetical order of countries): Australia (Cynthia Fan; Rogelia Pe-Pua; David Sang); Canada (John Berry; Kyunghwa Kwak); Finland (Karmela Liebkind); France (Colette Sabatier); Germany (Paul Schmitz); Israel (Gabriel Horenczyk); Netherlands (Paul Vedder; Fons van de Vijver; Colette van Laar); Norway (David Sam); Portugal (Felix Neto); Sweden (Charles Westin, Erkki Virta) and United States (Jean Phinney).

The Norwegian portion of the study was made possible by research grants from the Research Council of Norway, and from Young Investigators Grant, Johann Jacobs Foundation of Switzerland. The Swedish portion was made possible by a research grant from the Swedish Council of Social Research.

REFERENCES

Aguirre, B. E., Saenz, R., & Hwang, S. (1989). Discrimination and the assimilation and ethnic competition perspective. *Social Science Quarterly, 70,* 594–606.

Alsaker, F. D. (1990). Global negative self-evaluation in early adolescence. *Doctoral dissertation in psychology.* Bergen: University of Bergen, Norway.

Baron, R. M., & Kenny, D. A. (1986). The moderator-mediator variable distinction in social psychological research: Conceptual, strategic, and statistical considerations. *Journal of Personality and Social Psychology, 51,* 1173–1182.

Berry, J. W., & Kalin, R. (1995). Multicultural and ethnic attitudes in Canada: An overview of the 1991 national survey. *Canadian Journal of Behavioural Science, 2,* 301–320.

Berry, J. W., Poortinga, Y. H., Segall, M. H., & Dasen, P. R. (2002). *Cross-cultural psychology: Research and applications.* Cambridge, UK: Cambridge University Press.

Berry, J. W., & Sam, D. L. (1997). Acculturation and adaptation. In J. W. Berry, M. H. Segall, & C. Kagitcibasi (Eds.), *Handbook of cross-cultural psychology, Vol. 3. Social and applied psychology* (2nd ed., pp. 291–326). Boston: Allyn & Bacon.

Birman, D. (1994). Acculturation and human diversity in a multicultural context. In E. Trickett, R. Watts, & D. Birman (Eds.), *Human diversity: Perspective on people in context* (pp. 261–284). San Francisco: Jossey-Bass.

Brochmann, G. (1999). Redrawing lines of control: The Norwegian welfare state dilemma. In G. Brochmann & T. Hammar (Eds.), *Mechanisms of immigration control: A comparative analysis of European regulation policies* (pp. 203–232). Oxford: Berg.

Clark, R., Anderson, N. B., Clark, W. R., & Williams, D. R. (1999). Racism as a stressor for African Americans: A biosocial model. *American Psychologist, 54,* 805–816.

Crocker, J., Cornwell, B., & Major, B. (1993). The stigma of overweight: Affective consequences of attributional ambiguity. *Journal of Personality and Social Psychology, 64,* 60–70.

Crocker, J., Luhtanen, R., Blaine, B., & Broadnax, S. (1994). Collective self-esteem and psychological well-being among White, Black and Asian college students. *Personality and Social Psychology Bulletin, 20,* 503–515.

Crocker, J., & Major, B. (1989). Social stigma and self-esteem: The self-protective properties of stigma. *Psychological Review, 96,* 608–630.

Crocker, J., Voelkl, K., Testa, M., & Major, B. (1991). Social stigma: The affective consequences of attributional ambiguity. *Journal of Personality and Social Psychology, 60* 218–228.

Cross, W. E. (1991). *Shades of black.* Philadelphia: Temple University Press.

Cross, W. E. (1995). The psychology of Nigresence: Revisiting the Cross-model. In J. G. Ponterotto, J. M. Casa, L. A. Suzuki, & C. M. Alexander (Eds.), *Handbook of multicultural counselling* (pp. 93–122). Thousand Oaks, CA: Sage.

Diener, E., & Diener, M. (1995). Cross-cultural correlates of life satisfaction and self-esteem. *Journal of Personality and Social Psychology, 68,* 653–663.

Dion, K. L., Dion, K. K., & Pak, A. W-P. (1992). Personality-based hardness as a buffer for discrimination-related stress in members of Toronto's Chinese community. *Canadian Journal of Behavioural Sciences, 24,* 517–536.

Dion, K. L., & Earn, B. M. (1975). The phenomenology of being a target of prejudice. *Journal of Personality and Social Psychology, 32,* 944–950.

Floyd, M., & Gramann, J. H. (1995). Perceptions of discrimination in a recreation context. *Journal of Leisure Research, 27,* 192–199.

Hughes, M., & Demo, D. H. (1989). Self-perceptions of Black Americans: Self-esteem and personal efficacy. *American Journal of Sociology, 95,* 132–159.

Hammar, T. (1999). Closing the doors to the Swedish welfare state. In G. Brochmann & T. Hammar (Eds.), *Mechanisms of immigration control: A comparative analysis of European regulation policies* (pp. 169–201). Oxford: Berg.

Helms, J. (1990). *Black and White racial identity: Theory, research, and practice.* New York: Greenwood Press.

Ho, D. Y. F. (1994). Cognitive socialisation in Confucian heritage culture. In P. M. Greenfield & R. R. Cocking (Eds.), *Cross-cultural roots of minority children development* (pp. 285–313). Hillsdale: Erlbaum.

Inman, M., & Baron, R. S. (1996). Influence of prototypes on perceptions of prejudice. *Journal of Personality and Social Psychology, 70,* 727–739.

Jensen, G., White, C., & Galliher, J. (1982). Ethnic status and adolescent self-evaluations: An extension of research of minority self-esteem. *Social Problems, 30*, 226–159.

LaFromboise, T., Coleman, H. L. K., & Gerton, J. (1993). Psychological impact of biculturalism: Evidence and theory. *Psychological Bulletin, 114*, 395–412.

Liebkind, K. (1993). Self-reported ethnic identity, depression and anxiety among young Vietnamese refugees and their parents. *Journal of Refugee Studies, 1*, 26–39.

Marcia, J. (1980). Identity in adolescence. In J. Adeson (Ed.), *Handbook of adolescent psychology* (pp. 159–187). New York: Wiley.

Pak, A. W-P., Dion, K. L., & Dion, K. K. (1991). Social psychological correlates of expereinced discrimination: Test of the double jeopardy hypothesis. *International Journal of Intercultural Relations, 15*, 243 254.

Phinney, J. S. (1989). Stages of ethnic identity in minority group adolescents. *Journal of Early Adolescence, 9*, 34 49.

Phinney, J. S. (1990). Ethnic identity in adolescents and adults: A review of research. *Psychological Bulletin, 108*, 499–514.

Phinney, J. S. (1991). Ethnic identity and self-esteem: A review and integration. *Hispanic Journal of Behavioural Sciences, 13*, 193–208.

Phinney, J. S., Cantu, C., & Kurtz, D. (1997). Ethnic and American identity as predictors of self-esteem among African American, Latino and White adolescents. *Journal of Youth and Adolescence, 26*, 165–185.

Phinney, J. S., & Chavira, V. (1992). Ethnic identity and self-esteem: An exploratory longitudinal study. *Journal of Adolescent Research, 15*, 271–281.

Phinney, J. S., & Devich-Navarro, M. (1997). Variations in bicultural identification among African American and Mexican American adolescents. *Journal of Research on Adolescence, 7*, 3–32.

Phinney, J. S., Ferguson, D. L., & Tate, J. D. (1997). Intergroup attitudes among ethnic minority adolescents: A causal model. *Child Development, 68*, 955–969.

Phinney, J. S., Madden, T, & Santos, L. J. (1998). Psychological variables as predictors of perceived ethnic discrimination among minority and immigrant adolescents. *Journal of Applied Social Psychology, 28*, 937–953.

Porter, J. R., & Washington, R. E. (1979). Black identity and self-esteem: A review of studies of Black self-concept from 1968–1978. *Annual Review of Sociology, 5*, 53–74.

Portes, A. (1984). The rise of ethnicity: Determinants of ethnic perceptions among Cuban exiles in Miami. *American Sociological Review, 49*, 383–397.

Portes, A., Parker, R. N., & Cobas, J. (1980). Assimilation or consciousness: Perceptions of U.S society among recent Latin American immigrants to the United States. *Social Forces, 59*, 200–224.

Pratto, F., & Lemieux, A. (2001). The psychological ambiguity of immigration and its implications for promoting immigration policy. *Journal of Social Issues, 57*, 413–430.

Richman, C. L., Clark, M. L., & Brown, K. (1985). General and specific self-esteem in late adolescent students. *Adolescence, 20*, 555–566

Rogosch, F., Chassin, L., & Sher, K. (1990). Personality variables as mediators and moderators of family history risk for alcoholism: Conceptual and methodological issues. *Journal of Studies on Alcohol, 51,* 310–318.

Rosenberg, M. (1986). *Conceiving the self.* Melbourne, FL: Kreiger.

Rosenberg, M., & Simmons, R. (1972). *Black and White esteem: The urban school child.* Washington, DC: American Sociological Association.

Rosenthal, D. E., & Feldman, S. S. (1992a). The nature and stability of ethnic identity in Chinese youth: Effects of length of residence in two cultural contexts. *Journal of Cross-cultural Psychology, 23,* 214–227.

Rosenthal, D. E., & Feldman, S. S. (1992b). The relationship between parenting behaviour and ethnic identity in Chinese-American and Chinese-Australian adolescents. *International Journal of Psychology, 27,* 19–31.

Rotheram-Borus, M. J. (1990). Adolescents' reference-group choices, self-esteem and adjustment. *Journal of Personality and Social Psychology, 59,* 1075–1081.

Sam, D. L. (2000). The psychological adaptation of adolescents with immigrant backgrounds. *The Journal of Social Psychology, 140,* 5–25.

Sam, D. L., & Virta, E. (2001). Social group identity and its effect on the self-esteem of adolescents with immigrant background in Norway and Sweden. In R. G. Craven. & H. W. Marsh (Eds.). *Self-concept theory; research and practice: Advances for the new millennium* (pp. 366 – 378). Sydney: Self Research Centre, University of Western Sydney.

Sanchez, J. I., & Fernandez, D. M. (1993). Acculturative stress among Hispanics: A bidimensional model of ethnicidentification. *Journal of Applied Social Psychology, 23,* 654–668.

Segall, M. H., Dasen, P. R., Berry, J. W., & Poortinga, Y. H. (1999). *Human behaviour in global perspective: An introduction to cross-cultural psychology.* Boston: Allyn & Bacon.

Tajfel, H. (1981). *Human groups and social categories.* Cambridge, UK: Cambridge University Press.

Tajfel, H. & Turner, J. C. (1986). The social identity theory of inter-group behaviour. In S. Worchel & W. Austin (Eds.), *The social psychology of inter-group relations* (pp. 33–48). Pacific Grove, CA: Brooks/Cole.

Van de Vijver, F., Leibkind, K., & Vedder, P. (2000, August). *International comparative study of ethnocultural youth: Evaluation of the frame work.* Paper presented at the 15th International Congress of the International Association of Cross-Cultural Psychology, Pultussk, Poland.

Van Oudenhoven, J. P., & Eisses, A. M. (1998). Integration and assimilation of Moroccan immigrants in Israel and the Netherlands. *International Journal of Intercultural Relations, 22,* 293–307.

Verkuyten, M. (1988). General self-esteem of adolescents from ethnic minorities in the Netherlands and the reflected appraisal process. *Adolescence, 23,* 863–871.

Verkuyten, M. (1994). Self-esteem among ethnic minority youth in Western countries. *Social Indicators Research, 32,* 21–47.

Verkuyten, M. (1995). Self-esteem, self-concept stability and aspects of ethnic identity among minority and majority youth in the Netherlands. *Journal of Youth and Adolescence, 24,* 155–175.

Virta, E., Sam, D.L., & Westin, C. (in press). Adolescents with Turkish background in Norway and Sweden: A comparative study of their psychological adaptation. *Scandinavian Journal of Psychology.*

Virta, E., & Westin, C. (1999). Psychosocial adjustment of adolescents with immigrant background in Sweden. *Occasional papers, No. 2.* Stockholm: Centre for Research on International Migration and Ethnic Relations. Stockholm University.

Westin, C. (1999). *The context of immigration to Sweden: A brief survey.* Unpublished manuscript prepared for the ICSEY project, Stockholm: Centre for Research on International Migration and Ethnic Relations, Stockholm University.

Yu, P., & Berryman, D. L. (1996). The relationship among self-esteem. acculturation and recreation participation of recently arrived Chinese immigrant adolescents. *Journal of Leisure Research, 28,* 251–273.

Zak, I. (1993). Dimensions of Jewish American identity. *Psychological Reports, 33,* 891–900.

CHAPTER 15

THE NATURE
OF SELF-CONCEPTION

Findings of a Cross-Cultural
Research Program

David Watkins
with Adebowale Akande, Jorj Balev, Jim Fleming, Maria Klis,
Wilson Lopez Lopez, Konrad Lorenz,
Murari Regmi, and Tribhuvan

For over twenty-five years this writer has been conducting research in the area of self-concept. This was despite the best attempts of my Australian professors to dissuade me from becoming involved in what was regarded in the early 1970s as a rather discredited area of research. Mentalistic constructs such as self-concept were considered by behaviorists not to be amenable to scientific study and research and the area had become the domain of sociologists and clinical psychologists. Unfortunately, an extensive critique showed that the great majority of ensuing research was of poor quality (Wylie, 1974). In particular Wylie highlighted fundamental problems in the definitions, theories, measures, and research designs in this area, which led to conflicting findings in the literature.

Happily Wylie's critical review served as a wake-up call to psychology and a number of leading researchers became interested in this field. A real

International Advances in Self Research, pages 375–398
Copyright © 2003 by Information Age Publishing

turning point was the postulation of a hierarchical, multifaceted model of the self by Shavelson, Hubner, and Stanton (1976), which provided both a clear structure for the self and a number of accompanying theoretical propositions. This work served as the basis for the development of a number of instruments with strong psychometric properties (see reviews by Byrne, 1996; Hattie, 1992). Subsequent research using such instruments has done much to clarify our understanding of how self-concept develops. Other investigations have also provided a basis for understanding how self-concept can be enhanced and how it influences behavior (Hattie, 1992).

The self-concept has also played a central role in the cross-cultural psychology literature in recent years. Indeed the publication of Markus and Kitayama (1991), which quickly reached the status of one of the most widely cited papers in all of psychology, has been credited as leading to the acceptance by mainstream psychology of the cross-cultural area (Bond, 1996): previously treated with virtual disdain. In that paper Markus and Kitayama argued that the psychological literature at the time, such as that of Shavelson and colleagues portrayed the self as independent, autonomous, separate, and agentic. While this view of self, may be appropriate for Western persons, Markus and Kitayama (1991) and Triandis (1989) questioned its relevance for non-Western individuals. These writers claimed that the latter were more likely to view themselves as interdependent, communal, and relational.

An interesting parallel to these claims of cultural differences comes from the literature on gender differences in self-construals. Josephs, Markus, and Tafarodi (1992) and Cross and Madson (1997) argued that while men are likely to describe themselves in ways typical of the independent self, women are more likely to espouse interdependent self-conceptions. The question then arises as to whether cultural and gender differences in self-construal can be characterized by the same underlying psychological dimensions. Kashima and colleages (1995) argued that this is unlikely from a cultural evolutionary perspective. They contend that gender-related roles have arisen within particular societies primarily based on a gender based division of labor due to women's roles as child bearers whereas differences between cultures are more likely to reflect the ways different peoples have tried to cope with different ecological systems.

For me personally this literature brought together in dramatic fashion two of my major research interests: culture and the self-concept. However, while impressed with the quality of the writing of these authors I was much less impressed by the quality of the evidence for culture and gender differences in self-construal they provided (see below). Like Bond (1996), I questioned whether we may have been too willing to accept the claims of Markus and Kitayama (1991) without sufficient empirical support. I decided to undertake the research program on which this chapter is based[1] to provide a more adequate database to assess claims of culture and gender differences in self-construal. It should be noted that these claims might be fundamental to our understanding of basic psychological processes. Thus, Cross and Madson (1997), Markus and Kitayama (1991), and Triandis (1989) all argued that differences in self-construal may explain culture and gender differences in basic psychological processes such as cognition, emotion, and motivation. If true such claims would require rewriting of much of our literature on such processes.

CULTURAL DIMENSIONS AND SELF-CONSTRUAL

A number of recent in-depth indigenous studies of self-conceptions have provided rather different models of self than those developed in Western research (for example, Enriquez, 1993, with Filipinos; Hsu, 1985, with Chinese; Mpofu, 1994, with Zimbabweans; and Yamaguchi, 1994, with Japanese). These investigations have been relatively consistent in finding that non-Western subjects were more likely to report possessing a relational, collectivist, or interdependent self-conception, which contrasted with the idiocentric, independent, or individualistic self typically reported by Western (or at least American) subjects. Moreover, a number of other studies have concluded that respondents from the United States of America tend to provide qualitatively different self-descriptions than responses from China, India, and Japan respondents (Bond & Cheung, 1983; Dhawan, Roseman, Naidu, Thapa, & Rettek, 1995; Ip & Bond, 1995; Schweder & Bourne, 1982).

The cultural dimension of individualism-collectivism (I-C) seemed to be tailor-made as an explanatory variable for such findings. This dimension was used by Hofstede (1980, 1983) to describe a continuum from individualism, where persons are considered as distinct units clearly separable from their social context, to collectivism, where people think of themselves not so much as separate entities but rather as members of the groups to which they belong. Hofstede compared survey data from samples of IBM employees to construct an index of individualism-collectivism (I-C) and three other dimensions: power distance, uncertainty avoidance, and masculinity/femininity for over 50 countries (see Hofstede, 2001, for updated indices and descriptions of the dimensions).

However, the self-concept research discussed above involved either two-country etic-type research (typically America vs. India, China, or Japan) or contrasted findings from an emic study of the self in a non-Western society with Western models of self.[2] Such evidence is not sufficient to show that a generalizable cultural dimension such as individualism-collectivism underlies the differences found between respondents of the different countries

(Bond, 1996). Cross-cultural methodologists have pointed out that to avoid false generalizations based on irrelevant differences between any two cultures we need to do the minimum of a *four* culture study (Bond, 1994; Schwartz, 1994; Triandis, 1990). Data would be needed on the self-conceptions of matched participants from at least two individualist and two collectivist cultures. We could first test whether the self-conceptions of the two individualist (and also the two collectivist) culture subjects were *similar* to each other and then that there were *differences* according to the supposedly underlying I-C dimension. The larger the number of cultures sampled the greater the confidence that could be placed in such an interpretation.

Prior to the research program reported here there had been two three-culture and two larger studies conducted. In the former category, Bochner (1994) found as hypothesized that adults from a collectivist culture (Malaysia) gave statistically, significantly more group and fewer idiocentric self-description responses to the Twenty Statements Test (TST; Kuhn & McPartland, 1954) than did respondents from the individualistic cultures of Australia and Britain. However, the total sample size of 78 was rather too small for much confidence to be placed in an interpretation at a cultural level for the three countries concerned. The second three-culture study of university students, questions a simple I-C/self-concept relationship (Bond & Cheung, 1983). Very similar responses were found for their individualistic (United States) and one of the collectivistic samples (Hong Kong Chinese) but their other collectivistic sample (Japan) was very different. One of the larger studies was that of Triandis, McCusker, and Hui (1990) who, analyzed responses to the TST of Illinois, Greek, Hawaiian (of both European and Asian background), Hong Kong, and Chinese psychology college students. They showed that the percentage of the participants' responses that were linked to a social entity increased as expected by the supposed degree of collectivism of the cultural group to which they belonged. While this finding was encouraging, three of the groups sampled were American and participants were undergraduate college students (except for the People's Republic of China sample which was not only small in number but was also composed of older graduate students). Possible gender differences in the relationship between the I-C dimension and the self-concept were not considered.

Gender and the Self

Josephs and colleagues (1992) pointed out that little attention had been paid to gender differences in the basis of self-esteem. They argued that self-esteem is related at least in part to how well men or women feel they have satisfied culturally mandated norms, which differ according to gender. Whereas for men, being independent, autonomous, and superior to others are often expected; for women sensitivity, nurturance, and interdependence are more common expectations. So Josephs and colleagues (1992) proposed that men are more likely to have self-conceptions based on individualistic, independent self-cognitions, while those of women are relatively more likely to be based on the notion of a collectivistic, interdependent self. They supported their claims with data from three small studies of American college students of psychology. A more recent major review of this research area reached similar findings (Cross & Madson, 1997). However, the latter writers urged caution in generalizing these claims to non-Western cultures, as there was little relevant data.

Luk and Bond (1992) provided more direct evidence and concluded that their Hong Kong male and female university student participants based their self-esteem on the same dimensions of self-concept. Moreover, a recent article by Kashima and colleagues (1995) addressed the issue of culture, gender, and the self from the perspective of individualism-collectivism research. Kashima and colleagues analyzed the responses to questionnaire measures of individualistic, relational, and collective dimensions of self-construal originally developed from concepts emic to Japanese culture, by a total of about 1,000 introductory psychology students from five cultures: two supposedly individualist (Australia and mainland United States), two thought to be collectivist (Korea and Japan) and one 'in-between' culture (Hawaii). They concluded that whereas gender differences in self-concept were primarily due to differences in the extent that their respondents thought of themselves as emotionally related to others, such differences between cultures were primarily due to differences in the degree to which their respondents saw themselves as acting as independent agents.

Research Considerations

The research program described in this chapter was designed to provide a strong test of the claims that at least some of the self-concept differences between cultures can be explained by underlying cultural dimensions such as I-C and that consistent gender differences in the relative salience of individualistic and collectivistic self-conceptions will be found in different cultures.

In planning this research program the following considerations were taken into account:

1. Several different methods should be utilized so findings are not due to cultural differences in responding to the same method (Triandis, 1990). However, as the focus of this research was the nature of self-conceptions it was argued that respondents' views of themselves,

should be the basis of analysis but that these self-reports should be obtained in different ways. Thus, in this research program the open-ended TST approach was used together with the fixed rating scales of the Adult Sources of Self-Esteem Inventory (ASSEI; Fleming & Elovson, 1988).

2. Participants of different ages should be utilized so that any findings are not age specific (Western research indicates that the structure and content of self-concept tends to change by age; see, for example, Hattie, 1992). Therefore studies were planned to sample adolescents, college students, and older adults; and

3. As wide a range of cultures as possible should be obtained. Thus, the author contacted a number of cross-cultural psychologists from a range of countries which according to Hofstede's (1980) listing were clearly near one extreme or the other of the I-C dimension or could be sensibly placed on this continuum in such a way as based on existing research evidence. In particular we were careful to include Collectivist cultures varying in terms of dominant religion, geography, and ethnic backgrounds.

Exploring the Self-Concept

The Twenty Statements Test has been widely used for over 40 years to explore how individuals think about themselves in their own words. It is considered a valuable tool for understanding spontaneous self-conceptions and how these might vary according to variables such as gender and culture (Bochner, 1994; Dhawan et al., 1995; Triandis, 1989; Verkuyten, 1989). The TST typically provides rich data, which can be used to investigate various aspects of self-conceptions. However, problems arise when researchers try to categorize these responses. There are a number of different category systems, varying from 2 to 59 categories depending on the interests of the researcher (see Wells & Marwell, 1976, for further information). It has also been argued that respondents from non-Western, lesser developed, or non-English speaking backgrounds might have difficulty giving 20 responses about themselves and that the responses should be weighted according to the order of response on the assumption that those provided early in the order are likely to be more salient for the respondent's self-conception (Bochner, 1994).

Surprisingly given the hundreds of times the TST has been used by different researchers, little focus has been placed on such measurement issues for American let alone other respondents. Reporting of high inter-judge reliability for assignment of responses to the categories chosen by the researchers is as far as most studies go. Spitzer and Parker (1976) found that U.S. college students in the 1950s perceived the TST as the least valid but in the 1970s as the most valid of four established measures of self-concept they were asked to complete. These researchers also reported that the median number of responses to the TST rose from 8 in the 1950s to 20 in the 1970s. These findings were attributed to changes in the emphasis on self-discovery in US society over these 20 years. In a more recent U.S. study, Rentsch and Heffner (1992) reported that, when respondents were asked to rate the importance and satisfaction of TST responses, 18 of the 20 responses correlated significantly with the Rosenberg Self-Esteem Scale (RSE; Rosenberg, 1979) and overall self-esteem as estimated from the TST and RSE correlated an encouraging .66.

In research conducted by this author shorter, simpler versions of the TST have been used to explore the self-concepts of adolescents from Nepal, New Zealand, and the Philippines (see, for example, Watkins & Regmi, 1996). A pilot study for this research program with Hong Kong Chinese secondary school students found that the TST was too difficult for 12 year olds but was suitable for 17 year olds responding in their own first language. Analysis using the same categories as used throughout this research indicated that the number of items and weighting in terms of rank order did make a difference to the proportions of responses classified. The fewer the number of items analyzed (7, 10, and 20 items were examined) the fewer the proportion of Independent self-responses found. Weighting responses for order also had the same effect. However, testing of gender differences in self-conceptions were found to be consistent whatever the number of items, weighted or not (see Watkins, Yau, Dahlin, & Wondimu, 1997 for details). In another pilot study using the same coding system with 100 Swedish and 100 Ethiopian university student respondents to the TST, the weighting and number of items were found to have only very minor effects, which did not affect testing of cross-cultural differences. Whatever version of TST scoring (7, 10, or 20 items; weighted or unweighted) the Ethiopians were statistically, significantly less likely to describe themselves in independent terms than did the Swedes. For the Swedish data, no matter which TST estimate of the independent self was used, the correlations with a quantitative measure of the independent self via ASSEI were around .30, all statistically significant at the .01 level (Watkins, Yau, Dahlin et al., 1997).[3] It seems then that the number of items and weighting might affect the scoring of TST responses of participants from different cultures but there is no evidence which is best and any differences are consistent across gender and culture.

In this research, we found that the means of the number of different, codable item responses to the TST varied from 13.15 for Australian female university students to 19.88 for Ethiopian male university students. While the number of usable responses varied there was no evidence that those differences varied systematically according to I-C, gender, or type of student (secondary school v university). Given the above, we concluded that we could find no reason that the TST could not be used validly with our school and university samples from different countries and that our coding system was appropriate.

The TST has been the primary tool used to date to probe possible gender and culture differences in the nature of self-concept. However, analysis of responses to the TST is relatively subjective and research findings in this area may be instrument dependent. Moreover, the components of self-concept of men and women and between different cultures may well vary more in terms of salience rather than kind. Thus a measuring instrument is required which will allow exploration of the salience of possible self-components. ASSEI was designed to fulfill this function. This instrument contains two sections with 20 identical items (see Appendix). The first section asks respondents to identify how important each item is to their self-esteem while the second section asks them to rate how satisfied they are with that aspect of themselves (Markus & Kitayama, 1991, have argued that in a cross-cultural setting self-esteem is more appropriately seen as self-satisfaction rather than in self-enhancement terms). The items of ASSEI were chosen to represent a wide range of sources of self-esteem and to be capable of reflecting gender, developmental, and ethnic differences in the source of self-esteem.

ASSEI has the advantage over measures such as the TST of being objective in measurement but also allowing for individual differences in self-construal. However, it could be argued that the twenty items of ASSEI, while carefully selected to included a wide range of possible self-concept aspects throughout the adult life-span, may still not consider relatively unusual aspects of the self-concept valued by individual respondents or those not salient to American society where ASSEI was developed. Therefore pilot studies were conducted to explore the bases of self-esteem of students and adults in Australia, Hong Kong, Nepal, New Zealand, Nigeria, and the Philippines. These studies supported the appropriateness of the ASSEI items in a range of cultures. For example, content-analysis of the responses (in Chinese) of 281 Hong Kong adults averaging 30 years of age to the open-ended question "What areas of your life are important to you?" found most of the ASSEI items reflected the life areas reported by these respondents (Tam & Watkins, 1995). Of course, it is most unlikely that precisely the same 20 items would be the most salient for individuals within the same culture let alone across cultures. The aim of ASSEI was to include a range of life areas likely to include the most salient areas for as many adults as possible whatever their culture, age, gender, or religion.

For a U.S. sample the ASSEI Importance and Satisfaction items were found to have median test-retest reliabilities over a two-week period of 0.69

and 0.67, respectively: quite impressive for single items (Davis-Zinner, 1990). The overall unweighted self-satisfaction total score was found to have an excellent internal consistency coefficient alpha of 0.97 for Turkish students (Inelmen, 1996). ASSEI total satisfaction scores unweighted and weighted for importance, respectively, were also found in this former research to correlate as predicted moderately highly (0.37 and 0.52) with the Rosenberg Self-Esteem Scale and negatively (−0.14 and −0.37) with the Neuroticism scale of the Eysenck Personality Questionnaire. Social desirability as measured by the Marlowe-Crowne scale as expected had only a minor influence on these ASSEI satisfaction scores (respective correlations of 0.28 and 0.23). Further cross-cultural validity evidence comes from a study of 139 Turkisk university students (Inelmen, 1996) which found correlations of 0.65 and 0.55 between the ASSEI unweighted and unweighted satisfaction scores and general self-esteem as measured by the Coopersmith Self-Esteem Inventory and from a Swedish study (Watkins et al., 1996) which found a correlation of 0.45 with self-esteem as assessed by the TST (all correlations are significant at 0.01 level).

Independent qualitative pilot studies for this research conducted in Hong Kong and Turkey supported by factor analyses of response to ASSEI items from over 20 countries have shown that responses to ASSEI can be classified into two sub-components of the self: the independent self and the interdependent self. Internal consistency reliabilities for both importance and satisfaction ratings of these sub-components has consistently proved to exceed .80 in over 20 countries (and in all samples in this research). Exploratory multilevel factor analysis, based on data from 19 countries in this research program, supported the structural equivalence at individual and country levels of ASSEI as a measure of the independent and interdependent self (van de Vijver & Watkins, 2001). It was concluded that ASSEI provided a strong etic measure of these two components of the self: the first time that such a demonstration has been provided for any existing measure of these constructs. Such a demonstration strengthens the validity of individual and country level use of ASSEI such as in this research program.

METHOD

Research Design

To summarize, the aims of this research program were to investigate the relationships between cultural dimensions and gender and the degree to which respondents espoused an Independent or Interdependent conception of self. To accomplish this school and college student and adult participants from a wide range of countries were asked to complete the open-ended Twenty Statements Test and/or the fixed-response format, Adult Sources of Self-Esteem Inventory. The responses to the TST were content-analyzed to provide the percentage of each participant's responses classified as depicting the Independent self. Responses to ASSEI was also analyzed to provide scores on the Independent and Interdependent self. These TST and ASSEI summary scores were then analyzed for within- and between-country gender differences and correlated with the country level dimensions of Hofstede (1983) and Schwartz's (1994) value scores, and Gross National Product.

Participants

The TSST was completed by 3,228 respondents (2850 university first or second year undergraduates; 378 senior secondary school students) from 18 countries. The university students averaged 22 years of age and the school students 17 years. Forty-two percent of the sample was male (see Table 15.1 for breakdown of sample by country).

ASSEI was completed by 6,786 respondents from 24 countries (2043 male and 3081 university undergraduates and 868 male and 794 female adults). The students averaged 22 years of age while the adults 33 years. The latter were obtained by different sampling procedures in each country to be as representative as possible of middle class urban adults (see Watkins, Mortazavi, & Trofimova, 1999 for further details).

A breakdown of the ASSEI sample by country is given in Table 15.3. It can be seen that the countries involved ranged from Western countries such as Australia, Canada, Netherlands, New Zealand, South Africa (White), Sweden, and the United States all with high Individualism-Collectivism indices (Hofstede, 1983) of 90, 80, 80, 79, 71 and 92 to a range of non-Western countries such as Colombia, Ethiopia, Hong Kong, India, Iran, Malaysia, Nigeria, Philippines, Thailand, Turkey, and Zimbabwe with relatively low I-C indices of 13, 27, 25, 48, 41, 26, 20, 32, 20, 37, and 27 respectively. Four Eastern European, former communist, countries that had little country level data available, were also included in the sample. For Hong Kong adult samples, were also obtained for nurses and heart and mental patients.

The Instruments

ASSEI is a 20-item inventory that requests each respondent to rate on a 1 (very low) to 10 (very high) scale the importance for him- or herself and his or her satisfaction with different aspects of a person's self-concept such as the physical, social, ethnic, familial, and intellectual (see Appendix).[4] The items were translated into the local language by teams of bilingual social scientists using the approved translation/back-translation method

(Brislin, 1986) for the Bulgarian, Chinese, Dutch, Lithuanian, Hong Kong, Iranian, Russian, Polish, and Thai respondents. The items tapping the Independent self are 1, 2, 3, 9, 12, 13, 14, 15, 16, and 18.

Procedure

The student respondents were surveyed with the TST and/or ASSEI in their normal class groups (except in the case of Canada where they were selected randomly from a subject pool) and told that they were taking part in an international study comparing the self-conceptions of people from different cultures. They were requested to participate in the research by answering truthfully and were assured that their individual answers would not be identified. They were then asked to complete the survey form. For the TST the following instructions were also given:

> There are twenty numbered blanks on the page below. Please write twenty answers to the simple question 'Who am I?' in the blanks. Just give twenty different answers to this question. Answer as if you are giving the answers to yourself, not to somebody else. Write the answers in the order that they occur to you. Don't worry about the logic or 'importance' and go along fairly fast for time is limited.

In all but seven of the countries the students responded to the above questions in English but for China, Ethiopia, Hong Kong, India, Poland, Sweden, Taiwan and Turkey the instructions were translated into the relevant local language and the students responded in that language. Their responses were later translated into English by expert translators blind to the hypotheses of the study.

Analysis

The following criterion was used to code the TST responses[5]: Classify each statement according to whether it is an instance of the Independent Self which is defined as Statements about personal qualities, attitudes, beliefs, states, and traits that DO NOT relate to other people. Examples: "I am honest," "I am intelligent," "I am happy."

Each sample of TST responses were classified independently by the author and experienced post-graduate students majoring in psychology. Each respondent's totals for the Independent Self category was then calculated (in the few cases where fewer than twenty categories were given or one or more responses were unclassifiable, the totals were prorated to give scores totalling twenty). An inter-rater correlation of over 0.90 was obtained on all occasions.

RESULTS

Because of space limitations it will only be possible to summarize the main results in this chapter, so for further details on the TST readers are referred to Watkins and colleagues (Watkins & Regmi, 1996; Watkins, Adair, Akande, Gerong, et al., 1998; Watkins, Cheng, et al., 1999), while for ASSEI to Watkins and colleagues, (Watkins, Yau, et al., 1997; Watkins, Adair, Akande, Cheng, et al, 1998; Watkins, Mortazavi ,& Trofimova, 1999).

The percentage of responses to the TST classified as representing the Independent Self are shown in Table 15.1 by gender. Inspection of the data

Table 15.1.   Percentage of TST Responses Classified as Independent Self by Country and Gender

Country	Sample Size	Males	Females
University Students			
Australia	207	70.68	53.08*
Canada	206	64.12	56.87*
China	187	71.06	78.54
Ethiopia	165	72.65	69.93
Hong Kong	115	40.54	49.25
India	214	50.30	49.25
Nepal	73	65.30	62.50
Netherlands	139	73.12	75.19
New Zealand	152	64.88	55.86*
Nigeria	107	61.77	64.32
Philippines	157	63.83	71.84
Poland	181	54.28	40.33*
South Africa (black)	171	68.74	68.33
South Africa (white)	179	65.56	61.52
Sweden	149	71.35	75.96
Turkey	156	71.13	71.02
Zimbabwe	302	47.35	52.25
School Students			
Hong Kong	60	55.20	48.08
Hong Kong	76	61.27	64.22
Philippines	166	50.85	53.44
Taiwan	76	60.12	63.49

Note. * indicates within-country gender difference is significant at .05 level

in Table 15.1 shows that the percentage of responses varies considerably by country and gender. For the university data, the six Western countries sampled (Australia, Canada, Netherlands, New Zealand, South African white, and Sweden) the percentage of responses classified as Independent Self ranged from 53.08 to 75.96 with a median of 65.22. The corresponding percentages for the ten non-Western countries ranged from 40.54 to 78.54 with a similar median of 64.81 and for the one Eastern European country sampled, Poland, were 54.28 and 40.33 for males and females, respectively. For the school data the percentages ranged from 48.08 to 64.22 with a median of 57.66. (MANOVA) indicated that main effects for Gender and Country and interaction effects were statistically significant at .01 level (Watkins, Adair, Akande, Cheng, et al., 1998; Watkins, Mortazavi, & Trofimova, 1999). However, the effect sizes were much less for gender and there was no significant main effect for the I/C dimension. Analyses indicated that while the TST data from the Anglophone Western countries were rather similar, the self-conceptions of respondents even from closely related culturally and geographically collectivist countries such as China, Taiwan, and Hong Kong differed markedly.

Culture (I/C) × Gender and Country × Gender Multivariate Analyses of Variance

Interestingly the predicted gender difference (males providing a higher percentage Independent Self responses than females) was found only for three of the Anglophone Western countries (Australia, Canada, and New Zealand) and the one Eastern European country sampled, Poland. Correlations between the TST Independent Self percentages and cultural level variables are shown in Table 15.2. As can be seen 4 of the 24 correlations were significant at the .05 level (it should be noted that because of the country level analysis and as several of the country level variables were not available for some countries the degrees of freedom of the correlations reported in both Tables 15.2 and 15.4 were small requiring correlations of the order of .50 before statistical significance was reached). The TST Independent self-scores were significantly correlated positively with the Schwartz Harmony (males only) and Intellectual Autonomy scores and negatively with the Hofstede Masculinity-Femininity scores (females only).

The means of the ASSEI ratings of the importance of the Independent and the Interdependent Self by country and gender are shown in Table 15.3. As the midpoint of both scales 55.00 was exceeded in every case it is clear that the majority of the student and adult respondents from each of the countries whether Western or non-Western, male or female considered

Table 15.2.   Correlates of Country TST Independent Self Scores with Culture Level Variables for Males and Females

Variables	Males	Females
Affective Autonomy[a]	.13	.02
Conservatism[a]	−.38	−.43
Egalitarian Commitment[a]	.46	.20
Harmony[a]	.73*	.18
Hierarchy[a]	−.04	.42
Mastery[a]	−.20	.16
Intellectual Autonomy[a]	.66*	.55*
Individualism-Collectivism[b]	.48	.00
Masculinity-Femininity[b]	−.36	−.61*
Power Distance[b]	−.42	−.01
Uncertainty Avoidance[b]	.41	.25
Gross National Product	.21	.06

Note. * indicates correlation is significant at .05. [a] from Schwartz (1994). [b] from Hofstede (1983)

both aspects of the self as relatively important. In about 80% of the cases the Interdependent self was considered the more important.

The six highest ratings for the Independent self were provided by the black South African, Colombian, American, and Zimbabwean students and the Lithuanian and Turkish adults for the males and the Bulgarian, Iranian, Colombian, Filipino, black South African, and American students for the females. These countries are a mix of supposedly Individualist and Collectivist in terms of Hofstede's (1983) I-C indices.[6] The same is true for the countries rating the Interdependent self as very important. Indeed there were several samples such as black South African, Zimbabwean, and US students and Turkish adults who provided amongst the highest importance means for both aspects of the self for both males and females.

Gender differences within country were found to be statistically significant at the .05 level for 18 of the 64 instances, including 7 out of the 8 adult samples for the Interdependent self. There was an apparent trend for the females to rate the Interdependent self to be significantly more important than their male counterparts. Unfortunately in five cases the females also rated the Independent self as more important than their male peers. Therefore it appears that in some cases females rated both aspects of the self as more important than males. The correlations between the importance ratings of the Independent and Interdependent self and culture level variables

Table 15.3. Means of Independent and Interdependent Self Importance Ratings by Country and Gender for University Student and Adult Samples and Hofstede Individualism–Collectivism Indices (where available)

Country	Independent Self		Interdependent Self		I-C Index[a]
	Males	Females	Males	Females	
University Students					
Australia (34M, 170F)	64.17	71.60*	70.88	79.51*	90
Bulgaria (50M, 158F)	76.04	81.75	75.82	78.95	—
Canada (74M, 48F)	73.02	72.30	82.70	82.17	—
China (90M, 99F)	76.20	77.05	73.98	80.10*	80
Colombia (42M, 199F)	80.47	79.70	77.34	79.82	13
Ethiopia (147M, 18F)	69.56	65.11	79.57	76.73	27
Hong Kong (175M, 183F)	67.80	67.71	71.39	74.30	25
India (110M, 105F)	66.95	70.10	79.92	81.42	48
Iran (101M, 80F)	75.03	80.56*	77.84	82.11*	41
Malaysia (75M, 185F)	73.33	75.95	82.10	83.86	26
Nepal (205M, 177F)	70.62	62.22*	80.16	78.27	—
Netherlands (19M, 114F)	69.82	66.96	70.22	71.68	80
New Zealand (43M, 108F)	66.53	66.71	68.99	73.06*	79
Nigeria (71M, 122F)	76.20	75.23	77.00	77.57	20
Philippines (48M, 116F)	77.72	80.46	81.38	82.19	32
Poland (20M, 167F)	72.22	74.17	75.38	80.62	—
Russia (120M, 96F)	75.64	76.30	74.70	76.06	—
South Africa (black; 46M, 124F)	80.66	79.47	84.00	85.29	—
South Africa (white; 74M, 105F)	74.58	75.42	79.83	77.10	65
Sweden (31M, 117F)	64.58	65.34	73.48	80.01	71
Thailand (50M, 128F)	71.76	74.74	77.80	79.24	20
Turkey (80M, 132F)	76.19	78.86	79.40	82.86	37
USA (201M, 192F)	79.55	79.12	79.64	82.61*	91
Zimbabwe (147M, 138F)	79.34	78.02	82.02	83.56	27
Adults					
Hong Kong (58M, 88F)	66.28	66.97	74.82	79.65*	25
HK (heart; 82M, 69F)	60.31	67.47*	75.55	82.41*	25
HK (mental; 68M, 54F)	63.10	65.23	67.92	72.63*	25
HK (nurses; 56M, 256F)	70.68	72.93	76.29	80.20*	25
Iran (101M, 80F)	71.48	72.90	80.27	79.85	41

Table 15.3.   Means of Independent and Interdependent Self Importance Ratings by Country and Gender for University Student and Adult Samples and Hofstede Individualism–Collectivism Indices (where available) (Cont.)

	Independent Self		Interdependent Self		
Country	Males	Females	Males	Females	I-C Index[a]
Lithuania (96M, 40F)	78.83	73.33*	80.32	74.18*	—
Russia (52M, 51F)	69.50	70.59	67.63	74.64*	—
Turkey (20M, 30F)	77.56	78.91	82.49	85.83	37
USA (166M, 161F)	71.47	77.95*	75.20	84.41*	91

Note. * indicates within-country gender difference is significant at .05 level for corresponding aspect of self. [a] *Source.* Hofstede (1983)

Table 15.4.   Correlates of Country Importance Ratings of Independent and Interdependent Self with Culture Level Variables

	Independent Self		Interdependent Self	
	Males	Females	Males	Females
Affective Autonomy[a]	.24	.07	.01	−.05
Conservatism[a]	.38	.63*	.49*	.51*
Egalitarian Commitment[a]	−.12	−.18	−.42	−.29
Harmony[a]	.38	.47*	.07	.07
Hierarchy[a]	.31	.31	.51*	.31
Mastery[a]	.13	−.02	.35	.23
Intellectual Autonomy[a]	−.25	−.50*	−.28	−.35
Individualism-Collectivism[b]	−.09	−.07	−.29	−.06
Masculinity-Femininity[b]	.11	.30	.09	.16
Power Distance[b]	.20	.27	.51*	.31
Uncertainty Avoidance[b]	.62*	.58*	.39	.25
Gross National Product[c]	−.44*	−.31	−.58*	−.24

Note. * indicates correlation is significant at .05 level.
Source:
[a] from Schwartz (1994).
[b] from Hofstede (1983).
[c] from Encyclopaedia Britannica (1994).

for males and females are shown in Table 15.4. While 11 of the 48 correlations are statistically significant at the .05 level, there is little evidence of gender differences except in the cases of Intellectual Autonomy and Conservatism for the Independent Self; Hierarchy and Power Distance for the Interdependent Self; and Gross National Product for both aspects of the self (correlations being more highly negative for the males in this case).

Analyses of University Student versus Adult samples for Hong Kong, Iran, Russia, and the United States by Watkins and colleagues (1999b) found a complex picture. In America, contrary to our predictions, it was the older respondents who tended to rate the Independent self as more important than did the college students. The opposite (predicted) trend was found for both the Hong Kong and Iranian samples.

CONCLUSIONS

This research program was initiated in the hope of providing a sound database for inferring how the nature of self-construal varied according to culture and gender. To that end a large scale program was designed to improve on existing data by using two very different research instruments both subjected to rigorous pilot testing in a number of cultures; by obtaining evidence from a much wider range of cultures than ever before; and by utilizing samples of adults and school children rather than relying only on college student samples. In addition both in-depth content analyses, checked by independent raters, and sophisticated statistical techniques such as multilevel factor analysis, MANOVA, and multidimensional scaling were utilized.

The big question, of course, is what does all this data tell us about culture, gender, and the self-concept? Unfortunately the answer is clear: there is NO easy answer! While it may be comforting to believe that we can explain the basis of self-conceptions in terms of cultural level variables such as individualism-collectivism or Western versus Eastern cultures, etc. the data just does not support such a simple explanation.

In both studies it is clear that while there are clear differences between cultural groups these differences are not easily explainable by the cultural indices of Hofstede or Schwartz or indeed Gross National Product. Where such significant correlations were found in one study they were not supported in the other (indeed in some cases significant correlations in the opposite direction were found). Perhaps the main message here is not to be too easily persuaded by the wonderful rhetoric and even the sophisticated theoretical rationale provided by Markus and Kitayma.[7] I would have liked nothing better than for research program to have supported their claims (and so would many of the leaders of the cross-cultural psychology field who often would rather ignore my results). But it failed to do that or even suggest an alternative explanation.

This data does indicate how careful we need to be before inferring that our differences are due to an underlying cultural dimension from two country studies. Depending on which two countries were chosen a very different picture could be drawn about the I-C dimension and the self-concept from this database.

Moreover, the data also indicated that we should not be too ready to generalize claims about gender and the self-concept based on US research. In both studies occasional gender differences were found in non-Western countries but there was virtually no support for the hypothesis that males are more likely to espouse a more independent self-conception than females. Interestingly, such support findings for U.S. research based on the TST, came from other English heritage countries of Australia, Canada, and New Zealand. Although hardly supported by the ASSEI data this does suggest that it may be worth further study of English heritage cultures to investigate the possible impact on the self-conceptions of men and women.

Another intriguing finding was the age trend found in our analyses described in detail by Watkins and colleagues (Watkins, Mortazavi, & Trofimova, 1999). In that paper we speculated that our data was consistent with the contention that while in previously Western, individualistic countries the younger generation was becoming more collectivistic. In previously collectivistic countries the younger generations may be becoming more individualistic. Perhaps cultural differences are shrinking over time. It would be comforting to believe that this was due to a greater degree of intercultural understanding. Moreover these findings do indicate that we should be careful in over-reliance on college student samples. Also perhaps we need to be cautious of data collected many years ago and even the Hofstede data, which has been such a great boon to cross-cultural research, may be reaching its "use-by" date.[8]

APPENDIX

Using a scale of 0 to 10 where:

0 = "of no importance"   10 = "extremely important"

Please indicate how **IMPORTANT** to your self-esteem is your:

1. Looks and physical attractiveness:

   0   1   2   3   4   5   6   7   8   9   10

2. Physical condition, strength, and agility:

   0   1   2   3   4   5   6   7   8   9   10

3. Grooming, clothing, overall appearance:

   0   1   2   3   4   5   6   7   8   9   10

4. Being liked by others, your popularity and ability to get along, your social skills:

   0   1   2   3   4   5   6   7   8   9   10

5. Being a good person, your friendliness and helpfulness to others:

   0   1   2   3   4   5   6   7   8   9   10

6. Having a loving, close relationship with someone:

   0   1   2   3   4   5   6   7   8   9   10

7. Being a law abiding, responsible citizen:

   0   1   2   3   4   5   6   7   8   9   10

8. Being an honest and truthful person in your dealings with others:

   0   1   2   3   4   5   6   7   8   9   10

9. Having the courage of your convictions, speaking up for what you think is right, even when it is not popular to do so:

   0   1   2   3   4   5   6   7   8   9   10

10. Relationship with your family, being on good terms with your family, having good feelings for each other:

   0   1   2   3   4   5   6   7   8   9   10

11. Meeting or have met your responsibilities to your family, i.e., being a good parent, spouse, son, or daughter:

    0   1   2   3   4   5   6   7   8   9   10

12. Intelligence, how smart you are:

    0   1   2   3   4   5   6   7   8   9   10

13. Level of academic accomplishments, years of education:

    0   1   2   3   4   5   6   7   8   9   10

14. Being a cultured and knowledgeable person, knowing about art, music, and world events:

    0   1   2   3   4   5   6   7   8   9   10

15. Having special talents or abilities - artistic, scientific, musical, athletic, etc.:

    0   1   2   3   4   5   6   7   8   9   10

16. Earning a great amount of money and acquiring valuable possessions:

    0   1   2   3   4   5   6   7   8   9   10

17. Being recognized for your accomplishments, earning the respect of others for your work:

    0   1   2   3   4   5   6   7   8   9   10

18. Doing what you set out to do personally, meeting the goals you set for yourself:

    0   1   2   3   4   5   6   7   8   9   10

19. Having influence over the events or people in your life:

    0   1   2   3   4   5   6   7   8   9   10

20. Belief in a higher power, your spiritual convictions:

    0   1   2   3   4   5   6   7   8   9   10

NOTES

1.   The following also deserve thanks for their assistance in some aspect of this research program: John Adair, Chris Cheng, Andres Gerong, Kent Lefner, Dennis McInerney, Shahrenaz Mortazari, Elias Mpofu, Sunita Singh-Sengupta, Diane Sunar, Irene Trofimova, Sue Watson, Wen Qiu Fang, Habtamu Wondimu, Jeffrey Yau, and Yu Jiayuan.

2.   Etic studies involve several cultures and have a comparative objective while emic studies are conducted within one particular culture only.

3.   For convergent validity purposes it would have been preferable to correlate ASSEI and TST scores for respondents from each sample, which completed both instruments. Unfortunately my first Research Assistant's first act was to unstaple the ASSEI and TST responses for the first twelve such samples. Thus convergent validities could be checked for only four of the samples and as with the Swedish data reported here moderate TST/ASSEI correlations of .30 to .40 were found for each sample.

4.   As the focus of this chapter is the basis of self-conception only the results of the ASSEI importance ratings are discussed here. Readers interested in satisfaction ratings are referred to Watkins and colleagues (Watkins, Adair, Akande, Cheng, et al., 1998)

5.   This is a simplified version of the four categories into which TST responses were classified (see Watkins, Adair, Akande, Gerong, et al., 1998, for details)

6.   Multidimensional scaling produced a similar mix of country groupings

7.   A major review of the research in the Individualism Collectivism area (Oyserman, Coon, and Kemmelmeier, 2002) published after the completion of the research program reported in this chapter has also questioned simple interpretations of cultural differences in related constructs including the independent and interdependent self.

8.   This has now been done (see Hofstede, 2001).

REFERENCES

Bochner, S. (1994). Cross-cultural differences in the self-concept: A test of Hofstede's individualism/collectivism distinction. *Journal of Cross-cultural Psychology, 25*, 273–283.

Bond, M. H. (1994). Into the heart of collectivism: A personal and scientific journey. In U. Kim, H. C. Triandis, C. Kagitcibasi, S. C. Choi & G. Yoon (Eds.), *Individualism and collectivism* (pp. 66–76). Newbury Park, CA: Sage.

Bond, M.H. (1996). *Social psychology across cultures: Two ways forward.* Keynote address at International Congress of Psychology, Montreal.

Bond, M. H., & Cheung, T-S. (1983). College students' spontaneous self-concept: The effect of culture among respondents in Hong Kong, Japan, and the United States. *Journal of Cross-cultural Psychology, 14*, 153–171.

Brislin, R. (1986). The wording and translation of research instruments. In W. J. Lonner & J. W. Berry (Eds.), *Field methods in educational research* (pp.137–164). Newbury Park, CA: Sage.

Byrne, B. M. (1996). *Measuring self-concept across the life span issues and instrumentation.* Washington, DC: American Psychological Association.

Cross, S. E., & Madson, L. (1997). Models of the self: self-construals and gender. *Psychological Bulletin, 122,* 5–37.

Davis-Zinner, N. (1990). *Source differences in male and female self-esteem.* Unpublished doctoral dissertation, California School of Professional Psychology, Los Angeles.

Dhawan, N., Roseman, I .J., Naidu, R. K., Thapa, K., & Rettek, S. I. (1995). Self-concepts across two cultures: India and the United States. *Journal of Cross-cultural Psychology, 26,* 606–621.

Enriquez, V. (1993). Developing a Filipino psychology. In U. Kim & J. W. Berry (Eds.), *Indigenous psychologies* (pp. 152–169). Newbury Park, CA: Sage.

Fleming, J., & Elovson, A. (1988). *The adult sources of self-esteem inventory.* State University of California at Northridge.

Hattie, J. (1992). *Self-concept.* Hillsdale, NJ: Erlbaum.

Hofstede, G. (1980). *Culture's consequences: International differences in work-related values.* Beverly Hills, CA: Sage.

Hofstede, G. (1983). Dimensions of national cultures in fifty countries and three regions. In J. B. Deregowski, S. Dziurawiec, & R. C. Annis (Eds.), *Explications in cross-cultural psychology* (pp. 335–355). Lisse, Netherlands: Swets & Zeitlinger.

Hofstede, G. (2001). *Culture's consequences: International differences in work-related values* (2nd ed.). Beverly Hills, CA: Sage.

Hsu, F. L. K. (1985). The self in cross-cultural perspective. In A. J. Marsella, G., De Vos, & F. L. K. Hsu (Eds.), *Culture and self.* London: Tavistock.

Inelmen, K. (1996). *Relationship of sex-role orientation to two measures of self-esteem.* Unpublished master's thesis, Bogazici University.

Ip, G. W. M., & Bond, M. H. (1995). Culture, values and the spontaneous self-concept. *Asian Journal of Psychology, 1,* 29–35.

Josephs, R. A., Markus, H. R., & Tafarodi, R. W. (1992). Gender and self-esteem. *Journal of Personality and Social Psychology, 63,* 391–402.

Kashima, Y., Yamaguchi, S., Kim, U., Choi, S. C., Gelfand, M. J., & Yuki, M. (1995). Culture, gender, and the self: A perspective from individualism-collectivism research. *Journal of Personality and Social Psychology, 69,* 925–937.

Kuhn, M. H., & McPartland, T. S. (1954). An empirical investigation of self-attitudes. *American Sociological Review, 19,* 68–76.

Luk, C. L., & Bond, M. H. (1992). Explaining Chinese self-esteem in terms of the self-concept. *Psychologia, 35,* 147–154.

Markus, H. R., & Kitayama, S. (1991). Culture and the self: Implications for cognition, emotion, and motivation. *Psychological Review, 98,* 224–253.

Mpofu, E. (1994). Exploring the self-concept in an African culture. *Journal of Genetic Psychology, 155,* 341–354.

Oyserman, D., Coon, H. M., & Kemmelmeier, M. (2002). Rethinking individualism and collectivism: evaluation of theoretical assumptions and meta-analyses. *Psychological Bulletin, 128,* 3–72.

Rentsch, J. R., & Heffner, T. S. (1992). Measuring self-esteem: Validation of a new scoring technique for "Who am I" responses. *Educational and Psychological Measurement, 52,* 641–651.

Rosenberg, M. (1979). *The conceiving self.* New York: Basic Books.

Schwartz, S. (1994). Beyond Individualism-Collectivism: New cultural dimensions of value. In U. Kim, H. C. Triandis, C. Kagitcibasi, S. C. Choi & G. Yoon (Eds.), *Individualism and collectivism* (pp. 85–122) Newbury Park, CA: Sage.

Schweder, R. A., & Bourne, E. J. (1982). In A. J. Marsella & G. M. White (Eds.), *Cultural conceptions of mental health and therapy.* Dortrecht, The Netherlands: Reidel.

Shavelson, R. A., Hubner, J. J., & Stanton, G. C. (1976). Self-concept: Validation of construct interpretations. *Review of Educational Research, 46,* 407–441.

Spitzer, S. P., & Parker, J. (1976). Perceived validity and assessment of the self: A decade later. *The Sociological Quarterly, 17,* 236–246.

Tam, A. S. F., & Watkins, D. (1995). Towards a hierarchical model of self-concept for Hong Kong adults with physical disabilities. *International Journal of Psychology, 30*(1), 1–17.

Triandis, H. C. (1989). The self and social behavior in differing cultural contexts. *Psychological Review, 96,* 506–520.

Triandis, H. C. (1990). Cross-cultural studies of individualism and collectivism. *Nebraska Symposium of Motivation* (pp.41–133). Lincoln, NE: University of Nebraska Press.

Triandis, H. C., McCusker, C., & Hui, C. H. (1990). Multimethod probes of individualism and collectivism. *Journal of Personality and Social Psychology, 59,* 1006–1020.

Van de Vijver, F. J. R., & Watkins, D. (2001) *Structural equivalence at individual and country levels.* Invited speech University of Sussex.

Verkuyten, M. (1989). Self-concept in cross-cultural perspective; Turkish and Dutch adolescents in the Netherlands. *Journal of Social Psychology, 129,* 184–185.

Watkins, D., Adair, J., Akande, A., Cheng, C., Fleming, J., Lefner, K., Gerong, A., Ismail, M., McInerney, D., Mpofu, E., Regmi, M., Singh-Sengupta, S., Watson, S., Wondimu, H., & Yu, J. (1998). Cultural dimensions, gender, and the nature of self-concept: a fourteen country study. *International Journal of Psychology, 33,* 17–31.

Watkins, D., Adair, J., Akande, A., Gerong, A., McInerney, D., Sunar, D., Watson, S., Wen, Q., & Wondimu, H. (1998a). Individualism-Collectivism, gender, and the self-concept: A nine culture investigation. *Psychologia, 41,* 259–271.

Watkins, D., Cheng, C., Mpofu, E., Olowu, Singh-Sengupta, S., & Regmi, M. (1999). *Gender differences in self-construal: How generalizable are Western findings?* University of Hong Kong.

Watkins, D., Mortazavi, S., & Trofimova, I. (1999). *Independent and interdependent conceptions of self.* University of Hong Kong.

Watkins, D., & Regmi, M. P. (1996). Exploring the basis of self-esteem of urban and rural Nepalese children. In J. Pandey, D. Sinha & D. Bhawuk (Eds.), *Asian contributions to cross-cultural psychology.* New Delhi: Sage.

Watkins, D., Yau, J., Dahlin, B., & Wondimu, H. (1997). The Twenty Statements Test: Some measurement issues. *Journal of Cross-cultural Psychology, 28,* 626–633.

Watkins, D., Yau, J. Fleming, J., Davis-Zinner, N., Tam, A., Juhasz, A. M., & Walker, A. (1997). Gender differences in the basis and level of adult self-esteem: A cross-cultural perspective. *Psychologia, 40,* 265–276.

Wells, L. E., & Marwell, G. (1976). *Self-esteem: Its conceptualization and measurement.* London: Sage.

Wylie, R. C. (1974). *The self concept* (Vol. 1). Lincoln: University of Nebraska Press.

Yamaguchi, S. (1994). Collectivism among the Japanese: A perspective from the self. In U. Kim, H. C. Triandis, C. Kagitcibasi, S. C. Choi & G. Yoon (Eds.), *Individualism and collectivism* (pp. 175–188). Newbury Park, CA: Sage.

ABOUT THE EDITORS

Herb Marsh (BA, Hons, Indiana, MA; Ph.D., UCLA; DSc, University of Western Sydney, Australia Academy of Social Science) is Professor of Education and founding Director of the SELF Research Centre. He is the author of internationally recognized psychological tests that measure self-concept, motivation, and university students' evaluations of teaching effectiveness. He has published more than 230 articles in top international journals, 22 chapters, 8 monographs, and 225 conference papers. He was recognized as the most productive educational psychologist in the world, as one of the top 10 international researchers in Higher Education and in Social Psychology, and the 11th most productive researcher in the world across all disciplines of psychology. His major research/scholarly interests include self-concept and motivational constructs; evaluations of teaching effectiveness; developmental psychology, quantitative analysis; sports psychology; the peer review; gender differences; peer support and anti-bullying interventions. Email: h.marsh@uws.edu.au

International Advances in Self Research, pages 399–400

Rhonda Craven (Dip.Teach., Alexander Mackie CAE; B.A. (Hons), University Medal; Ph.D. (Ed. Psych.) University of Sydney) is Deputy Director of the SELF Research Centre, is Associate-Professor in the School of Education and Early Childhood Studies, and is Honours Research Degree Coordinator, College of Arts, Education and Social Science, University of Western Sydney. As an Educational Psychologist her research focuses on large-scale quantitative research studies in educational settings. She is a highly accomplished researcher having successfully secured over 1.4 million dollars in prestigious, external competitive funding for over 19 research projects. Her research has resulted in scholarly publications in books and academic journals of international repute. Her research interests include: the structure, measurement and enhancement of self-concept; the relationship of self-concept to desirable educational outcomes; the effective teaching of Aboriginal studies and Aboriginal students; and interventions that make a difference in educational settings. Email: r.craven@uws.edu.au

Dennis McInerney is Professor of Educational Psychology at the University of Western Sydney, Australia. Dennis has a strong interest in cross-cultural research and has published extensively in refereed international journals, written numerous book chapters and conference papers, particularly in the area of motivation and learning. His textbook Educational Psychology: Constructing Learning (3rd ed., 2002, Prentice Hall Australia, coauthored with Associate Professor Valentina McInerney) is the top selling educational psychology text in Australia and is widely used as a standard text in most Australian universities. Dennis's latest texts are *Helping Kids Achieve Their Best: Understanding and Using Motivation in the Classroom* (Allen & Unwin, 2001), *Publishing Your Psychology Research: A Guide to Writing for Journals in Psychology and Related Fields* (Sage, 2001), and *Research on Sociocultural Influences on Motivation and Learning Vols. 1 & 2* (with Shawn Van Etten, Information Age Publishing, 2001 & 2002). Email: d.mcinerney@uws.edu.au

ABOUT THE CONTRIBUTORS

Mimi Bong is Associate Professor of Educational Psychology, Technology, and Research in the Department of Educational Psychology at the University of South Carolina. She received her PhD from the University of Southern California in 1995. She is originally from Seoul, Korea, where she received her BA from Ewha Woman's University. Her research interests include academic motivation and learning, cross-cultural comparison of motivation, measurement of self-perceptions, and technological applications in the classrooms. In particular, she has published extensively on the similarities and differences of academic motivation across multiple domains, predictive utility of self-efficacy judgments at different levels of measurement specificity, theoretical and empirical comparisons of self-concept and self-efficacy beliefs, and gender differences in attitudes toward information technology. Mimi Bong currently serves on the editorial board of *Journal of Educational Psychology* and *Contemporary Educational Psychology* and as Consulting Editor of *Child Development.*

Email: mimibong@sc.edu

Paul Burnett is Pro Vice-Chancellor (Research and Graduate Training) at Charles Sturt University, Wagga Wagga Campus, Australia. Prior to this he was Professor of Education and Head of the School of Teacher Education at Charles Sturt University's Bathurst Campus, Associate Professor and Senior Lecturer in Research Methods, and Director of the Centre for Cognitive Processes in Learning within the School of Learning and Development at Queensland University of Technology. He is a Counsellor, Counselling Psychologist and Educational and Developmental Psycholo-

International Advances in Self Research, pages 401–409

gist. Additionally, he has been a Registered Teacher and Psychologist in Queensland and a former Vice-President of the Queensland Guidance and Counselling Association. He has five degrees in Education and Psychology with his PhD in Counsellor Education. He has authored or co-authored over 100 publications in a variety of academic and professional forums. Professor Burnett has researched and written in the areas of self-concept, self-esteem, self-talk, childhood depression, bereavement reactions, decision-making and the wish to hasten death in the terminally ill. He has national and international repute in the field of self-concept and self-esteem research in children.

Email: pburnett@csu.edu.au

Barbara Byrne is Professor Emeritus in the School of Psychology, University of Ottawa, Canada. Substantively, Dr. Byrne's research focuses on construct validation issues related to the structure and measurement of self-concept, burnout, and depression. Methodologically, her research centers on the sound application of structural equation modeling in the validation of measuring instruments and psychological constructs. Dr. Byrne has published extensively in the area of self-concept and is the author of *Measuring Self-concept Across the Lifespan: Issues and Instrumentation*, an important reference book related to self-concept measurement. She is also the author of four introductory-level books dealing with basic concepts and applications of structural equation modeling. Dr. Byrne is the recipient of the Canadian Psychological Association 1995 Distinguished Teaching Award, the 2002 American Psychological Association (APA) Distinguished Contributions to Education and Training Award, and the 2002 Division 5 (APA) Jacob Cohen Award for Distinguished Contributions to Teaching and Mentoring.

Email: bmbyrne@swfla.rr.com

Jason Crabtree received his PhD entitled Educational Inclusion: *The self-concept of students with moderate learning difficulties* in 2002 from Brunel University, England. His PhD research focused on the structure of self-concept and the impact of social environment on the formation of self-concept in individuals with mild learning disabilities. He is currently working for the learning disability department of the health service in the capacity of researcher and assistant psychologist. As a component of his current post he is involved in developing service delivery for individuals with learning disabilities as part of the British Government's 2001 White Paper entitled *Valuing People*. His current research interests include the self-concept and quality of life of individuals with learning disabilities.

Email: jcrabt01@hotmail.com

Rhonda Craven is Deputy Director of the SELF Research Centre, is Associate-Professor in the School of Education and Early Childhood Studies, and is Honours Research Degree Coordinator, College of Arts, Education and Social Science, University of Western Sydney. As an Educational Psychologist her research focuses on large-scale quantitative research studies in educational settings. She is a highly accomplished researcher having successfully secured over 1.4 million dollars in prestigious, external competitive funding for more than 19 research projects. Her research has resulted in scholarly publications in books and academic journals of international repute. Her research interests include: the structure, measurement and enhancement of self-concept; the relationship of self-concept to desirable educational outcomes; the effective teaching of Aboriginal Studies and Aboriginal students; and interventions that make a difference in educational settings.

Email: r.craven@uws.edu.au

Vicente González-Romá is Associate Professor in the Department of Methodology of the Behavioral Sciences at the University of Valencia, Spain. He has published in refereed international journals (including *Multivariate Behavioral Research* and *Journal of Applied Psychology*) and his articles relate to analysis of multitrait-multimethod matrices, item response scales, differential item functioning, work-team climate, and validity studies. In collaboration with Inés Tomás, he has developed a Spanish version of the Physical Self Description Questionnaire (PSDQ), and has carried out several studies regarding the measurement of physical self-concept in Spanish adolescents, and the cross-cultural validation of the PSDQ. His research interests include: measurement equivalence in translated tests; differential item functioning; analysis of middle categories in polytomous response scales; structure of affect; and work-teams.

Email: Vicente.Glez-roma@uv.es

Jessica Grainger is Senior Lecturer in the Clinical Program in Psychology at Wollongong University, Australia, specializing in Child and Adolescent Work and in particular in areas of research in ADHD, Conduct and Reading Disorders and Parent Training. Jessica has worked as a school psychologist and was previously director of a specialist child and adolescent assessment and treatment clinic in NSW. Jessica has a background in clinical and educational psychology and is the author of several books and research articles in a range of topics associated with the special needs of children and adolescents. Her main interest is in the nature of self-talk and internal cognitive self-evaluation and the development of self-management skills. This is particularly related to her research and publication in relation to children with behavior and conduct disorders as well as with children with ADHD and learning problems.

Email: Jessicag@uow.edu.au

John Hattie's main areas of research and scholarship are self-concept, educational measurement, and the application of measurement models to educational practice. He specializes in self-concept research and has written the most highly regarded research monographs in the field. Since 1998 he has been Professor of Education at the University of Auckland in New Zealand. Between 1994 and 1998 he was Professor and Chair of Educational Research Methodology, University of North Carolina at Greensboro (USA) where he was also the Associate Director of the Center for Research and Evaluation and Psychometric Advisor to National Council for Accrediting Teacher Education Washington D.C. Throughout his distinguished career, he has been one of the premiere quantitative Australian educational researchers, a conclusion supported by studies of citation rates in both international and national journals. Professor Hattie has made important contributions to the areas of structural equation modeling, meta-analysis and item-response theory. His application of measurement models to a wide variety of substantive areas of educational research has led to conceptual advances in a variety of fields. He has authored over 200 journal articles and nine books and serves on editorial boards of 26 highly respected international journals.

Email: j.hattie@auckland.ac.nz

Kit-Tai Hau is Professor and Chair of the Department of Educational Psychology and Associate Director of the Hong Kong Institute of Educational Research, at the Chinese University of Hong Kong. His research interest includes structural equation modeling, academic achievement motivation, policy on educational assessment and adolescent suicide. He is one of the international founding members of the SELF Research Centre and has made frequent visits, including long stays under the sponsorship of the Australian Research Grant Council. Some of his recent articles appeared in *Journal of Educational Measurement, Journal of Educational Psychology, American Educational Research Journal, Journal of Personality and Social Psychology, Harvard Educational Review,* and *Applied Psychological Measurement.* He has also run a great number of national workshops on structural equation modeling in China and has participated actively in the debates as well as policy formation on ability segregation of students, computerized assessment, medium of instruction, public examination systems, and gender discrimination in school place allocation.

Email: kthau@cuhk.edu.hk

Olaf Köller is a full Professor of Educational Psychology at the Faculty of Education, University of Erlangen-Nuremberg. After graduation in psychology in 1991 he started his scientific career at the Institute for Science Education (IPN) at the University of Kiel, Germany. In 1996 he moved to the Max Planck-Institute for Human Development (MPI), where he finished his dissertation in 1997. In 2002 he accepted the offer of a full Professorship at the University of Erlangen-Nuremberg. During his time at the IPN and MPI, he was involved in the Third International Mathematics and Science Study (TIMSS) and the Programme for International Student Assessment (PISA). His major research interests are reciprocal effects of academic self-concepts and achievement, the development of academic interests and their effects on achievement, and the role of academic self-concepts for coursework selection and occupational choices. Olaf Köeller has published more than one hundred national and international journal articles, book chapters and monographs.

Email: koeller@ewf.uni-erlangen.de

Chit-Kwong Kong has been a part-time lecturer in science teaching at the Chinese University of Hong Kong. He also worked at the Educational Research Section of the Hong Kong Education Department in analyzing various large-scale data sets to help educational policy decision-making. His research interest includes self-concept development, multilevel analyses, structural equation modeling, and chemistry teaching. He has published in the *Journal of Educational Psychology, American Educational Research Journal, Journal of Personality and Social Psychology,* and *Harvard Educational Review.*

Email: markong@netvigator.com

Herb Marsh is Professor of Education and founding Director of the SELF Research Centre. He is the author of internationally recognized psychological tests that measure self-concept, motivation and university students' evaluations of teaching effectiveness. He has published more than 230 articles in top international journals, 22 chapters, 8 monographs, and 225 conference papers. He was recognized as the most productive educational psychologist in the world, as one of the top 10 international researchers in Higher Education and in Social Psychology, and the 11th most productive researcher in the world across all disciplines of psychology. His major research/scholarly interests include self-concept and motivational constructs; evaluations of teaching effectiveness; developmental psychology, quantitative analysis; sports psychology; the peer review; gender differences; peer support and anti-bullying interventions.

Email: h.marsh@uws.edu.au

Dennis McInerney is Professor of Educational Psychology at the University of Western Sydney, Australia. Dennis has a strong interest in cross-cultural research and has published extensively in refereed international journals, written numerous book chapters and conference papers, particularly in the area of motivation and learning. His textbook *Educational Psychology: Constructing Learning* (3rd ed., 2002, Prentice Hall Australia, co-authored with Associate Professor Valentina McInerney) is the top selling educational psychology text in Australia and is widely used as a standard text in most Australian universities. Dennis's latest texts are *Helping Kids Achieve Their Best: Understanding and Using Motivation in the Classroom* (Allen & Unwin, 2001), *Publishing Your Psychology Research: A Guide to Writing for Journals in Psychology and Related Fields*, and *Research on Sociocultural Influences on Motivation and Learning Vols. 1 and 2* (with Shawn Van Etten).

Email: d.mcinerney@uws.edu.au

David Lackland Sam (B.Sc Hons, University of Ghana; PhD (Dr. Psychol.), University of Bergen, Norway) is a Ghanaian by birth, and migrated to Norway in 1984 as a student. David is currently a Professor of Cross-Cultural Psychology at the University of Bergen, Norway, where he divides this position between the Department of Psychosocial Science, and the Centre for International Health. He teaches several courses, including culture and human development, culture and psychopathology, and acculturation. As an immigrant, one of his research interests has been the psychology of acculturation where he has published extensively on the topic. He is currently completing a book together with other researchers (including the co-author of this paper) on a large-scale comparative study involving 13 Western countries. He is also involved in another large-scale research project on socialization in a number of countries, including his native country of Ghana.

Email: david.sam@psysp.uib.no

Einar Skaalvik, holds the position of Professor of Educational Psychology at the Norwegian University of Science and Technology (formerly the University of Trondheim). He has his MA (1969) and PhD (1974) in Education from the University of Oslo, Norway. Dr. Skaalvik specialists in self-concept, self-efficacy, and motivation, where he has done basic research related to conceptual analysis, how self-concept and motivation are affected, relations between self-concept and motivation, and how self-concept and motivation affects emotional responses, behavior and achievement. His research also expands to areas such as learning, special education, adult education, prison education, and curriculum and teaching methods. Professor Skaalvik has published six textbooks, eleven research reports, some 50 research articles (more than two dozen in international journals). He has also presented more than 30 conference presentations and invited addresses at international research conferences. He has reviewed articles for 10 international journals and serves on the review board of *Journal of Educational Psychology*.

Email: Einar.Skaalvik@SVT.NTNU.NO

Waheeda Tabassam is a Lecturer, Counsellor and Researcher in Applied Psychology at the Punjab University, Pakistan. She has a Masters in Applied Psychology and her PhD in Psychology is from University of Wollongong, Australia. She is a member of the Australian Psychological Society. Her research focuses on the assessment and enhancement of self-concept in children, attributional style and self-efficacy in children with LD and ADHD. Her main interest is in the cognitive interventions for self-concept enhancement of children with learning and behavioral difficulties. Waheeda has many years of experience in psychological test-development and has developed tools for the assessment of temperament, attributions, adjustment, aptitude and self-efficacy. She has presented her work in many conferences and has published extensively in the area of parent-child relationships, antisocial behavior in children and self-perceptions of children with learning and behavioral difficulties.

Email: wtabassam@hotmail.com

Inés Tomás-Marco is Associate Professor in the Department of Methodology of the Behavioral Sciences at the University of Valencia, Spain. She has developed a Spanish version of the Physical Self Description Questionnaire (PSDQ), and has carried out several studies regarding the measurement of physical self-concept in Spanish adolescents, and the cross-cultural validation of the PSDQ. This last subject has resulted in two recent publications in academic journals of international repute (*Journal of Sport and Exercise Psychology*, and *Research Quarterly for Exercise and Sport*). Her major research interests focus on differential item functioning (DIF) issues related to test translation and the development of psychometrically equivalent versions of questionnaires for use in cross-cultural research. Methodologically, her research centers on the application and comparison of structural equation modeling and item response theory models in the detection of DIF and validation of measuring instruments.

Email: Ines.Tomas@uv.es

Danielle Tracey, received her PhD in 2002 from the SELF Research Centre, University of Western Sydney, Australia. Her thesis investigated the self-concepts of preadolescents with mild intellectual disability, with particular reference to structural and measurement issues, and the impact of the inclusion movement as supported by the big fish little pond effect. Other research interests include the social and emotional development of children with special needs, and transitions such as returning to school after serious illness and starting school. She currently serves as the Director of School Age Services for a leading New South Wales charity specializing in helping children with learning difficulties.

Email: dtracey@learninglinks.org.au

Erkki Virta (MA in psychology at the University of Helsinki, Finland; PhD in Psychology at Stockholm University, Sweden; authorized psychologist in Sweden) is Finnish by birth, and migrated to Sweden as a researcher of stress and psychology of work. From 1994 to 2002 he was a researcher at the Centre for Research in the International Migration and Ethnic Relations at Stockholm University. In 2003 he is a researcher at the Centre for Research in Ethnic Relations and Nationalism at the University of Helsinki, Finland. Recently, he has been occupied with two international projects, one concerning the psychological and socio-cultural adaptation of immigrant adolescents in 13 Western countries, the other one dealing with Finland and Sweden in psychological, social, historical, linguistic and economical perspectives. Previously, Erkki was involved in research on bilingualism and the issue of language and thought. He has also worked as a journalist and a psychologist.

Email: erkki.virta@ceifo.su.se

Walter Vispoel received his BA in Psychology and Music and his MEd in Educational Evaluation from the University of Illinois at Chicago, USA and his PhD. in Measurement and Statistics from the University of Illinois at Urbana-Champaign, USA. He is currently Professor of Educational Psychology and Professor of Measurement and Statistics at the University of Iowa, USA. Prior to that, Professor Vispoel worked as a professional musician and music teacher in the Chicago area and as Director of Research and Testing for High School District 214 in Mount Prospect, Illinois. Professor Vispoel's research has emphasized extensions of self-theory and instrumentation into artistic domains and the use of computers in improving the validity and administrative efficiency of assessment tools. He is the author of computerized and paper-and-pencil forms of the Arts Self-Perception Inventory and the Music Self-Perception Inventory.
Email: walter-vispoel@uiowa.edu

David Watkins is a Professor in the Faculty of Education at the University of Hong Kong. He has had a long interest in the self-concept area beginning with his Masters degree at the University of Melbourne some thirty years ago. He is the author of over 250 journal articles; book chapters, and five edited books. His other main research area is the cross-cultural investigation of conceptions of teaching and learning. He has been an executive committee member of the International Association of Cross-cultural Psychology and International Association of Applied Psychology. His PhD is from the Australian National University.

Email: hrfewda@hku.hk

INDEX

International Advances in Self Research, pages 411–416
Copyright © 2003 by Information Age Publishing